CULTURE, POLITY AND ECONOMY

CULTURE, POLITY AND ECONOMY

Editors

Varsha Joshi
Surjit Singh

Institute of Rajasthan Studies, Jaipur

RAWAT PUBLICATIONS

Jaipur • New Delhi • Bangalore • Mumbai • Hyderabad • Guwahati

ISBN 81-316-0206-0

Published by
Prem Rawat for **Rawat Publications**
Satyam Apts, Sector 3, Jawahar Nagar, Jaipur 302 004 (India)
Phone: 0141 265 1748 / 7006 Fax: 0141 265 1748
E-mail: info@rawatbooks.com
Website: www.rawatbooks.com

New Delhi Office
4858/24, Ansari Road, Daryaganj, New Delhi 110 002
Phone: 011 2326 3290

Also at Bangalore, Mumbai, Hyderabad and Guwahati

Typeset by Rawat Computers, Jaipur
Printed at Chaman Enterprises, New Delhi

Contents

Section II
Culture and Tradition

Section III
Environment and Institutions

Section IV
Social and Gender Issues

Acknowledgements

This volume is a result of commitment of the scholars who are dedicated and selflessly involved in Rajasthan studies. We are obliged to the contributors for not only participating in the Fifth International Conference on Rajasthan with the theme "Multiple Histories, Ethnicity, Pluralism and Institutions" but also for their scholarly contribution in the form of papers. The select papers in this volume are revised versions of those presented in the conference.

Prof. Satish Chandra, Chairman of Institute of Rajasthan Studies, Jaipur as usual has been the source of inspiration. This venture would not have been possible without his guidance. The Institute has continued the tradition of providing an interdisciplinary platform for scholars to discuss their researches on Rajasthan in the footsteps of Prof. Rajendra Joshi. Prof. Dilbag Singh of Centre for Historical Studies, Jawaharlal Nehru University was always there before and during the conference to lend the helping hand. His encouragement had resulted in a successful conference. The Rajasthan Studies Group, USA has always extended academic support in the past and also in this venture, for which we are extremely grateful. In particular, we would like to thank Professors Susanne and Lloyd Rudolph, Lawrence A. Babb and Frances Taft, with whom we had many interactive meeting to give shape to the conference. The conference also saw younger generation of Rajasthan scholars rubbing shoulders with veterans of

Rajasthan Studies. This is a welcome sign for Rajasthan Studies Group. Ranvir Sinh ably supported us in this venture and we owe him our thanks. We are also grateful to Mr. Rakesh Hooja for his support and Prof. Pratibha Jain for giving her valuable time during the conference.

We would like to thank the Indian Council of Social Science Research, New Delhi for the financial support. Finally, we thank Shri Kailash Rawat and Pranit Rawat for standing by us as usual and ably bringing out the present volume.

Varsha Joshi
Surjit Singh

1

Introduction

Varsha Joshi and Surjit Singh

Rajasthan has a rich historical, cultural and religious past. The polity and economy of Rajasthan has been influenced by its history, culture and society. People talk about its culture, history and polity. It has been an abode for diverse religions, and over the centuries the society of Rajasthan has evolved into a well-knit fabric. In recent years, the importance of regional studies, complimenting existing 'mainstream' history, has largely been accepted and recognised. Along with this, interdisciplinary approach to research has also been encouraged and there has been a major shift in incorporating folk literature and oral traditions as primary sources. Rajasthan studies today have certainly moved from just chronological arrangements of events and incidents to an integrated and interdisciplinary understanding of grass roots history, gender issues, literature and religion and much more. The five international conferences on Rajasthan have been successful in providing an interdisciplinary approach in understanding Rajasthan. This has been specially in cases of understanding of both existing structures and the processes of social change. There is certainly a need to shift from studying the structures and systems to social change including local diversities and specificities of socio-cultural life. We find that ethnographic and field studies, particularly anthropology, have led to a better realisation of the importance of the tribes and the tribal forms in the evolution of such institutions as the caste. However, unlike sociology and anthropology, the Indian historians have been comparatively slow to assimilate the techniques of social anthropology and adapt them for this purpose. The papers included in this volume attempt to look at Rajasthan in a wider perspective. The pairing of culture, polity and economy should not be surprising. If culture has been the core of Rajasthan, issues of power and economy have a significant role in the complex feudalistic society.

Oral history is another area that needs attention. Folk songs and *Bat Sahitya* form an important source of understanding the community interactions, gender issues etc. For instance, in Rajasthan, we find that there is lack of written evidence, especially on gender issues. It is the state's oral tradition that provides immense information to understand existing feudalistic patriarchal structure of the families. Similarly, community co-existence can be best understood by studying the oral history of the state. Thus, there is need to establish the importance of oral history in the writing of history. Interestingly, in understanding social and economic development in Rajasthan, one has to look it in a historical perspective. As a researcher, one who looks at the modern state of Rajasthan, with its long history, cannot look at the 21st century in isolation. There has been a counting link between the past and the present. Any development initiative in the state has to keep in mind the past social scenario, without which these initiatives will end up in a "throwing the baby out with the bath water" situation. Even though deserted and disseminated elements of feudalism, caste disparities and similar accompanying paraphernalia with traditional knowledge system and ways of life and certain in-built acceptance and rational, which cannot be ignored in the then context. This needs to be understood in the contextual framework and thus cannot be just out rightly rejected.

Keeping this in mind, the present collection of papers is an attempt to unravel the interdisciplinary studies, pointing towards its productive possibilities, not only in past and the present but also in the times to come.

The structuring of the volume reflects four distinct sections. Section I deals with the issues of history and polity with Tod and Tessitori as a reference points. Section II covers issues concerning culture and traditions. Section III deals with environment and institutions, and the Section IV concerns social and gender issues in the economic context.

Rajasthan, with rich cultural and historical past, was considered a common entity/region with Tod's *Annals and Antiquities* in the early 19th century only. Only Tod's writings have become a source of inspiration for researchers to look at Rajasthan with a lens that helped clear its unhidden cultural historical past. Not all researchers go all hog with Tod in his perception and interpretation and this is reflected in papers in Section 1. Tessitori too has contributed to the understanding of Rajasthan's past but in a limited sense. The papers in this section throw much light on writings of these individuals.

Elena Karachkova in her paper "Multiple Histories of Amber: Tod's Annals versus Local Oral Tradition" illustrates and discusses some specific ways, in which oral traditions co-exist and sustain a dialogue with written sources in a semi-literate community—the population of Amber. The author notes that the most paradoxical aspect of Tod's account is that (although Khoh and Manch were just temporary strongholds, while Amber remained the capital of the kingdom for seven centuries) no developed narrative associated with the conquest of Amber is represented in the *Annals*. Tod simply states that it was Dhola Rae's grandson—Maidul Rao—who captured Amber from the Susawat Minas in the 11th century. Tourist literature also does not elaborate on the issue in question, the paper notes. It does say that contrary to Tod, it attributes the conquest of Amber to the reign of Kakil Dev—Dulha Rai's son. So far as Tod is concerned, it is argued that one of the two versions of Manch/Ramgarh tradition follows Tod in placing *Dhola* and *Maru*, rather than Dulha Rai, in the midst of the dramatic events. It nevertheless rejects the version of the Kacchawa cultural hero's death for it contradicts the logic of the *kuldevi, Jamwai Mata* tradition. But, most importantly, the oral tradition borrows the Khoh episode from Tod to fill in the gap in his own narrative—lack of the circumstances associated with the conquest of Amber proper. While the Manch/Ramgarh oral tradition is constantly reinforced in the collective memory of the Kacchawas, who visit the place to worship their *kuldevi* in the temple of Jamwai Mata, contemporary Khoh is but an insignificant village with no monuments to remind Rajputs of their glorious past.

G.S.L. Devra's paper "Mongols and Rajputs: A Study of James Tod on the Historical Ethnicity of Martial Races of Rajasthan and Central Asia" points out that James Tod and several scholars of 19th and early 20th centuries were of the opinion that a study of the mythological descriptions, martial manners, language and poetry, and even music and architectural ornaments of the early settlers in India, China and Mongolia speak about their common origin. In this context, Tod tried to compare the genealogical histories of the Mongols and

Rajputs given in the accounts of Abul Ghazi (Genealogy) and *Puranic* literature of India respectively and comes to a conclusion that they had almost similar kind of inferences for their racial origin. Whereupon, the traditional accounts of the Rajput courts came out strongly in favour of the origin of these ruling races from the established Kashtriya families of the Epic and Puranic periods. The paper argues that at no stage these descriptions have tried to compare the origin or histories of these races with that of the other parts of Asia or Europe. The emphasis of their theory remained on the centre of the theme of pure royal races of ancient Aryan India. It also says that during the modern times, the theories of Brahman and tribal origin of the Rajputs also found the place in the span of long and continuous debate. The view expressed is that in the present time the writings of Tod either got challenged, spared or could not be considered serious at all. It further argues that the observations of James Tod, however, deserve attentions. Although on the plain surface one finds it difficult to accept whatever he has proposed, as his writings lack the support of historical evidences and moreover the names of the various clans of the Rajputs or Kshatriyas do not match with the names of tribes, clans or communities of any part of Asia or Europe. The paper points out that Tod has tried to place his theory on the ground of the presence of similar types of the social customs and traditions prevalent both in the Rajput and Indo-Scythians or Mongol societies but such observations failed to find favourable response from the Indian authors. According to the critics of Tod, such customs and social practices were already present in the Indian Kshatriya societies. In fact, Rajputs, despite their new names and identities are the Kshatriyas of the early periods and like their predecessors fought against all those who came from the outside of the country. Indo-Scythians were treated as foreigners in the country and Kshatriyas had challenged their arms for the independence of the country. The paper cites the popularity of the legend of the tale of Vikrmaditya in the support of this trendy version

V.K. Vashishtha in his paper, "James Tod's Reflections on History and Society of Rajasthan" points out that it may not be an exaggeration to conclude that Tod's *Annals* were solely swayed by the view of showing the British as the saviour of Rajputana states, its people and Rajput aristocracy from the oppression and exploitation of the Marathas. This imperialistic view of history has been reflected throughout the *Annals* in describing the social, economic and political life of the people of Rajasthan around the dynastic history of each state. Tod's predictions towards the Rajputs is further revealed in his criticism of the Emperor Aurangzeb and Muhammadans as intolerant (bigoted), as well as dubbing the Marathas as plunderers, and responsible for the chaotic condition before the British intervention in Rajputana. This effort to differentiate between the cultural and territorial boundaries of Rajputs, Marathas and Muhammadans on the notion of insider, outsider or native from foreigners, was aimed at winning the Rajputs to the British side, and turning them against the Marathas and the Muhammadans. Tod's personal narrative in the *Annals,* repeatedly emphasised that the dismal condition of Rajputana states of the Maratha period had subsided after the Anglo-Rajput treaties, that peace and tranquillity was restored in these states, and the establishment of the British paramountcy had proved a boon for the people of Rajputana. He had toed the same policy to win over the Rajput rulers to British side, as he highlighted their loyalty for the British government in the dedication of the first volume of the *Annals* to King George IV. Tod, being a keen observer, for the first time, pointed out in the *Annals* about the virtue of the Rajput princes of remaining loyal to the British throne. His predilections do come true. The Rajput states remained loyal to the British government in 1857 and took a leading part in the First World War, and one of their princes, Maharaja Ganga Singh of Bikaner, had participated in the Imperial Conference at Paris. This revived the interest of the British government in Tod's *Annals* and William Crooke brought out its new edition in 1920 for the use of modern scholars and students of Indian history and antiquities, the paper argues.

Marco Fattori's "James Tod and the 'Rajpoot Feudalism': The Case of the Bhumiya Chiefs in Mewar" highlights the genesis and the political impact of one 'feudal' category in the 19th and 20th century Rajasthan, that of the Bhumiya chiefs as 'allodial tenants' in the rigidly stratified colonial framework of 'Rajpoot feudalism'. It focuses on the history of historical and administrative category in Mewar, because of the specific tribal background of most Bhumiya chiefs in the south-western Bhumat (or Bhomat) region of the former princely state of Udaipur, and because the strained relations between the Mewar Darbar and these petty chiefs throughout the 19th century about respective rights of sovereignty led the colonial British administration to become more and more involved in mediating different attitudes.

As Tod interested many scholars working on Rajasthan, his counterpart from Italy, Tessitori has also generated interest in certain quarters. Enrico Fasana in his paper on "Luigi Pio Tessitori: His Historical Research and the Rajasthan of His Time" provides detailed analysis of the long journey that Tessitori's investigations took. The paper takes refuge in various events that marked his presence in Rajasthan and India. The paper refers to various documents/papers produced by Tessitori that bring out social, political and economic history of Rajasthan. It is argued that Tessitori's attempt to catalogue the historical manuscripts and the bardic poems of Rajasthan is the first historically ascertained effort. It is observed that the *Annals* of Tod, the *Ras Mala* of Forbes, the *Gazetteers* of Walters, and of P.W. Powlett, the *Census Report* of Jodhpur of 1881, and *the Annual Administration Reports* of a single state never dealt scientifically with the question of the historical sources of Rajasthan. The relevance of Tessitori, it is argued, is not only as a collector but also because within the cultural heritage which he rediscovered, he made the ideals of that world known as well as a type of behaviour which was connected to those ideals. For the cultural environment of Rajasthan in general and of the Charans in particular, the commemorative poems are traditional ways of expression and education which underline hospitality, the sense of duty, honouring one's word, the protection of cattle, and the sacrifice of one's own life as a point of reference for heroism and loyalty to the above-mentioned ideals. Tessitori's studies of the language help us to understand the history of the people, it is maintained.

Fatima Imam's paper "Law and Administrative Practices: Institutionalising Sovereignty in 18th Century Jaipur" critiques theories of oriental despotism by analysing administrative practices of Jaipur's rulers. According to colonial administrators, who are still echoed in historical scholarship, Indian rulers could only legitimise their rule with the help of priests and theories of divine kingship. The pre-colonial notion of kingship and authority has been related to the will of Muslim rulers, especially Mughal emperors; and religions, customs and traditions of non-Muslims rulers. This concept of the nature of Indian states is examined by looking at the dynamics of Jaipur's legal administration. The discussion on roles of *Shastric* law elaborates cases of state interference in customary laws, and decisions of caste councils. Evidence provided by official records of Jaipur State demonstrates that administrative policies were not dependent on divine law or the will of rulers. Pre-existing Mughal institutions, however, were reinterpreted by this state to legitimise and institutionalise sovereignty. Her analysis adds to the existing historiography on

18th century states, where questions on the nature of state control are assessed and analysed. The paper deals with organisation of the justice system in the 18th century and emphasises that Jaipur's rulers drew parallels from both Mughal and *Shastric* models. Jaipur rulers' administrative practices poignantly point out the extent of state control. In addition, a study of policies negates the powerful critique that pre-colonial states failed to centralise their rule or cogently legitimise their power. This view resented by colonial rulers, in the early 18th century, focused primarily the system of fines, which led to venal practices. Rich and influential people could bribe the ministers of justice to buy freedom, while the poor and less fortunate could be imprisoned for life if they were unable to pay. Also, the British criticised Jaipur's mild laws, which were full of loopholes and allowed criminals to be inadequately punished. Cruelty was evident in mutilation sanctioned by religious law (both Islamic and *Shastric* laws prescribed this form of punishment). However, if these criticisms are reassessed in the light of available evidence, it becomes apparent that mutilations for crimes such as petty thefts were always discouraged. Jaipur records, the paper argues, indicate that most criminals were liable to fines or imprisonment.

Madhu Sethia's paper "Forms of Resistance in 18th Century Villages of Rajasthan" examines the forms of resistance adopted by various sections of the village society in the Hadauti (south-eastern Rajasthan) region. She argues that this region has very fertile land, low subsistence level and free peasant production had created relative stability in India's society and economy and that there was hardly any concentrated social effort to change completely the means, the methods and the relations of production and that a kind of equilibrium in the village society helped the state to appropriate the peasant's surplus. The paper focuses on the reaction of peasants, artisans and menials to an unequal distribution of economic resources, power and position. Since the big dramatic uprisings or movements have already been highlighted and studied in detail by many leading historians, the author feels that now there is a need to explore the day-to-day resistance within or outside the process of production in various forms. The paper finds that people resisted high-handedness and transgression of authority in various ways and the state found itself increasingly answerable to resolve the issues confronting the people. It points out that the forms of protest except in the case of Bheels hardly questioned the basis of state power. Most of the time forms of resistance adopted by settled peasants and artisans were non-violent with an underlying hope of getting justice. The methods and ways of cheating the system, as survival strategy, show beyond doubt that it was not easy to survive and the system was certainly questionable but individual solutions were practised instead of non-compliance. But it would not be fair to think that everything or anything was acceptable as is clear from the threatened or real migrations. The state was by and large able to check discontentment and anger by making timely intervention and necessary adjustments.

Rajasthan's culture has been enriched by the diversity it presents in terms of music, crafts, and epics like Dhoḷa-Maru and Mira. Section II has contributions that reflect on Mira Bai, Dhola-Maru, and cross-border influence of music and crafts. The papers offer new interpretations and reflections.

Frances Taft in her paper "Six Incarnations of Mirabai" says that it is truly astonishing that a woman who lived in the first half of the 16th century and was largely obscure in her own times has become almost a household name in early 21st century India. Mira is now known in many, overlapping and contradictory incarnations. The author lists six of them viz., the *bhaktan* Mira, the literary Mira the media Mira; the socio-political protest Mira, Gandhi's ideal Hindu wife Mira, and author's own, the historical Mira. It is argued that there may be many more faces, but these six serve to illustrate how wide are the interests and concerns of those who invoke her name. It is perhaps not surprising that the young widow whose family were devout *Vaishnavas* and who was herself pious from childhood should turn to her lord Krishna Giridhar in her bereavement and reduced circumstances. The paper points out that Mira's path was different from that of so many other Rajput widows. One knows Mira today in her various modern incarnations because in her own time she had the courage to defy her in-laws, ignore social disapproval, associate with other devotees of whatever origin, leave Chittor, and dedicate the rest of her life to singing the praise of her lord Giridhar and her devotion to him.

Aleksandra Szyszko in her paper "Is the *Dhola-Maru ra duha* only a Poetic Composition" points out that *Dhola-Maru ra duha* is an interesting elaboration on two levels—both as a poetic composition, which occupies an important place in both Rajasthani and Hindi literature and as a relict of image of the society and culture of medieval Rajasthan. The poem mentions multiple Rajasthani cultures. One comes across people from various social strata (e.g., from the castes of

Rebari, Dom, Jogi, Dhadhi, Banjara). There is also description of certain folk beliefs, fauna, flora, etc. *Dhola-Maru* is presented in two traditions—literary and oral. The latter is still popular today.

Vijay Verma in his "The Music of Western Rajasthan: A Wider Regional Context" tries to observe Rajasthani music in a wider regional context. The paper, while dealing with music and musicians, the *Mand, Asa, Sameri, Sub and Jog, Maru, Prabhati* song type or *raga,* brings out the various nuances and interpretations. In doing so, Verma only scratches the vast subject area. There are many other aspects one could think of. For example, the types of instruments used; the ubiquitous *Tandura,* the type of songs sung with it and the *Durga* which often surfaces in them; the highly evolved art of *Manjira* (cymbals)—playing in Gujarat and its adaptation in the *Terahtali* 'dance' of Rajasthan, the popularity of the *Derun* in north-west Rajasthan and the use by the *Dhadhis* of Punjab of a diminutive *Derun*; the musician communities and their numbers and role in the various sub-regions; vestiges, if any, of the seemingly lost art of *Kadkha—singing by the Kadkait-bards,* and so on. Perhaps, there is need for a larger, coordinated, cooperative effort.

Varsha Joshi in her paper on "Changing Profiles of Crafts in Rajasthan" argues that certainly, crafts sector is undergoing changes with need and demand in the market. Though, on one hand, the handicrafts industry has been treated as a neglected industry in the government policies, yet on the other hand it is proving to be one of the major sectors of employment and financial gain. This has brought about another change where professionalism has also entered this sector. Unfortunately, what is happening is that we are losing on the traditional skills, designs and colours. There is certainly now a need to preserve the traditional handicrafts and this could be done primarily through government interventions in the form of crafts museums, etc.

Rajasthan is located in an environmentally fragile region. The land, on the one hand, has communities preserving environment, but on the other hand modern development and high population pressures have rendered the environment unsustainable. There is erosion of old institutions and emergence of new ones. The papers in Section III provide an insight into environmental issues and the role of human beings and animals in protecting Rajasthan's environmental legacy.

Paul Robbins and Anil K. Chhangani's paper "Protecting Wolves from Sheep: People and Wildlife in the Rajasthani Aravalli" is located in Kumbalgarh Wildlife Sanctuary in Pali district Rajasthan. The paper points out that the problem at Kumbhalgarh is that a co-evolved ecological system cannot be suddenly turned into a wilderness, either in practical terms or ecological ones. The fundamental issue more generally is the problem inherent in the insistence on enforcing an *ecological misunderstanding*, one that presupposes a case of people *versus* wildlife, a zero-sum choice, with limited historical precedent. This understanding is based on the assumption that one size fits all rule for ecologically diverse areas and an unstable ontological distinction between 'human beings' and 'nature' exists. It is argued that the latter problem, fundamental to conservation conflicts and failures elsewhere in the world, is one deeply rooted in modernist partitions of the world that tend not only to lead to poor science, but also impoverished democracy. Nor does it by any means necessarily fit the indigenous cosmologies of Rajasthan. The authors believe that enforcement of the Supreme Court's order of banning and criminalising all human activity in every wildlife reserve in the nation may lead to an increasing rate of conservation failures in many areas: a decline in the species it is designed to protect, a deterioration in the potential for participatory ecological democracy, and an erasure of dynamic cultural practice. However, the authors caution that their findings do not suggest that totally free and open use of forests is ecologically sustainable. On the contrary, the historical elimination of encroachments on forest areas, a crack-down on commercial exploitation of these areas, and a full effort to halt poaching, are all prerequisites to the survival of key endemic species, including wolves, panthers and a host of other fauna. They also argue that data do not suggest that the plantation protection, and enclosure practices of the Forest Department are wholly inappropriate; at least not where they (like local subsistence practices) follow a rotational 'shifting mosaic' that mimics historical disturbance patterns. The authors commend the Rajasthan Forest Department as it has performed heroically in attempting to implement crucial conservation efforts with extremely constrained budgets and limited operational opportunities. The paper finally suggests that the success of some recent conservation efforts has largely been afforded by subsidies provided by some of the country's poorest and most politically marginal people, and that the temporal and spatial variability afforded by extant (pre-2004) local practices is likely essential to the conservation of the region's flora and fauna. In the absence of ecologically and politically sensitive planning and practice, a wholesale ban on human disturbance will likely do more harm than good. The future of Rajasthan's wildlife heritage thus hangs in the balance in their view.

Trevor Birkenholtz, in his paper "Murky Waters: Mediating Local Institutions for Demand Side Solutions in Rajasthani Irrigation Systems" tries to evaluate the potential success of future groundwater management in Rajasthan by comparing and contrasting existing local and technical groundwater knowledge, and irrigation practices and institutions. It draws out the tensions and contradictions between local and bureaucratic ways of thinking and doing. The paper provides a brief history of the tubewell in Rajasthan and the problem of groundwater management as through the eyes of the state and the World Bank. It argues that resource privatisation as the remedy for demand side management is a forgone conclusion in the usual discourse. The state's acceptance of funding from the World Bank ensures that the problem of groundwater is framed so that privatisation is the solution, because the World Bank's solutions to natural resource management rest on an ideology of market-based or neo-liberal approaches. On the obverse, local people conceive of groundwater not as something to be privately held but as something to be collectively managed, as illustrated by the cooperative use of tubewells. The paper also brings out that the localisation of governance is problematic because the three-tiered Groundwater Authorities set up through the State Act consist of appointed consultants at every level of governance rather than democratically elected representatives. The localising of governance in this way will simply result in a more efficient means to subject local people to state control, while reproducing the beneficial political economic positions of local elites. Technological expansion is of concern for several reasons, viz., local distrust in government expertise and past government failures to follow through on projects, frustrates both local land managers and hinders the prospect of future collaboration. On the other hand, the knowledge and techniques of tubewell drilling firms and that of the *Sungha* hold more currency for locals because they are more accessible, both in terms of the approach and method of implementation. Additionally, the paper points out that technologies, such as tubewells, are historically not adopted neutrally but benefit those with the ability to adopt them and to control the political apparatus. The paper also shows that sprinkler and drip irrigation technologies can significantly increase irrigation water-use efficiency. Finally, it argues that the successful dissemination of technologies to ensure long-term equity and efficiency in their adoption and implementation depends on the cultivation of local institutions through democratic government intervention.

The camel population of Rajasthan, and of India as a whole, is experiencing a steep decline. While water-intensive animals, such as buffalo, are increasing in numbers significantly, camel breeding is rapidly being abandoned. These trends would render Rajasthan more vulnerable to droughts, increase dependence on non-renewable energy and have severe negative impacts on the livelihoods of many poor families depending on working camels as a source of livelihood. The paper by Ilse Köhler-Rollefson and Hanwant Singh Rathore entitled "The Camel in Rajasthan: Agricultural Biodiversity under Threat" argues that in order to prevent a further decline and eventual near-extinction of this species in India, it is necessary to adopt participatory approaches and focus research and development efforts on the needs and worries of the people whose livelihoods depend on camels, especially the *Raika* camel breeding community. Equally or even more important, the government urgently needs to create a supportive policy framework by providing secure access to grazing areas and encouraging the marketing of camel products. In doing so, the paper probes the economics of camel in Rajasthan's context, its social significance, role in people's livelihood, ecological benefits that camel gives, camel breeds and host of other related features. As camel is vital for Rajasthan and people's livelihood, especially poor, it articulates for non-discriminating policy towards camel.

Then, Nirmal Kumar's "Camel-Theft in 18th Century Rajasthan: Some Observations" deals with the prevailing trend in Rajasthan's historiography that it would be only expected to presuppose a wholly Mughal type judicial administration and crime situation in the state. The author tries to test this assumption in the essay. Taking camel theft as a centre point, the paper points to the fact that camel theft was in existence in 18th century Rajasthan. The state, though aware of the problem, took serious action in limited cases. People used all available methods to retrieve the stolen animal. Caste/community did play a role in tracing and fining the camel thieves. The discussion also leads one to believe that camel theft was an organised business for many. Retaliations also took place in certain cases when the stolen animal, when traced, was not returned to the owner. Judicial system in the Mughal era was only partially helpful in controlling the crime, the author argues.

Women in Rajasthan have played a vital role in its history, culture, society and economy. However, their true role has not been given due place. This vibrant half of Rajasthan's population is looked into afresh through contributions in Section IV. Women in Rajasthan have added role in the modern development process and management of resources.

Kathleen O'Reilly, through her paper "Gendered Participatory Approaches to Drinking Water Supply: Power and Practice", explores participatory approaches to development as negotiated practices that encompass women fieldworkers' understanding of the (in)significance of women's participation to project success and their own personal understandings of participation. The author argues that participation is a form of power, wielded by women fieldworkers and reflective of tensions between them, their co-workers and their clients. The paper demonstrates that development projects are sites of struggle, where the politics between actors impact project outcomes. As the work of a project unfolds, staff and constituents engage in constant negotiations over meanings of terms like 'participation'. The author argues that the outcomes of these struggles have importance not only for meanings of participation, but project outcomes (e.g., will women become empowered or clean stand posts or both?). Shifting meanings of participation cannot be pinned down by training and policies, it is maintained. Instead, relationships of power between staff and between staff and their constituents provide clues for understanding what meanings emerge, when and why. The paper raises, many issues that require further investigations in the context of the social complexities of development implementation. Given their increasing focus on women, it is critical we move towards a richer understanding of participatory programme impacts on meanings, spaces and relationships.

The labour market in developing countries is segmented into formal and informal. The attributes of both these sectors are different. One encounters regional and gender differentiations in employment in the informal/unorganised sector. Surjit Singh, in his paper on "Female Employment in Unorganised Sector in Rajasthan" examines female employment in unorganised sector in Rajasthan. The paper finds a decline in share of female workers in total main workers during the eighties. In urban areas, though, the share has improved, it has deteriorated in rural areas. The work participation rates in most activities have improved, but service activities have concentration of female workers. There are occupations, which are only urban in nature, and that shift towards rural Rajasthan of such occupation has not taken place over time, though few exceptions are there. This also means that increased opportunities are available in urban centres only. An important finding of the paper is that 84 per cent of female workers in Rajasthan have education of higher secondary or below with majority being illiterate. More educated female workforce is found in urban areas compared to rural areas. In case of employment of females in Rajasthan, employment rate according to principal status was 27 in rural Rajasthan compared to just 9.3 in urban Rajasthan. In Rajasthan, women constitute 31 per cent of rural unorganised sector workforce and 27 per cent of urban unorganised sector workforce. At the aggregate level the percentage is 29. There is concentration of unorganised sector female workers in rural areas, non-agricultural enterprises and establishments. Female child workers' proportion is higher in case of agricultural enterprises compared to non-agricultural enterprises. The proportion of female workers in total workers is higher in urban agricultural enterprises, while it is higher in case of rural non-agricultural enterprises. Besides, share in total workforce is lower of female workers in non-agricultural enterprises. Female workers in own enterprises are concentrated in three activities, viz., manufacturing, retail trade and community, social and personal services. Women are significant contributors in raising of livestock and manufacturing in terms of employment share. The other activities where women workers in own enterprises are relevant are mining and quarrying, wholesale trade, community, social and personal services and retail trade. Community, social and personal services, manufacturing and raising of livestock in non-directory enterprises employ about 84 per cent of all female workers.

Food security implies several aspects of hunger, including famine, energy deficiency, micronutrient deficiency and nutrients depleting illness. Food security questions are tackled at global, regional, national, household and individual levels. Food security largely depends on access and entitlements to food, which depend on improved incomes for many. Women in developing countries are the principal, if not the sole, economic support to themselves and their children and they are increasingly responsible for food security. Women play a crucial role, though constrained and undervalued, in ensuring food availability for household members, in both normal times and in periods of stress. Achieving household food security is concerned with enough food for all members at all times. It implies freedom from future vulnerability to food and other shocks, as well as a guarantee of adequate current consumption. World Bank looks at food security in terms of access by all people at all times to enough food for active healthy life. However, nutrition security is broader than food security that requires broadening and diversification of our food base. At the present juncture, the extent and depth of food security in the developing countries remains unquestionable. One-sixth of the developing world's population, mainly children and women, do not have access to sufficient food to lead healthy, productive lives. The progress in tackling food insecurity is slow. Micronutrient deficiencies (iron, iodine and vitamin A) also remain widespread among children and women, especially poor women. Besides, there is neglect of zinc, riboflavin and calcium, and the global extent and consequences of their deficiencies are unknown. The consequences of micronutrient malnutrition include mortality and morbidity, lower cognitive ability and work production and impaired reproduction. Varsha Joshi and Surjit Singh in their paper "Crisis, Food and Nutrition Security: Some Gender Concerns" attempt to look at issues related to gender and food and nutrition security in times of crisis. It also presents nutrition situation in India and Rajasthan. The paper argues that India's nutrition problem is not so much of lack of food grains, but of lack of adequate access to food in over 30 per cent of poor households whose family incomes are so low that even with 70 per cent of family income spent on food, nutritional needs are not met. Over time, food security problem has been handled effectively, though nutrition security is found wanting. In the context of household food security, food security is necessary but not sufficient condition for adequate nutrition, the other conditions like care and health are also important. The paper argues that though during the times of crisis, improvement is observed in food and nutritional security, though women and poor are still vulnerable. There is also no doubt that women are nutrition mediators. The paper suggests a way out to ensure household food and nutrition security.

The last paper by P.R. Sharma and G.S. Narwani "Two-Child Norm in Panchayati Raj: Evidence from Rajasthan" maps the administrative changes that took place in adoption of two-child norm in Rajasthan. It is argued that population stabilisation cannot be viewed in isolation from poverty, illiteracy, status of women in society and living conditions. No doubt, panchayats at the grass roots are expected to become effective instruments for population stabilisation. In Rajasthan, 82 per cent male and 18 per cent female PRI representatives have been removed on account of having a third child during the last 10 years. Experience of southern states, the paper points out, has shown that education and people's participation are key to success for small family norm. Since divergent views have been expressed in different quarters advocating that PRI representatives should not suffer from coercive measure. In fact, this sort of coercion goes against the National Population Policy, 2000, which does not prescribe any size of the family. The public health system needs to be strengthened. Awareness creation of the merits of the small family is also required and couples should be offered a variety of contraceptive options. If the government takes care of the people, population will take care of itself. There are host of programmes geared at family planning but no programme of national significance can succeed without political will. Looking to declining population growth rates in southern states and even China shifting from compulsion to choices now, disqualification on account of small family norm in limited number of states and that too limited only to PRI representatives, as role models for society, can hardly make any visible impact. Education, communication, awareness generation, along with political will, can be a model for success in the field of family welfare.

Rajasthan today is a rapidly changing society. Within a span of two generations, people have seen bigger changes in their pattern of life than the several preceding centuries. Despite the many old habits, customs and traditions have been preserved. It is this that makes Rajasthan a wonderful laboratory for studying the processes of change. In order to understand the processes, contributions in this volume have greatly been successful.

Conclusively, it can be stated that all the papers with their inherent diversity significantly contribute to the understanding of Rajasthan's culture, society, polity and economy. Women empowerment has been core of all recent debates in Rajasthan and would lead to unshackling of age-old *purdah* system in the Rajasthan's society. On the economic front, Rajasthan is coming out of the 'BIMARU' tag attached to it, through slowly. The challenges that Rajasthan faces are immense and the modern process of change has to be continued.

Section I

History and Polity with Tod and Tessitori

2

Multiple Histories of Amber

Tod's Annals versus Local Oral Tradition

Elena Karachkova

In this paper I intend to illustrate and discuss some specific ways, in which oral traditions coexist and sustain a dialogue with written sources in a semi-literate community.[1] The community in question is the population of Amber—a town situated about six miles to the north-east of Jaipur. Together with the magnificent fort-palace, built high on the mountain range, the town at the bottom remained the capital of the Kacchawa Rajputs' kingdom from 11th until early 18th century, when the court moved to the newly-built city of Jaipur. While the fort-palace complex, initially under the supervision of the Archeological Survey of India and now the State Ministry of Tourism, is kept in a relatively good condition, the town suffers from neglect of the above-mentioned authorities. This neglect results in chaotic construction right in the old part of Amber, within the town walls—"the only surviving model of a medieval town that exists today in Rajasthan" (Nath, 1996: 5).

Along with other heritage landmarks around Jaipur, such as Galta and Gaitor, the fort of Amber is routinely included into the itineraries of domestic and foreign tourists, who visit Jaipur. Travel literature acknowledges the town, but selectively: it briefly mentions two or three of its most outstanding heritage monuments. So the majority of the so-called 'organised tourists' comes to Amber and leaves it unaware of the town's existence. Only backpackers can be seen browsing Amber's streets, but even their favourite publication—*The Lonely Planet Guide*[2]—does not provide any help: it does not even mention the town. But even this limited exposure to the 'tourist gaze'[3] affects the local oral tradition.

The data for this presentation was collected in the course of two brief fieldtrips to Jaipur/Amber area of Rajasthan: four months in winter of 2000–2001 and four months in winter of 2002–2003. On more occasions than I can count I browsed the streets of Amber, asking questions about the town's history and particular temples, wells or residential buildings. My respondents and volunteer guides through the town were men and women, young and old, literate and illiterate, as well as school children; Hindus, Muslims and Jains; Rajputs, Brahmans and Minas; temple priests, store owners and school teachers. On several occasions I hired trained and licensed guides working at the fort/palace complex above to hear the intended-for-tourist-consumption version of Amber's history. I also conducted a lot of interviews in Jaipur, but mostly with professionals—historians, art historians, anthropologists and museum curators.

My discussion of 'oral tradition' is theoretically based on Jan Vansina's path breaking study *Oral Tradition as History,* 1985.[4] The author did extensive fieldwork among non-literate societies of Africa. He explores the potential value of oral traditions for historical reconstructions. David Henige's monographs *The Chronology of Oral Tradition: Quest for a Chimera, 1974, Oral Historiography, 1982*, and the "Introduction" to his recently published *Princely States of India: a Guide to Chronology and Rulers, 2004,* discuss similar issues. Vansina defines oral traditions as "verbal messages, which are important statements of the past beyond the present generation" (Vansina, 1985: 27). My usage of the term meets a stricter criterion suggested by David Henige. He insists that to constitute an oral tradition these verbal messages about the past "(...) should be commonly or universally known in a given culture. Versions that are not widely known should rightfully be considered as 'testimony' (...)" (Henige, 1982: 2).

Oral historians believe that in this day and age, with the advent of literacy, uncontaminated oral traditions no longer exist. Contamination occurs as a response and adaptation of oral traditions to new information, contained in written sources. David Henige suggests a term 'feedback' for this process (Henige, 1982: 81–87). In colonial and post-colonial situations feedback often stems from writings of missionaries, colonial administrations, or early European travellers.

Without a doubt, Tod's *Annals and Antiquities of Rajasthan*, constitute the most important source of such feedback in the oral traditions of the former princely states of Rajputana. But as residents of Amber and Jaipur kept narrating their glorious history to me, I started to realise that with a few exceptions their perception of Amber's past was shaped not so much by what Tod actually wrote in his *Annals of Amber* (Tod, 1997: II, 279–354), but by their own idea of what he may have written as an outstanding and perceptive historian. Marzia Balzani's recently published study of court ritual in Jodhpur supports my observations. She writes:

> In response to some of my questions, Rajputs in contemporary Jodhpur would, typically, lead me to their remarkably unworn and underused copies of Tod's *Annals and Antiquities of Rajasthan* to find the answer. In these instances it was evident that part of the modern Rajput's sense of history and historical worth is now derived from the historical-romantic writings of a nineteenth century Briton, who himself sought the truth of history in the songs of the bards of Rajasthan. (...) The niceties of the post-colonial, post-orientalist, non-essentialising, post-modern strategies and approaches used by some contemporary academics are not on the whole known or of interest to the Rajputs, who provided the materials for the ethnography that follows. An unreconstructed Colonel Tod and Dr Luigi Tessitori were, however, known and held up, despite what often turned out to be little actual knowledge of the works, produced by these men, as models of exemplary scholarship and historical truth (Balzani, 2003: 13–14).

My interlocutors in Amber (both Rajputs and non-Rajputs) would also often refer to Tod as the source of their knowledge about particular events of the past, but their narratives would follow the spirit rather than the letter of Tod's writings.

As the town gradually gets incorporated into the tourist space, travel literature and narratives offered by the licensed guides on site, i.e., 'the marketing discourse of Amber' becomes another important source of feedback for the oral tradition. I found out that my respondents, who obviously do not read guidebooks or take guided tours through their native town, did not remain oblivious of or indifferent to the marketing discourse of Amber's history. At the same time they do not reproduce it uncritically. Local oral tradition contests a number of parametres of the travel literature.

Oral traditions, being messages about the past, are at the same time commentaries to the existing situations. "All sorts of existing situations,—writes Vansina,—prompt explanations as to why they exist. (...) One set of explanations is often given for remarkable features in a landscape or to explain monuments" (Vansina, 1985: 10). He refers to this type of explanations as *iconatrophy*. Since 'tourist gaze' is normally drawn to the heritage landmarks, residents of Amber, both literate and illiterate, frequently find themselves in a position, when they have to 'explain', i.e. *interpret* the 'when' and 'why' of particular heritage landmarks to the outsiders. During our 'heritage walks' through the town my respondents would always chose a particular site—a *haveli*, a *kund* or a temple—to narrate a relevant, in their opinion, episode in Amber's history. It would be fair to say, that architectural monuments of Amber are more than important means of sustaining collective memory: simply by being there they constitute visible and tangible 'evidence' of the past events.

Consequently, for this presentation I organised some of my findings as my respondents would—around an important heritage landmark of Amber—one of its oldest step-wells. This was the site, which one of my volunteer guides chose to narrate to me one of the most glorious episodes in the history of the ruling clan—the conquest of Amber.

The Step-well of Minas or How Amber was Won

It may be in a short paragraph or a whole chapter, depending on the genre of the publication, but marketing discourse always addresses 'historical' circumstances of the establishment of the Dhoondhar kingdom. It is said that in the 10th-11th centuries A.D. the territory of the future kingdom was taken from the local tribe of Minas through a series of decisive battles. Before Amber became the capital of the Kacchawas in the 11th century, their temporary strongholds were—not necessarily in this order—Khoh,[5] Dausa[6] and Manch.[7] The alliance with Dausa's Birgujar Rajputs was established through the marriage of Dulha Rai—the leader of the Kacchawas, while Khoh and Manch were captured in battles. The travel literature's 'narrative of conquest' is generally 'borrowed' from Tod's *Annals of Amber* with or without references to the author.[8]

As far as academic discourse is concerned, most Indian historians argue, that the verifiable history of the Kacchawas starts in the 16th century, during the reign of Raja Bharmal (r. 1547–1573), who established an alliance with the Mughals by giving his daughter in marriage to Emperor Akbar. They quote from Tod only to dismiss his writings as myth making. Jadunath Sarkar was a particularly harsh critic of Tod. In his still influential monograph on the history of Jaipur (Sarkar, 1984) he calls Tod's *Annals of Amber* a 'cock-and-bull story' (Sarkar, 1984: 23) and a 'classic howler' (Sarkar, 1984: 27). He is particularly impatient with Tod for confounding, most likely because of the consonance of names, the cultural hero of the Kacchawas Dulha Rai (the Groom Prince), who led his clan from Narwar to Dhoondhar, with Dhola, the hero of Rajasthani folk epic *Dhola-Maru ra duha.* Sarkar expresses the prevailing opinion among Indian historians, when he says:

> With the coming of the Mughal Emperors and their highly civilised court in the middle of the sixteenth century, Rajput history emerges from the delusive mists of oral tradition and bardic exaggeration, into the clear light of authentic contemporary record (Sarkar, 1984: 31).

Since the "delusive mists of oral tradition" are precisely the concern of this paper, I will, following the example of the marketing discourse, quote from Tod at some length and compare his written narrative of "how Amber was won" with living, breathing and ever changing local lore. It is important to realise that Tod's narrative is also based on oral tradition, but fixed and frozen by the 17th–18th centuries in *khyats* (chronicles) and *vamshavalis* (clan or lineage genealogies).

According to Tod

> On the death of Sora Sing (Singh),[9] prince of Nurwar (Narwar), his brother usurped the government, depriving the infant, Dhola Rae, of his inheritance. His mother, clothing herself in mean apparel, put the infant in a basket, which she placed on her head, and traveled westward until she reached the town of Khogong (Khoh gaon) (...) then inhabited by the Meenas (Minas) (Tod, 1997: 281).

After many trials on the road the woman finally reached Khoh and found an "employment for food" in the house of the Mina chieftain.

> (...) As soon as the Meena chief discovered the rank of the illustrious fugitive, he adopted her as his sister, and Dhola Rae as his nephew. When the boy had attained the age of Rajpoot (Rajput) manhood

> (fourteen), he was sent to Delhi, with the tribute of Khohgong, to attend instead of the Meena. The young Cuchwaha (Kucchwaha) remained there five years, when he conceived the idea of usurping his benefactor's authority. Having consulted the Meena *d'hadi,* or bard, as to the best means of executing his plan, he recommended him to take advantage of the festival of the *Dewali* (Diwali), when it is customary to perform the ablutions *en masse*, in a tank. Having brought a few of his Rajpoot brethren from Delhi, he accomplished his object, filling the reservoirs in which the Meenas bathed with their dead bodies. The treacherous bard did not escape; Dhola Rae put him to death with his own hands, observing, "He who had proved unfaithful to one master, could not be trusted by another". He then took possession of Khogong (Tod, 1997: 281).

Dhola Rae's next move was to establish a strategic alliance with Dausa, ruled at the time by Birgujar clan of Rajputs. He married the daughter of the ruler, and "as the Birgoojur (Birgujar) had no male issue, he resigned his power to his son-in-law" (Tod, 1997: 282).

> With the additional means thus at his disposal, Dhola determined to subjugate the Seroh (Sira) tribe of Meenas, whose chief, Rao Natto, dwelt at Mauch (Manch). Again he was victorious, and deeming his new conquest better adapted for a residence than Khogong, he transferred his infant government thither, changing the name of Mauch, in honour of his great ancestor, to Ramgurh (Ramgarh). (Tod, 1997: 282)

Tod then Proceeds to Describe the Death of Dhola Rae

On the way back from the temple of Jamwai Mata, Dhola Rae's procession was attacked by an army of Seera Meenas. The ruler was killed, and his followers fled.

> Maroni[10] escaped, and bore a posthumous child, who was named Kankul (Kakil), and who conquered the country of Dhoondhar (Dhundhar). His son Maidul Rao, made a conquest of Amber from the Soosawut (Susawat) Meenas, the residence of their chief, named Bhatto, who had the title of Rao, and was head of the Meena confederation (Tod, 1997: 282).

The local tradition regarding the conquest of Manch, which is currently in circulation among the Kacchawas of Jaipur/Amber area, differs considerably from the version reproduced in Tod's *Annals of*

Amber. The most important difference is, of course, that Dulha Rai does not die. He is either healed after being heavily wounded or, resurrected—as in the temple tradition, which I wrote down in March of 2003—due to the divine interference of Jamvai Mata herself. The oral tradition of conquest of Manch is a well-known and normalised narrative, which does not allow for too many variations, because it establishes an important moment in the Kacchawa identity discourse—how Jamwai Mata became the *kuldevi* or the patron goddess of the clan. The most typical account—by a Kacchawa Rajput male—is reproduced in Lindsey Harlan's study (Harlan, 1992):

> The Kachvahas came from Navar (Narwar) near Gwalior in Madhya Pradesh. They fought their way to Dosa (Dausa), which they won from the Gujar Rajputs. They took some land from the Mina tribe by treachery. Finally, at (...) Rajgarh,[11] they were defeated. Dularai, their leader, was badly injured. He lay unconscious and dying on the battlefield. Jamwai Mata appeared to him in a vision. She said, "I am the *kuldevi* of Minas, but I am angry with them. I am a vegetarian but they offer me meat and wine in my temple." Jamwai Mata then turned herself into a cow and sprayed milk on Dularai's face. She revived the rest of the Kachvahas in the same way. Meanwhile the Minas were rejoicing over their victory. They were drunk. The Kachvahas successfully attacked them. Since then Jamvai Mata has been our *kuldevi* (Harlan, 1992: 55–56).

Tod's account of conquest of Manch seems to be a corrupt version of the above: it shares and logically connects two central motifs of the more popular version—Jamwai Mata (a visit to her temple) and death (or near death) of the ruler—but connects them through different logic and with a different outcome. Yet Tod's *Annals* did leave their impact on this oral tradition. In another version, reproduced in Harlan, 2000 it is Dhola, not Dulha Rai, who lies dying on the battle-field. His wife Maru prays to the Goddess, who appears and heals the hero with the sprinkle of cow's milk (Harlan, 2000: 81).

But note the most paradoxical aspect of Tod's account: although Khoh and Manch were just temporary strongholds, while Amber remained the capital of the kingdom for seven centuries, no developed narrative associated with the conquest of Amber is represented in Tod's *Annals*. He simply states that it was Dhola Rae's grandson—Maidul Rao[12]—who captured Amber from the Susawat Minas in the 11th century. Tourist literature does not elaborate on the issue in question either, but, contrary to Tod, attributes the conquest of Amber to the reign of Kakil Dev, Dulha Rai's son.

Local oral tradition—dozens of accounts I have heard from my respondents in both Amber and Jaipur—creatively overcomes this gap. It borrows the Khoh episode as depicted by Tod and transplants its central theme—the *Diwali* massacre of Minas—on Amber soil. A licensed guide of the Fort/Palace complex, himself a resident of Amber, told me the following story, while we were looking down at the town from the fort above:

> Before the tenth century this territory belonged to the tribe of Minas. They worshipped Amba Mata, who is a form of Kali. That is where the ancient name of the town—Ambavati—comes from. See the two rows of fort walls, surrounding the town? They were built by the Minas. Minas are a ferocious tribe and good warriors, except for Deepawali,[13] when they drink and engage in festivities. It was on the night of the Deepawali that the Kacchawas attacked and captured the town.

Some of the narratives I recorded are richly embellished by details, narrating past and commenting on the present. For example, an elderly Rajput woman concluded the already familiar story, saying that since that time Kacchawa Rajputs always wear black jackets on the eve of the Diwali to commemorate that fateful night, because the night of Diwali is the darkest night of the calendar year. For my respondent the tradition of wearing black on Diwali constituted the 'proof' that Amber had been conquered on Diwali, just like for the licensed guide quoted above, the old fort walls were in themselves an 'evidence' of Mina's presence on this soil before it was seized by the Kacchawas.

Furthermore, as I found out, the Khoh story was not simply borrowed from Tod's *Annals of Amber* and transplanted on Amber's soil, but metaphorically—and literally—inscribed on one of its most famous heritage monuments. I am referring to the controversy surrounding one of the *kunds* or step-wells, located in the heart of the old town. It is one of the oldest water sources in Amber. The well's water basin is about thirty feet deep. It is surrounded by a square platform with *chhatris* (kiosks) at its four corners and a two-level verandah on its western side. Archeologists and historians, as well as tourist guidebooks, attribute the well's construction to early 18th century. It has been established, that the well was built by a eunuch of

Sawai Jai Singh's *Zenani Deorhi* (harem)—Panna Miyan, hence its name—*Panna Miyan ka kund.*[14]

One of my first local guides through the town chose this particular site to tell me about the *Diwali* massacre of Minas, suggesting that this may have been the reservoir, where they had been performing their ritual ablutions, when the Kacchawas attacked and filled it with their dead bodies. He said that the name of the step-well was *Panna Mina ka kund* (The Ancient[15] Step-well of Minas) and pointed to a *devanagari* inscription—stating the same, hand painted on the side of the platform. When I objected, that the structure did not look that old, he said that one of the *chhatris* was made of stone, which had been mined here in Amber in 11th-12th century.

Although none of my other respondents explicitly connected the events of the fateful Diwali night to the step-well in question, the issue of its true name remains a matter of principle for the local residents. Two years later I unexpectedly became involved in a contest of narratives, the details of which I reproduce below, based on an entry in my field diary:

February 14, 2003

> This trip to Amber was inspired by an article in *Dainik Bhaskar*,[16] stating that the dispute between the local bureaucratic authorities over the issue of the Heritage Walk in Amber was finally over, and preparations to launch the walk were underway. So, armed with the article and playing the role of a nosy foreign tourist, I went to the Tourist Information booth in the Fort/Palace museum complex and asked to provide me with a guide, who would take me on the Heritage Walk through the town. (...) My guide readily admitted that no one had informed or instructed him regarding the Walk, but he was willing to do his best. (...) Despite his best intentions, the guide, who does not live in Amber, but resides in a village, ten km away from Jaipur, could not add any information to what I already knew. Very soon, as it often happened, several local residents, including an elderly Rajput, joined our small procession. From this point on our walk turned into a fascinating contest of narratives. The Rajput immediately seized the initiative. He knew a lot of stories about particular temples. According to him, each and every temple on our way was built in the ninth century, and not a century earlier or later.[17] The guide, who must have read something about the town, presented the marketing discourse, albeit, in a radically

> abbreviated and simplified form. The Rajput, on the other hand, presented the rich counter narrative—the local oral tradition.
>
> (...) A particularly heated argument started at the famous step-well. The Rajput insisted that the step-well was built in the ninth century, i.e. before the Kacchawa Rajputs invaded the area, and its proper name was Panna Mina ka kund. To prove his point he drew everybody's attention to the recently repaired side of the platform: while the cement was still fresh, someone has scratched "panna mina ka kund" on its surface. This could not have happened more than two years ago, because I clearly recall, that during my previous field trip the same inscription was painted in the same spot with red oil paint. My guide argued, like most tourist publications do, that the proper name of the well was Panna Miyan ka kund, but could neither explain the meaning of the name, nor produce any proof. Other locals, who joined our walk in the process, took the Rajput's side. So, in the end of the Heritage Walk, the Rajput and his counter narrative emerged victorious out of this contest of narratives.

The local oral tradition of conquest of Dhundhar reveals signs of feedback from two kinds of written sources: Tod's *Annals of Amber* and the marketing discourse.

As far as Tod is concerned, one of the two versions of Manch/Ramgarh tradition follows Tod in placing Dhola and Maru, rather than Dulha Rai, in the midst of the dramatic events. It nevertheless rejects the version of the Kacchawa cultural hero's death for it contradicts the logic of the *kuldevi* Jamwai Mata tradition. But most importantly, the oral tradition borrows the Khoh episode from Tod to fill in the gap in his own narrative—lack of the circumstances associated with the conquest of Amber proper. While the Manch/Ramgarh oral tradition is constantly reinforced in the collective memory of the Kacchawas, who visit the place to worship their *kuldevi* in the temple of Jamwai Mata, contemporary Khoh is but an insignificant village with no monuments to remind Rajputs of their glorious past.

In tourist destinations heritage monuments are the focus of 'the tourist gaze'. Consequently, they also become the focus of concentration of competing narratives. Vansina writes:

> Speculation about the why of a landscape, a monument, a name, or a custom sometimes became so convincing that it was accepted as

truth and added to the information of tradition, in which the original datum now became 'proof' of the truth of the information (Vansina, 1985: 157).

The controversy surrounding the true name of the step-well perfectly illustrates this point. Written sources established the name of the well as *Panna Miyan*. Collective memory preserved the name of the tribe—*Mina*—as first rulers of these lands. Oral tradition incorporated the new datum, but edited it by virtue of consonance according to the original information, stored in the collective memory. The step-well became known as *Panna Mina* and today constitutes the 'proof' of the original oral tradition that Minas resided in these lands before the Kacchawas.

Notes

1. By stressing the semi-literate state of the community in question I follow, rather uncritically, the notion shared by some oral historians, that oral tradition survives as long as literacy is not general (Vansina, 1985: 156). But I am not totally convinced. For example, in Moscow—a hundred per cent literate city—stories about mystical or mysterious events of the past, surrounding several historically important landmarks, are widely known. They meet all the requirements to be identified as oral traditions.
2. The *Lonely Planet Guide*, positions itself in the market as a tourist publication, which leads its readers off and beyond the beaten tourist tracks.
3. John Urri's term (See Urri, 1990).
4. I worked with the second, revised edition. The book was originally published in 1961.
5. Currently Khoh-Nagoria, a village 5 miles east of Jaipur.
6. A town east of Jaipur.
7. Currently the village of Jamwa-Ramgarh, 32 km to the northeast of Jaipur. The place is famous for its Jamwai Mataji temple—the *kuldevi* (tutelary deity) of the Kacchawa clan.
8. See for example Nath (1996: 15–16) and Dhama (1955: 74–76).
9. In brackets is the currently accepted spelling of geographical and proper names.
10. Maroni or Maru—the bride, and later—the wife of Dhola in *Dhola-Maru*.
11. Apparently, the author's mistake. She keeps referring to Jamwa-Ramgarh as 'Rajgargh'.
12. It is not clear where the name came from. Maidul Rao is not even mentioned in *Kacchwaha Vamshavali*. According to the *Vamshavali*, Dhola Rae's grandson was Hanut Dev.

13. Another name for Diwali.
14. N.K. Pareek provides additional details about this historical figure. Panna Miyan used to be a eunuch in the Mughal court. It was Sawai Jai Singh's father who brought him to Amber. He had purchased landed property on behalf of the Jaipur Maharaja in Vrindavan and Mathura. His own property was also quite considerable. Several paintings in Jaipur's City Palace bear his personal seal (Pareek, 2000: 55).
15. My guide derived the etymology of the word 'panna' from 'puran' (old, ancient).
16. *Amer men heritage walk ko hari jhandi* (Green Light to the Heritage Walk in Amber), *Dainik Bhaskar,* 10 February, 2003
17. In other words, my volunteer guide attributed the monuments to pre-Kacchawa times. There is a general tendency among Amber's residents to exaggerate the antiquity of landmarks in question.

References

Balzani, Marzia (2003) *Modern Indian Kingship: Changing Traditions and Rituals of Legitimation in Jodhpur,* Oxford: James Currey.

Dhama, B.L. (1955) *A Guide to Jaipur and Amber,* Jaipur: The Hanuman Press.

Harlan, Lindsey (1992) *Religion and Rajput Women: The Ethic of Protection in Contemporary Narratives,* Berkeley and Los Angeles: University of California Press. 2000 *Battles, Brides, and Sacrifice: Rajput Kuldevis in Rajasthan,* in, Alf Hiltebeitel and Kathleen M. Erndl (eds.) *Is the Goddess a Feminist: The Politics of South Asian Goddesses,* Sheffield Academic Press.

Henige, David P., (1974) *The Chronology of Oral Tradition: Quest for a Chimera,* Oxford: Clarendon Press. (1982) *Oral Historiography,* New York: Longman Group Ltd. (2004) *Princely States of India: A Guide to Chronology and Rulers,* Bangkok: Orchid Press.

Nath, Aman (1996) *Jaipur: The Last Destination,* London: Taurus Parke Books.

Pareekh, Nand Kishore (2000) *Jaipur That Was: Royal Court and the Seraglio,* Jaipur: Subodh Sahitya Sadan.

Sarkar, Jadunath (1984) *A History of Jaipur,* Delhi: Orient Longman.

Tod, James (1997) Annals of Amber, or Dhoondhar, in, *Annals and Antiquities of Rajasthan,* Vol.II Calcutta: Rupa & Co.

Urri, John (1990) *The Tourist Gaze: Leisure and Travel in Contemporary Societies,* London.

Vansina, Jan (1985) *Oral Tradition as History,* Madison: The University of Wisconsin Press.

3

Mongols and Rajputs

A Study of James Tod on the Historical Ethnicity of Martial Races of Rajasthan and Central Asia

G.S.L. Devra

I

The theory of *Shaka* or Indo-Scythians origin of the Rajput races of Rajasthan and elsewhere in India propounded by James Tod and other European writers has been challenged and debated since the beginning of the last century.[1] Rather, James Tod and several scholars of 19th and early 20th centuries are of this opinion that a study of the mythological descriptions, martial manners, language and poetry, and even music and architectural ornaments of the early settlers in India, China and Mongolia speak about their common origin.[2] In this context Tod especially had tried to compare the genealogical histories of the Mongols and Rajputs given in the account of Abul Ghazi (Genealogy) and *Puranic* literature of India respectively and come to this conclusion that they had almost similar kind of inferences for their racial origin.[3] Whereupon, the traditional accounts of the Rajput courts came out strongly in favour of the origin of these ruling races from the established *Kashtriya* families of the epic and Puranic periods.[4] And at no stage these description have tried to compare the origin or histories of these races with that of the other parts of Asia or Europe. The emphasis of their theory remained on the centre of the theme of pure royal races of ancient Aryan India. Subsequently, during the modern times the theories of Brahman and tribal origin of the Rajputs also found the place in the span of long and continuous debate. In the present time the writings of Tod either got challenged, spared or could not be considered serious at all.

The observations of James Tod deserve our attentions. Although on the plain surface one finds it difficult to accept whatever he has proposed, as his writings lack the support of historical evidences and moreover the names of the various clans of the Rajputs or Kshatriyas do not match with the names of tribes, clans or communities of any part of Asia or Europe. He has tried to place his theory on the ground of the presence of similar types of the social customs and traditions prevalent both in the Rajput and Indo-Scythians or Mongol societies[5] but such observations failed to find the favourable response from the Indian authors. According to the critics of Tod such customs and social practices were already present in the Indian Kshatriya societies. In fact, Rajputs despite with their new names and identities are the Kshatriyas of the early periods and like of their predecessors fought against all those who came from the outside of the country. Indo-Scythians were treated as foreigners in the country and Kshatriyas had challenged their arms for the independence of the country. The popularity of the legend of the tale of Vikrmaditya may be cited in the support of this trendy version.[6]

II

(A) Muhnot Nainsi, the famous Khyat writer of the 17th century Rajasthan has vividly described the genealogies of the ruling dynasties of the Rajput houses of northern India. While doing so it appears that he not only had used the traditional material preserved in the families of ruling houses especially those prepared by the Bhats, family account keepers but also consulted the other available sources before preparing the genealogical lists and related accounts of them.[7] Some of his remarks in such descriptions are very interesting. For example, while giving the history of the Bhatis of erstwhile Jaisalmer State at one stage he had outlined that the Mughals are Chakita or Chagata Bhati(s).[8] According to him Mughal-Chakita was son of Bhopat and grandson Balbandh and great grandson of Shalivahan. It is said that Shalivahan had ruled over Punjab and the frontier regions of the country, perhaps just before the coming of Huns in these parts. The fort of Ghazni in Afganistan was under their possession, rather it was an important seat of the kingdom. The writings of Nainsi came out at the time when Mughal power was at its zenith in the Indian subcontinent and Rajputs had been accepted socially as a distinct warrior and ruling class, like that of Kshatriyas.[9]

Moreover, the family records of the Bhatis of Jaisalmer also corroborate this view that Chaghtay Mughals have a descent from their family. Even the modern works on the Bhatis of Jaisalmer and other areas do not contradict these versions, rather most of them have come out with such references or details which overall support such claims and genealogies. These Bhatis are treated as respectable clan of the Rajputs and their bards have bracketed them into the group of lunar Kashtriya races of the country. It is also well documented that once they had their sway on the both sides of the Frontier Mountains.[10]

(B) So far the history of Chaghtay people (or *ulus*) who ruled over most parts of central Asia during the intervening period of the rule of Chinggis Khan and Amir Timur is concerned, it is well documented that they were the progeny of Chaghtay, second son of Chinggis Khan.[11] Mughals of medieval India are also reputed as Chaghtay and claim their descent from the families of both Chinggis Khan and Amir Timur, and draw their succession line more specifically from Amir Timur.[12] Mongols have their origin from the races of the Mongolia and as per their secret history their descent was from the divine forces.[13] Looking to this kind of historical and mythological background one finds it difficult to place the ancestors of Bhatis in the social realm of the Mongols. Or should we accept that remark tauntingly pressed by the Mongols of 'Eastern Mongols'(Semirechye and East Turkistan, on the border of China) that the Mongols of Western Regions (Central Asia) are of mixed descent.[14] Whereupon most of the historians find that the family history of Amir Timur is obscure, rather the ancestors of Timur belonged to a mixed horde.[15] James Tod is of this opinion that both Mongols and Bhatis had mixed descent and that materialised before the advent of Chinggis Khan.[16] The accounts of Bhatis admit that Jadams or Bhatis had solemnised marriage relations with the Turkish ruling families of Bukhara.[17] The details given about this development elaborate that Bijal, son of Chikita and grandson of Bhopat, ruler of Ghazni most likely during the period of early medieval centuries had married the daughter of the Turkish king of Bukhara. Shahasmad, son of Bijal succeeded the throne of Bukhara as the king of Bukhara died without leaving any male issue. Perhaps after this development, Chikita branch of Jadams popularly known as Bhatis became the part of Turkish ruling society. (Shahsamand grandson of Chikita, who, in turn, was son of Bijal and grandson of Bhupati—son of Balbandh and brother of Bhati, progenitor of Bhatis) thenceforth their old identity got ceased and they merged into the tribes of Turks and then of Mongols.[18] Incidentally, Timurs also belonged to the Gurkhans (or son in law) branch of the Barla tribes of the Mongols.[19] All these aspects present an exciting condition for the further investigation before making any final judgment on the origins of both Mongols and Rajputs. Tod on the basis of these observations believes that the origin of Bhatis was from Indo-Scythian group.[20] A. Cunningham also suggests that the lower and south part of Afghanistan, near to Sistan and upper course of the Helmand River was under the possession of the Shakas. Sistan was already under the possession of them.[21] At the time of Gupta and Huna rule Shakas along with the later Kedarite kings had occupied the parts of modern Punjab and now new researches had established that Gupta ruler, Chandra Gupta had fought not only with the Shakas of western India but prior to that in the beginning of his rule faced the Shakas of Punjab and frontier regions. After great difficulties he could overcome from their attack.[22]

III

Abul Fazl and other Mughal historians trace the origin of the great Mughals of India from that family or race, which in their opinion claim the descent from both Chinggis Khan and Amir Timur of central Asia. Particularly, Abul Fazl in his genealogy of the house of Mughals of India draws such conclusion and according to that one Prince Toman Khan, fourth ancestor of Chinggis Khan had two wives and from second wife he had twins. One of the twins was named Qabal Khan, who was the great grandfather of Chinggis Khan and the other was named Qaculi, the progenitor of Amir Timur and Great Mughals of India. Qabal Khan succeeded the throne of his father but his brother Qaculi under the obligations of an agreement (*Ahad-nama* or *Altamgha* of Toman Khan), which was designed to remain in the force from generation to generation, was made Commander-in-Chief and Prime Minister, of both the realms. At the time of Chinggis Khan Qaracar Nuyan performed these duties.[23] After that it seems that the title of Nuyan became attached to the names of family members of Qaracar Nuyan.[24] Before his death Chinggis Khan had nominated his elder son Okadai as his successor but gave central parts of his empire comprising Transoxiana Turkistan, some parts of Khwarizm to his second son Chaghtay Khan. He also placed the services of Qaracar Nuyan in this newly created dominion.[25] According to Abul Fazl, he (Chinggis Khan) also appraised his son about the covenant made between Qabal Khan and his brother Qaculi Bahadur and advised him for not departing from these sacred traditions and added that regard Qaracar Nuyan as the partner in rule and realm. Chinggis Khan, according to the author went further and established the relationship of fatherhood and sonship between them (perhaps Chinggis Khan did it by marrying Qaracar to a daughter of Chaghtay). In the words of Abul Fazl, "In this way the noble line (Akbar's) came to be called as Chaghtayees".[26] The successor of Qaracar Nuyan was his son Aijal Nuyan who happened to be the great grand father of Taragai, father of Amir Timur. Amir Timur's third son, Jalalu-d-din was the great grand-father of Umar Shaikh Mirza, father of Babur. The mother of Babur was from the family of Chaghtayees and she was daughter of Yunus Khan, who ruled over parts of Chaghtay domain during the suggested period.[27] Babur himself in his biography has given the details of the family of his mother and feels proud in claiming that she was from the aristocratic Chaghtay tribe. He also used to boast about his Timuri blood but more or less looks silent on the progeny from Chinggis Khan.[28] The argument advanced by Abul Fazl on the noble line from the Toman Khan and Chinggis Khan and particularly on calling them as Chaghtayee from the period of Qaracar Nuyan is not convincing. The contemporary writings also do not mention this kind of social arrangement and elevation. Equally it is not acceptable that Amir Timur was from the family of Chaghtay. Modern researches on the history of the origin of Amir Timur's family, too, do not subscribe to such ideas. Rather some of them remarked that, "Sultan Babur withdrew to India and founded there one of the most brilliant Muslim kingdoms which by tradition was also called 'Chaghtay', although there were none of Chaghtay's descendants in it".[29]

The origin of the family of Amir Timur is not clear and henceforth the entire issue is debatable. Opinions put forth about it include that both he and his father were shepherds; belonging to a mixed horde. His father was a poor smith. His name also signifies 'iron'. Further, they belong to a tribe accustomed to travel hither and thither and courageous, who lived in Transoxiana. Again, they were from the one clan of high Asia that were named Scythians in the elder days and sometimes Turks. With the Mongol horde they had come from the northern plains to this fertile mountain land. Generally, it is accepted that Timur was son of Taraghai, chief of Gurkan branch of the Barlas, a Turkish tribe. Through his mother's family he claimed his descent from Chinggis Khan.[30]

It appears that the name of Chaghtay became so popular and synonymous with such several activities, which had no direct connection to the family of Chinggis Khan or his son Chaghtay. V.V. Barthold, the famous Russian scholar on central Indian history, long back had come out with this conclusion that 'Chaghtay' was the name adopted by the nomads on whom depended the military strength of the dynasty, and they remained known under this name even after no Khans of the Chaghtay branch were left. The literary language that towards that time was created in central Asia also became known as 'Chaghtay'.[31] In fact, no other name connected with the Mongol conquest achieved a similar fame. He, further, writes that the nomads of Mawarannuhar called themselves 'Chaghtay' and looked upon their eastern neighbours as free looters—Jata. At the same time the nomads of Khashgariyas and of the Semirechye called themselves Moghul, while referring to their western neighbours as qaraunas, i.e., half-breeds, men of mixed descent.[32] Early history of the family of Amir Timur like of the other nomads of the region, in fact, went through a number of political and social changes and they came out with a mixture of several ethnic groups. C.E. Bosworth, another expert on the history of these regions, rightly remarks that the westward migration, from the later 10th century onwards, of Turkish tribal nomads were to have long-term effects on the ethnic and social composition of the 'northern tier' of the east, i.e., the lands running westward from Afghanistan through Iran to Anatolia regions which had been Iranian in population and language since the time of Indo-Aryan migrations into central Asia in the second millennium B.C., now felt the impact of Turkicisation. Turkish and, to a much lesser extent, Mongol military expansion south of Oxus river into what is now Afghanistan and northern India was also to have lasting political effect on these regions.[33] In the 7th century the land of the west of Kabul was under the influence of a Turk ruler. Hiueun Tsiang writes that king of Kophene was Turk. The King of Ghazni was a Buddhist.[34]

Bosworth while elaborating his point, further, adds that, "The changes brought about by the movements of Turkish people were accelerated by the Mongol invasions of the 13th century, which had an immediate and cataclysmic effect on the economic and social organisation of the lands which they over-run … . In Transoxiana and the northern regions of the Islamic middle east, the effects of the Mongol invasion were sharply felt in such fields as social organisation and land tenure, and the pastoralism of many parts of Iran and Anatolia were accentuated".[35] Thirteenth century travellers confirm that disunity and conflict were rife among the Mongol tribes. The whole nation was in rebellion. The kinship group lost its homogeneous character as a result of the constant plundering and retaliating campaigns; defeated tribes and clans were incorporated into the victorious confederation. Rashid-d-din remarks that such economic uncertainty and poverty motivated young, adventurous men to leave their clan and become followers (nukhid) in the service of any leader. It seems that the difference between the master and his servant (serf) greatly reduced during this period.[36]

IV

Bhatis, before coming into the regions of Sind and Rajasthan were the residents of Punjab and frontier regions. These Bhatis had followed their own calendar, popular as *Bhattik Samvat* that was contemporary to the *Hijri* calendar of Islamic faith. Now researches have confirmed that their rule in Zabul (Ghazni) and Punjab had finally ended after the first wave of Muslim aggression sometime in the early part of the second half of the 7th century, which penetrated through the region of Sivistan or Sistan and that happened before the invasion by the Arabs on Sind and Multan.[37] Bhati records elaborate that at that time a good number of Bhatis were converted into Islam but somehow after sometime they succeeded in recapturing the fort of Ghazni. It remained in the hands of Chakita branch of Jadams or Bhatis who did not move along with other groups of their clan towards the interior parts of the subcontinent.[38] In the *Chachnama* of Sind the references of Bhatis as a ruling clan have come up repeatedly but the description of them in the form of various hordes suggests that in the parts of Sind and its neighbouring regions of South Punjab and Rajasthan they had re-emerged but in small groups.[39] This development suggests that they had disintegrated both socially and politically. Of course, they in due course of time succeeded in establishing a kingdom to rule for their credit but by that time the division among them became decisive. The kingdom of Ramel was ruled by one Bhati king Sohan or Sursen that was lying between the regions of Sind and Hind whereupon other small chiefs recruited themselves either into the services of the king of Sind and others or operated independently in the difficult terrains of the region. Sursen was contemporary of both Chach and his successor Dahir.[40] When Arabs occupied the various parts of Sind and Multan they made several agreements with these local Bhati chiefs and succeeded in enlisting the services of them.[41] Such information available from Chachnama confirms that the Jadams of the frontier regions and Afghanistan now had become popular as Bhatis in the western and north-western parts of India. Another important seat of the Bhatis was the fort of Bhatner, now known as Hanumangarh and situated on the northern part of Rajasthan, close to Haryana and Punjab. According to the Bhati sources Prince Bhati had established this fort after their sufferings from the hands of power of Khurasan (Huns) which, in turn, compelled them to migrate from the frontier regions and find the respite only in the south of Sutluj.[42] The fort as per their traditions was founded sometime after 455 A.D. In fact, this Bhati was the prince, after his name all of them came to be called as Bhatis. As written earlier before that they were known as Jadams.[43] So it was the one branch of Jadams that remained behind in Ghazni and, later on, that became known as Chakita or Chagta or Chagtay. Since most of the branches of Jadams had identified themselves with the name of Bhati for that reason Chakitas were also remembered as Chakita or Chagta Bhatis.[44]

Thus, the process of social and political disintegration of Jadams or Bhatis which was started during the 5th century took more or less a definite form by the time of 7th century especially that happened after their reversals from the hands of the Arabs and Turks. Perhaps, after such major political debacles they could not find the proper space and opportunities for them to regroup again at the clan level. Bhatis had certainly re-emerged but they could not unite the other branches of the Jadams. From 8th century onwards they ruled from Bhatner, Marot and later on from Ludreva and Jaisalmer, rather they could only find the home in the Thar Desert of Rajasthan and Sind.[45] Although Bhati is credited for the foundation of the Bhatner fort yet there are strong archeological evidences that support the human settlement in this part prior to the advent of the Jadams. The country was known as Bang or Band. Chinese traveller has listed it as Satadru, might be on account of that the river Sutluj was running on its western border.[46] The other branches of Jadams who moved towards the Sind and Saurashtra and spread over there, either became famous as Samas and Jadechas or remained known as Bhatis. Chakitaa remained in Ghazni and other parts of Afghanistan. Similarly Janjas remained in the parts of Punjab.[47] This branch of Bhatner or Bhatis, after the decline of Huns, again became powerful in Punjab and thenceforth felt the brunt of first invasion of the Arabs in Zabulistan and north-west parts of Punjab. Yet after their continuous defeats first by the Arabs and then from the local powers of Punjab (Takkas, Gurjjars, Varhas and Vardhans) during the last decades of the 7th century, compelled them to find place only in the region lying between Sutluj and Ghaggar rivers. Their power remained centred around the forts of Bhatner, Marot (Bhawalpur, Pakistan) and Mumanwahan (Panjnand), but where they, too, remained in constant struggle with the Varhas of South Punjab, Chiefs of Sind and Parihars or Gujjar Partihars of Mandor. At this time they almost lost connection with the other branches of their clan.[48]

V

The information regarding the branch of Chakitas of Ghazni in the Bhati records is very succinct and in the absence of proper genealogy it is difficult to describe the developments that took place at their level after the defeat from the Arabs. As written earlier the progenitor of Chakita or Chagtay was Chikata or Chagta, who was son of Bhopat and nephew of Bhati. Baland or Balbandh, the ruler of Shalivahanpur or Sialkot and Bhatner had entrusted the fief of Ghazni to his son, Bhopat. Chakita, the son of Bhupati got Ghazni in succession. When the other branches of Jadams or Bhatis had been trying hard to recover their lost territories in Punjab and other parts of the frontier region these Chakitas somehow succeeded in maintaining their control over Ghazni.[49] It is just possible that they had accepted the suzerainty of the Huns and after that of Sassanians of Iran. Chakita or Chagata had seven or eight sons and one of his sons, Bijal got married to the daughter of the (Uzjbek) king of Balkh and Bukhara. It appears that he was the king of Turckic Sammanid dynasty who ruled from Bukhara and succeeded in establishing the empire in Transoxiana. Ghazni had accepted the sovereignty of this dynasty.[50] Again, as per the information available in the Bhati literature since the king of Bukhara had no male issue the son of Bijal, Shahsamand succeeded his maternal grandfather on the throne of Bukhara (Vahalik). The descendants of Shahsamand on being the offspring of Chakita, through Bijal, adopted Chakita or Chaghtay as their clan name.[51] At the time of first Arab invasion on Sistan, Ghazni was worst affected. It is only a matter of pure conjunction that with the passage of the time when and how these descendants of Chakita or rulers of Ghazni got converted into Islam. Bhati records just add that they embraced Islam but it appears that this event took place after the first Arab invasion on Zabul. In the records those Bhati groups who were converted at the time of first invasion are more or less in the different contexts has been mentioned. As written earlier this information is rather categorical in their statement that Mughals are Chakita or Chagta Bhatis.[52] This situation leaves two possibilities that either at the time of 9th or 10th century when this part of Afghanistan and central Asia came under the influence of Islam or at the time Chaghtayees became the followers of Islam, these Chakita Bhatis also embraced Islam. James Tod put on additional information here that one of the conditions of the marriage with the Princesses of Bukhara was that Bijal would embrace Buddhism, which eventually he did. Since there is no definite information available about the religion of Jadams of Ghazni so the authority of the statement of Tod could not be ascertained. Even during the 7th century, according to the Hieun Tsiang the king of Ghazni, himself, was Buddhist. Otherwise, it is a fact that most of the ruling tribes of central Asia even after the spread of Islam there, were followers of Buddhism. Chinggis Khan was one of them.[53] *Khyat, Tawarikhs and Vansavalis* of Bhatis or Jaisalmer State add significant information that Ghori, another son of Bijal and younger brother of Shahsamand founded the city of Ghor in the land situated between Ghazni and Heart, almost 100 km away from Balkh. His descendants were called Ghoris who later on had embraced Islam.[54] As we know that the Ghorids who emerged from the remote village in the middle of Hindukush had no definite kind of decent.

It appears that the influence of Islam came to the eastern parts of Iran and Afghanistan sometime in the 9th century.[55] These Bhatis either at the time of first wave of Islamic influence or in the subsequent period, possibly in the 9th-10th century got converted into Islam. After their succession at Bukhara they must have become the part of Turkic polity and society. Cunningham on the basis of his study on Chinese accounts and other classical literature of the earlier periods has suggested that the region of Kaofu or Afganistan, during the second century before Christ was divided among the Parthians, the Indians and the Su or Sacae (Indo-Scythians) of Kipin. The lower part of Afghanistan remained under the control of Indo Scythians.[56] Gazni was located in their dominion. They accepted the suzerainty of Greeks, Parthians, Kushans and Huns. They succeeded in giving the defeat to the Huns only after getting the military support from the Persians. Interestingly in the Bhati literature too, the reference of the alliance between them and Parihar (Partihar or Parthians), which was concluded against the Huns has been given.[57] The history of the town of Begram (Karsana of Ptolemy *KIu la sa pang* of Chinese accounts) may be quoted in order to understand the nature of political and social upheavals undergoing through this period. According to Cunningham towards the end of the 10th century and especially after the Muhammadan conquest of Kabul by Sabuktugin the city of Begram began gradually to decay as its inhabitants started shifting to Ghazni and it was finally deserted about the beginning of the 13th century. At this time the invasion of Chinggis Khan also took place over these territories and as a result of that either people went to other parts or had joined the army of the Mongols.[58]

Well, it is not tenable that Bhatis of Ghazni became Chaghtay simply because of their lineage from the Prince Chakita or Chagata. We have already discussed that how this particular expression of 'Chaghtay' was first applied to the Ulus of Chaghtay, second son of Chunggis Khan and after that those who lived in this area of historical Ulus also got the name of Chaghtay, irrespective of that whether they belong to that particular clan or not. Similarly the land of Ghor bears the name of hill ranges, Ghur or Ghurchistan. It appears that after the settlement of the families of Bijal and Shahsamand in this part of the North-West Afghanistan they came to be started calling as Ghor. Historians on the basis of local sayings forwarded that the family of the rulers of Ghor was from East Persia (near Afghanistan and south west of Ghazni) and their ancestor was Shansab (Shahsamand) a supposed descendant of the legendary monarch Zuhuk or Jadu. According to the local traditions Kabul was the country of Zohak or Zuhuk.[59] The Bhati records emphatically claim that some of their families moved towards Persia and parts of central Asia from Ghazni and had settled down there. They embraced Islam in due course of the time. On the other hand there are enough evidences to suggest that the people of Chaghtay and other regions of central Asia were composed of mixed hordes and races, which penetrated into their society from time to time. The family of Amir Timur in the elder years was called as the people from Indo-Scythian races.[60] In this background the claims of Bhati records, well supported by the scholar like James Tod deserve serious attentions and have the scope for further study. It is important that when other ruling houses of Rajasthan during the periods of recent centuries have practically denounced their relations with the Mughals and particularly social and matrimonial relations with them, these records raise their voice in different historical perspectives. Of course, all these findings also press us to think that Bhatis or Jadams are from the Indo-Scythians stock. Tod has already recommended for such assumption. The modern historians on the annals of Bhatis or Jaisalmer State do agree that the ancestors of Bhatis came from Ghazni and Punjab but they are from the famous clan of Yadus, and Mathura was their principal fort. Now it has been accepted that those Yadus or Jadus or Jadams who crossed the frontier passes might have mingled up with the Shaka hordes.[61] But the chronology and sequence of the events given in the Bhati records do support that they were from the Indo-Scythian group.

Notes

1. James Tod, *Annals and Antiquities of Rajasthan* (Ed. by William Crooke), Vol. I, Oxford University Press, 1920, for the detailed study, see, pp. 72–96. Also see, "Introduction" of William Crooke, pp. xxxi–xxxvii; V.A. Smith, *Early History of India*, pp. 103–05.
2. James Tod, *Annals and Antiquities of Rajasthan,* Vol. I, op. cit. pp. 68–71.
3. James Tod, *Annals and Antiquities of Rajasthan,*Vol. I, op. cit. pp. 68–71. Especially see the notes of William Crooke, pp. 55–68 (Chapter V); Abul Ghazi Khan (1643–63)' was minister in the Uzbek Khanate wrote Genealogy and

covered the history of Mongols and the family of Amir Timur; V.V. Barthold, *Four Studies on the History of Central Asia,* (Translated by V. and T. Minorsky), Vol. I, Leiden, 1962, p. 65.

4. Jagdish Singh Gehlot, *Rajputana Ka Itihas* (Hindi), Part I, pp. 11–22; For the discussion, see, J.N. Asopa, *The Origin of the Rajputs,* Delhi, 1976, Chapter I,
5. James Tod, op. cit., pp. 72–96.
6. G.S.L. Devra, Changes in Perspectives of the Legends of Vikramaditya (From Raja to Rajpoot) "Historicity of the tale of Jug Dev Parmar of Malwa", Paper presented in the Indian History Congress, Bareileye, December, 2005.
7. Manohar Singh Ranawat, *Itihaskar Muhnot Nainsi Aur usake Itihas Granth* (Hindi), Jodhpur, 1981, pp. 82–96.
8. *Muhta Nainsi Ri Khyat,* (Rajasthani-Hindi; Edited by Badri Parsad Sakaria), Vol. III, Jodhpur, 1984, p. 37.
9. *Muhta Nainsi Ri Khyat,* op. cit., p. 37; Laxmichand, *Tawarikh Jaisalmer,* Jodhpur, 1999 (First Print, 1891), p. 11, (Hereafter, *Tawarikh Jaisalmer*) He is the same Shalivahan who is credited for the foundation of Shalivahanpur in Punjab.
10. *Jaisalmer ri Khyat* (Ed. by Dr Narayan Singh Bhati), *Parampara,* Part 57–58, pp. 30–31, Jodhpur, 1981, *Tawarikh Jaisalmer,* p. 11; Hari Singh Bhati, *Annals of Jaisalmer,* Bikaner, 2002, pp. 113–17.
11. V.V. Barthold, *Four Studies on the History of Central Asia,* op. cit., pp. 45–46, 51–52; B. Akhmedov and D. Sinor, *Central Asia under the Rule of Chinggis Khan's Successors, (History of Civilisation of Central Asia),* Vol. IV (*The Age of Achievements,* Editors, M.S. Asimov and C.E. Boswoth), UNESCO, 1996, pp. 263–67.
12. H. Brveridge, *The Akbarnama of Abul Fazl,* Vol I, Delhi, pp. 185, 187–88, 192–95; S.A.A. Rizvi, *Mughul Kalin Bharat* (Hindi), Aligarh, 1960, pp. 475–76.
13. *The Secret History of the Mongols,* (Translated, Annotated and Introduction by Urgunge Onon), Curzon, Great Britain, 2001, pp. 42–44.
14. V.V. Barthold, *Four Studies on the History of Central Asia,* Vol. I, op. cit. p. 54.
15. See the references of No. 29.
16. James Tod, Vol. III, op. cit., pp. 1182–83.
17. *Tawarikh Jaisalmer,* p. 13; Hari Singh Bhati, *Annals of Jaisalmer,* Bikaner, 2002, pp. 113–17. cf.
18. *Jaisalmer ri Khyat,* op. cit., p. 31; *Tawarikh Jaisalmer,* p. 13; Hari Singh Bhati, *Annals of Jaisalmer,* Bikaner, 2002, pp. 113–17.
19. Harold Lamb, *Tamerlane—The Earth Shaker,* New Delhi, 1989, p. 22.
20. James Tod, Vol. III, op. cit., pp. 1171–72, 1182–83.
21. Alexander Cunningham, *Ancient Geography of India,* Calcutta (Kolkata), 1924, pp. 46–48.
22. GSL Devra, *Chandra ka Mehroli Stambh-eak Adhyanan* (Hindi) (Mehroli Pillar of Chandra), *Shodh Patrika,* No. 216–17, July–December. 2003, Udaipur.
23. H. Brveridge, *The Akbarnama of Abul Fazl,* Vol I, Delhi, pp. 185, 187–88, 192.
24. Ibid., p. 198.

25. Ibid., pp. 197–98.
26. Ibid.
27. Ibid., pp. 219–21, 224.
28. S.A.A. Rizvi, *Mughul Kalin Bharat* (Hindi), Aligarh, 1960, pp. 475–76.
29. V.V. Barthold, *Four Studies on the History of Central Asia,* op. cit., p. 64; V.V. Barthold, further, writes that, "Like his predecessors, Timur set upon the throne puppet Khans of the House of Chaghtay and cloaked his acts with their authority. These Khans no longer enjoyed even the outward honours due to the supreme ruler, and a legend was invented in favour of Timur who had no hereditary right to the supreme power. His ancestors were said to have been independent amirs under Chingiz–Khan's successors, on the strength of a treaty several times renewed and forgotten during the troublous times. By this marriage with the Amir Husayn's widow, who was a daughter Qazan Khan, Timur became related with the Khan's family and acquired the right to the appellation of '*gurkan*' (son-in-law) which gave him precedence over the other amirs.", (p. 58); Regarding other opinions, see, Tamerlane-Life of Timur (tr. by J.H. Sanders from the Arabic written by Ibn Arabshah), Lahore (Reprint), 1976, pp. 1–2.; Harold Lamb, *Tamerlane—The Earth Shaker,* New Delhi, 1989, pp. 22, 104.; Paul Ratchnevsky, *Genghis Khan–His Life and Legacy,* (Tr. and Ed. by Thomas Nivison Haining), Blackwell, USA, 1991, pp. 12–14.
30. *Tamerlane—Life of Timur,* (tr. by J.H. Sanders from the Arabic written by Ibn Arabshah), op. cit., pp. 1–2.; Harold Lamb, op. cit., pp. 22, 104.
31. V.V. Barthold, *Four Studies on the History of Central Asia,* p. 51.
32. Ibid., p. 54.
33. *History of Civilisation of Central Asia,* Vol. IV, op. cit., Introduction.
34. Samuel Beal, *The Life of Hiuen Tsiang,* New Delhi, 1998 (Reprint), pp. 57–59; Alexander Cunningham, op. cit., pp. 44–45.
35. *History of Civilisation of Central Asia,* Vol. IV, op. cit., Introduction.
36. Paul Ratchnevsky, *Genghis Khan—His Life and Legacy,* (tr. and Ed. by Thomas Nivison Haining), Blackwell, USA, 1991, pp. 12–14.
37. K.A. Rashid, "The first Muslim invasion of North-West frontier of the Indo-Pakistan sub-continent" *Journal of the Asiatic Society of Pakistan,* Vol. VIII, No. 2, 1963, pp. 25–32; see also the work of S.Q. Fatimi published with the same title and in the same Journal (Vol. VIII, No. 1, 1963, pp. 37–46); GSL Devra, "Political Zone Vs Historical Zone", Presidential Address, Punjab Historical Conference, Patiala, March 2001.
38. *Jaisalmer ri Khyat,* op. cit., pp. 33–34; *Tawarikh Jaisalmer,* pp. 15–16.
39. The *Chachnama, An ancient history of Sind,* (Tr. From Persian by Mirza Kalichbeg Fredunbeg), pp. 32, 40, 43, 55, 157, Delhi, 1979 (Reprint).
40. The *Chachnama, An ancient history of Sind,* op. cit., pp. 32, 40, 43, 55, 157; GSL Devra, *Identification of Ramel—a forgotten kingdom of early medieval India,* Indian History Congress Proceeding, Bhopal, 2002.
41. The *Chachnama, An ancient history of Sind,* pp. 32, 40, 43, 55, 157.
42. *Jaisalmer ri Khyat,* op. cit., pp. 30–34; *Tawarikh Jaisalmer,* pp. 11–16.

43. Ibid.
44. Ibid.
45. Ibid.
46. Samuel Beal, *The Life of Hiuen Tsiang,* op. cit., pp. 57–59; GSL Devra, *Chandra ka Mehroli Stambh-eak Adhyanan* (Hindi), Mehroli Pillar of Chandra, op. cit.
47. *Jaisalmer ri Khyat,* op. cit., pp. 33–34; *Tawarikh Jaisalmer,* pp. 15–16
48. *Jaisalmer ri Khyat,* op. cit., pp. 33–34; *Tawarikh Jaisalmer,* pp. 15–16; *Rajasthan ke Pramukh Abhilekh* (Ed. by Sukhveer Singh Gehlot) pp. 83–84, Jodhpur, 1988 (The inscription was discovered by Munshi Devi Prasad); GSL Devra, *Varhas "Political Wilderness And Social Dismemberment";Varhas: A Forgotten Clan of North-West India (Pre-Medieval Period)*, IHCP, 2004.
49. *Muhta Nainsi Ri Khyat,* op. cit., p. 37; *Jaisalmer ri Khyat,* op. cit., p. 31; *Tawarikh Jaisalmer,* p. 13; Hari Singh Bhati, *Annals of Jaisalmer,* Bikaner, 2002, pp. 113–17.
50. N.N. Negmatov, *The Samanid State, History of Civilisation of Central Asia,* Vol. IV, op. cit.
51. *Jaisalmer ri Khyat,* op. cit., p. 31; *Tawarikh Jaisalmer,* p. 13; Hari Singh Bhati, *Annals of Jaisalmer,* Bikaner, 2002, pp. 113–17.
52. *Jaisalmer ri Khyat,* op. cit., p. 34; *Tawarikh Jaisalmer,* pp. 15–16; Hari Singh Bhati, *Annals of Jaisalmer,* Bikaner, 2002, pp. 113–17.
53. Samuel Beal, *The Life of Hiuen Tsiang,* op. cit., pp. 57–59
54. *Tawarikh Jaisalmer,* p. 13; Hari Singh Bhati, *Annals of Jaisalmer,* Bikaner, 2002, pp. 113–17.
55. Alexander Cunningham, op. cit., pp. 33–35.
56. Alexander Cunningham, op. cit., pp. 33–35.
57. Alexander Cunningham, op. cit., pp. 33–35; *Jaisalmer ri Khyat,* op. cit., p. 32; *Tawarikh Jaisalmer,* p. 14. In the *Khyat* and *Tawarikh* it is mentioned that one Bhati king Satorao of Punjab in the collaborations with the Parihars (Parthians) defeated and had driven back the *Javanas* (*yavans* or Huns) from Punjab and rehabilitated the towns like, Multan and Lahore.
58. Alexander Cunningham, op. cit., p. 35.
59. Alexander Cunningham, op. cit., pp. 33–35; Stephen Tanner, *Afghanistan*, New York, 2002, pp. 74–75.
60. Harold Lamb, op. cit., p. 22.
61. *Jaisalmer ri Khyat,* op. cit., pp. 17–18. According to *Khyat*, Bhatis or Jadams are *Somvamsi* and originated from *Adi Prayag*; Hari Singh Bhati, *Annals of Jaisalmer,* Bikaner, 2002, pp. 113–17. Shakas are Yaduvanshi, p. 108; J.K. pp. 30–35.

4

James Tod's Reflections on History and Society of Rajasthan

V.K. Vashishtha

James Tod's *Annals* of Rajasthan is a 'classical account'[1] of the history and society of Rajasthan. During the colonial period it was "naturalised, treated as a foundational text and given canonical standing".[2] It gives encyclopaedic view of Rajput history covering the study of Rajput polity and society, religion, Bhil and Mina tribes, architecture and antiquities, forts, temples, cenotaphs and cairns, agriculture, natural productions, flaura and fauna, traditional water resources, trade and commerce, and several other aspects of society. It is based on primary Rajasthani and Persian sources, inscriptions, ballads, and baradic literature. It was written in the period of transition, marking the liquidation of Maratha paramountcy and emergence of the modern era in Rajasthan under the Anglo-Rajput treaties of 1818. Moreover, Tod's *Annals* and his narratives of journey covering several parts of urban and rural Rajputana, would remain a reference media of abiding value and importance for the researchers on History of Rajasthan. However, the errors of facts or theories in the *Annals* would not "detract the real value of the work".[3] The critics and admirers of the *Annals* such as, William Crooke, G.H. Ojha, Sukumar Bhattacharya, J.S. Grewal, Lloyd I. Rudolph and several others have unanimously advocated this.

Tod's Career

The Herodotus of the History of Rajasthan, James Tod, was born at Islington on March 20, 1782. His father James Tod First was of a Scottish descent and was an indigo-planter at Mirzapur (Uttar Pradesh). His mother, Mary Heatly also belonged to Scottish family; her father Andrew Heatly had migrated to Rhode Island. In 1798, James Tod joined the service of the East India Company as a Cadet.[4] After completing his training at the Royal Military Academy, Woolwich, young James Tod joined his Commission in the 2nd European Regiment at Calcutta on 9 January 1800. Adventurous by nature and desirous of gaining experience of a soldier's life, he volunteered for the expedition to the Molucca Islands.[5] On his promotion as Lieutenant on 29 May 1800, he was transferred to the 14th Regiment of the Native Infantry. In 1801, he conducted a survey of an ancient canal near the city of Delhi. In 1805, he joined as the Commander of the Escort of Graeme Mercer, Envoy and Resident at the Court of Daulat Rao Sindhia at Gwalior.

The sojourn of Tod at Sindhia's perambulating Court, first in the capacity of the Commander of the Escort (1805–1815) of the Resident, and subsequently as the latter's First Assistant (1815–1817), acquainted him with the affairs of Central India and Rajputana States. In 1814–15, he had sent to his government a *Memoir of the rise, progress and existing condition of Pindaris in Malwa and Rajputana,* which was later published in the form of a book.[6] Subsequently, he submitted to Lord Hastings, the Governor-General of India, a map of these regions, with an account of their physical and political history along with a general plan for the extermination of the Pindaris.[7] During the period from 1817–1818, Tod assisted Lord Hastings in military operations against the Marathas and the Pindaris with the cooperation of Rajrana Zalim Singh, Prime Minister of Kota, and other rulers of Rajputana. In 1818, he concluded a treaty with the Rajput State of Bundi.

In appreciation of his services and experience of the Princely States of Rajputana, Lord Hastings appointed James Tod as Political Agent of the Western States of Rajputana comprising the charge of conducting British relations with the States of Mewar (Udaipur), Kota, Bundi, Jodhpur (Marwar), Jaisalmer and Sirohi. On his failure to conduct British relations with the State of Kota and his growing differences with David Ochterlony, the Resident in Malwa and Rajputana, he was left only with the charge of the State of Mewar. In view of his partisan attitude towards Rajput Princes, even in the capacity of the Political Agent in Mewar, he was placed in subordination to David

Ochterlony. He considered the continuous reduction of his political powers and jurisdiction humiliating, as it degraded him in prestige and influence in the eyes of the Rajput rulers. Above all, he found it galling to work in subordination to Ochterlony specially when without intimating him, the latter sent a *Vakil,* Ganesh Narain, directly to the Maharana of Mewar, informing about Tod's being deprived of an independent charge of Political Agent in Mewar. Tod could not brook this insult. In the pangs of self-mortification, he took leave from his post on the pretext of ill-health.[8] He left Udaipur on 1 June 1822, arrived at Bombay in January 1823, and in the following month he sailed for England.[9]

After May 1824, James Tod was given rapid promotions. It was on 2 June 1826 that he attained his last promotion on the rank of Lieutenant Colonel, when he was transferred to the 2nd European Regiment, the Corps in which he had commenced his military career. He retired from the service of the East India Company on 28 June 1826 and on 16 November 1826 married Julia Cluttbuck of a Dutch family that came to England in the 16th century.[10] In his zeal to collect source-material on Rajputana, he paid a two-day visit to Count Benoit de Boigne,[11] the former French General in Sindhia's army, at Savoy in France.[12] He died on 17 November, 1835 at the age of fifty-three.

James Tod devoted much of his time and energy to literary pursuits and research during his stay in England from 1823 to 1835. He was actively associated with the *Royal Asiatic Society* in London and also served as its librarian for sometime. He presented to it numerous manuscripts, inscriptions, coins and a series of drawings of sculptures and collection of his paintings, which he had used as a source-material for writing the history of Rajasthan.

Tod's Emergence as a Historian of Rajasthan History

Tod proved himself a failure as a Political Agent but he made a mark as a historian of the Rajasthan history. The intellectual atmosphere, which was created by the efforts of Sir William Jones, Captain Francis Wilford, and several other scholars in the *Asiatic Researches* (1788), and also by T. Maurice in the *Indian Antiquities,* had influenced the mind of young Tod, He gradually developed taste for the study of history and antiquities, The writings of Montesquieu, Henry Hallam's *View of the State of Europe during the Middle Ages,* Gibbon's *History of Europe,* etc., had posted him well with the trends of historical writings in Europe. Tod's strong linkages with Scotland drove him to write the *Annals* under the spell of Hellenistic writings of Scottish writers—Lord Byron and Sir Walter Scott, he constructed his *Annals* with a 'romantic world view' and 'romantic nationalism'.[13] He saw in the Greek War of Independence of 1821 against Ottoman Turks, resemblance of Mewar's struggle against Mughal Imperialism, which dissuaded him to call the battle of Haldighati similar to that of the valley at Thermopylae.[14] Along with these internal and external influences, Tod had developed special interest among the rulers of Rajputana, during his official tenure from 1805 to 1822 in Central India and Rajputana. The plundering raids of the Marathas and the Pindaris in Rajputana had made him a critic of the Marathas and Cornwallis-Barlow policy of non-interference there. The overbearing behaviour of Daulat Rao Sindhia with Maharana Bhim Singh of Mewar in the meeting at Eklingji in June 1806 infused in him hatred for the Marathas and a desire for restoring the State of Mewar to its pristine glory.

Thus, Tod developed interest in the Rajputs about whom the Europeans had hardly any knowledge except what little they could gather from the stray references in the works of Major General John Malcolm pertaining to Malwa and its adjoining territories of Rajputana States.[15] He fulfilled his zest for research and antiquarian pursuits during his official duties in Central India and Rajputana from 1805 to 1822. He published his famous book entitled *Annals and Antiquities of Rajasthan or the Central and Western Rajput States of India,* in two volumes in 1829 and 1832. Besides, his travel account entitled: *Travels in Western India,* embracing *A visit to the Sacred Mounts of the Jains and the most celebrated shrines of Hindu Faith between Rajpootana and the Indus;* with an *Account of the Ancient city of Nehrwalla, was* published after his death in 1839.

Tod's Reflections on Rajput Society

Tod's *Annals and Antiquities of Rajasthan* contains the dynastic history of the seven Rajput States viz., Mewar (Udaipur), Marwar (Jodhpur), Amber, Bikaner, Jaisalmer, Kota and Bundi from their origin to their relations with the Mughals, Marathas and the British Government till 1821. It is notable for reflecting over the origin and growth of the *jagirdari* system in Rajputana, nature of the relations of *jagirdars* with their liege lords, and condition of the people in the rural areas. Tod considered the oppressions of *Patels* and *Patwaris* responsible for the abject condition of the peasants in Mewar. His description of the caste *panchayat* of Rasmi (in Mewar) reveals the mechanism of social control in the rural society. He has published a fragment of patriarchal legislation from village Rasmi, prohibiting the ladies from carrying away under their *ghaghras* (petticots) any portion of *Sadh* (village feast).[16] He had great appreciation for the virtues of the Rajputs, such as, their loyalty, valour and self-sacrifice for righteous cause but he has also condemned them for their weaknesses as "their instability of character, their tendency to yield to panic on the battlefield, their inability, as a result of their tribal system, to form a permanent combination against a common enemy, their occasional faithlessness to their chiefs and allies, their excessive use of opium".[17] He desired the British Government "to prohibit the use of opium by a legislation" so that the progeny of the Rajputs would have "just reason to praise us (the British) for this mercy". Moreover, he describes the prevalence of social evils like *sati,* female infanticide and slavery among the Rajputs. He examines the social relations of the Charans with the Rajputs and describes the practice of *Chandi* (self-sacrifice) among the Charans for safeguarding their privileges and customs in the feudal society of Rajputana. Further, he has written about the celebration of the festivals, especially in Mewar, viz., *Nauratri, Bhan Saptami, Holi, Sitala, Gangor, Tij, Nagpanchami, Rakhi* and *Diwali.*[18] The *Annals* are specially useful for writing the history of the tribes of Bhils, Minas, Saharias and Girasias. The social customs of the Bhils and their role in resisting the Mughal forward policy towards the State of Mewar has been described in the *Annals.* The contribution of Maharaja Sawai Jai Singh of Jaipur to astrology and science, and Rajrana Zalim Singh of Kota to protect the Kota State against Maratha plundering raids are noteworthy. The effects of the treaties of 1817–18 on the Rajputana States are also analysed and their text have been given in appendices. In fact, the *Annals and Antiquities of Rajasthan* provides useful source-material on the socio political history of Rajasthan from the ancient period to the early 19th century.

The *Travels in Western India* contains the travel account of Tod's journey in 1822–23 from Udaipur (Mewar) to Sirohi, Mt. Abu, Anhilwara, Ahmedabad, Baroda, Junagarh, Kutch and Bombay. He had dedicated this travel diary to Mrs. Colonel William Hunter Blair in appreciation of her visit to the sacred Mt. Abu and as a gratitude for presenting him a photograph of the famous Jain temple of Vastupal of that place. This travel account gives information about the Rajput aristocracy of Rajputana and Kutch, their customs, their traditional tales, dress and habitations. It also describes the mode of life and social customs and superstitions of the tribes of Bhils, Minas and Saharias. Further, it gives information about agriculture, pattern of crops and vegetation.

The *Travels in Western India* also gives a vivid account of the history and architecture of Brahmanic and Jain temples lying between

Mt. Abu and Bombay. This travel diary contains useful source-material for the socio-religious and urban history of Rajputana and other parts of Western India during the early 19th century.

Historical Approach

James Tod belonged to the Romanticist school. He had sympathy for Indian customs and institutions like his contemporary historians—Mountstuart Elphinstone, Grant Duff, Edward Thornton and Alexander Kinloch Forbes. In his historical writings, he is speculative. He has taken a broad view of human history in narrating the history of Rajasthan. He has compared several events, customs and institutions of Rajputs with those of Central Asia, Egypt, Greece and Europe. It is because "like many of his contemporaries, he believed that mythology of Egypt or Palestine influenced the beliefs of the Indian people".[19] These presumptions induced him to formulate erroneous views on the origin of Rajputs and feudalism in Rajputana, which have become obsolete in view of the researches in the modern period.

Tod was aware of his speculative style in analysing the history of Rajasthan. Of course, he confessed that he never intended to "treat the subject in the severe style of history", although he claimed that he had drawn "a faithful picture of the States". The intellectual atmosphere of his times and the objectives of his writing the *Annals* were responsible for this presumption. The *Annals* were published at a time when in India the study of archaeology, sociology and numismatics was in its initial stage. This resulted in his committing some errors in his formulations. He had published the *Annals* (i) for the politicians and students, (ii) for acquainting the Europeans about the mode of life of the Rajputs and (iii) for providing source-material for future historians.

Christian Lassen (1800–1876), L.P. Tessitori, William Crooke and several other scholars have stated that Tod had relied mainly on the bardic literature in writing his *Annals and Antiquities of Rajasthan.* This presumption is not correct especially on the ground that he had adopted a scientific and balanced approach in utilising the source-material for writing the *Annals.* Tod himself was conscious of the defects of bardic literature but he was also aware of its utility for the social history as is also emphasised by the modern historians. He was of the opinion that anecdotes and events in the bardic literature specially provided source-material to him for writing social history of the Rajput aristocracy. Moreover, he subscribed to interdisciplinary approach in consulting the sources for writing the *Annals.* It was clearly reflected in his writing the *Annals* on the basis of the inscriptions, copper plates, coins, Persian works, and bardic literature, such as, *Khyats, Rasos* and ballads, besides his personal interviews with the Rajput rulers and *thakurs* and his meeting the people during his journey and field survey in the various places of Rajputana. Tod had also consulted the archival records of several Rajput States and one could even glean the use of British archival records in the *Annals* pertaining to Mewar, Marwar and Mers of Merwara. He has consulted the archives of the Maharana of Mewar and had obtained several books and taken notes from them for writing the *Annals.* He had received copies of several historical works from Maharaja Man Singh of Jodhpur, such as, the *Vijay Vilas,* the *Surya Prakash,* the *Marwar-ri-Khyats,* etc. He had secured copies of several manuscripts from the Jaipur State, such as, *Jagat Vilas, Jaivilasa, Rajprakash, Rajaprashati, Navsahasanka Charita, Kumarpala Charita, Man Charita, Hammir Kavya, Rajavali, Rajatarangini* and *Jaisingh Kapadruma.* He had collected copies of the *Ramayana, Mahabharta, Prithviraja Raso, Khumman Raso, Hammira Raso, Ratan Raso,* etc. He had also acquired copies of the translated Persian works, such as, Ferishta's *History* by A. Dow and Jona Khan, *Ain-i-Akbari* of F. Gladwin and *Memoirs of Jahangir* by Major David Price.[20] Moreover, Tod explored the temple sites of Badoli, Bhanpura, Chandravati, Mt. Abu, Bijoliya, Menal, Kansua and Nadol; obtained their drawings with the help of Ghasi and Captain Waugh and wrote in detail about them. These temple sites belonged to 8–10th century A.D., and their documentation has provided information to the scholars about their conditions in the early 19th century. These examples are enough to show that Tod's *Annals and Antiquities of Rajasthan* was not merely based on Bardic literature but also on contemporary Rajasthani and Persian sources. If Tod had committed a few mistakes in writing the *Annals,* it was natural in such a pioneer work on Rajasthan.

Tod had committed mistakes in reading the inscriptions because he did not know Sanskrit and had only working knowledge of Rajasthani. His Jain guru Yati Gyanchandra and Brahmin Pandits committed atrocious blunders in reading the inscriptions. Many of the mistakes which James Tod had committed were due to his "rashness in following their guidance" and his erroneous calculations of the dates of the *Samvat.* William Crooke remarked that inconsistencies between some dates in the text was due to Tod's "habit in adopting the dates of the *Samvat* to those of the Christian era, to deduce 56, not 57 from the former, contrary to the practice of modern historians".[21]

Modern scholars like Shyamaldass, G.H. Ojha, Dasharatha Sharma, G.N, Sharma and several others have pointed out the mistakes, which Tod had committed in deciphering the inscriptions. For instance, Tod wrongly stated that the inscription of the Brahmin Raja Shivagana found at Kansua (Kota) is of 597 V.S. Ojha has rightly considered the date of the inscription as 795 V.S.[22] Tod wrongly believed that Buddhism was introduced from Central Asia. Further, he wrongly mentions that Mira Bai was married to Kumbha. Harbilas Sarda and G.N, Sharma state that she was not the wife of Kumbha, but of Bhojraj, son of Rana Sanga. Tod had considered Bharat (who was son of Sakuntala) as the husband of Sakuntala and Dusyant (her husband) as her father. He has also used wrong names for cities, such as, Mandodari for Mandor (Mandavyapur), Jalindra (Jabalipur) for Jalore and Nisipta for Narwar (Nalpur).[23]

Non-Prejudice against Jaipur

William Crooke and Sukumar Bhattacharya[24] have stated that Tod had expressed marked sympathy with Mewar and Marwar and had shown "decided prejudice" against the Kachhawas of Jaipur for their "hesitation in accepting the British alliance". The opinion seems to be far-fetched. First, it is erroneous to consider that Tod deliberately allotted less space to the dynastic history of the Jaipur State in comparison with the other Rajput States. It is clear from the recent researches of Dasharatha Sharma, V.S. Bhatnagar and several others that there is a paucity of source-material on the pre-medieval period of Jaipur State and Tod could write about its history on the basis of the literary works, which were provided to him by Sawai Jai Singh III. Tod has admired Maharaja Sawai Jai Singh II (1693–1743) as a statesman, legislator and man of science and has called the city of Jaipur, the new capital of Dhundhar as the seat of science and art". Of course, he has rightly not accorded similar distinction to Maharaja Jagat Singh (1803–18), as he had proved a failure in conducting the administration of the Jaipur State. Tod's remarks about this ruler as the "most dissolute prince of his race or of his age", has not been questioned by any of the modern historians of Rajasthan. He is not critical of Jaipur's hesitation in accepting the treaty of 1818, rather he has questioned the British right to demand the surrender of Wazir Ali from the Jaipur State in 1803, as it cast an indelible stain on the Kachhawa rulers. Tod had admired all Rajput States, but called Jaipur State with the epithet of *Jhuta darbar* (lying court). His views on Jaipur State are testified by the travel account of Bishop Heber and James Sutherland's official report (1842).[25] It is rather surprising that Tod is silent about the legitimacy of Sawai Jai Singh III, the posthumous son of Jagat Singh. It is alleged that Maharaja Sawai Jai Singh III was ushered in the palace secretly and was not the natural son of Jagat Singh.[26] Perhaps Tod did not give any credence to this rumour. These facts clearly show that Tod wrote the dynastic history of the Jaipur State objectively and without any prejudice.

Tod was also criticised for giving less space and importance to Bikaner State in comparison with Mewar. This made Maharaja Ganga Singh of Bikaner to publish a voluminous book entitled: *House of Bikaner,* as a rejoinder to Tod's *Annals.*[27] The House of Bikaner reflected over the high position of Bikaner State among Rathors and its conspicuous role during the Mughal and British periods.

Tod devoted more space in his *Annals* to Mewar because he could profusely secure source-material for writing its history. Besides, he considered Mewar and Jaisalmer States more ancient and older States as the other Rajput States had attained their settlements subsequent to the Mohammedan invasions.[28] He himself made it clear that he proposed to touch upon the *Annals* of all the Rajput States but Mewar and some other States would be treated copiously to provide a specimen to the historians.

Tod's analysis of British reflections with the States of Rajputana is full of contradictions. In the beginning he considered the non-interference policy of the British Government responsible for the deplorable condition of Rajputana between 1806 and 1817. Among the Rajputana States, he had concluded treaty with the State of Bundi in 1818 and, thus, he was instrumental in bringing the Rajputana States under the British paramountcy. But within a period of eleven years by 1829, his political views changed and he transformed himself as a protagonist of freeing the Rajputana States from the British treaties. At the time of dedicating the First Volume of the *Annals* to King George IV in 1829, he advocated that the Rajput States should be restored to their "former independence".

It is surprising to note that in the *Annals,* Tod criticises the British policy of interference in the States of Rajputana after 1818 but does not mention that he himself was the protagonist of this policy in Mewar as Political Agent during 1818–1821. His interference in Mewar resulted in offending the Maharana, *ryot* and the *thakurs.* The Mers of Merwara revolted against his stringent measures, while the Bhils of Mewar resented his orders to deprive them of their traditional right to collect *Rakhwali* (protection tax) and *Bolai* (travellers tax), and ultimately, revolted for the restoration of their rights in 1821.

Tod had not only ignored to mention these points in the *Annals* but he is also silent about his differences with his Government relating to Kota State. For instance, during the conflict between Rajrana Zalim

Singh and Maharao Kishore Singh of Kota in 1821, Tod showed marked sympathy with the latter in defiance of the order of his government. For this deviation, the British government censured him and deprived him of the political charge of the Harauti States of Kota and Bundi, resulting in his holding only the charge of Mewar Sate as Political Agent.[29]

Earlier to Tod's publication of the *Annals,* the historical writings on Rajasthan were confined to bardic literature and the Khyats. The Khyats generally narrated the dynastic history, and were parochial in outlook, narrow in approach and panegeric in nature and feudal in content. Tod attempted to write the history of Rajasthan in an integrated manner. His *Annals* certainly discarded the tradition of Khyat writing. He showed the path of writing comprehensive history of Rajasthan on a scientific basis, conveying the genesis of historical events and their cause and effects. By using inscriptions, coins, copper plates, monuments, archival material and Persian and Rajasthani sources of writing the *Annals,* he showed that a historian required the skill of an archaeologist, a sociologist, an anthropologist and a geographer. He combined in him all these qualities. He not only initiated a new approach to historical writings in Rajasthan but also influenced the research methodology of the historical works of Kaviraja Shyamaldass, Munshi Jwala Sahai, Munshi Sohanlal, G.H. Ojha and several others. Under the influence of James Tod and other European scholars, Shyamaldass, a Charan historian, discarded the panegyric style of Khyat writing and wrote the history of Mewar and other Rajput States critically and on an objective basis. Of course, he rectified several historical errors of Tod's *Annals,* but he certainly blended the method of narration and research methodology of Tod's *Annals.* Like Tod, Shyamaldass admired the martial action and noble ideals of the Rajputs, and gave the texts of inscriptions, letters and relevant documents in the appendix of his book for the reference of posterity.

Tod's Imperialist View of Rajasthan History

It may not be an exaggeration to conclude that Tod's *Annals* were solely swayed by the view of showing the British as the saviour of Rajputana States, its people and Rajput aristocracy from the oppression and exploitation of the Marathas. This imperialistic view of history has been reflected throughout the *Annals* in describing the social, economic and political life of the people of Rajasthan around the dynastic history of each State. Tod's predictions towards the Rajputs is further revealed in his criticism of the "Emperor Aurangzeb and Muhammadans as intolerant (bigoted)",[30] as well as dubbing the Marathas as plunderers, and responsible for the chaotic condition before the British intervention in Rajputana (1818). This effort to differentiate between the cultural and territorial boundaries of Rajputs, Marathas and Muhammadans on the notion of insider, outsider or native from foreigners,[31] was aimed at winning the Rajputs to the British side, and turning them against the Marathas and the Muhammadans. Tod's personal narrative in the *Annals,* repeatedly emphasised that the dismal condition of Rajputana States of the Maratha period had subsided after the Anglo-Rajput treaties (1818), that the peace and tranquillity was restored in these States, and the establishment of the British paramountcy had proved a boon for the people of Rajputana.[32] He had toed the same policy to win over the Rajput rulers to British side, as he highlighted their loyalty for the British Government in the dedication of the First Volume of the *Annals* to King George IV.[33]

> The Rajput princes, happily rescued, by the triumph of the British arms, from the yoke of lawless oppression, are now the most remote tributaries to Your Majesty's extensive empire; and their admirer and annalist may ... hope that the signs of this ancient and interesting race for the restoration of their former independence, which it would suit our wisest policy to grant ... .

With the same imperialist motives, Tod presented the Second Volume of the *Annals* to King William IV in 1832 stating that:[34]

> The throne has always been the watchword and rallying point of the Rajputs ... . It will not I trust, be deemed presumptuous in the Annalist of these gallant and long oppressed races thus to solicit for them a full measure of Your Majesty's gracious patronage; in return for which, the Rajputs making Your Majesty's enemies their own, would glory in assuming the "saffron robe", emblematic of death or victory ...

Tod was a keen observer as it was he, who had for the first time pointed out in the *Annals* about the virtue of the Rajput princes of remaining loyal to British throne. His predilections came true. The Rajput States remained loyal to the British Government in 1857 and took leading part in the First World War, and one of their princes, Maharaja Ganga Singh of Bikaner, had participated in the Imperial Conference at Paris, This revived the interest of the British Government in *Tod's Annals* and William Crooke brought out its new edition in 1920 for the use of modern scholars and students of Indian history and antiquities.

Tod's *Annals* also became a source of interest during the Indian National Movement. R.C. Datta extracted material from this book and wrote *Rajput Jivan Sandhya;* the hero is Maharana Pratap of Mewar, who struggled for the independence of his patrimony.

Notes

1. James Tod, *Annals and Antiquities of Rajasthan,* vol.I, ed., by William Crooke, Motilal Banarsidass, Delhi, Reprint 1971, Preface p. ix.
2. Lloyd I. Rudolph, *Producing and Reproducing Rajasthan: Why Col. Tod Represented Rajasthan the Way he Did and Its Consequences for Imperial, Nationalist and Rajput Historiography,* Institute of Rajasthan Studies, Jaipur, 2001, p. 5.
3. Tod., op. cit., Vol. I, p. x.
4. James Tod, *Travels in Western India:* Oriental Publishers, Delhi, First Indian Reprint, 1971, p. xvii. William Crooke mentions that James Tod procured the Cadetship through the influence of Patrick and S. Heatley, brothers of his mother who were members of the Civil Service of the East India Company. Cf. James Tod, *Annals and Antiquities of Rajasthan,* ed. by William Crooke, Motilal Banarsidass, Delhi, Reprint 1971, Vol. I, p. xxv.
5. The expedition was not carried into execution.
6. This *Memoir* was revised and published by him in the form of a book. It is available in the Library at the National Archives of India, New Delhi. This *Memoir* was included in a chapter of Tod's *Annals and Antiquities of Rajasthan.* The manuscript of this monograph can be consulted in the series of Miscellaneous Records at the National Archives of India, New Delhi. Cf. S.No. 150, List No. 1124, Miscellaneous Records, National Archives of India, New Delhi.
7. James Tod, *Travels in Western India,* p. xxvi.
8. For details see, V.K. Vashishtha. "Tod's Role as Political Agent in the States of Rajputana", Proceedings of the Rajasthan History Congress, Fourth Session, Bikaner, 1970. pp. 62–77.
9. For details about Tod's travel account from Udaipur to Bombay during 1822–23, See, James Tod, *Travels in Western India,* Delhi, Oriental Publishers, Reprint 1971.
10. Julia was a daughter of Dr Henry Clutterbuck, a physician in London.
11. De Boigne died in 1830. The Maratha army, which had fought under his command had defeated the ruler of Jodhpur in the battle of Mairta (1790).
12. For details about the biographical sketch of James Tod, see, James Tod, *Travels in Western India,* pp. i–ix.
13. Rudolph, op. cit., pp. 3–4.
14. Ibid., p. 7.

15. Major General John Malcolm had published the following two works which contained information about the society and political condition of Central India and Rajputana States:
    (i) *A Memoir of Central India including Malwa and Adjoining Provinces with the History and Copious illustrations of the Past and Present Condition of the Country* (London: Parbury, Allen & Co., Third edn. 1832), in two volumes.
    (ii) *The Political History of India from 1784 to* 1828 (London, John Murray, Albemarle Street, 1828), in two volumes.
16. James Tod, *Annals and Antiquities of Rajasthan,* Motilal Banarsidass, Delhi, Reprint, 1971, Vol. III, p. 1729.
17. Ibid., p. xxxviii.
18. Tod, op. cit., Vol. I, pp. 652–95.
19. Tod, *Annals,* Vol. I, p. xi.
20. Ibid., p. x.
21. Ibid., pp. xii–xiii, xxiv.
22. G.B. Ojha has pointed out that out of seven inscriptions used by Tod, four were misrepresented. Cf. G.H. Ojha, *Colonel James Tod ka Jiwan Charita,* Khadvillas Press, Bankipur, 1902, p. 32.
23. Ibid., pp. 32–34.
24. Sukumar Bhattacharya, "James Tod", in *Historians and Historiography in Modern India,* ed. by S.P. Sen, Calcutta, Institute of Historical Studies, 1973.
25. V.K. Vashishtha, *Rajputana Agency,* 1832–1858, Aalekh Publishers, Jaipur, p. 172
26. For details see, A.H.E, Boileau, *Personal Narrative of a Tour through the Western State of Rajwara in 1835, Comprising Beekaner, Jesulmere and Jodhpur,* Calcutta, 1837, p. 35.
27. K.M. Pannikar, *His Highness the Maharaja of Bikaner. A Biography,* Oxford University Press, London 1937, p. 353.
28. Tod, *Annals,* p. ixiv.
29. For details see, Vashishtha, op. cit., p. 69.
30. Tod, op. cit., Vol.I, p. xxvii.
31. Rudolph, op. cit., pp. 7–14.
32. Tod, op. cit., Vol. III, pp. 1700–01.
33. Dedication of the First Volume of the *Annals* by James Tod to King George IV. Cf. Tod, op. cit., Vol. I.
34. Dedication of the Second Volume of the *Annals* by James Tod to King William IV. Cf. Tod. op. cit., Vol. I.

5

James Tod and the 'Rajpoot Feudalism'

The Case of the Bhumiya Chiefs in Mewar

Marco Fattori

> *The Bhumia does not renew his grant, but holds on prescriptive possession.*[1]

> (...) *these allodial tenants, the yeomen of Rajasthan, who constitute, as in the districts of Kumbhalmer and Mandalgarh, the landwehr, or local militia.*[2]

> *Kaulnamah* of 1854, art. 10, 2nd par.: *Bhoomias (or landholders) from the Maharana are, as hitherto, to be responsible for the protection of their villages, and for all losses by theft and robbery.*[3]

The aim of my paper is to highlight the genesis and the political impact of one 'feudal' category in 19th and 20th centuries Rajasthan, that of the 'Bhumiya' chiefs as 'allodial tenants' in the rigidly stratified colonial framework of 'Rajpoot feudalism'. It is well known that the interpretation of Rajput history as an archetypal process of feudal rise and fall owes much to the political activity of James Tod, as well as to his masterwork *Annals and Antiquities of Rajasthan, or the Central and Western Rajpoot States of India* (1829–32). In this paper I want to focus on the history of this historical and administrative category in Mewar, because of the specific tribal background of most Bhumiya chiefs in the south-western Bhumat (or Bhomat) region of the former 'Princely State' of Udaipur, and because the strained relations between the Mewar Darbar and these petty chiefs throughout the 19th century about respective rights of sovereignty led the colonial British administration to become more and more involved in mediating different attitudes. In doing so, British officers regularly regarded Tod's work as a major authority. But what is particularly striking is to detect how promptly the Mewar Darbar referred to Tod's letter in order to enforce its power vis-à-vis the nobles of the kingdom.[4] Indeed, the construction of a feudal model as the natural, 'national' pattern of concurring political legitimations in Rajasthan proved a major tool for the centralisation of power, an effort shared by both ruling Maharajas and Political Agents. In this process, petty chiefs as the Bhumiya from Bhumat were to be generally regarded as minor relics of an age of 'anarchy' supposed to have come to an end since the stipulation of a treaty of subsidiary alliance between the East India Company and the Mewar Darbar. The '*Rajpoot* feudalism' came to mean a pyramidal pattern of political hierarchy, and on the other hand it was functional to a new representation of power, the Maharaja's rule being identified with the political fixed boundaries of the 'Native State'.

The Bhumiya Chiefs of Mewar as a Case of 'Rajputisation'

The Bhumat region stretches to the west of the city of Udaipur, impending on the borders of Dhar, Sirohi and Jodhpur States. The Aravalli range stretches longitudinally within the region and thick forests covered the hilly landscape throughout the 18th century. The main centres of the region were and are the towns of Kherwara and Kotra.

The local political system of the Bhil and Garasiya groups, as far as we know, had never been brought entirely under the effective administration of the Mewar Darbar. The local chiefs were bounded to the payment of a tribute, whose regular collection depended much on the effective capability on the part of the Maharaja of imposing his will in the region.[5] In fact, we do not possess any valuable historical source to detail the social and political history of the local tribal chiefdoms.[6] On the other hand, since the 1820s much colonial evidence is available in the form of administrative acts and correspondence. British administrators from the very beginning of the colonial influence in the area were much concerned with how to deal with the local petty chiefs of these hilly 'little kingdoms' in order to dispel the 'turbulent proclivities' of the local Bhils.

The Bhils of the region had an established tradition as guides, escorts and protectors of the traders who were passing along their homeland. Tod himself in his *Travels in Western India* wrote that the

Bhils were popularly referred to as *Mairote* (born of mountain), *Goind* (lord of caves), *Pal Indra* (lord of the pass).[7] The legitimation of these local tribes through a specific appeal to the value and practice of protection can be considered as a specific form of the general process labelled as 'Rajputisation' by historians and anthropologists. The continuous tension by groups of uncertain or tribal background and status to enjoy in the long run a Rajput status is a well-known historical trend in all-northern India. The adoption of Rajput ethos, names, titles, customs and (more or less fictive) genealogies is a common pattern, yet quite difficult to record in its historical development, and one has mainly to refer to local oral traditions in this 'ethno-historical' approach. In the case of the Bhil groups based in Mewar's Bhumat, we can point out how their 'Rajputisation' in one of its most striking features is thoroughly inscribed in the local ecology. This is to say that the ideal and the praxis of protection which is the backbone of each and every *Go-Brahman-Pratipalak* (protector of cows and Brahmans) is locally translated in the customary protection afforded by local chiefs with their retinue to travellers and merchants venturing through the hills. In this perspective, the *bolai* and the *rakhwali*, the sums in cash or kind to be corresponded by travellers and villagers were much more of a contribution to the maintenance of this kind of protection than 'blackmail'.[8]

The British could not appreciate the fact that local tribal groups claimed a Rajput-like status through protection of traders in the passes of the Aravalli range. The *bolai* and *rakhwali* system was to be condemned as petty banditry, preventing the flourishing of regional trade. Indeed, the presence and the influence of several 'little kings' within the political boundaries of the 'Mewar State', undermined the royal prerogatives of the Maharaja restored to his full powers by the providential aid of the British and by the insightful interpretation of Rajput history and society by James Tod.

The 'Rajpoot Feudalism': History and Colonial Administration

Much has been written about James Tod, his cultural background, his historical and literary models, and his lasting influence as a major authority in both history and anthropology of Rajasthan. However, the impact of his interpretative legacy and the foundation of the Company's paramountcy in Rajasthan have been dealt with only in very general terms. In this sense, I think that we are facing here one of the main shortcomings of 'post-colonial' studies, to wit, the fact that the personal profile of major colonial administrators and scholars is extensively examined in order to trace the intellectual roots of a consistent 'discourse' on history, politics and society, but the effects of this same 'discourse' in the local context are not detailed.

The case of the 'Rajpoot feudalism' coined by Tod is somehow revealing. The idea of Rajput society as a continuum of rigidly hierarchised levels of political power provided the British colonial administration with a simple frame of action, which could embrace all the variety of local and regional politics. Yet, British colonial officers became in due course of time conscious of the limitations of so lineal an interpretation. One of the successors of Tod as Political Agent in Mewar, Colonel Lawrence, expressed his discomfort with such feudal categories, which in 1854, appeared obsolete and even misleading in their application:

> My views differ materially from those of Captain Brooke; as he, though condemning Colonel Tod's support of the feudal system, himself supports it throughout and argues upon our being pledged for its continuance. I consider it in no way adapted to the present state of things, as entirely opposed to the welfare of the country, and that we are not bounded by treaty to support it. It has had a long trial and been found to fail (...)[9]

Sir Alfred C. Lyall, who had a personal experience as a colonial administrator, pointed out as early as 1882 his criticism to Tod's influence on the colonial policy vis-à-vis Rajput *rajas* and chiefs:

> Although he (Tod) clearly understands the connection of those whom he calls "vassals" with their suzerain to be affinity of blood, still he insist that the working system of Rajpútana of all those medieval terms (escuage, reliefs, Knights' fees, subinfeudation, &c., &c.), which were seised upon as convenient phrases by others who had not Tod's intimate qualifying acquaintance with the facts. Now in these days the difficulty of eradicating a convenient theory is enormous, because the habit of general reading disseminates it so widely, and because even men who could collect and examine their own facts find it so much easier to go to the standard books of reference, where they can find some ready-made theory which helps them to arrange their facts (...).[10]

Some fifty years later, in another Rajasthan context, Jaipur State, a dispute arose between the Maharaja's government and the 'rebellious' *thakurs* of Shekhawati who firmly defended the 'mining rights' in their *thikanas* from any encroachment on the part of the Jaipur Darbar.[11] In this conflict the *thikanedars* backed their claims mostly on the representation of the local history contained in Tod's *Annals*, a representation of ancestral independence from (or against) the court of Jaipur. The Jaipur Darbar engaged a retired officer of the Indian Civil Service (ICS), C.U. Wills, to produce a report detailing the respective prerogatives of both the Maharaja and the thakurs.[12] The Wills Report recognised the impact of Tod's assumptions on "almost every social and historical question in Rajputana", and particularly on Amber (Jaipur) and Shekhawati history. Generations of colonial officers had been misled by his "immature conclusions" on a supposed "Shekhawati Confederation". Starting from the specific case of the Jaipur/Shekhawati controversy, Will's analysis focalised on the general theory of 'Rajpoot feudalism':

> It was Tod who misled the British Government of his day into thinking that, in a Rajput State, the Thakurs formed, by ancient custom, a Political Order ready, with a little encouragement, to stand forth as a constitutional check upon the autocracy of their sovereign.[13]

Tod had formulated his theory on the political system of the Rajput tribes mainly on the basis of his own administrative experience in the region as well as on the historical (epigraphical, bardic, genealogical) sources he found throughout the years spent in the service of the Company. Much has been written on Henry Hallam's influence on Tod's ideas on feudal politics.[14] The 'King', or Maharaja was visualised as the prime and sole source of honour and political legitimacy, though, in the case of Rajput polity, the common genealogical tie was also duly stressed. But the whole interdependence of king and nobility was definitely flawed by a marked preference for the former, who embodied the continuity of a territorially bounded power. Acting on Mewar's political stage just after the defeat and the submission of the Maratha commander Daulat Rao Sindhia, Tod was persuaded of the disruptive tendencies of Mewar *sardars,* who in the previous generation had encroached substantial portions of *khalsa* lands in favour of their own estates. The spirit and the letter of both the Treaty of 1818 and "Captain Tod's Kaulnamah" of the same year testify that the restoration of the "lands seised by one Chief from another" was a major concern for Tod. In the same "Kaulnamah" the restoration of the "old" order in the control of the soil was backed by the integration of the local nobles in the court system (*darbar*), and this integration was fully sanctioned and conceived of by Tod as a necessary check to the political initiative of the nobility. Throughout the 19th century the British were presented with dozens of petitions on the part of the Rajput nobility to the clear definition of their rights and duties vis-á-vis the Mewar Darbar. In the same way, the Maharajas regularly decried the insubordination of the nobles in disregarding these same duties.[15]

Writing fifty years after the publication of the *Annals of Rajasthan*, Alfred C. Lyall lamented the fact that the political and legal frame established by the British to the benefit of the ruling Rajput chiefs had proved utterly ineffective in consolidating the role and the authority of Rajas and Maharajas. In fact, the British paramountcy had done much—in Sir Alfred's view—to destroy the traditional process of 'selection' of the ruling chief too much protected by colonial guarantees against the "turbulent and reactionary nobles".[16] These same nobles in good old days would pose a challenge to the capability of the new king on his accession to the gaddi,[17] ensuring in this way that only the fittest of the clan would rule.

In Search of the Bhumiya: A Marginal 'Feudal' Category

Bhumiya is a traditional title common in all northern India to denote a local petty chief who controls the land without the legitimation of some grant (*patta*) from a superior political authority, but relying on the ancestry of the connection between his family or clan and the local tutelary *saktis*. In this sense, the title of Bhumiya is widespread in all contexts, which have been influenced by Rajput models of social legitimation. It may refer either to groups hailing from a tribal background or from minor branches of some Rajput clan defeated in the course of time, surviving as local, minor powers in peripheral areas. In both cases, one may detect a local strategy of social and religious legitimation through the control of local forms of the *devi*. Indeed, Bhumiya was the common denomination for the thakurs of Mewar's Bhumat.[18]

The semantic connection with the mother-earth (*bhumi*) is evident. The set of traditional warrior values as protection and sacrifice is also central in another important respect, i.e. the fact that Bhumiya (or *bhomiyo*) is also the general name of a large number of deified local heroes.[19] These sanctified heroes act as major protectors of villages and routes. The ancient warrior fallen while rescuing the cattle or defending some village against 'dacoits' is regularly represented as mounted on his horse, bearing his weapons as a 'memento' of Rajput ethos. Often, his wife is depicted as a *sati*, to stress the complementary sacrifice of both the warrior and his *sakti*. Most interestingly, the name of the warrior as an individual is rapidly forgotten: what lasts is the connection of his clan or lineage with that particular tract of land, a connection legitimised by the sacrifice of one ancestor. In this perspective the intimate coherence of Bhumiya as a term referring both to the actual holder of power in a hilly tract and the ideal model of warrior sacrifice and tutelary village god is evident.

British knowledge of India was based, in many respects, on the knowledge of local 'land tenures', and in the case of Rajasthan and Western India in general we find that the early reports on the region were very rich in information about local land systems.[20] 'Definitions' of the Bhumiya chiefs so often met in these explorations are quite interesting, because of the British perception of the peculiarity of these 'tenures', on the one hand, and the absence of any written legal evidence to certify their ancestry on the other. I want to quote here from Lieutenant James Holland's journal, written while exploring western Rajasthan in the early months of 1831, in order to inquire, *inter alia*, whether a Russian invasion from the Thar Desert would have been feasible in terms of military logistics.[21] The pages of his journal provide an anthropological sketch of the region he traversed, and reveal the keen interest of the British officer in local institutions:

> From the time that I first entered Marwar I have been making enquiries into the nature of Putta and Bhoom lands and their difference but the ignorance of the people and the difference of custom in different district have frequently baffled me. As far as I am understand now the Bhoomiah are proprietors of old date, whose grants are beyond record, and as their name implies they are *actual proprietors of the soil*. There are some few of modern creation to whom lands have been granted in this manner for some extraordinary service, or "the price of blood" a small tribute or tax, generally triennial, is claimed from most of them and from some military service is also required, but either one or both of these claims are frequently denied, and seldom paid except when compelled. (My emphasis)

Lieutenant Alexander Burnes, who led the same mission, also gave some account of the Bhoomiah tenures in Marwar in his report:

> Boomeeas hold their possessions by grant of an old date and which have been conferred on them for ever for services rendered and who are relieved thereby from all taxes, duties or calls of service.[22]

The definition of 'property' for the lands controlled by the Bhumiya chiefs as opposed to the concession of a royal grant, yet in the absence of any written legal document to testify this private right, will continue up to the 20th century, as in the case of Lt. Col. Pinhey's *History of Mewar:*

> (...) the hill tracts of Mewar are inhabited by wild and restless tribes of Bhils under petty Chiefs of Rajput origin who, while owing nominal allegiance to Udaipur, have for generations held rights of property in the land over which the Maharana has no powers of interference.[23]

When Tod tried to encompass all land tenures and political bonds of allegiance in a 'feudal' frame, the Bhumiya category was to comprise all petty Rajput chiefs who could not rely on any *jagir* grant (or similar), but boasted a right to the control of the soil, which pre-dated the establishment of any major dynasty. Conquest, sacrifice and intimate connection with local *saktis* were thus opposed to the 'feudal' rigid formulation of the 'royal' court as the sole source of honours and titles. The label of 'allodial tenants' was thus introduced to tally with these Rajput or "Rajputising" tenants. The social and political profile of these Bhumiyas was spelled on the basis of land property and the set of court obligations imposed to the other thakurs and jagirdars. The 'terms of service' of the Bhumiyas were thoroughly detailed: attendance to court, fees on successions, and recognition of adoptions.[24] On the other hand, the juridical formulation of 'prescriptive rights' for defining their traditional forms of control over certain tracts of land proved to be an effective legal-historical *escamotage* to deal with all consolidated rights which could not be traced back in any 'royal grant'. Indeed, declaring that these rights were 'prescriptive' meant that they were on the verge of actual prescription, because traditional modes of protection as bolai and rakhwali had to be considered as mere exaction or 'blackmail'.[25] Thus this kind of traditional ways of protection were considered in themselves as just causes for the prescription of the ancient 'rights' enjoyed by the Bhumiya chiefs. This impending prescription would then lead to a new systemisation of these areas in the framework of a consistent feudal scheme, based exclusively on 'royal grants' and vassalage.

Colonial Recruitment

Since the inception of the British paramountcy in the region, great political and military effort was dedicated to the pacification of the Bhumat region. The main disturbance in these tracts was, as we have seen, the Bhil groups who were labelled as "wild and restless". The scheme for the pacification of the Bhumat was implemented through frequent raids against tribal hamlets (*pal*) to disband the gangs of 'robbers'. Then, another imperial strategy to bring the whole region under the new order was the project of enrolling the same Bhils of the area as a local, cheap police force to be used against other Bhil bands unwilling to dismiss the old ways of living. The 'Mewar Bhil Corps' (MBC) was then to be founded in 1841, on the blueprint of other similar local tribal forces in Western India: the main model for Mewar was James Outram's 'Khandesh Bhil Corps', founded in 1825 and which had proved quite effective in checking the Bhil raids in that country.[26] The MBC was to be encamped in Kherwara and in Kotra, under the command of the Political Superintendent for the 'Hilly Tracts Mewar' (HTM), as the Bhumat region had since been labelled in British documents, leaving the civil administration with the Mewar Darbar. In fact, since the establishment of the MBC all political authority in the region was to be in the hands of the Superintendent.

The enrolment of Bhils in the MBC would also entail, in the pacification project, the establishment of the families of the soldiers as sedentary cultivators in the surroundings of the camp, thus progressively leaving the life in forest. In this way it was deemed that in due course of time the whole tribal population of Mewar would abandon their 'barbarous' habits to transform in a loyal, quiet and productive peasantry. Indeed, the MBC proved to be an efficient body of local surveillance, and stood loyal during the 'Mutiny' of 1857. The history of the MBC goes beyond the merger of the Mewar State in independent India, as it was to be integrated in the new police forces of the State of Rajasthan. As far the 'pacification' of the 'rebellious' Bhils is concerned, enrolment in the MBC and the correlated settlement of a portion of the tribes as sedentary peasants did play an important role in the whole process.

'Men on the Spot': Defence of the Bhumiyas' Rights by British Officers

The experience of an effective executive authority on a large forest region, much on the contrary of the ideal standard of service of Political Agents, led many of the British officers who acted as Political Superintendents and Commanders of the MBC to develop a sympathetic attitude towards the local Bhil population. In particular, the desire of pacifying the hilly tracts of Mewar was to be coupled, in the views of these 'men on the spot', by the protection of the tribes and the improvement of their condition.[27] In this sense, the tribal hamlets had to be guarded against the Mewar Darbar's officers, whose exactions in collecting the tribute were unbearable for the local population. In a certain way, the colonial officers who had a local experience in the Bhumat tried to resist to the strict application of the feudal political framework in that region: the political authority of the State of Udaipur was deemed to be a nuisance for the local tribes and the British should appropriate of the direct administration of the district, in civil as well as in military matters. I shall quote the words of Col. Brooke, in his reflection on the British engagement in the Hilly Tracts Mewar:

> The object was by conciliation, and just treatment, to reclaim a savage race; and it was expected that the Native States would move hand in hand with us, in so doing; but as the government of the Bhils was left with them, the chief means of conciliation and improvement were taken away from the British officer sent to carry out the reform. A constant struggle has been going on between the native authorities seeking to oppress the Bhils, and the British Superintendent to protect them. This may have been prevented a few outbursts and insurrections, but the general condition of the mass of the population has not been ameliorated as much as was the expectation of the Government, when it consented to the sacrifice of so large a sum for the maintenance of the Bhil Corps. During sixteen long years of peace and generally favourable seasons, in a country possessing far greater capabilities than Merwara, not a tank, or one might even say, not a well, has been constructed in the crowded districts, nor has the energy of the Bhils called out or directed to an extension of agriculture.[28]

In the ensuing discussion, we shall see how the British officers in charge of the military and, unofficially, of the political and administrative authority in the Bhumat were to be the major protectors of the interests of the Bhumiya chiefs vis-á-vis the Mewar Darbar.[29] The contestation of the established autonomy of the local chiefs came in due course of time also to mean the drastic reduction of the effective powers of the Political Superintendent and his Assistant. Being reduced to the standard duties of British colonial officers ("to advise and criticise when they deem it necessary to do so"), they were to lose any direct control in the *thikanas* under "minority administration", in framing the budgets of the chiefs and supervising their expenditure.[30] They maintained, however, the command of the MBC.[31]

Mewar's Centralisation in early 1930s

The contestation on the part of the Mewar Darbar of any independent authority of the Bhumiya chiefs in the Bhumat and the resistance of the latter to any claim of sovereignty from Udaipur became manifested in the early 1930s.[32] In fact, since 1922 Darbar nominated *kamdars* (administrative officers) as agents in the region,[33] but the local chiefs lamented the fact that these kamdars were regularly absent, and did not act properly as mediators in local disputes. The Government of India did not consider favourably the prolongations *sine die* of the political anomaly of the Hilly Tracts Mewar, where British officers were de facto invested with all executive powers in dealings, which were normally the exclusive competence of 'native authorities'. In the spring of 1931 the Agent to the Governor-General (AGG) proposed once more to restore all 'effective authority' in the Bhumat to the State of Udaipur in the person of a Hakim *(hakim)* of the Darbar. This transfer of authority from the Political Superintendent to an Udaipur officer would eventually consist in introducing posts for the collection of customs duties in that region, and dispossessing the local chiefs of any judicial power. The Mewar Darbar backed its claim to the restoration of its powers by quoting exactly the formula '*An, Dan, Khan*', exalted by Tod as the resume of the feudal Rajput sovereignty: all customs duties are the exclusive privilege of the Maharaja.[34] The Bhumiya chiefs replied acknowledging the sovereignty of the Mewar Darbar, but at the same time denounced the formula as a 'false saying' and proclaiming their ancestry and originality vis-á-vis every 'feudal' institution, addressing at the same time the colonial power to protect their traditional rights:

> (...) we have not received Bhumat in Jagir, but have got it in our own power (...) we have every hope that the British Government which has always been famous in siding the weak will help us in maintaining our rights, as they did with the weak Government of Belgium against the powerful Empire of Germany in the late Great World War.[35]

In the defence of their position vis-à-vis the State, the local chiefs referred to the agreement of 1894 between the Darbar and the *Solah-Ka-Sardars*, the highest nobles of the reign, with regard to customs duties in their thikanas.[36] Other significant claims on the part of the Bhumiya chiefs was the right to maintain their own 'police' and judicial powers and to get an 'appropriate seat' in the Darbar, which had not been the case on the last succession.

The position of the Mewar State was exposed through a letter by the *Musahib Ala* (*Musahab Ala*) or prime minister, who had his doubts about the actual authorship of the chiefs' petition, suspecting that they had been manipulated against the Darbar by some 'outsider agitator'.[37] The paramountcy of Mewar on the Bhumiya chiefs was expressed in terms of actual 'ownership' of the land on the part of the State, and the whole argumentation is based on a legalistic examination of the extant 'Bhum tenures' against the feudal model:

> A study of Bhum tenure, as it exists in Rajputana, will show that its essential features are:
>
> (1) No right of primogeniture. "The tenure is of a gavel kind, i.e., the estate id divided equally among sons".
> (2) No definite partition of the land produce is paid to the Ruler of the state, but a quit-rent is paid in the name of 'Bhum Bat' or 'Bhum Barar'.
> (3) In rendering service, the Bhumia personally attends, but does not supply a quota of troop as well, as the Jagirdars do.
> (4) Bhum is not a self-acquired land but is a grant from a superior authority.
>
> One and all of these features are absent in their case and hence they do not legitimately fall within the category of Bhumias (...).
>
> History shows that it is a land self-acquired, on which the Mewar Durbar, by virtue of conquest, have superimposed their sovereign rights and Thikanedars have accepted the general obligations of *Jagir* tenure, such as payment of Chhatoond, rendering of service,

> and the supervision and control by the Mewar Durbar on their judicial proceedings, and other concomitant obligations.[38]

The position of the Darbar was also favourable to the maintenance, on the part of the Bhumiya chiefs, of "what they call their police", in order to keep "peace and order in their *Jagirs* (...)" (My emphasis). As far as the tribute was concerned, a fresh assessment of the lands was proposed to be every 25/30 years. Judicial powers in minor cases, both civil and criminal, could be left with the chiefs, still with the chance of appeal, revision and confirmation by the Darbar.

Indeed, the British files on the dispute are quite indicative of the different attitudes on the part of the officers and administrators in charge of the Residency of Mewar and the Political Superintendents of the HTM, much more sympathetic with the views of the Bhumiya chiefs. In a letter, D.M. Field, then Resident in Mewar and in close contact with the court and its pretensions, expressed his scepticism on the judicial autonomy of the chiefs:

> The exercise of non appealable jurisdiction by *a number of ignorant and petty chiefs* is a condition which will cause grave injustice and difficulty and will be increasingly difficult to countenance (...) (My emphasis)[39]

On the other hand, the chiefs received the constant support of the Political Superintendent HTM, Lt. Col. G.M. Ayscough, and the Assistant Political Superintendent, Capt. R.M.S. Barton. Their correspondence states that they had a detailed cognition of the different grievances of the chiefs:

> The Judicial Officer states that the Bhumat Chiefs have been assigned their seats in the Darbar below the "Battis" and above the "Charans", (...) and know that the Chiefs have resented the treatment accorded to them on the last occasion.[40]

The Bhumiya chiefs, anxious to get some definite reply to their questions about their future political status directly addressed the Hon'ble the AGG in Rajputana, with a petition which traced the history of the dispute and invited to a perusal of many letters by Political Agents, dating back as early as 1851:

> (...) the Bhumia Thikanedars in the southern and western parts of the Mewar were so independent that they exercised unrestricted powers so much so that they awarded death sentences. They have been in political relations with the Superintendent Hilly Tracts

> Mewar and his Assistant at Kotra and (these) Political Officers are in political relations with them in the same manner as the Resident is with other States.[41]

In the end, the AGG in Rajputana intervened in the issue by stating that the policy of the Government of India was the restoration of all executive authority to the Mewar State. In doing so, the AGG also supported his views on a reflection about the character of the 'Bhum tenures'. Once again, 'Bhum' and 'Bhumias' were strictly identified with feudal categories and administrative examples in other Rajasthan contexts with no regard for the local history of the Bhumat region:

> (...) I agree with the Darbar that (...) the practice which has grown up of describing these Chiefs as Bhumias and their Estates as Bhum is incorrect. Their position appears to me to approximate very closely to the jagirdars of Mallani in Marwar and the Thakurs of Sheikhawati in Jaipur all of whom claim peculiar privileges on the ground that their estates were acquired prior to the establishment of the power of the suzerain Darbar and were not held as grants directly made by it.[42]

By the end of 1931 the official sanction by the Government of India to the "extension of the authority of the Mewar Darbar in the Bhumat" was to be delivered to the AGG in Rajputana meaning the end of the large executive power exercised for decades by the officers of the MBC, and of course the end of any status of semi-independence for the Bhumiya chiefs. These were to be integrated as *jagirdars* of the State, enjoying all the formal marks of reference due to the "first class Umraos" of Mewar.[43] Since the 1st of March 1932 the "transfer of power" in the Bhumat was effective, with new customs posts as a major signal of the resumption of every administrative authority in the hands of the Mewar Darbar. The Bhumiya chiefs could only address once more by petition the Resident in Mewar, and then petition again for the lack of any reply:

> Sir, with due respect, we the Thikanedars of the Kotra Bhumat beg to place the following points before your honour's justice and fair play.
>
> That our forefathers established our Thikanas even before the existence of the City of the Udaipur (*sic*) and since then we have been the sole authorities in fixing and realizing the duties in our

> Thikanas. (...) in eighteen hundred and eighty (1880) the Mewar State authorities wanted to establish Customs Chawkis in our Thikanas but this resulted in a general discontentment among the Bhils and Garasiayas who afterwards openly revolted against the State.[44]

Conclusion

In this paper, I have tried to point out the impact of James Tod's conceptions about 'Rajpoot feudalism' on the social and political context of Mewar's Bhumat since the 1820s up to the 1930s, with special reference for the last period. In particular, I wanted to sketch the history of the dispute about the identity of the Bhumiya a chiefs, the 'little kings' who were ruling in a semi-independent status and who were reduced, in the feudal framework, under the category of 'allodial tenants' provided with 'prescriptive rights' on the land. In the early 1930s they were to lose any power in favour of the Mewar Darbar and be absorbed in the formal political hierarchy of the "Princely State" of Udaipur: in the colonial correspondence on the dispute between the chiefs and the Court of Udaipur we may detect the point of view of the *bhumiyas* themselves, trying to denounce the formality of the feudal construction.

Notes

1. Tod J. (1829–1832), *Annals and Antiquities of Rajasthan or, the Central and Western Rajpoot States of India*, 2 Vols., Routledge & Kegan Paul, London. All references from this work in my paper will be drawn from the 1997 edition, published by Rupa & Co., New Delhi. The quotation is from Vol. I, p. 133.
2. Tod J., ibid., Vol. I, p. 393. For further reference to the "Bhoomias" in Tod's work, see Vol. I, pp. 136–138.
3. Aitchinson C.U. (1909), *A Collection of Treaties, Engagements and Sanads*, Vol. III, Superintendent Government Printing, Calcutta, p. 51. 'Kaulnamah' (*qaulnama*) is the Persian term, which denoted all engagements between the *Maharana* of Udaipur and his nobles, negotiated through the authority of the Political Agents. The paragraph quoted was to be reaffirmed in the 'Kaulnamah' of 1854, art. 10, 1st par.
4. One interesting example of the acceptance of Tod's narrative as a final reference is given by the words of Babu Ram Narayan, compiler of "*Rajasthan Ratnakar. History of the Guhil Princes of Rajputana*" (Udaipur, 1913): "The manners and customs of the Guhil House and their old administrative systems have been adequately and admirably described by Colonel Tod in his

'Rajasthan' and no further repetition of them was deemed desirable'. (Introduction, p. X).

5. For a scheme of the sums of tribute in cash or kind due by the Bhumiya chiefs to the Mewar Darbar from 1843 up to 1931, see IOR R/2/146/A101, letter of 13 October, 1971 from D.M. Field, Resident in Mewar, to C.P. Hancock, Secretary to the AGG.
6. In their effort to understand the social and political conditions of the region, the British became fully aware of the fact that the claim of a Rajput status on the part of the Bhumiyas was contested. I quote from a 1898 letter: "(...) with the exception of Serwan, all the Magra Chiefs under this Superintendency are Bhumia chiefs of the Grassia Caste. The Chiefs would most indignantly deny this statement but the fact remains. They are of Rajput and Bhil descent and are therefore Grassias. They only marry amongst themselves and their poorer brethrens are known as Grassias.", in IOR R/2/146/A101, copy of letter No. 417–G of 8 September, 1898 from Lt. Col. E.D.F. Bignell, Political Superintendent HTM, to Lt. Col. C.W. Ravenshaw, Resident in Mewar.
7. Quoted by Nandini Sinha Kapur (2002), *State Formation in Rajasthan: Mewar during the Seventh-Fifteenth Centuries*, Manohar, Delhi, p. 129.
8. Tod considered 'rekwalee' as a feudal institution, akin to the European mediæval *salvamenta*, connected with 'bhoom' tenures. See Tod J, (1829–1832), op. cit., Vol. I, pp. 142–43.
9. Quoted in Pinhey, A.F. (1996, first published 1909), *History of Mewar*, Books Treasure, Jodhpur, p. 88.
10. Lyall, A.C. (1882), *Asiatic Studies. Religious and Social*, London, John Murray, p. 211.
11. For the administrative correspondence on the dispute, see IOR R/2/134/27 and 28.
12. Wills C.U. (1933), *Report on the land-tenures and Special Powers of Certain Thikanedars of the Jaipur State*, Delhi, T.M.H. Press. For the history of the establishment of these *thikanas* see also Taft, F.H. (1999), "The Origins of the Shekhawat Thikanas of Jaipur", in Singhi N.K. and Joshi, R. (eds.), *Religion, Ritual and Royalty*, Rawat Publications, Jaipur and New Delhi.
13. Wills, C.U., op. cit, par. 49.
14. See Peabody, N. (1996), " Tod's Rajasthan and the Boundaries of Imperial Rule in Nineteenth-Century India", *Modern Asian Studies*, 30, pp. 185–220.
15. For a concise history of these protests, from a British viewpoint, see Pinhey, A.F. (1909), op. cit., pp. 80–97.
16. Lyall, A.C. (1882), op. cit., p. 225.
17. The *gaddi* is the name of the cushion, which in Rajput tradition is the seat of authority.
18. In fact, in most colonial documents, the Bhumiya chiefs were referred to as 'Thikanedars' (*thikanedar*), as the major nobles of the State. In fact, the chiefs of Jawas, Pahara, Madri, Jura and Oghna were known as *rawats*, those of Chani, Thana and Umaria as *thakurs*, and the chief of Panarwa was known as *raja*: see IOR R/2/146/A101, letter of 10 March, 1932 from Lt. Col. G.M.

Ayscough, Political Superintendent HTM, to Lt Col. R.J. Macnabb, Resident in Mewar.

19. See Smith, J.D. (1991), *The Epic of Pabuji. A Study, Transcription and Translation*, Cambridge, Cambridge University Press, pp. 89–91.
20. Pinhey, considering retrospectively the history of Mewar in the Nineteenth century, admitted that "[i]t should be observed that hardly anything was known of the relations subsisting between the Rajput Thakurs and their Bhil subject, or of the position and rights of the Grassia chiefs.", Pinhey (1909), op. cit., p. 98.
21. "Lieutenant Holland's Journal during the period he was employed in the survey beyond the frontier. Journal of a route through Parkur, Jeysulmeer, Joodhpoor &cc &cc &cc", IOR L/PS/19/24.
22. "Information regarding the Territories of Scinde and the Navigation of the Indus 1830", IOR L/PS/19/25. What is note-worth in both Holland's and Burnes' reports are that they were composed when James Tod had not yet completed his work. In this sense, the two officers did not resent the overbearing authority of the "*Annals*" in their effort to understand more of the political and social system of Western Rajasthan.
23. Pinhey, A.F. (1909), op. cit., p. 108. We find almost the same formulation in Aitchinson, C.U. (1909), op. cit., p. 13.
24. We may recall that all 'Princely States' all over India had to face the issue of cataloguing rights and duties of the local nobility. Sometimes this process led to the creation of detailed handbooks at the benefit of *diwans* and Political Officers: such is the case of the major Maratha State of Gwalior, which from 1913 was provided with its own *Manual for Jagirdars of the Gwalior State*, IOR L/PS/20/F169. In its pages, we find that the category of "Bhumia of an entire village or villages" was listed amongst many other entries (Sardar, Istumrardar, Darakdar, Nemnobkar, Tankedar, Ubaridar, Nankar, Girasia and Inamdar) under the simple entry of 'Jagirdar'.
25. This policy was summed up by Pinhey as follows: "Colonel Tod, with the view of increasing the resources of the State and encouraging trade, shortly after his arrival in Udaipur, endeavoured to resume all the taxes levied from time immemorial by the Bhils on their neighbours and to which they considered themselves entitled by *prescriptive rights*." [My emphasis], Pinhey, A.F. (1909), op. cit., p. 97. Beyond the protection of trade and the necessary fiscal regeneration of the Mewar Darbar, by this policy Tod also wanted to strengthen the actual territorial sovereignty of the Darbar itself within the fixed boundaries of the 'Princely State'.
26. For an account of the foundation and the exploits of the Khandesh Bhil Corps, see Simcox, A.H.A. (1912), *A Memoir of the Khandesh Bhil Corps 1825–1891*, Thacker and Co., Bombay,. See also Pinhey, A.F. (1909), op. cit., p. 104.
27. The Political Superintendents HTM also produced accurate profiles of the local chiefs, to detail their attitudes towards both the British and Udaipur officers, as well as their personal character; see IOR R/2/146/A101, "List of Leading Bhoomia and Grassia Chiefs of this Superintendency", in a letter of 22 July, 1898 from Lt. Col. E.D.F. Bignell, Political Superintendent HTM, to Lt. Col. C.W.

Ravenshaw, Resident in Mewar. Bignell observed at the end of his report that "[a]s far as the records show in 1827–28 when the British first entered the Magra they found the chiefs called Rao Rawats etc. and accepted that title. *Whether the title was self assumed or granted by any Native Government or Darbar there exists no record nor have I been able to trace any reliable tradition.*" (My emphasis).

28. Pinhey, A.F. (1909), op. cit., p. 107
29. We find an expression of the confidence of the Bhumiya chiefs in the British officers in charge of the Bhumat region in this translation from a '*hindi kagaz*' of 6 September, 1931, a petition by the Rawatji of Oghna, Uday Singh, to the attention of the Assistant Political Superintendent HTM, lamenting the delay in getting any reply to previous petitions about the respective rights of the chiefs and the Darbar: "We are living under your protection for the last 100 years and used to get appropriate replies immediately. We lived happily under the British Government for which we are much thankful to you and Jai to British Sarkar."
30. The title of Political Superintendent was also to be changed in that of Assistant to the Resident.
31. "Although the Officers of the Corps will no longer exercise any executive function in the Bhumat, the Resident will continue to watch the development of Darbar policy in this tract with sufficient attention to ensure that the Bhil Corps is not used to support the Darbar policy of oppression towards chiefs who have hitherto relied on our protection.", letter of 31 October, 1931 from the AGG in Rajputana to Lt Col. R.J. Macnabb, Resident in Mewar.
32. All references have been drawn from IOR R/2/146/A101, "Relations of the Bhumia Chiefs of the Hilly Tracts Mewar with His Highness the Maharana of Udaipur".
33. In the letter of 19 November, 1930 the Kotra Bhumat chiefs pointed out that "since 1901 our rights have been curtailed in favour of the Darbar".
34. *An-Dan-Kan* is a triple figurative expression, which comprehends the sum of sovereign rights in Rajasthan, being *allegiance, commercial duties, mines'*, (Author's emphasis), *Tod*, p. 10. On the other hand, *the* Bhumiya chiefs argued that "[t]he Kotra Bhumat Chiefs have always levied and are still levying Customs duties and no question has ever been raised. In 1881 Customs posts were forcibly established in the Bhumat but were abolished as soon as they came in existence"., translation of a Hindi letter by the *Raja* of Panarwa and the *Rawats* of Jura and Oghna, 19 November, 1930.
35. Translation of a Hindi letter from the *Raja* of Panarwa and the *Rawats* of Jura and Oghna, 19 November, 1930. The Assistant Political Superintendent HTM, Capt. R.M.S. Barton, recalled in his letter to the Political Superintendent, HTM, (7 January, 1931), that in a talk in Kotra the Bhumiya chiefs declared that "their intention was, that their rights and position with the Mewar Darbar may be defined, and as they themselves said, times are now changing, they wish to know how they stand." In the same letter, a note of 26 January, 1920 by R.E. Holland, former AGG in Rajputana was referred to, in which the "representations of the Thikanedars" had been recognised as "reasonable and justified".

36. For a sketch of the nobiliary hierarchy in early twentieth century Mewar, see Narayan R. (1913), op. cit., p. 203.
37. So the *Musahab Ala*: "The very wording of the document will show that it is not the product of their brain but the work of an outsider agitator. The metaphorical expression "Chiriyan kah rahi hain ki" (translated as: "sparrow chirps in our ears" in the English version) is foreign to these Thikanedars whose educational qualifications are not unknown to you."
38. Letter to Lt. Col. D.M. Field, Resident in Mewar, 30 April, 1931. In the following of the Musahab Ala's letter, one finds that the Mewar Darbar also legitimised its claim for full sovereignty in Bhumat through a reference to its own mission for the "opening of the country and sympathetic handling" in order to mitigate the "turbulent proclivities" and "wild habits" of the Bhils. The prime minister also criticised the fact that "[t]he Political Superintendent and his Assistant (...) were supposed to be the trustees and guardians of the Durbar rights and interests", but they created, much on the contrary, a sort of "imperium in imperio" in the Hilly Tracts." By the way, the formula "imperium in imperio" was also used by Tod in the same pages on 'Bhoomias', see Tod J. (1829–1832), op. cit., p. 392.
39. Letter of 15 June, 1931 from D.M. Field, Resident in Mewar, to the Secretary to the AGG.
40. Letter of 24 June, 1931 from Ayscough to Field.
41. Translation of a Hindi petition of 17 October, 1931 from the Thikanedars of the Bhumat to the Hon'ble the AGG in Rajputana. In the translation most references to correspondence with the British officers are referred to as 'not traceable' by the translator. At the end of the petition the names of the chiefs are found: "Rawat Shiv Singh of Jura, Runna Mohbat Singh of Panarwa, Rawat Udai Singh of Oghna, Rawat Badan Singh of Pahara, Thakur Manohar Singh of Chani".
42. Letter of 31 October, 1931 from the AGG in Rajputana to Lt Col. R.J. Macnabb, Resident in Mewar. See also the letter of 25 February, 1931 from Macnabb to the 'Musahib Ala', to transmit the views of the AGG to the Udaipur court.
43. In a letter of 14 April, 1932 from G.M. Ayscough to the Musahib Ala, we find "a plan of the seating arrangements of a Darbar held on the occasion of the Hon'ble the AGG's visit to Kherwara in January 1914", forwarded as a reliable precedent for placing the chiefs' seats.
44. Letter in English, manuscript, of 5 February, 1933, to the Resident in Mewar (W.A.M. Garstin) from Rawatji Uday Singhji of Oghna and Rawatji Rao Shiv Singhji of Jura.

6

Luigi Pio Tessitori

His Historical Research and the Rajasthan of His Time

Enrico Fasana

An important part of the Indian stay of Dr Tessitori (as Luigi Pio is known in India)[1] was dedicated to research on the history of the Rajput clans and heroes, and on the customs and traditions of Rajputana (as Rajasthan was called in his time). The territory, the archaeology, the languages and the cultures of that country fascinated him. He was attracted by the Rajasthani manuscripts at the Regia Biblioteca Nazionale (Royal National Library) in Florence, where he was studying, and his correspondence with a Jain monk, Vijaya Dharma Suri, and the friendship of young Indian colleagues.

Soon after obtaining his degree at the Regio Istituto di Studi Superiori (Royal Institute of Higher Studies) in Florence, his desire to go to India, in particular to Rajasthan, was so strong that he wrote to Sir George Grierson,[2] the chief editor of the *Linguistic Survey of India.*[3] Their voluminous correspondence starts from September 1911 and is uninterrupted, so swift and interlinked are the answers.[4] Thanks to Sir George, new correspondence began: with Frederick Thomas, the librarian of the India Office Library; with Sir Richard Temple, chief editor of *The Indian Antiquary;* and, finally, with Sir John Marshall, Director of the Archaeological Survey of India, the only one whom he met personally, at Simla during summer leave in 1917. They were the first, Grierson in particular, to be his sponsors at the Department of

Education. The links between Tessitori and the Department of Education are to be found in the correspondence with Grierson and in the reports of that Department, whose permission was necessary to go to India as a foreign expert.[5] The first employment request was refused in November 1913 because "not being a British subject Dr Tessitori is not eligible for appointment to the Indian Educational Service, but it is possible that an opportunity may occur for making use of his services". After further correspondence between the Society of Bengal and the Department on 15 January, 1914, it was decided to employ him for the period of one year.[6]

The Asiatic Society of Bengal

The position of Tessitori in India always remained anomalous, that of a 'double stranger' for the British and for the Indians, and was the cause of many difficulties. Permission was granted but the stipend was entrusted to the Asiatic Society of Bengal for the initial period, during which he had to undertake the task of being the editor of the Rajasthani manuscripts. On 13 September, 1904, Grierson had written to the Viceroy Lord Curzon on the necessity of keeping, assembling, editing and publishing the manuscripts of the *Bardic Chronicles* of Rajasthan. Lord Curzon had put at the disposal of the Society 2,400 rupees. Tessitori, willing to leave as soon as possible, paid the travel expenses in advance and accepted the contract. The work scheme was approved by the Department of Education. Tessitori sailed from Naples on 24 March, 1914 and reached Bombay on 8, April.

The idea of his Scheme for the collection and the studies of those texts was not a novelty. Mahamopadhyaya Haraprasad Shastri had already drawn up a project in 1908 and was in touch with the local Bardic Committees of the Rajasthani and Gujarati States after his resignation as Principal of the Sanskrit College of Calcutta. The Shastri was an expert on Sanskrit and admitted that he could not allow himself more than three months a year for the research. From 1909 to 1913, he submitted four *Reports*. On the first *Tour*,[7] he stayed in Jaipur, Baroda and Jodhpur. The major interest seems to have been in Baroda, because the local *dewan* (minister of finance), Romesh Chandra Dutt, was interested in preserving the 'National literature'.[8] Some *thakurs* (noblemen) of Jaipur were also interested in the research. In Jodhpur the *dewan* Rao Bahadur Sukhdeo Prasad and Murari Dan, *kaviraj* (court poet), gave their support, Sukhdeo Prasad became the president of the Bardic Committee and Murari Dan the vice-president. In the *Report of the Second Tour*,[9] *Pandit* Ramkaran

Sarma, secretary of the Committee,[10] who had prepared a very useful grammar of the *marubhasa* (the Marwari language), which forms the basis of *dingal,*[11] is introduced.

The Historical Departments

In 1911 the Shastri again visited Jaipur and Baroda, where the All India Literary Conference was in session. Bikaner, where the Maharaja Ganga Singh gave Kamta Prasad (Home Member) the task of preparing a list of the manuscripts already collected, and finally, Jodhpur, where Sir Pratap Singh, the Regent, assigned the task of supervisor to the thakur, Guman Singh Khichi and gave a copy of 200 manuscripts already catalogued to the Shastri. The Mahkma and Tawarikh Khas (the historical department) was doing excellent work according to the Shastri, but "half of the State of Marwar yet remains unexplored".[12] The research of the Shastri also covered Gujarat, Kathiawar, and Malwa, where the Bardic literature was flourishing. In the Scheme proposed in 1912, the Shastri underlined the task of the various historical departments of the single states (in particular, Jodhpur gave 2,500 rupees and Bikaner 1,500 annually) and the necessity of fieldwork (once or twice a year), based in Calcutta. "Their publications and translations would remove one of the greatest wants of the historical student, namely the Hindu view of the great historical movements during the Musulman and the early British rule".

There is no doubt that the work of the Shastri introduced Tessitori to the primary sources of information of Rajasthan for this type of collection—the castes of the Charans and of the Bhats (bards and genealogists)—and produced the awakening of a certain local and 'national' interest for their own history. Quite a few of these historical departments were active at the beginning of the 20th century, when many Rajas were looking forward to building a state infrastructure.

The Scheme of Tessitori

Tessitori complains in his correspondence with Grierson about the misunderstandings that he had with the Shastri. The differences were not so much in the purposes but in the process of working. In his Diary,[13] there is no apparent animosity towards him. In the correspondence Tessitori underlines the possibly excessive fear of the Shastri of losing control of the project and the personal ties that linked him to the people responsible for the historical departments. Furthermore, he notices a certain haughty Brahmanical attitude (the Sanskrit side) vis-á-vis the local languages, a remarkable sympathy for the Bhats (the genealogists), and most of all the limited scientific outlook in the selection of the texts and in their philological analysis.

The task of being the editor of the *Bardic and Historical Literature of Rajputana* was given to Tessitori but the manuscripts available in Calcutta were only foolscap copies. On 22 July, 1914, he left for Jodhpur, proposed to the Royal Asiatic Society a new work scheme and immediately faced the problem of the language.[14] The Scheme, though approved by the Society, was not received favourably at the Department of Education. Not even the travel expenses were reimbursed: a journey to Rajputana was made before the administrative decisions. Tessitori was then compelled to reduce his wide research and publication project, writing a *Summary Report for the Bardic and Historical Literature in Rajputana* in 1915. Submitted in July 1916 to the Department of Education and recommended by the General Director of the Archaeological Department, the reduced Scheme was approved with effect from 1 April, 1917 for a period of five years with the allotment of 6,000 rupees a year and the economic participation of the Department of Archaeology, "leaving entirely to the discretion of the native states concerned whether they should supplement this grant or not".[15] The Scheme would have been enforced only in the six principal States of Rajputana: Bikaner, Udaipur, Jodhpur, Bundi (including Kota), Jaipur and Jaisalmer. A full year would have been dedicated to each state with residence in each capital.

No history was to be compiled, with the exception of Bikaner, which would have required two or more years of residence. The engagement with the Department of Archaeology would require the preparation of a list of the monuments of Rajputana and the research for the Sanskrit manuscripts, Rajput paintings and other antiquities. Control was transferred from the Asiatic Society of Bengal to the Agent of the Governor General in Rajputana, but the publications were to be edited by the Asiatic Society in a separate section of the 'Bibliotheca Indica'. The Agent for the Governor General, Sir Elliot Graham Colvin, accepted the proposals and responsibilities of Tessitori on 23 September, 1916.[16]

The Sources of Rajasthani History in the Progress Reports

Part of his working plan for the publications, the Bulletin of the Bardic and Historical Survey, which had to be bi-annual, was never published. The Progress Reports appeared in the "Journal of the

Asiatic Society of Bengal": *A Progress Report on the Preliminary work done during the Year* 1915 *in connection with the proposed Bardic and Historical Survey of Rajputana, of* 1916; A Progress Report of the work undertaken in 1916 was published in 1917, that of 1917 in 1919 (two years later) and that of 1918 in 1920 (two years after his death).[17]

The Progress Reports were entrusted to the scientific committee of the Asiatic Society and published as articles in a much more reduced form than was the original intention.[18] In the different Progress Reports, Tessitori specifies the collection and the research made for the various manuscripts and the Tours in the areas. In the Appendices, he dwells upon some texts in particular and on stories both of places and of characters. In the Appendices of the Progress Reports of 1915 he deals with a *gita* (song), which praises the deeds of Jasavanta Sonigaro, a brave Rajput, and in which his acts of heroism are blended with the events of Mahadev and Parvati. He dwells on the descriptions of Phalodi, an area rich in inscriptions, and on the story of the hero Pabuji.

In the Report of 1916, Tessitori mentions his transfer to the court of Bikaner (6 December, 1915), an appointment received on the 17 March, 1916 for the edition of the "History of Bikaner" and for the publications of the most important Bardic poems related to the State. The most interesting side of his task, besides the list of the manuscripts received and acquired, is the writing of the Touring Report. We have the description of twelve localities in the area of Bikaner. It is like an accurate 'Gazetteer' compiled on the basis of local chronicles, oral information, legends and traditions, steles and inscriptions. In particular he mentions these localities: Jangalu, which had been the most important fortress of the Sankhala Rajputs before the advent of the Rathors, Morkhana with the description of the life and temple of Susani, *kuladevi* (clan deity), of the Suranas,[19] a merchant caste of Marwar, Kodamdesara, the place from where *rava* Biko left for the conquest of the territory which became Bikaner, after having given homage to Bherun (Siva Bhairava), who became the protective deity of the royal family of Bikaner.

In the Appendix to the same report, Tessitori underlines the historical relevance of the *Sakha ri kavita* (or just *kavita*), the commemorative poems, in particular those which refer to the history of Bikaner: from *rava* Biko, the founder, up to Raja Raya Singha, the famous general who served under Akbar. It consists of ten *kavitas* in the *gita* metre composed in the 15th and 16th centuries. In particular a song shows that the *ravas* of Jodhpur (Rathors), Jaisalmer and Pugal

(Bhati Rajputs) and the *khan* of Nagor were many times allied against Bikaner (which is not mentioned in the chronicles of Jodhpur). It is interesting to note how the Rathors are identified as Kanaujas, thanks to their roots from Kanauj, and the Muslims as Kabulis (evidently due to their *pathan* origin). Tessitori collects all this documentation to compile the history of Bikaner (as if it were a *Vikanera ri kavita).*

In the Progress Report of 1917, Tessitori deals with the publication of the Catalogues, of the explorative tours, in particular with the collection of the inscriptions (192 of them), of the steles named *devlia,* praising the heroes fallen on battlefields and heroines, mostly *satis* (widows who offered the supreme sacrifice). Tessitori also started exploration of the Ghaggar basin, where plenty of traces of the ruins of the Gandhara civilisation could be found.

Tessitori continues the classification of the sources of Rajasthani history and, in particular, of the chronicles (prose chronicles) which he was the first to examine in a scientific way. He refers to an illustrious predecessor: Colonel James Tod, in India from 1806 to 1823.[20] Colonel Tod was the first to make the Rajput world both of Rajasthan and Malwa (Central India) known to the general public. Published in two volumes in London (1829 the first, 1832 the second) the *Annals and Antiquities of Rajasthan* remain the primary and widest source of information of the time, both for their capacity for assimilating history and myth, and for their sympathetic approach on a human and institutional level.[21] Tod in his plentiful reflections throughout the volumes writes upon the analogies with the European feudal world. He warns the British authorities not to destroy that system which, not being centralised was not dangerous and assured at the same time the loyalty of the allies.[22]

Tessitori collects much material and at the same time underlines the necessity for a critical examination of the sources, in particular the Chronicles, for whose collection he had received a commission from the Department of Education and the Mahkma and Tawarikh Khas of Bikaner. According to Tessitori, the most appropriate unifying title for various prose sources was *Rajasthani Chronicles.* They did not include all the Rajput chronicles (these would have included other areas), and their scope was larger than the Marwari one (a limited part of the Rajasthani linguistic area) and the bardic too (limited to the literature of the Charans, even though they formed the most significant part).

Tessitori is inclined to exclude as historical sources the *vatas* (tales or historical novels, biographies and short reflections on particular events), while he underlines the importance of the *khyathas* (fame, celebrity) and of the *pidhiyan* or *pidhiyavali* (generations, lines of ancestors). The first relate the principal events of the history of the Rajput States in chronological order, kingdom after kingdom, while the second group is a list of names without dates, transmitted in a descending order, first the principal line followed by the secondary ones. A progressive number marks every generation, both in the principal line and in the lateral ones, according to the degree of so-called 'seniority' (precedence of age).

The most important genealogists are the Bhats, who served not only the kings, and the Jatis (or Yatis), the ascetics of the Jaina group, who kept regular registers of the families, which supported their institutions.[23]

Both the *khyathas* and the *pidhiyavalis*, according to Tessitori, go back to the 16th century and are influenced by the need for the right of precedence at the court of the Muslim emperors of Delhi. Tessitori ascribes them to the officials of the princes *(mutsaddis)*[24] rather than to the genealogists and bards. He is inclined to distinguish the *pidhiyavalis* from the *vamsavalis.*[25] These, enriched by legends and quotations, were brought together into the *khyatas.*

Tessitori underlines how the *charan* literature (that of the bards) leans towards encomium, privileging own group as the source of legitimacy.[26] On the other hand, Muslim court chroniclers largely compiled the history of mediaeval India, who never did sufficient justice to the Rajputs, so that in the chronicles written by them they appear rarely and often are ignored. Tessitori hoped, therefore, to fill the gaps with the Rajasthani chronicles thanks to the enlightened support of a few Rajput kings (in his case the maharaja of Bikaner). The Rajasthani literature on the other hand allowed that part of it could continue to be oral.[27]

In the Report of 1918 things seem to be going better as regards the working programme. In Bikaner, the *Darbar* (administration) had decided the establishment of an archaeological museum in the Fort.[28] Besides the usual necessity of finding competent assistants, the work concentrated on the *History of Bikaner;* in particular the history of the Rathor conquest of the Marwar territories. The material collected in Bikaner was useful for both the States.

The archaeological explorations continued. The list of the localities touched in his own tours reached 55 in the year 1917, at least according to the Report, but in fact there were many more. The most interesting discoveries were made in the area of Ghaggar under the *theris,* mounds of various heights, which covered tombs of varying antiquity.[29] The most conspicuous collection is that of the inscriptions (more than 550) from 950 to about 1850 A.D.[30] Many of them give an insight into the history of the Mohilas, perhaps the most ancient invaders among the Rajputs, and on that of the Brahmana Palivalas (at Kolayat and Jhajju), a caste of desert farmers until now scarcely examined.[31]

The Descriptive Catalogues

His second proposal was the publication of the *Descriptive Catalogues of Bardic and Historical Manuscripts.* The Asiatic Society in the series Bibliotheca Indica of Calcutta published them: A *Descriptive Catalogue of Bardic and Historical Manuscripts.* Section 1.: *Prose Chronicles;* Part I: *Jodhpur State,* issue I: Bibliotheca Indica (1917) 1–69; Part. II: *Bikaner State,* issue I: Bibliotheca Indica (1918) 2–94; Section II: *Bardic Poetry.* Part I: *Bikaner State,* Issue I: Bibliotheca Indica (1918) 1–87.[32] The volumes were published at the expense of the Darbar (administration) of Bikaner, with the exception of the first volume of Jodhpur, which was at the expense of the Asiatic Society.

In the *Prose Chronicles* of Jodhpur of 1917, twenty manuscripts and among them many *phutkar,* a term denoting miscellanea, are analysed. They contain *khyatas, pidhiyans, vamsavalis, vatas,* etc. The historical character of many texts is evident as are many non-historical themes, in particular, caste histories (of the Oswal merchants, of the Khichi, Sankhala, Bhati Rajputs), of famous heroes such as Amar Singh Nagori, of areas and of battles. A great part of the events spans the period up to and including the reign of Man Singh (1803–1843), the famous, controversial Raja who was deposed by the British and who had been the great patron of the Nath Sampradaya and of the Charans. Many of the *khyatas* were composed during his reign.

In the *Prose Chronicles* of Bikaner, 25 miscellanea of manuscripts are analysed. The lion's share belongs to the Charan Sindhayaca Dayala Dasa (1798–1891) one of the greatest Bardic chroniclers. His *Bikaner re Rathoran ri khyat,* the *Desadarpana tatha paththan ra gauvan ri vigat* (the mirror of the country and the description of village concessions), the *Arya Akhania Kalpadrumna* (which deals with the mythical wishing-tree) are taken into consideration.[33] Inside ms. 3, very important from the historical viewpoint, are the *Jodhpur ra Rathoran,* and the text in Marwari of the treaty made between Charles Theophilus Metcalfe, representative of the East India Company and Vyasa Asopa Visena Rama, representative of the Maharaja Man Singh.

The same treaty appears as *kaulnama* (names of the family groups) in ms. 5.[34]

There are also *Thakurana ra namas* (lists of noblemen) *vamsavalis, pidhiyans,* horoscopes *(janampatriyans)* and various catalogues *(pothis)*. There are 32 manuscripts of poetical texts found in Bikaner and catalogued. Among them the most important are the *duhas* dedicated to the loves of Dhola and Maru (mss. 3, 9 and 12) the *veli* of Krsna and Rukmini (mss. 10 and 16) a *chand* dedicated to Pabuji (ms. 2) the *vacanika* of Siva Dasa on Achaldas Dasa Khichi (ms. 15), and two *kavitas* in honour of Karniji, the *charani* goddess (mss. 2 and 17). Also there is the description of the women of different castes at the well by the poet Chihala (ms. 18) and the poem by Sidhi Nathi, a famous *rajputni* belonging to the Nath Sampradaya.

The Published Texts

In "Bibliotheca Indica" Tessitori published three poetical and historical texts belonging to the series *Bardic and Historical Survey of Rajputana.*

The first volume, *Vacanika Rathora Ratana Singhaji ri Mahesadasota ri Khiriya Jaga ri Kahi* (Part I: *Dingala Text with Notes and Glossary:* Bibliotheca Indica—Calcutta, 1917: 1–139), with text in Dingala, was written on the basis of the choice of thirteen manuscripts and published at the expense of the Darbars of Ratlam, Sitamau and Sailana, whose Rajas descended from the hero Ratana Singh immortalised in the poem.

It is, in fact, one of the most well-known works of the Charan bards which commemorated the battle of Dharmat near Ujjain between the maharaja Jaswant Singh of Jodhpur at the head of the imperial troops of Shah Jahan, and Aurangzeb and Murad, his sons, at the head of the rebel troops. The battle went against Jaswant Singh but the historical episode (1658) showed Rajput loyalty to the imperial cause.[35] At his death (1678), Aurangzeb, in revenge, put the territories of the Raja directly under his own rule.[36] Among the Rajputs who fell on the battlefield there was Ratana Singh, Raja of Ratlam, himself a *rathor* and related to Jaswant Singh, through Mahes Dasa, his father. The author of this first volume was Jaga Mala, *charan* of the clan Khiriya. Tessitori made a research journey to familiarise himself with his life and to trace back his descendants (and other manuscripts) outside Rajputana, at Semalekhara, in the state of Sitamau (19–28 October, 1914).[37] The text was partly translated into English by Tessitori and is still today in a manuscript form.[38]

The second volume, *Veli Krisana Rukamani ri* (part–I: *Dingala text with Notes and Glossary,* Bibliotheca Indica, pp. 1–143) was published in Calcutta in 1919. The work was composed in 1580 by the *rathor* raja Prithi Raja[39] brother of Raya Singh of Bikaner who ruled under Akbar. The subject is the story of Rukmini who falls in love secretly with the god Krsna. Betrothed against her will to Sisupala, she was kidnapped by Krsna and married by him. The story ends with the birth of Pradyumna.[40]

The third volume, *Chanda Rau Jeta si ro Vithu Suje ro kiyo,* (part–I), with Dingala text and notes, was published in 1920 (Calcutta). It was written by Vithu Sujo, a *charan* and follower of Jeta Si of Bikaner c. 1535 to celebrate the victory obtained the previous year over Kamran, son of Babur and brother of Humayun, Mughal emperors.[41] The fact that the Muslim historians do not mention this unfortunate adventure of the son of Babur, then governor of Lahore, increases the value of the poem, which in this way has the credit of filling a gap in the history of India. The history of the battle follows the military deeds of the *rathor* ancestors, from Chudo, the first *rava* of Marwar, founder of Mandor up to Biko, the founder of Bikaner (1488).[42] Prominent are the deeds of Biko against the Bhatis of Pugal, the Sankhalas of Jangalu, the *khans* of Nagor and Fatehpur, the imperials of Jhunjhunu, the defeat of the Lodis from the Mughals and finally the entry of Kamran into the desert, the attack and the capture of the fortress of Bhatner, the defence of Bikaner, the sally from the fort and the final victory of Jeta Si shouting 'Jai Rama' (victory to Rama), riding the matchless mare Sampa, just like a new Garuda.

The History of Bikaner

The programme of completing the history of Bikaner, after the collection of so much historical material, was interrupted by the unexpected and sudden death of Tessitori. Only a manuscript copy of the *History of Bikaner*[43] remains but it would be better to call it "History of the Rathors".[44] It was evidently written after 1917 because it deals with the *rathor* conquests and from the 14th to the 16th centuries with the foundation of the Forts of Jodhpur and of Bikaner. The other written History of Bikaner a manuscript found in the Bikaner Archives deals with the beginnings of the deeds of Ganga Singh, renowned protector.[45]

Financial and Logistical Difficulties

Regarding the cost of the publications, the Education Department continuously reminds him of the difficult situation (war time) and passes it on to the ordinary budget of the Asiatic Society and to a possible interest of the Native States.[46] Otherwise he would have to go through the Department of Education via the local political officer (Col. C.J. Windham in Bikaner) or via the Agent to the Governor General in Rajputana (Sir Elliot Colvin) resident at Ajmer, whereas finance from the Native States would be through the local *darbars* of Jodhpur and Bikaner via the Historical Departments where the Bardic Offices or Committees were located.

The Darbar of Jodhpur was not in favour of his research and he soon lacked the necessary help.[47] Tessitori was informed about the intrigues and the plots against him: he writes about it to Grierson.[48] Guman Singh Khichi, the *thakur* responsible for the Bardic Office, on the specific request of the vice president of the Council of Jodhpur, Zalim Singh, was called back from the French front to prevent Tessitori from doing it by himself.[49]

Tessitori found in this case more hospitality and help in Bikaner where he remained from 6, December, 1915 until the end of his life, and where he was buried. Here his *Scheme* and his studies seemed to be much more appreciated and the *darbar* intervened to cover half of his expenses (6,000 rupees).[50]

The Assistants

The help given to Tessitori was essentially for translation and collection of the material. The Assistants he had in Jodhpur were the Brahman Pandit Rama Kama Sarma, already mentioned, and the Charan Kishor Dan.[51] The first had been the mediator between the Historical Department of Jodhpur and the Asiatic Society of Bengal. The second is mentioned many times and in the *Diario* as "forse l'unico amico che io mi abbia in questi deserti" (may be the only friend I have in these deserts).[52]

Other Charans in Jodhpur provided the manuscripts to copy and to catalogue while in Bikaner he could catalogue directly part of the material found in the Darbar Library of the Fort. His assistants went to meet him in Bikaner; we know about it from the pages of the *Diario*.[53] Notwithstanding the steps taken directly by the Maharaja of Bikaner, the stay of Pandit Rama Kama and Kishor Dan was shortened because the *thakur* Guman Singh called them back to Jodhpur.[54]

The Jaina Friends

The other significant help came to him from the Jaina group with whom he came in touch immediately. In particular, we have the correspondence with Vijaya Dharma Suri and Indravijaya, his successor,[55] both of them Svetambara *murtipujak.*[56] Tessitori wrote the biography of the spiritual master: *Vijaya Dharma Suri, a Jain Acharya of the Present Day,* Calcutta 1917.[57]

For Tessitori, Northern India is a wide itinerary of Jaina meetings from the moment of his arrival in Calcutta, then at Pali in Rajasthan, at Talaja in Kathiawar; followers, disciples, monks close to Vijaya Dharma ply him with attention and solicitude. Tessitori demonstrates openly in his *Tour* that he was particularly close to the sect, staying in the Jaina monasteries *(upasraya)* and witnessing the initiation ceremonies of the monks.[58] For Tessitori their spiritual contribution is the occasion to allow the Jains into the history of Rajasthan. In their case, too, it was difficult to distinguish the myth, the fantasy and the eulogy from the historical side. Here the genealogies are substituted by the succession of the Acharyas, the heads of the various schools of thought.

The Contribution of Tessitori to Rajasthani History and Literature

Tessitori's attempt to catalogue the historical manuscripts and the Bardic poems of Rajasthan is the first historically ascertained. The *Annals* of Tod, the *Ras Mala* of Forbes, the *Gazetteers* of Walters,[59] of P.W. Powlett,[60] the *Census Report* of Jodhpur of 1881,[61] and the *Annual Administration Reports* of a single state never dealt scientifically with the question of the historical sources of Rajasthan.

The relevance of Tessitori is not only as a collector but also because within the cultural heritage which he rediscovered, he made the ideals of that world known as well as a type of behaviour which was connected to those ideals. For the cultural environment of Rajasthan in general and of the Charans in particular, the commemorative poems are traditional ways of expression and education which underline hospitality, the sense of duty, honouring one's word, the protection of cattle, and the sacrifice of one's own life as a point of reference for heroism and loyalty to the above mentioned ideals.

He is the first writer who deals with Pabuji[62] both in the *Progress Report* of 1915,[63] and in the *Bardic Poetry of Bikaner*. All the stories of the Rathor heroes have something of the stories of Pabuji, who represents their archetype.[64] Like Pabuji, *Sant* Ramdevra, whose tomb in the desert attracts both Hindus and Muslims, is venerated as a Pir (Muslim saint). It is one of the most popular places of pilgrimage in Rajasthan.[65] Tessitori also collects plenty of commemorative material on Amar Singh Rathor sent by his father Gaj Singh because of his son's restless character, to the court of Shah Jahan. Amar Singh received from the emperor the fief of Nagar. Feeling his honour insulted in full Darbar court in Delhi, he attacked his defamers and was in the end killed.[66] The loves in the desert with the happy ending between Dhola and Maru and the more tragic story of Mahendra and Mumal praise the deeds of the swift camel-drivers, messengers of love beyond the rules.[67] In the *veli* of Krsna and Rukmini, Tessitori discloses the *bhakti* components. In other poems he speaks of the Nathas, the other big pan-Indian sect, which mingles Shivaism and Tantrism. All the material collected, be it in manuscript form or as archaeological pieces, has a major historical relevance.

The Field Research

Tessitori's studies of the language help us to understand the history of the people. The ancient *dingal* is maintained 'pure' by the Jains, while that of the Charans keeps changing because it is rewritten, copied and utilised many times. It is a living language, changing with the times. While the examples offered by the Charans are taken as a model of behaviour, their language also changes but when the same language is no longer currently utilised (and the royal and 'dominant' caste patronage comes to an end), it remains fixed as it was at the moment of its demise.[68] Every description of the *Tours* of Tessitori is historical material in its own right, which was only partly published in the *Progress Reports*. The same is true of the journeys made in Malwa to Semalekhara, to Udaipur, in the territory of Marwar to the extreme north of Bikaner, to Bhatner—Hanumangarh, the most advanced fortresses, which more than once passed from the hands of Delhi to Bikaner and vice versa, to Pugal where the love of Dhola for Maru started and where the mythical throne of Kanauj[69] is located. The steles *(devlia, viragal, paliya)* commemorate the heroes fallen protecting cattle and *satis* who became deities. The inscriptions on the walls of the Fort prolong the remembrance of the sallies from the besieged castles, of the *johars* (the collective sacrifice of the princesses when flight was impossible), those of the *govardhans* (the pillars dedicated to Krsna) point at the places of the entombments with dates and *prasasni* (epigraphies with genealogies).[70] A synthesis of the material was published in the *Reports* of the Archaeological Service thanks to the help of Sir John Marshall.[71] Tessitori calls into question many times the history as it was treated by local historical committees, in particular that of Jodhpur which in thirty years of activity before his arrival had never published anything. For the collection of archaeological material, he had some problems. One of his last missions was contested by Bhairon Singh, the vice president of the Council of Bikaner who enjoined the return to the Fort of Suratgarh of one Buddha locally considered as Vinayak (Ganesa) and of two other *murtis* (statues) defined as of Hanuman and Siva, while they were of Buddhist appearance. The local beliefs frustrated his desire for scientific collection.[72]

The Rajasthan of Tessitori's Times

The stay of Tessitori in India happened to be in a period of great economic difficulties for the immense military effort of the British Empire in the First World War and also a period of personal psychological difficulties, because of the death of his brother and the invasion of Friuli, his homeland, by the troops of the Habsburg Empire. These events emerge again and again from the *Diario*. On one hand, the Department of Education complained of poverty, haggling over funds, on the other, it was impossible for him to go back to his own country.

For the warlike Rajputs (especially those locally in power) the war was a great military opportunity which for a time substituted the boring *shikari* (hunting) organised in a near ritual way with Residents, guests, Political Officers, agents, Governors and the like. Isolated in fixed territories under the unrelenting and strict observation of officials, tutors, governesses, technicians, polo and physical training teachers, the imperial bureaucracy fatally caged in their caste honour. The Imperial Conference of 1911 is the effective prelude to the Chamber of Princes of 1921. Ganga Singh, Maharaja of Bikaner, was one of its keenest supporters. Since 1877, Queen Victoria had been proclaimed by the Viceroy Lord Lytton (thanks to the policy of Disraeli) *Kaiser-i-Hind* and there had been many visits by the Prince of Wales and the Emperor King to India.

The difficulties in Jodhpur were also due to 'minor' kings.[73] Sardar Singh (1895–1911) was only fifteen years old when he ascended the throne, Sumer Singh (1911–1918) was only eight and Umed Singh (1918–1947) sixteen. There were long periods of regency. Some strong characters: Pratap Singh,[74] Regent at Jodhpur from 1878 to 1900; and *pandit* Sukhdeo Prasad Kak[75] from 1910 to 1922, with other duties from 1900 to 1910, while *Maharaj* Zalim Singh, vice president of the Council during the absence of Pratap Singh was engaged on the war-front in Europe. During the war, when the Regent of Jodhpur was absent, the court intrigues were frequent and Tessitori, too, was involved in them.

Ganga Singh in Bikaner

In Bikaner, there was the long stable reign of Ganga Singh (1880–1943), a patron of the State and on very good terms with the imperial government. He took part in the colonial wars in China (1900–1901), in Somaliland (1903–1904) and with the camel troops *(Ganga Risala)* in both World Wars.[76] A lover of the arts and guardian of the historical and architectural heritage of the State, he gave total liberty to Tessitori, encouraging him in his research.[77] Ganga Singh went to London to represent the Indian Princes at the Imperial War Conference of 1917. Tessitori wrote in his *Diario* (Bikaner, 5 February, 1917): "Sono tornato pieno di mestizia dalla stazione, dopa aver vista il mio maharaja partire per Londra. Oggi ho conosciuto tutto l'affetto che mi stringe a lui. Gli ho data nel mio cuore il primo posto dopa quello del mio Re. *Jaya Jangaladhara Patisaka* ... Good bye Tessitori" (I came back full of sadness from the station after having seen my maharaja leaving for London. Today I have known all the affection, which ties me to him. I gave him in my heart the first place after that of my King ...).[78] After his absence the vice president or the Council Bhairon Singh, close to Tessitori, took his place.[79]

In Rajputana throughout the 19th century there took place a change from a 'feudal' state to a bureaucratic one, both in the relations between the States and the Indian Imperial Government (1858, proclamation of Queen Victoria; 1878, Victoria *Kaiser-i-Hind;* 1913, Imperial Darbar and Conference in Delhi, new capital of the Empire) and in relations between the individual 'protected' states and the noblemen, their vassals.[80] From the problems of caste, of clan, of land control there was a shift towards the bureaucratisation of many noblemen *(thakurs, thikaneders, chaudhuris),*[81] to the dismantling of their forts with the transfer of their residence to the capitals (where at first they built their fortified houses in separate quarters), to the substitution of the *nazar* (gift, homage to the king) with a fixed land tax *(rekh),* and from the effective control of horses and soldiers to the mere form of honour, titles and donations. While Man Singh in Jodhpur[82] at the beginning of 19th century was unsuccessful in this type of centralisation, Pratap Singh in Jodhpur and Ganga Singh in Bikaner managed it at the end of the century. The last revolt of some Jagirdars in the desert happened to take place in the same period.[83]

Tessitori in the manuscript *History of Bikaner,*[84] which is actually the history of the reign of Ganga Singh, goes hack to the rebellion of the *thakurs* or 1882–1883 (Bidasar, Mahajan, Ravatsar, Sandwa) and 1904 (again Bidasar, Gopalpur, Ajitpura). Their forts were dismantled. The submission of the *thakurs,* thanks to British forces, tied the Raja more strictly to the imperial policy.[85]

Tessitori requested on several occasions from the Tawarikh and Mahkma Khas material which could help in the outline of its history: *Annual Administration Reports, Khalsa Villages Settlement Reports, Rajputana Agency Administration Reports, Lists and Biographies of rulers, nobles and gentlemen; Detailed Accounts of China Expeditions and Somaliland Campaign, Ganga Rissala Troops History, etc. ...*[86]

Imperial and State Bureaucracy

For the *thakurs* devoid of political and judicial power there remained glory without responsibility. The effective military control of the land was lost to the advantage of the economic benefit (from land to control to land to manage).[87] Once conquered or occupied land appears as being granted; from *thikana* to *jagir.* The Mughals had done the same thing with the Rajas called 'Zamindars', appointing them 'Mansabdars' (officers and officials of the empire), trying to legitimise their position as subaltern. At the imperial level, the rulers of the little kingdoms[88] became part of a vast bureaucratic system. The idea was to make them British Noblemen and the Chamber of Princes to become a House of Lords. Some kings were reduced in some areas to *mahajan* (merchant) kings owing to the Marwari merchant influence,[89] others were considered 'bureaucrats' of the Empire.

The foundation of colleges for the sons of the noblemen (Thakurs, Sardars, Nobles colleges) and for the sons of the kings (Rajkumar colleges such as that of Rajkot, the Mayo College of Ajmer, the Daly College of Indore, the Aitchison College of Lahore etc. ...) on the model of British Public Schools made, or wanted to make, gentlemen of the future kings as the best *British gentlemen.*[90] In Jodhpur the Pawlett Nobles' School was founded in 1886, it then moved to Chopasni on the line of a residential public school and in Bikaner the Walter Nobles' School in 1896 was modeled on the basis of the Jodhpur Nobles' School of Mount Abu.[91]

The presence of tutors, ministers and experts of various types took the place of the traditional intelligentsia, which was essentially brahmanical. It is interesting to note that the local *pirohitas (purohita, upadhyaya* etc. ..., the title conferred to the Brahmans) where nearly totally absent from the political scene of Rajasthan. This is the opposite of what happened in Maharashtra (in particular for the contribution or the Chitpavan Brahmans) or in other groups or the Native States. The Brahmans in power in Rajputana at the time of Tessitori are of Bengali or Kashmiri origin (Kaks in Jodhpur and Udaipur, Mukerjees and Atals in Jaipur),[92] and were prime ministers or finance ministers.

Charans and Bhats

What remains in Rajasthan among the classical tasks of the good king *(go-brahmanpratipalak,* protector of cows and Brahmans) is probably only the first term of reference (and in the desert the protection is of cattle alone), while the second term can be substituted by the Charans, who take the place of the Brahmans as the medium of legitimating of power. But during the 19th century, after British penetration and protection, there is a steady decline of the Charans' position. Tessitori notes this many times because the historical material comes from them. He makes a distinction between them and the Bhats, the genealogists, often nomads, whom he considers historically less reliable and more 'bribe-prone'.[93]

It is interesting to note as usual the complementarity between the various caste groups. The Charans appear historically in Rajasthan as those who can legitimise the power of the Rajput kings and even the martial groups, also of farmer stock, including the Jats, but they needed the help of the Brahman copyists to have their lore written down.[94] In fact in the manuscripts catalogued by Tessitori the names of both authors and copyists are quoted. However, between Charans and Rajputs the relationship is more than complementary. The history of the Charans had been of caravan leaders[95] and bards, of the medium of the Rajput power and of the witnessing of the heroic and protective virtues of the kings.

One of the most dramatic customs of the Charans was that of the *tragu* a collective suicide.[96] Being the living hostages and witnesses of broken pledges (economical and military, of hospitality and protection), of the keeping of the given word of their own king, they took the responsibility on themselves. Their death commemorates the failure of their king.

The values of Rajasthan and likewise of traditional India, are based on mutual trust, on the certainty of relations and on commitments formally made.

Karniji Devi

The presence of the Charans exalted the *sakti* (the vital force) of the kings. It is peculiar that many Charanis (the women of the Charans) were the living expression of the *devi* (the personified *sakti)*. The most famous of them, Karniji, lived, according to tradition, a hundred and fifty years.[97] The dates are controversial but certainly the legend and the miracles of this exceptional ascetic woman of the desert concern the history of many *rathor* dynasties, the dominant Rajput clan of Marwar, and the foundation of the forts of Bikaner and of Jodhpur.[98] There is no work of the bards, to whom she belongs, which does not refer to her. One of the legends of Desnoke (a village located a few miles south of Bikaner) where, in a temple dedicated to her, hundreds of rats are fed and protected, the *kahas* (his little ones), reminds us of the tragic custom of the *tragu.* The suicide results in a compulsory stage as a little rodent, very low but never ending and therefore immortal, just like the king's fame, which the bards, reborn, will hand down through generations. They can in this way escape from the noose of Yama, the god of death.[99]

The Charani women, in history and in legend, also in that of Pabuji, are the privileged witnesses of the absolute priority of the defence of the cattle, even before marriage. This is understandable in an ecological pastoral world such as that of the Rajasthani desert. There is no doubt that as the Charans took after the Rajputs, so the Rajputs took after the Charans, adopting Karniji as *kuladevi* (family goddess) besides the traditional Nagnechi.[100] Karniji provided protection and Desnoke enjoyed a special right of asylum.

The *kaviraj,* the charan court poet, received *lakhs* (hundreds of thousands) and also *crore* (tens of millions) of rupees and the *sasana,* a benefit in lands and villages[101] From 1818 onwards during the reign of Man Singh in Jodhpur and Surat Singh in Bikaner, British protection substituted the legitimating of the Charans and the protection of Karniji.

The Honour (Izzat) of the Rajputs

There is no doubt that the Charans enjoy this right of pre-emption on the family and dynastic histories of the Rajput.[102] They were so aware of this custody right that they extended it to all the historical memories in their possession. They were, we might say, more royalist than the king. Kishor Dan himself in a letter to Tessitori was aware of this. He did not want to be *rajdrohi,* a betrayer of his country, disclosing its secrets to a stranger. Tessitori is compelled to assure him that he himself was a friend of the British and so was his king.[103]

Tessitori was greatly in sympathy with the heroic virtues of the Rajputs but scientific concerns compelled him to an objective evaluation of the facts. It is clear that the function of the Rajputs has always been antithetical to an authoritarian and centralised government, in particular those arising from Agra, Delhi or Calcutta. The most famous exploits are those against the Mughal emperors, but not in an anti-Islamic sense, not even during the period of Aurangzeb, whose systematic destruction of Hindu religious places led to occasional rebellions.[104] In the case of Bikaner, Karan Singh (r. 1631–1669) declared himself *Jangaladhara Patisaka* (Emperor of the Desert)[105] after breaking off relations with Delhi, but Aurangzeb succeeded in calling him back to the court, granting him his privileges again. In the end Karan Singh left for Deccan to fight the Marathas.[106] Only Udaipur-Mewar was hostile to the imperial regime and remained so even during the British period. Their descendance from Suryavamsis, the 'sons of the Sun' seemed unquestionable.

The legitimation for a higher status in Indian society is antiquity, which is strengthened by genealogy. In the case of no written tradition (Bhat), the Bards (Charans) witness it, i.e., a neutral tradition.[107]

Tessitori did not consider with particular sympathy what was one of the most peculiar traits of the Rajput caste, the sacrifice of widows *(satis).*[108] A great part of the tales and feats recalled also in the manuscripts and mainly in the inscriptions *(devlia)* "found everywhere in Rajasthan" has this trait.[109] The *sati* often was mixed with a cult or the *devi* (goddess) and her sacrifice used to bring *sakti* (vital force) to those who venerated her. Unfortunately, Tessitori did not have enough time to deepen the content of the manuscripts, which deal with the history and the people of Rajasthan, nor his personally acquired knowledge.

The Political Relevance of the Local Histories

The Bardic texts recalled unpleasant episodes of ancestors, acts of cowardice, pilgrimages and expiations, marriages with exchanges between castes and clans, which gave or received wives (and to give them implied a hierarchical inferiority),[110] of concubines and sons born out of wedlock, of adoptions, of infinite gradations of status and of behaviour, as well as of seniority and juniority. In a world of hierarchies, of precedencies and of honours these facts had an enormous social and political relevance. It is certain that the scientific concerns of Tessitori clashed with the need to prevent family secrets related to the previous generations from being published because this could imply a *deminutio capitis* and of status.

In one particular, but extremely significant, case Tessitori found himself at the centre of the secular dispute on the 'seniority' between the two *rathor* states of Jodhpur and Bikaner, whose founders were the descendants of Jodha, Jodho in Marwari, States with similar castes and environmental characteristics, both 'integrated' during the Mughal period and at the time of Tessitori both pro-British, thanks to the strong personalities of Ganga Singh and of Pratap Singh. The dispute for honour and precedence, which existed at the Mughal court continued under the British Empire.

In the long correspondence between the Government of Jodhpur and the British Government came the request from Zalim Singh, vice president of the Council of Jodhpur, to obtain the KCSI (Knight Commander Star of India), one of the highest imperial honours already received by Bhairon Singh, his equivalent in Bikaner. The merits were underlined to the benefit of the King of Jodhpur. He was more powerful and more loyal, had paid a bigger contribution and had sent colonial troops right from 1887.[111] Pratap Singh intervened directly. The King of Jodhpur was the head of all the Rathors, which was the highest Rajput clan. The comparison with Bikaner was continuously implied, like the personal one between Zalim Singh, son of a Maharaja, and Bhairon Singh, son of a Maharaj, and so of a cadet branch of the dynasty.[112]

The year 1916 was also the year when Tessitori was researching in Bikaner. In the *Progress Report* of 1917 (published in 1919) in Appendix III,[113] *The ruling families of Bikaner and Jodhpur and their controversy about seniority,* Tessitori reported in detail the Rajasthani chronicles and arrived at the following conclusion: "There is some indirect evidence which tends to show that *rava* Biko was elder than *rava* Sujo, the progenitor of the descendants of Jodho who have been sitting on the gaddi of Jodhpur, and consequently the ruling family of Bikaner is senior to the ruling family of Jodhpur".[114] Tessitori still underlined: "it is not a futile question to the eyes of the modern rajput to whom seniority in respect to a rival lateral branch means a condition of inferiority and almost humiliation". Bhairon Singh requested from the Society on 20th August 1920, ten copies of the *Report.*

In 1933 the official publication of the kingdom of Bikaner was issued: *The House of Bikaner and its Antiquities, being a narrative of the Antiquity, Lineage and Traditions, the high Izzat and Dignity and Rank and Status, the Potential Political and Military Power and the Prestige, Influence and Importance of the Bikaner State and its Rulers from Ancient Times, compiled under the Orders of the Government of Bikaner.*[115] The entire Appendix II of *the Progress Report* of 1917 by Tessitori is reported in pp. 229–234 with the same underlinings and bold type.[116] The response of the "official" writer of Jodhpur *(sahityacharya)* Visvesvar Nath Reu,[117] responsible to the "historical committee for the compilation of the history of Marwar"[118] came later.

It is interesting to note that in estimation of the British at the time (thanks also to Ganga Singh) Bikaner surpassed Jodhpur. Tessitori consciously or unwittingly continued the tradition of the bards and genealogists who used to legitimise the power of the kings.

The Rajput State and Nationalism

Bikaner was an isolated world where news of the events, which happened elsewhere in British India arrived slowly. Tessitori was busy in his research and far from that feverish world. He had a strong perception of it (in a negative way) when he happened to spend the night of the 14th April 1919 at Ahmedabad, on the road to Bombay, from where he would continue for his leave in Italy. The same day the situation at Amritsar with the massacre of Jallianwala Bagh had taken place and *mahatma* Gandhi was staying in the *asrama* of Sabarmati at Ahmedabad "Nella citta e proclamato lo stato di assedio. Ieri fu per Ahmedabad una giornata di anarchia" (In the city the state of siege has been proclaimed. Yesterday was a day of anarchy for Ahmedabad).[119]

In Jodhpur after the death of Pratap Singh and the resignation of *pandit* Sukhdeo, who left for Udaipur, the Indian National Congress started its activities.

Ganga Singh and Bhairon Singh distinguished themselves in spreading the Hindi language: a *Nagar Bhandar* (Library of the Texts in that language) had been founded in 1909 and Bhairon Singh became the president of the society, which managed it.[120] In 1921 Hindi became the official language of the State of Bikaner.[121]

The States of the desert entered also albeit slowly into the trend of the national history of India.

After the death of Tessitori the research of the *Bardic and Historical Survey of Rajputana* was interrupted while that of the

Archaeological Survey was proceeding thanks to the efforts of Sir John Marshall. The *dingal* language ran the risk of oblivion again.

The impact of Tessitori and the relevance of his linguistic discoveries have a more evident dimension in the contemporary world than during the nationalist period owing to the constitution of the federal structure of independent India on a linguistic basis.[122] His example is not isolated. From Udaipur the *Vir Vinod,* the epic of the *kaviraj* Shyamaldas Charan was a model even if suppressed and censured.[123] The intention of Tessitori was to continue his research in Udaipur after Bikaner. Today there is a revival of interest in Rajasthani and a wide knowledge of Rajasthani Bhasa and Sahitya Academies.

Research into the activities of Dr Tessitori may hold other surprises in the correspondence received and sent (in places and with people who were often difficult to find) and in the material present in the Archives of Bikaner, in Jodhpur, in Ratlam and Sitamau, in the Jain monasteries frequented by Vijaya Dharma Suri and Indravijaya, at the various libraries and research institutes in India, in particular the Asiatic Society of Calcutta and the Archaeological Survey of India in Delhi, at the India Office Library of London, at the Peano Family at Reana del Roiale (a massive quantity of manuscript material) and in the Fondo Tessitori of the Biblioteca Civica of Udine (the Municipal Library).

Notes

1. Udine, 22 December, 1887, Bikaner, 22 November, 1919. The Tessitori family hails from Moggio Udinese, a village north of Udine. This is well known in the Indian world, which is always in search of the *gaon,* or ancestral village.
2. The outcome of the vast research work of Sir George Grierson (1851–1941) was published with the collaboration of Sten Konow, in eleven volumes edited by the Government of India, Calcutta 1903–1927.
3. Tessitori obviously knew vol. ix of the *Linguistic Survey* published in 1908 because he asked Grierson to study the "vernaculars of Rajasthan". Grierson answered that this was tantamount to a mine to be explored. After the publishing of *Phrithviraj Raso* by Chand Bardai, no other study had been written on the topic: "I fear that the only students of Rajputana history for many years to come will be insects and white ants".
4. The correspondence, albeit incomplete, between Tessitori and Grierson is to be found at the India Office Library of London. It consists of 43 letters of Tessitori and other documents (and some copies of Grierson's letters) catalogued as Europe Collection 1/83 IOR 2/1/1/32 Linguistic Survey of India with the following introduction by Grierson himself: "Signor L.P. Tessitori employed by the Government of India at *my* recommendation to search for and edit the

Bardic Chronicles of Rajputana". The first letter is dated 11 September, 1911 and refers to a previous one. The last one is the copy of his sister Antonietta' s letter of 7 January, 1920 after the death of Luigi Pio in Bikaner. The originals of Grierson's letters are to be found mostly at the residence of Dr Guido Peano's, nephew of Tessitori and son of his sister Elena, at Reana del Roiale (Udine), hereafter quoted as *Archivio Peano.*

5. All the documents concerning the connections between Tessitori and the above mentioned Department are published in the *Proceedings of the Department of Education, Government of India* ref. IOR/P/1916, 9443–4, 979, 9943 to be found at the India Office Library. After 1917, it seems that relations were directly between the government of Bikaner and Tessitori.
6. In a letter of Tessitori to Grierson from Naples (14 February, 1914) the official communication by the Government of India of 6 February 1914: "An opportunity has now arisen for utilizing your services in connection with the work of editing the *Bardic Chronicles* of Rajputana which has been undertaken by Asiatic Society of Bengal and the Government of India have asked that you may be offered employment under that Society for a year in the first instance on a stipend of Rs 500 a month. This appointment has been offered to you on the understanding that your employment, if continued for more than one year, would remain purely temporary, that it will not be regarded as employment under Government, and that it will not entitle you, to any pension ...".
7. *Report of a Tour in Western India in Search of MSS. of Bardic Chronicles,* 1–6, c. 1910.
8. Romesh Chandra Dutt (1848–1909) Bengali nationalist, *Amatya* (local name for *dewan)* well known for his books on economics and history. He also knew Italy from a tour in 1871.
9. *Report of a Second Tour in Rajputana in Search of Manuscripts of Bardic Chronicles*, September–October 1911.
10. The *Pandit* is the brahman who together with the bard Kishor Dan gave the most consistent help to the research of Tessitori. His grammar *Marwari vyakaram,* Jodhpur 1901, had been quoted by Grierson. The *Pandit* was also the author of articles in the *Indian Antiquary:* May 1911, April 1912.
11. According to Tessitori, the *dingal* is the local *marwari,* which differs from the colloquial form only in the complexity of the diction and the usage of poetical and obsolete terms and the *pingala* is nothing but Braj Bhasa with infiltrations of Rajasthani terms. Tessitori calls the *marwari* language *Old Western Rajasthani;* the term *dingala* is a simple adjective meaning 'irregular' which does not follow the standard poetry and so is 'vulgar'. The period of its development can be considered as being between the 13th and the 17th centuries. After this period the language became the monopoly of the bards, a heritage transmitted from father to son.
12. The scheme of his work proposed in 1912 corresponds to the *Preliminary Report on the Operation in Search of MSS. of Bardic Chronicles,* 1–51, Calcutta 1913.
13. The *Diario,* lost in its original form and rewritten by the sisters Elena and Antonietta for the official commemoration of the Academy of Udine in 1925,

fills 229 pages. It begins on 24 March, 1914 after the departure from Naples and ends 5 November, 1919 on his return to Bikaner after a leave of six months in Italy during the same year. The *Diario* is stimulating and interesting at the same time. It balances passions and affections, love for his homeland, and a 'D' Annunzian' style, after the main Italian poet of his time, a strong aesthetical feeling and a genuine interest for his own research and the people who surrounded him. It offers important historical and psychological insights.

14. *A Scheme for the Bardic and Historical Survey of Rajputana,* later published in Journal of the Asiatic Society of Bengal N.S. 10 (Calcutta 1914) 373–419.
15. *Department of Education Proceedings*—Edn. B. May 1916 n. 1215–130. *Appendix to notes:* "Dr Tessitori is extraordinary well fitted for this survey to continue after 31 March, 1917".
16. *Department of Educational Proceedings,* op. cit., n. 5552–1368, letter 23 September, 1916: "I have the honour to state that I agree with the proposals by Dr Tessitori formulating a scheme for a summary survey of the Bardic Chronicles".
17. In order: N.S. 12, 57–116; N.S. 15, 5–79; N.S. 16, 251–79.
18. The publications of the Progress Report concern only a part of the Notes taken in his *Tours.*
19. The description of "L.P. Tessitore" (sic) is reported wholly (pp. 31–41) in *Surana Vans, utpatti evan itihas* edited by Siddharaj and Harakarj Surana, Jodhpur, which deals with the history of the same caste.
20. The title of *Colonel* is of Indian usage. In the same sphere as Tod's research is A.K. Forbes', *Ras Mala or Hindoo Annals of the Province of Goozerat,* 2 vols. London 1856.
21. Tessitori underlines how Tod aims at the exaltation of the Rajputs more than at the analysis of the chronicles, preferring to mingle facts and legends.
22. "The desire of every liberal mind as well as the professed wish of the British Government, is to aid in their renovation and this will be best effected by not meddling with what we but imperfectly understand", Vol. I, 155; "Reduced in power, circumscribed in territory, compelled to yield much of their splendour and many of the dignities of birth, they have not abandoned an iota of the pride and high bearing arising from a knowledge of their illustrious and regal descent", Vol. I, 112.
23. It is interesting to note that the great patrons of Rajasthani literature are the kings and the merchants (mostly Jaina), groups, which seem to be opposite but in fact are very close. In reality the good Indian king is often the one who dons the saffron robe of the renouncer, before going into the last battlefield.
24. Among them Tessitori mentions especially Muhanota Nenasi, prime minister of the Maharaja Jasavanta Singh of Jodhpur, faithful to Shah Jahan, the Mughal emperor.
25. The *vamsavalis* seem to be accompanied by a religious legitimacy (connections with the deities: Surya, the sun, Chandra, the moon, Agni, fire, Nagas, the snakes). The dynasties of the great epic poems are directly connected with them. The imperial *mughal* legitimacy seemed more a political question of etiquette and alliances than a religious one. *Vamsa* seems to be an intermediate

value between the *jati* (caste group) and the *kula* (clan) subdivided into *sakhas* (branches) and *khampas* (local divisions).

26. The local histories, which had to be written by the various historical departments, did not succeed in distinguishing the facts from traditions and fantasy and Tessitori was a witness of this in Jodhpur.
27. For the different types of commemorative songs and prose writings in Rajasthani literature a classification by metres, and the biographies of some eminent poets and chroniclers, see Manohar Prabhakar, *A Critical Study of Rajasthani Literature (with exclusive reference to the contributions of Charanas),* Jaipur 1976. According to Prabhakar the *vacanika* has a particular dignity of rhymed prose, i.e., of prose with alternate verses, while he distinguishes the *kavitas* from the point of view of metres between *gita* (recitative song) and *duha* (distich). As usual the different forms can occur together in the same poem. We could also add the *chand* with its military character and the cracking rhythm.
28. The present museum is the result of further collections and research. Until now the most conspicuous collections—the terracottas of the Gandhara style, of the Ghaggar valley, the marble Jaina statues of Pallu (in particular the famous Sarasvati), the *devlias* with the inscriptions—go back to the time of Tessitori.
29. His explorations at Kali Banga and the discovery of figurines, seals and coins point to a civilisation akin to that of Mohenjo Daro. In this case Tessitori would be 'the first' to have heard the news of that civilisation (discovered 'officially' in 1922).
30. Tessitori fixes the dating of the archaeological remains and of the Rajasthani texts on the Vikramaditya Samvat *(S.)* chronology, for whose reckoning it is necessary to add 57 years to the date of our calendar.
31. P.C. Senarya and others, *Palivala Brahmanon ka Itihas,* Jodhpur 1973.
32. Part II for the State of Jodhpur is missing and there is only one issue. It remains uncertain where these manuscripts are located. Many of those acquired and recopied came into the possession of the Library of the Asiatic Society in Calcutta. According to the *Government of Bikaner Notes and Orders* n. 467 of 1921, pp. 311–13 *(Tessitori files*-Bikaner*),* on the death of Luigi Pio, 42 manuscripts passed to the Society, another 134 manuscripts were requested unsuccessfully by the Agent of the Governor General from the Government of Bikaner. Those catalogued in the Darbar Library of Bikaner should have been handed to the Anup Sanskrit Library and to the Sadul Research Library of Bikaner, those of Jodhpur to the Maharaja Man Singh Pustak Prakash Library of the Mehrangarh Fort or to the Rajasthan Research Institute of Chopasni.
33. Ms. I, pp. 1–16. ms. 3, pp. 21–24, pp. 89–93 in *Bikaner Prose Chronicles,* cit.
34. Jodhpur Prose Chronicles, cit., 10 and 17.
35. *Swamidharma,* the loyalty to their own king, Hindu or Muslim, is one of the features of the rajput honour *(izzat).*
36. In the chapter on Shah Jahan by Sir Richard Burn, Vol. iv, *The Mughal Period,* in *Cambridge History of India,* Delhi 1963, he just hints at it.
37. In the *Sitamau State Gazetteer* (by C.E. Luard, Bombay 1908), Semalekhara is classified as a *jagir* of *charan* origin (p. 80). I went myself in February 1986 to

Semalekhara where the local Charans (a few families who have kept till now the role of a dominant caste thanks to the land grants given to their ancestors), claim to be the descendants. Unfortunately I did not receive confirmation of the presence of Tessitori in the Archives of Sitamau (Shri Natnagar Shodh Samsthan). There is instead the correspondence with the *dewan* Yaswant Raoji Tombre (1912–1921) during the long reign of Raja Ram Singh (1900–1967).

38. Jodhpur 5 April, 1915. The 40 page manuscript is to be found in the Archivio Peano and is waiting to be edited and published.
39. Prithi Raja is represented as a pious man endowed with supernatural powers. The poem for its content is not characteristic of the bards, but the form *(veli)* and the language *(dingala)* is typical of them. Tessitori utilised 8 manuscripts.
40. Tessitori also wrote the English translation of those texts (the manuscripts are still at the Archivio Peano).
41. There is no mention of the battle in the contributions on Humayun (pp. 21–41) by Sir Richard Burn in the Vol. iv, *The Mughal Period,* op. cit.
42. In 1988, the 500th anniversary of the foundation of the city was enthusiastically celebrated.
43. The manuscript of pp. 63 is located at the Archivio Peano.
44. Both the term *rathor* and their lineage, as we can gather from a manuscript catalogued by Tessitori (ms. 23, *Bikaner Prose Chronicles,* cit.), seem to derive from *ratha,* the spine of the *rsi* Gautama. The origin of other Rajputs clans appears to be of a later date and mysterious. The documents and epigraphies confirm their existence in the 10th, 11th, 12th centuries. They reappear in the 14th century during the period of the Muslim expansion of Alaud-din Khalji (1361). Their original title is *raula.* Thanks to a series of marriages and successful battles, the Rathors extended their territories at the expense of the other *rajput* clans in the area of Marwar.
45. *Manuscript History of Bikaner,* n. J 565, *bundle* n. 63, in *Tessitori files*, Bikaner Archives.
46. The Society provided the funds for the publication of Jodhpur's catalogue, the Native States for all the other publications.
47. From the *Diario* (Jodhpur 2 September, 1915): "II Consiglio di Reggenza dello Stato di Jodhpur ha rifiutato ogni contribuzione e ogni aiuto a me nel mio compito di pubblicare i poemi eroici del Marwar e di compilare una storia dell a stirpe reale dei Rathor ... Sir Elliot Colvin mi comunico che tutti i suoi sforzi non avevano approdato a nulla". (The Council of Regency of the State of Jodhpur has refused to give any contribution and any help to me in my task of publishing heroic poems of Marwar and of compiling a history of the royal lineage of the Rathors ... Sir Elliot Colvin informed me that all his efforts did not achieve anything).
48. Letter to Grierson of 28 October, 1914: "In Jodhpur there are so many rivalries among the most influential natives that it is impossible to please everybody. By selecting as my assistant Pandit Rama Karoa (the most intelligent marwari) I have fallen under the displeasure of many people". Grierson advised him to address himself directly to the British Resident.

49. Letter to Tessitori from Zalim Singh (21 May,1915), Archivio Peano: "Dear Mister Tessitori, ... as Rao Bahadur Thakur Guman Singh has come back from the war and the work of the compilation of the History of Marwar as also of the Bardic Chronicles will be conducted under his supervision, P. Ram Karan and Charan Kishor Dan may be allowed to revert to the Historic Office after the expiry of their leave".

50 *Progress Report* of 1917, cit., 29.

51. After several difficulties and wrong information which reported the family as dispersed in different villages, in February 1987, I succeeded in meeting in the area of the old Polo Ground of Jodhpur the great grandsons of Kishor Dan. With their permission the seals of a box, in which according to them held his records, were broken and a day later I was surprised to find fourteen letters written by Tessitori to Kishor Dan between 1915 and 1918, eleven of which were in Hindi and three in Marwari. The letters were very interesting, both as documents on Tessitori's personality, and as a reward for my efforts in searching for them.

52. *Diario,* Bikaner 13 August, 1916. The first meeting with the other Charan Jait Dan was dated 9 August, 1914.

53. *Diario,* Bikaner 21 July, 1916: "E' venuto il mio amico, il poeta Kishor Dan. Da tempo lo avevo desiderato. II Maharaja ha telegrafato al Maharaja di Jodhpur e l'ha fatto mandare" (My friend, the poet Kishor Dan has come. I had wished for it for so long. The Maharaja of Bikaner had cabled to the Maharaja of Jodhpur and had him sent).

54. Letter of Guman Singh to Bhairon Singh, 30 April, 1917: "Kindly instruct him (Barath Kishor Dan) to return to his duty in my office without any further delay" in Bikaner *Notes and Order, Tessitori files,* Bikaner Archives, cit. In a letter addressed to me from Jodhpur, 17 May, 1989, Gopal Singh Khichi, grandson of Guman Singh remembers his grandfather in a short biography, mentioning the names of Tessitori's Indian assistants, but not Tessitori's own name.

55. The correspondence is kept in the Archivio Peano.

56. This is the Jaina group closest to Hinduism since it does not reject *(ad abundantiam)* the cult of the statues *(murtis),* though it highlights the monastic stage of the *upasrayas.*

57. Suri was the head of one of the 84 schools *(gacchas)* of the sect: "It is to him that I am indebted for having had an insight into the monastic life of the Jains which probably no European ever had before", op. cit., p. 3. Tessitori also wrote a review of Suri's work *Aitihasika Rasa Samgraha,* in the Indian Antiquary, June 1917, pp. 135–136.

58. There is the evidence of many *Tours* in the *Diario.* Some letters of Tessitori to Vijaya Dharma Suri were found in a Jain *upasraya* in Agra. Thanks to this, Hazarimal Banthiya in recent times found reason to partly dedicate his life to kindling the memory of Tessitori in India. Many committed Jains consider Tessitori as a disciple of Vijaya Dharma Suri.

59. C.K.M. Walters, *Gazetteers of Marwar, Mallani and Jaisalmer,* Calcutta 1877. Besides this A.D. Adams, *Western Rajputana States,* London 1899, K.D. Erskine, *Rajputana Gazetteers: Jodhpur,* Ajmer 1909, *Bikaner,* Ajmer 1910.

60. *Gazetteer of the Bikaner State,* Bikaner 1874 (with a genealogical tree).

61. Published in Hindi as *Majmui Halat va Intijam Rajmarwar (S.* 1940) under the supervision of the Maharaja Jaswant Singh and of the *Musahib-Ala* (Regent) Pratap Singh.
62. According to the Rajputs he is a Dandhalota *rathor,* but according to some anthropological experts he may be a *raika,* a camel-driver. The place where he was born and lost his life, visited by Tessitori (and by myself) is Kalu, a small village which can be reached from the salt-mines of Phalodi on the road to Jodhpur. The Bhopas, his bards, celebrate the glory of Pabuji who saved the honour of his sister, protected the farmers, the women and the cattle of the Charans from the dacoits and humbled the pride of the arrogant *thakurs.* Faced with the choice between success in life and fame beyond-life itself he preferred the latter, flying into the sky on the fabulous Keval Kesari, the black mare, herself a goddess. Pabuji is the local Rama and every battlefield is a Kurukshetra, of the Mahabharata epic.
63. Pp. 110–115, Calcutta 1916.
64. John Smith, 'Where the Plot Thickens: Epic Moments in Pabuji', in *South Asian Studies* 2 (1986, pp. 53–66). He is the main authority on the legends or Pabuji.
65. Mira Reym Binford, '"Mixing in the Color of Ram of Ranuja: A Folk Pilgrimage to the Grave of a Rajput Hero-saint", in *Hinduism: New Essays in the History of Religions,* edited by Bardwell L. Smith, Leiden 1976, pp. 120–142.
66. In his case the story of the archetype is handed down by the *katputlis* (the nomadic puppet players of Rajasthan) who portray him as an example for other caste groups, mostly farmers. Amar Singh escaping from the formal etiquettes (both in Jodhpur and in Delhi) overcome the caste barriers in the name of a common ideal, just like Pabuji who has among his allies some Thori robbers.
67. The love stories of Dhola, son of Nala, raja of Narwar, in Malwa and of Maru, or Marwani, the daughter of Rao Pingala of Pugal, represent the conflict and union between the regions of Marwar and Malwa. In other famous love story Mahendra crosses many times the desolate expanses of the desert to visit his beloved Mumal (from Umarkot, now in Sindh, to Lodurva, close to Jaisalmer). In their time the desert was only a physical challenge, now the territory is divided by a political boundary. For a description of these legends: Vijay Verma, *The Living Music of Rajasthan: A Census of India Monograph,* New Delhi 1987.
68. The preservation of archaic words in *dingal* is also explained by the existence of glossaries and a poetic vocabulary of Sanskrit origin, hence the extraordinary wealth of synonyms. The Dingala Kosa (vocabulary) by B. Misrana Murari Dan of Bundi records 55 synonyms referring to land, 50 referring to swords, 59 to kings, 55 to elephants, 70 to horses, 59 to the sun, 45 to the moon, 48 to fire etc. ... See also Manohar Prabhakar, *Cultural Heritage of Rajasthan,* Jaipur 1972, pp. 74–75.
69. Now entry to the area is forbidden by military order, because to the proximity to the border.
70. Many of these inscriptions are collected in the Museum of which a catalogue has been published, V.S. Srivastava, *Catalogue and Guide to Ganga Golden Jubilee Museum,* Bikaner, Jaipur 1961.

71. *Annual Report of the Archeological Survey of India,* 1917–1918, edited by B.D. Spooner, Calcutta 1920 where Tessitori is mentioned mainly for the work, which regards the commemorative steles. Sir John Marshall in his *Annual Report of the Director General of Archaeology of India 1918–1919,* Calcutta 1921, lamented the death of Tessitori and the interruption of the archaeological research in the area. For an analysis of the material still to be published it will suffice to quote the *Report on Tours in Search of Archaeological Remains Made in the Bikaner State during the year 1917*, dated 29 March, 1918 with 90 (!) localities visited (Archivio Peano).
72. It is the last correspondence left by him at the Bikaner Archives. The last letter answering the debated question is dated 12th November 1919. Tessitori died on the 22nd November. The same episode can be found in the correspondence in *Government of Bikaner Notes and Orders, Tessitori files,* cit.
73. Pandit Visvesvar Reu, *Marwar ka Itihas,* 2 Vol. Jodhpur 1938, 1940; Nirmala M. Upadhyaya, *The Administration of Jodhpur State,* 1800–1947, Jodhpur 1973.
74. Maharaj Sir Pratap Singh (1845–1922) brother of the Maharaja Jaswant Singh (1873–1895), who had been in China with the Jodhpur Lancers during the revolt of the Boxers (1900–1901) ruled Idar as Maharana between the 1900 and the 1910. He abdicated to return to Jodhpur. See R.B. Van Wart. *The Life of Lieut. General H.H. Sir Pratap Singh,* London 1926 and V. Gundoj, *Sar Pratap aor unki den,* Jodhpur 1983.
75. Already mentioned as president of the Bardic Committee, he maintained very good ties with the Asiatic Society of Bengal through Haraprasad Shastri. For some time he opposed Pratap Singh and served later as Revenue Member (finance minister) in the Council of Regency under Umed Singh. During the war (1914–1918) he was Prime Minister in Udaipur. See R. Venkoba Rao, *Ministers of Indian States,* Trichinopoly 1928, p. 68.
76. He opened the first irrigation canal in Rajasthan (the Ganga Canal), railways, hospitals, schools and various other institutions.
77. H. Goetz compiled under his patronage *Art and Architecture of Bikaner State,* Oxford 1950.
78. "Long life to the king of the territory of the desert" is the motto of the Maharajas of Bikaner.
79. Ganga Singh had opened in 1912 a Legislative Council whose advice was consultative. Bhairon Singh was a cousin of Ganga Singh, his personal secretary and a *great jagirdar.* He favoured the Hindi language as the official language of the State.
80. Sir William Lee Warner, *The Protected Princes of India,* London 1894, reprinted in 1910 with the title *The Native States of India.*
81. S. Hoeber, and Lloyd I. Rudolph, *Essays on Rajputana: Reflections on History, Culture and Administration*, New Delhi 1984.
82. Padmaja Sharma, Maharaja Man Singh of Jodhpur and his Times (1803–1843 A.D.), Agra 1972.
83. The complex situation of Sekhawati in the State of Jaipur and the traditional interdependence of the *Maharana* of Udaipur and the *thikanedars* of the kingdom prevented the centralisation of his States. We can say the same for

Alwar. See Robin Jeffrey, ed., *People, Princes and Paramount Power: Society and Politics in the Indian Princely States,* Oxford 1978: in particular, the articles by Edward S. Haynes about Alwar and by Rajat K. Ray about Udaipur-Mewar.

84. The grandson of Ganga Singh, Karni Singh, wrote the history of the kingdom in the *Relations of the House with the Central Powers* 1465–1949, Delhi 1974. The Prime Minister, K.M. Panikkar had published *His Highness the Maharaja of Bikaner, A Biography,* London 1937.

85. The initial historical situation of the first treaty of 9 March, 1918 signed by C.T. Metcalfe for the East India Company and Kashinath Ojha for Surat Singh, *Treaty of Bikaner State with the British Crown of Perpetual Friendship, Alliance and Unity of Interests,* occurred again later. It entailed the submission of the revolting Thakurs. The Maharaja had to pay the expenses (from the term 'subsidy', the treaties were called subsidiary) and furnish the troops to the British Government according to its needs.

86. Dr Tessitori's *Bardic Work and Preparation/or the History of Bikaner,* Pol. A 816–915, 1921, *Tessitori files*, Bikaner Archives.

87. Walter C. Neale, "Land is to Rule", in R.E. Frykenberg, ed., *Land Control and Social Structures in Indian History,* Madison 1969, pp. 1–15.

88. B.S. Cohn, "From Indian Status to British Contract", in *The Journal of Economic History,* 21 (1961), pp. 613–28; Id., "Political Systems in Eighteenth Century India: the Banaras Region", in *Journal of The American Oriental Society,* 82 (1962), pp. 312–20.

89. A typical example was the area of Sekhawati from where many Marwari merchants used to come. See Ratanlal Misra, *Sekhawati ka Itihas,* Mandawa 1984.

90. A full study on the history and the curricula of these schools has not been made as yet. A good beginning is Agostino Mansutti's, *L 'Indirect Rule in India: gli Stati Nativi e l'Educazione dei Principi,* Tesi di Laurea, Un. di Trieste, a.a. 1996–1997. The "Indian Public School Conference" joins these Colleges with the other Public Schools.

91. Ganga Singh, *Speech delivered by H.H. the Maharaja at the Prize Distribution of the Walter Nobles' School,* 7 September, 1912, in *Bikaner Annual Administration Report,* Bikaner 1913, pp. 96–97.

92. S.H. Rudolph and Lloyd L. Rudolph, op. cit.

93. They were much more appreciated by his predecessor Haraprasad Shastri because of their stricter dependence on the orthodox genealogical canons. In fact, Tessitori often criticises the Charans for their excessive use of 'fantasy' in order to obtain the Rajputs' favours.

94. Manohar Prabhakar, *A Critical Study of Rajasthani Literature,* cit. claims that the Charans "came out" of the nose of Brahma (the Vedas, a brahmanic monopoly, came out of his mouth). Ham Prasad Shastri wrote the Appendix I in *Preliminary Report,* cit. on *Charanas and Bhats,* pp. 7-) 3. He dates the Charan influence on the Rajputs as from the XV century. A more recent text is by Mohanlal Jighyasu, *Charana Sahitya ka Itihas,* in two volumes, Jodhpur 1973, 1977.

95. Initially the term *charana* seems to have derived from *chalna* (to move, to travel). The Charana's presence in the caravans could neutralise the most dangerous robbers because they would have carried the responsibility, the guilt and the curse ensuing the death of the Charans for generations.
96. Many see a affinity between *tragu* and *dharna,* passive resistance, fasting to death for the extinction of a debt, or to obtain a grace. According to H. Spodek, "On the Origin of Gandhi's Political Methodology, The Heritage of Kathiawad and Gujarat", in *Journal of Asian Studies*, Vol. 30, No. 2, 1972. pp. 361–72, Madras 1969, the influence of these traditions was also strong in Kathiawar and indirectly influenced Gandhi.
97. Karniji Singh, op. cit., dates her life between 1387 and 1538. For her present relevance Kailash Dan Ujwal, today's *rajcharan* (court bard), *Bhagwati Shri Karniji Maharaj, a Biography,* Ujlan.
98. Tessitori does not appear to have a great liking for Karniji, who appears in the most meaningful moments in the history of the Rathors to jeopardise what he considers to be the objective quality of a source he has found. Yet, she is undoubtedly a further factor enhancing the authority of the Rajputs.
99. E. Fasana, *Ratto e sacro,* "Airone" 45, January 1985, pp. 60–65.
100. It is interesting to note that the Rathors, though *Suryavamsi* (descendants from the sun) have as a *kuladevi* Nagnechi, i.e., a *sakti* of Nagas (cobras), a trace of a Nagbansi origin.
101. According to *charan* tradition, the villages granted as *sasana* were 350.
102. In one of the interviews given to me in January 1982, Sriraj Maharaja of Dhrangadhra, recalled his own *rajbharot* (an other title of the bard of the royal chronicles) Chatur Singh, untying the knot of the *vahi,* the big bundle of the family and caste history of the Jhalas of the State. To read an episode of it he had the hereditary right to compensation.
103. Letter of Tessitori to Kishor Dan, Bikaner 7 January, 1918: "Apko rajdrohi kam men maddat nahin dena chahta hun ... Hamara Maharaja Sumer Singhji Sahib angrezion ka dost he", op. cit. I remember also the tiny and frail Keshav Gangadhar Nirkhe, the diarist of the Sindhyas of Gwalior who had in his hand the *rojnisi* (diaries) of the family: 135 volumes. One had to request permission from Maharaja Madhaw Rao. He gave me the assurance that the material would be preserved.
104. Naturally the *rajput* were for the emperor Shah Jahan and for Dara Shikoh in the fight for the succession which opposed them against Aurangzeb, who on his part too had to maintain an alliance with the Rajputs.
105. K.K. Sehgal, *Bikaner, Rajasthan District Gazetteer,* Jaipur 1962, the latest gazetteer. The most famous episode of his life is that of the destruction of the ferryboats on the Indus river at Attock, pp. 37–39.
106. The temple of Karniji at Aurangabad built by Karan Singh bears witness of these facts.
107. The more ancient the genealogy, the higher is the status. Antiquity is connected with some deity or myth of creation. Royal birth also becomes a divine one.

108. The custom was imitated by some brahmanical castes, in particular the Palivalas. *Sati* remains at the centre of debate especially in Rajasthan.
109. The *devlias* are connected both with the warriors fallen while fighting and the *satis*. According to Rajasthani tradition, fame is greater where there is a belief in the ideals. Success is of the living but this is ephemeral while the glory of the fallen lasts for ever. The *dingal* is a eulogy of the losers, at least according to European logic.
110. For the caste system in general I follow the point of view of L. Dumont, *Homo Hierarchicus, un essai sur le systeme des castes,* Paris 1966.
111. Malta, Tirah, Mohmand, Transvaal, China; their military activities were not only outside India, but also against the Pathan tribes of the North-West.
112. All the correspondence is to be found in *Foreign and Political Dept. Confidential B.,* internal Branch, section c., 1916, n. 3, ref. R/1/1/1293 at the India Office Library of London.
113. Pp. 67–69.
114. Tessitori was here in disagreement with Tod who had written about Bikaner as detaining: "A secondary rank among the principalities of Rajputana".
115. Bikaner Government Press, Bikaner 1933, p. 254
116. In another Appendix we find: "Some further particulars regarding the House of Bikaner being the elder branch of the Jodhpur and Bikaner dynasties", op. cit., pp. 214–19.
117. Tessitori had met him in Jodhpur and he was invited at his home: "Un giovane brahmano kashmiriano dai modi franchi e simpatico" (a young kashmiri brahman with open and pleasant manners), *Diario,* Jodhpur 29 July, 1914; with him, on 3 August, 1914, he had visited Mandor.
118. 'False challenge against the seniority of the Jodhpur House', in *Journal of the Indian History,* Vol. 20, No. 1, 1941, pp. 22–27.
119. *Diario,* Ahmedabad, 14 April 1919.
120. The history of these efforts had been explained by the Maharaja in a speech of 1911 to the Nagar Bhandar Society, in *Bikaner Annual Administration Report,* 1912, cit., pp. 84–85.
121. *The State Gazette* was published in Hindi (Rajpatra), starting from that year.
122. A Rajasthani poet, Shrilal Nathmalji Joshi, in a novel, *Ghoran ro ghori,* Udaipur 1965, mentions that the three poets, who became the founders of the contemporary Rajasthani, literature were attending together the funerals of Tessitori and were meditating the example of his life (a foreigner who had sacrificed his life for their language).
123. Shyamaldas Kaviraj, 1836–1893, court poet at Udaipur and historian during the reign of three maharanas. He descended from a family of Charans who migrated to Mewar during the reign of rana Kumbha (15th century). His *Vir Vinod* (the deeds of *rajput* heroes) in process of preparation since 1875 was published in 1891–1892, censured during the reign of Maharana Fateh Singh till 1930 and at last in circulation only after the Second World War. For his biography, S.H. Rudolph and L.I. Rudolph, op. cit., pp. 176–77; *Vir Vinod* has been published in four volumes, New Delhi, 1986.

7

Law and Administrative Practices

Institutionalising Sovereignty in 18th Century Jaipur[1]

Fatima Imam

This paper critiques theories of oriental despotism[2] by analysing administrative practices of Jaipur's rulers. According to colonial administrators, who are still echoed in historical scholarship, Indian rulers could only legitimise their rule with the help of priests and theories of divine kingship. The pre-colonial notion of kingship and authority has been related to the will of Muslim rulers, especially Mughal emperors; and religions, customs, and traditions of non-Muslim rulers. This concept of the nature of Indian states is examined here by looking at the dynamics of Jaipur's legal administration. The discussion on roles of *shastric* law elaborates cases of state interference in customary laws and decisions of caste councils. Evidence provided by official records of Jaipur state demonstrates that administrative policies were not dependent on divine law or the will of rulers. Pre-existing Mughal institutions, however, were reinterpreted by this state to legitimise and institutionalise sovereignty.

Historiography

Pre-colonial Indian political systems were thought to be absolute and arbitrary in nature, unchecked by any political or social institution, with all authority derived from the will of the emperor. Giovanni Carreri, who came to India in the 17th century and lived in the courts of Aurangzeb, remarked, "The great Mughal is so absolute that, there being no written laws, his will in all things is law, and the last decision on cases both civil and criminal. He makes tyrannical use of this absolute power."[3] Alexander Dow, in his introduction to the translated history of Firishta (written in the 16th century), commented, "The history now given to the public presents us with a striking picture of the deplorable conditions of people subjected to arbitrary sway, and instability of the empire itself, when it is founded neither on law nor upon the opinions and attachments of mankind. Honours and property were solely based on the will of despotic rulers. Justice was dependent not on rule of law, but on the rule of men (clerics) who could be influenced by money, status and connection."[4] Bernard Cohn criticises this notion of oriental despotism and points out that "India was ruled by despots and was re-valorised in the 19th and 20th centuries as one of several paradigms that formed the ideological infrastructure of British rule in India."[5]

The other strand of the same argument is about ancient Indian kings and mostly non-Muslim states. The writings from the colonial period presents these kings as figureheads of political authority, and priests or Brahmans as state administrators. "The political institutions of Gentoos are so blended with the idea of religion, that this is generally affected where these are concerned. Soft manners focused people's attention on the solace of domestic life. There are not more tender parents, or better masters, in the world: Such a people made wills in favour of their offspring; and the prince found himself restrained by policy from establishing rights that were utterly shocking to the nature and disposition of his subjects."[6] It is interesting to note that these works were published during the 18th century when the states of Mysore, Awadh, Jaipur, and Marathas institutionalised political power by centralising their administrative framework.[7] The intention of this paper is not to critique the colonial writings on Indian judicial systems; that theme has already been successfully covered by Bernard Cohn, Thomas Metcalf, Jorg Fisch, and Radhika Singha.[8]

Critics of oriental despotism focused on the assumptions and logic of discourses characterising pre-colonial Indian states. This paper, in contrast, ventures outside the worldview of colonial rulers and seeks to redefine the ideology of Indian rulers by examining how they established their administrative institutions. In addition, this paper analyses the role of law in exposing political authority and moralising claims. Mughal administrative and political institutions have usually been studied as homogeneous institutions. It is commonly agreed that these institutions were influenced by Islamic law (*sharia*).[9] For example, the success of Mughal rule is generally attributed to its military skills and aggressive rulers. Very little analysis exists of the processes and negotiations through which the rule was legitimised in the 16th and the 17th centuries.[10] Similarly, the overarching argument about 18th century states has been that they were governed by statesmen who were only concerned with extracting revenue to maintain large armies.[11] Measures introduced by Tipu Sultan in Mysore and the meticulously gathered administrative data of Marathas are accredited to their military ends.[12] Questions about institutionalisation of sovereignty in these states have yet to be examined. In addition, arguments about military fiscalism can be refuted by noting that these states were able to govern their subjects even after suffering humiliating defeats by the English East India Company.

This analysis adds to the existing historiography on 18th century states, where questions on the nature of state control are assessed and analysed. Did decentralisation of central authority mean that regional powers lost control over fiscal and judicial functions? Radhika Singha points out that the picture is not clear for the Bengal and Awadh regions. However, existing historiographical works mention the success of the regional rulers in effectively performing these functions. For example, Gordon Stewart has worked on the nature of conquest of Marathas in the Malwa region. He comments, "Maratha revenue-collecting apparatus was the exact antithesis of marauding raids in the previous two decades. Malwa had come to full circle. By 1745, it was the Marathas who held towns and roads. It was their garrison troops who walked the ramparts and anxiously watched for marauders. Their civilian officials made surveys, collected revenues, tried cases, and regulated bazaars. Now the Peshwa and his *kamavisdars* (revenue officials) worried over and depended upon the very communication and trade they had so recently disrupted, and committed themselves to the economics of rebuilding of the province they had plundered."[13] Narendra Wagle's articles on the administration of Pune, capital city of the Peshwas, delineate the state's role in social and caste issues.[14]

The military fiscalism of Haider Ali and Tipu Sultan has been critically examined by Sumit Guha and Irfan Habib. They agree that the state of Mysore was successful because of the rulers' administrative policies, which helped legitimise their power.[15] Royal orders issued by Tipu Sultan deal with state policies regarding revenue, trade monopolies, market rates, and explicates the state's role in the administration of Mysore.[16]

On the contrary, scholars have emphasised a traditional clan and kinship form of political system for the rulers of Rajasthan (in pre-colonial times it was known as Rajputana). Rajput rulers are portrayed as upholders of *dharma-shastras and were* totally involved in caste and clan lineages.[17] Most scholars writing about the Rajputs either criticise James Tod or follow his conceptual framework for these states. James Tod was the first Englishman to write a detailed history of all the states of Rajputana and succinctly compared them with old European feudal lords. Comparisons highlighting the conventional picture of Rajput chieftains have been repeated in several other works, like those of Norbert Peabody and more recently, Gyan Prakash Pilania.[18] Non-Muslims are commonly portrayed as rulers subordinate to the priests or Gods, and played a hesitant political role. Ronald Inden puts in this way: "Royal authority in the Indian context was inextricably bound up with notions of divine power, material prosperity, and moral well-being. Therefore, it is problematic to class Hindu kings with kings of Egypt or Japan as transcendent divinities or sources of authority. Nor, on the other hand, can a Hindu king be grouped with a monarch of Persia and China, or medieval Europe, as an immanent administrator of his kingdom or a 'mere human agent or servant' of the transcendent divine. Rather, the Hindu king appears as a contradictory combination of the two. On one hand, he is a figure who is expected to transcend the world as a divine, yet humble, almost ascetic worshipper and passive focus of authority. On the other, he must make himself a divine administrator and warrior, decisive in everyday concerns of his realm."[19] This point of view is criticised here by analysing archival records of Jaipur rulers.[20] In addition, he questions the notion of universal kingship by pointing out that pre-colonial rulers did not follow a uniform policy in defining political authority is being re-assessed as well. Most of the 18th century states such as Marathas, Nizamates of Awadh and Hyderabad, and Rajput had inherited Mughal institutions.[21] Non-Muslim rulers never regarded themselves as separate political entities, nor referred to any other administrative model.[22]

Critique

The vast archival data available pertaining to revenue, trade, taxes, fines, decisions taken on caste and clan issues, and most importantly, official correspondence have been systematically examined here as a record of the administrative apparatus of Jaipur state. Evidence provided by official records demonstrates that laws and administrative policies in Jaipur were not dependent on divine law, or even on the will of rulers; on the contrary, rulers reinterpreted and codified these texts to suit their needs and purposes. A ruler's success was based on acceptance of his subjects and application of the texts.

Sawai Jai Singh (1700–1743 A.D) established his rule over territories which had been previously administered by Mughal *mansabdars*. These mansabdars were theoretically required to conform to Mughal systems of administration. However, effective execution depended upon the efficiency of centralised authority. When the imperial control began to weaken in early decades of the 18th century, Sawai Jai Singh and his successors started enforcing their own laws in Jaipur and its surrounding areas. He ruled over a predominantly clan-based Rajput society, where laws were largely localised despite being rooted in normative *Dharmashastras*.

Alliance with Mughals in the last decades of the 16th century brought many changes in the Rajput polity. Having been exposed to Indo-Muslim cultural ethos and employed by Mughals in different parts of the Indian sub-continent, these rulers adopted a lifestyle that was more bureaucratic and autocratic.

Rajputs imbibed the centralised control of Mughal emperors over their subjects. Akbar (1556–1605) was able to create a multiregional empire with innovative, durable centralised institutions. Akbar's radical political orientation injected dynamic energy into imperial expansion and consolidation initiatives. In formulating his interests, Akbar gave precedence to states over the narrowly defined interests of Islam. In every possible way, Akbar and his dynasty made the imperial system inclusive rather than exclusive. Mughals were engaged in a continued campaign of political socialisation, aiming to assimilate the local aristocracy (*zamindars*) and dominant peasant groups to the imperial revenue system's demands. Mughal officials combined threats and rewards to induce local warrior-aristocrats, or village lords, to assist in collection of imperial revenues.[23]

The Kachchawahas of Amber were in the forefront of this political assimilation of Mughals. They had a thorough understanding of the Mughal Empire's political and administrative institutions. As Mughal vitality dwindled after Aurangzeb's death (1658–1707 A.D.), factional conflicts severely tested the nobles' loyalties. Constant wars, retreat on the frontiers (Kabul and Qandhar in North-Western India), loss of confidence, and low morale of Mughal officials accentuated decentralisation of the imperial system into autonomous regional kingdoms. Mughal emperors were unable to deploy and control their nobles to meet imperial needs, as they had done in the past. Nobles of the highest caliber were unable to maintain their personal ties with emperors. John Richards explains that in order to survive, they shaped regional systems of power.[24] The state of Jaipur under Jai Singh was one such example of a regional kingdom; it was based not only on Mughal imperial institutions, but also on the innovative features he introduced.

Administrative records of Jaipur indicate that the state (*raj*) intervened and controlled all levels of society and economy. Individuals of every caste and status had to abide by the rulers' laws. When a violation of laws occurred, the matter was taken up by civil and criminal officials, such as the faujdars, kotwals, diwans and their subordinates, amils, and amins.

State policies regarding crimes, infractions of social norms, rebellions, theft, non-payment of taxes, family matters, marriages, sexual relations, religious crimes, and slaughter of animals can be ascertained through an inventory of all income and expenditure of the state, known as *arhsatta* documents. A section called farohi, or miscellaneous income, falls under the 'income head' section of *arhsattas.* State officials collected fines, fees, and dues from the population and submitted details under this section. The data are largely statistical in nature but can be corroborated from other sources, such as letters exchanged between state officials and rulers, or daily records maintained at their court. In addition, the records contain important *parwanas,* or official orders issued by the rulers.[25] These documents collectively discuss the incidence of various criminal activities and actions taken to control or punish individuals.

These archival diaries of 18th century Jaipur contain the state's administrative structure. The documents under survey belong to a period from 1728 to 1794 CE. They were written in the Dhundhari Rajasthani language with Persian administrative terms. The following information is based on 2,000 cases reported in the *arhsattas* about different crimes committed by individuals who belonged to different castes. Collection of fines varied from one individual to another and were based on their ability to pay, rather than on their castes. The records showcase offences committed by everyone from high caste Brahmans and Rajputs to lower castes, such as Baniyas, Sarrafs, Ahirs, Lohars, Gujars, Bhujars, Telis, Malis, and even Minas. Other religious communities were also represented quite well in these records especially the Muslims (referred to as Mussalmans not identified as religious community but as a separate caste).[26]

Questions about the establishment and entrenchment of sovereignty in 18th century Jaipur are grouped into three broad categories. Specifically, how did the state envision its role in the lives of its subjects? First, it was interested in providing a well-planned administrative structure, as it is demonstrated by the judicial system's organisation. Second, the rulers used moralising elements to legitimise their position, especially during the reign of Sawai Jai Singh. The third category deals with the way the state looked after problems of law and order; especially, what actions and offences were regarded as lawful or unlawful by these rulers. The records describe ways in which these problems were presented and controlled by state officials. This discussion also delineates the comparable elements of sovereignty in other states to explicate how they implemented and appropriated Mughal administrative set-up.[27]

Organisation of the Justice System in the 18th Century

Administration of justice was efficiently organised in 18th century Jaipur. Several *chaukies* (police stations) were established by offices of the Faujdar in provinces, the Kotwal in towns, and Amins and other officers in villages. When people lodged their complaints to these *chaukies,* officials investigated the matter. The multifarious functions of the *kotwali chabutra* (urban police station) were described quite aptly by Robert Orme: "At this place are perpetually heard the clamours of the populace: some demand redress for the injury of a blow, or a bad name; others for a fraud in the commerce of far-things; one wants assistance to take; another has taken a thief; some offer themselves for bondsmen; others are called upon for witnesses. Gentoos who have commerce with public women; Moors who had been addicted to drinking spirituous liquors; all persons who hazard money in gambling such are subject to be narrowly watched by the Catwall (Kotwal)."[28]

All complaints and actions taken at various locations were recorded and sent to the Maharaja. The *arhsatta* documents have a continuous record of all state activities from 1728 to 1798 CE. State officials or caste councils usually settled civil and criminal cases, and in some cases, the ruler personally intervened.[29]

Offenders were required to pay fines; those who were unable to pay were detained in jails. Taking their family members into custody was another method of coercing offenders into submission. When offenders surrendered or paid the fine, their family members were released. Krishna Brahmin wrote an *arzdasht* to Sawai Jai Singh asking for release of his wife, who was in the Maharaja's custody. He said he had paid Rs 45 of his debt and would pay the remaining Rs 25 later.[30] Government authorities also levied additional fines for late payments or non-payment of fines. The records contain many references to these charges. For example, Khushla Sunar of Jaipur owed Rs 71 for paying a fine late, and Gauri Khan Patwari (revenue official) of Tapa Khoh was fined Rs 33 for the same offence.[31] Bhagwan Agarwal of *qasba* Saganer had to pay Rs 58 as a late charge on his original fine of only Rs 15.[32]

By contrast, Sharia law in Mughal practices forbade payment of fines. Fine extraction had become a recurrent feature of 18th century states and was strongly criticised by the colonial authorities.[33] Mughal policies discouraging officials from fine collection caused the central administration to break down in the early part of the century.[34] Aurangzeb's *Farman* of 1661 refers to exaction of fines and fees for various functions, i.e., putting seals on official documents, recovering loans or stolen property, arbitrating between parties, performing marriages, or giving death and birth certificates. His order forbade collection of these cesses and fines, and officers in charge were instructed to pay the state back. However, this Mughal policy was not very successful. Reports from Bengal and Gujarat provinces gave evidence that illegal exactions had become a permanent feature. Ali Mohammad Khan, Diwan of Gujarat, complained, "Many innovations in illegal exactions took place during my governorship. None of the succeeding Nazims were graced in eradicating them. Now they have reached to the utmost height. Information about them, God the great willing, will be given as far as possible. Fines imposed in patrolling Faujdar of Nainpur, and what happened in the chabutra of Kotwali, was beyond man's power."[35]

By the early 18th century, fiscalisation of criminal activities was prevalent in the states of Bengal, Awadh, and Maratha territories. In Bengal and Awadh, where *nawabs* theoretically followed Islamic law, fine payment occurred frequently and was only abolished by colonial criminal codes.[36] Marathas levied fines on all criminal activities and cases of non-payment; criminals were either detained or imprisoned until full payment was made.[37] The 18th century regional states like Bengal, Awadh, Jaipur, and Hyderabad inherited Mughal institutions; otherwise, states such as Marathas, Ruhellas, and Jats adopted them.

These states did not just transport these systems in their entirety, but made substantive changes according to local customs, traditions, and needs. Most states were heavily involved in military conflict with each other for survival; hence, they needed more money to sustain their armies. Fiscalisation of criminal punishment became an avenue of cash flow for their economies and also facilitated the justice system in those changing times.[38]

Shifts in political authority from centralised to regional governments led to more coordination and efficiency. Changes resulted, for instance, in imposing fines for criminal offences. The original procedure of sending offenders to court and establishing defendants' and victims' claims was in place, but offenders paid costs of administration of justice. Laws became elaborate as states became more involved in day-to-day activities of their subjects. Criminal justice systemisation significantly institutionalised sovereignty as fine collection continued in these states throughout the 18th century. As a result, even when they became militarily weak, states were still able to administer and levy fines on their subjects. This analysis also negates the thesis of military fiscalism forwarded by many historians.[39]

Through an analysis of *arhsatta* documents and state correspondence between officials and rulers, the nature of state control over Jaipur and its surrounding areas becomes evident. The extent of state control over activities of individuals was distinguishable in every aspect of life.[40]

State's primary role was to establish peace and maintain law and order in society. Authorities properly investigated any violations of established laws and regulations, and meted out due punishments. Maintaining order in the kingdom meant that taxes could be collected from peasants, traders could bring commodities in and out of the state, merchants could carry on commercial activities, and more revenues could be accumulated for the Maharaja.

Jaipur inherited Mughal institutions for its administrative purposes, but it was ruled by non-Muslim rulers who were great patrons of *shastric* learning. Their knowledge and interest in the *dharma-shastras* helped them institutionalise Mughal administrative policies with local customs and traditions. Mughal rulers were also attentive to local customs. This aspect of Mughal rule is underdeveloped in the writings on Mughal sovereignty, which reiterate that Muslim rulers left adjudication of their non-Muslim subjects to local or religious authorities. Theories on Mughal legitimisation of sovereignty have emphatically repeated that Muslim rulers, whether Turkish or

Mughal, never interfered in the social and religious matters of their non-Muslim subjects; instead, they let local or religious authorities handle them.[41] However, Muslim rulers enforced Islamic law in criminal justice. Ideologically, *sharia* was the guiding force behind Mughal institutions. In practice, these customs were derived and implemented from local customs, traditions, and above all, sovereign decisions.[42] Rulers had the right to interfere in administration of justice in cases of public interest where *sharia* had not made provisions. This intervention was known as *siyasa,* or extraordinary justice.[43] Turks, and later, Mughals integrated many *shastric* maxims into their political ideologies when they came to India, which helped them legitimise their rule. Muslim kings did not present themselves as lawmakers for their non-Muslim subjects, but as their protectors who guaranteed continuity of traditional social and economic institutions. Moreover, Mughals adopted a general policy of tolerance vis-à-vis the largely non-Muslim population. These rulers elaborated an entirely new system of cultural ethnic integration, thereby introducing a new quality of imperial rule in India. They claimed to be responsible for the welfare of all their subjects, defending the realm and maintaining peace, justice, and prosperity, regardless of the population's origin or religion. Emperor Akbar (1556–1605), in a rare official document known as *dastur-amal* (regarding the duties of officials), wrote: "The best service to god in this world is the growth of relations and accomplishments of works of people's welfare which are performed without regard to personal friendship, enmity, or relationship."[44]

This paper emphasises that Jaipur's rulers drew parallels from both Mughal and *Shastric* models. The idea of a universal monarch, or *chakravartin,* was always prevalent in the *Dharma shástras,* and qualities of this king were elaborated so the role could be fulfilled by any capable person.[45] It was also a king's duty to apply certain rules and balance political and economic structures of his state, as mentioned in the *shastras*.[46] According to Manusmriti, "In politics, the two (*dharma/ artha*) are balanced, and if the loss of *artha* would be greater than the gain of dharma, *artha* is to be pursued, and if necessary, a penance performed for the breach of *dharma*."[47] Jaipur's rulers followed shastric political ideology by choosing certain sets of jurisdiction to uphold social order. Thus, they could interfere in religious, social and cultural affairs of their subjects and control them effectively. To establish control over a more traditional Rajput society, Jaipur rulers successfully utilised the moralising aspect of sovereignty. Sawai Jai Singh, in particular, promulgated laws to check activities of priests, social organisations, lavish expenditures on marriages, and abolition of certain practices. His changes continued to be the corner-stone for policies of later rulers.[48]

The following description of crime incidence, along with a categorisation of offences, illustrates ways in which the state of Jaipur administered its subjects.

Moralising Sovereignty Homicide/Murder

Safeguarding life is the most crucial aspect of any administrative set-up, constituting the basis of its justice system. Rulers' capabilities depend on placement of officials and deployment of armies to keep and maintain peace and security. Criminalising elements are targeted, and punishments are inflicted to deter or eliminate crimes. Pre-colonial Indian states established elaborate systems of justice where laws protected their subjects' lives. States punished offenders by imposing penalties such as fines, confiscation of property, payment of compensation, or imprisonment. Significantly, murder and homicide were not capital offences and were usually taken as crimes against another person. States interfered in murder cases to arrange penalties and give compensation to the victims' families, sometimes donating money to temples.[49] Here they followed Mughal administrative practices, as did other states such as Bengal, Hyderabad and Awadh. Islamic law also restricted capital punishment to wilful murder, but it was so complicated that it was virtually impossible to give any offender a death sentence.[50] According to Jorg Fisch, when the British took over administration of Bengal and Awadh, the widespread conviction existed that a family's satisfaction was the most crucial form of justice in homicide cases. A magistrate of Bakargang noted: "It is agreeable to the Law, and a Maxim likewise among the Hindoos that, in cases of Murder, if the perpetrator can find means to satisfy the next Heir of the murdered and obtain from him what is called a *Razeenamah,*[51] no prosecution can, or ought to be carried on against him." This aspect of Indian judicial systems drew the most criticism from colonial rulers, because at least two hundred capital statutes in England signified that protection of property was more important than protection of life.[52] Murders in the 18th century Jaipur society were settled by either payment of fines or agreements involving compensation for the victim's family. This also seems to be a common feature in other states. James Forbes comments that in Gujarat, "Capital punishments are seldom inflicted under these administrations; fines are more frequent and more acceptable to all parties; pardons can generally be purchased for the most atrocious crimes between man and man, where the prince and his rulers are not affected."[53] The Punjab reports some cases where a murderer's property was handed over to the victim's family in compensation.[54] Radhika Singha deftly covers cases of compensation paid by offenders in Banaras and Awadh, and Jorg Fisch describes those in Bengal. In the following examples of homicide cases from Jaipur, most perpetrators were fined, and one was imprisoned. These cases were all reported by the faujdar's offices, complete with names of defendants and the accused. In addition, reports contained details about their castes and locations of their offences. Fine collection differed significantly from Mughal procedures, where murder cases were dealt with either by capital punishment, imprisonment, dismissal and diminution from rank, or expulsion.[55]

The Maharaja of Jaipur, as head of a state, was notified and he sometimes intervened personally to reach agreement (*razinama*) with the victim's family. Balchand, a banker from Pargana Chatsu, was poisoned by two other bankers, Mukunda and Ajmeri, over a dispute involving a mansion (*haveli*). Bhikari Das Diwan requested the Maharaja to negotiate for a *razinama* from Balchand's heirs to solve the case.[56] In another instance, Sitaram Kotwal fined Dewa Gujar Rs 46 on a charge of poisoning a man, resulting in his death.[57] In the previous century, murder by poison merely resulted in severe verbal warning and imprisonment.[58] Mughals paid the deceased's heirs compensation if the victim was murdered by any kind of poison.[59]

As Jaipur records mention, the offenders' castes it seems, fewer reports accuse Brahmins as compared with people from, other castes, possibly because of the privileges and position they enjoyed. It can be inferred from British complaints that people were hesitant to report cases against Brahmins for fear of religious discredit.[60] However, some murder cases were reported in Jaipur where Brahmins were involved; they were fined for their crimes. For example, Faujdar Dalel Singh collected a fine of Rs 250 from Nandlal Brahmin of Tappa Khoh, for committing a murder.[61] Another Brahmin, Dharmatulcha of Pargana Chatsu, was fined Rs 50 for murdering and cremating an unnamed victim without informing government authorities.[62] Rajputs reported homicide cases involving other high castes. Kesri Singh Rajput was called to Jaipur from qasba Saganer to answer murder charges. He was ordered to pay the state Rs 33 to cover costs of the inquiry, and was told to get a *razinama* from the deceased's family.[63] Mansa Singh (Rajput) and his associates in Jaipur murdered Sona

Brahmin (place unknown) and were ordered to pay Rs 201 as a fine. In this case, the state negotiated for reconciliation with the deceased's family.[64]

Faujdars and Qazis usually investigated homicide cases and reported the deliberations to their rulers. For example, Shyam Singh (faujdar) reported Bhim Singh's Gujar murder in qasba Saganer to the Maharaja; the report gave full details of the investigations. Records indicate that the *qazi* was trying to reach a settlement with the Gujar (caste) community in obtaining a *razinama*.[65]

In cases of murder or suicide, officials led inquiries that involved family, and sometimes extended family, members. Jangla Gujar was convicted of murdering his daughter-in-law when her body was found in a well near his house in qasba Jaipur. He was imprisoned and fined Rs 63.[66] In a similar case, Dhanya Mali was accused of pushing his daughter-in-law into his village well in Pargana Lalsot. He was questioned by the Faujdar's men, but it was learned later that the woman had committed suicide. Dhanya was then fined Rs 10 for not informing government authorities about her death and cremation.[67]

This paper will later present many cases involving sword fights. One such fight led Dewi Singh to murder Kohri. Both men, from Pargana Jaipur, were Rajputs by caste. Officials found Dewi Singh guilty of murder; he was ordered to pay a fine of Rs 51.[68] According to cases reported in Awadh, these types of murders were decided in favour of retaliation (*kisas*) under Mughal administrations. Victims' families could demand either capital punishment or mutilation of any of the perpetrator's body parts. However, official records from Jaipur contain no references to mutilation, and very few to capital punishment.

Protection of private property and public safety were important elements of state administrative structures. The following examples of highway robbery and procedures used to prevent and punish this type of crime reinforce the overall argument. It is clear that Jaipur rulers were capable of enforcing authority and discipline for law-abiding subjects; they were also effective in dealing with recalcitrant elements.

Highway Robbery

The state considered thefts of any kind to be severe offences, and officials were instructed to deal sternly with culprits. One standard action was to exact fines from the culprits. However, the faujdar and revenue officials were authorised by Sawai Jai Singh to pronounce death sentences in serious theft cases. If proof was found that a theft was committed on highways, roads, or in a market, the thief would be deprived of one hand as punishment. To prove charges, either the thief was forced to produce stolen items or witnesses were called to testify against him. If the theft was less serious in nature, a hot iron rod branded the word 'thief' on his hands.[69]

It is clear that Jaipur's rulers followed Mughal policies in dealing with thefts and highway robberies.[70] Islamic law prescribed the loss of one limb for theft, two limbs for highway robbery, and, if weapons were used with intent to murder, the death sentence was received as punishment.[71] Akbar's Farman delineated a kotwal's duties as follows: "Investigation and pursuit of thieves, cut purses, and wagerers, etc. No trace of them of should be left. Whatever articles are lost or plundered in that locality should be found out along with thieves, or else, he (kotwal) should come out of that responsibility and give a reply."[72]

Jahangir followed his father's policy of dealing with theft and highway robbery: "Whenever a thief or plunderer steals or robs one of God's creatures of his wealth, that wealth should be made good by persons of that place. If there is no population, I order that a town should be built so that it may be populated, so no harm accrues to God's creatures."[73] In other words, those in charge of the area's law and order were held responsible when cases of robbery and theft were reported. Jahangir ordered uninhabited areas to be rehabilitated and properly supervised to be kept safe from thieves and robbers.

Aurangzeb made some changes in punishments given to thieves, instructing, "If a man stole an article not worth ten *dirhams*, and for which he incurred no *hadd* or legal punishment, he, in the first instance, was to be chastised. In case of repetition of the crime, he was, after *tazir*, to be kept in prison till he repented. If he committed theft again, he was to be sentenced to life imprisonment or executed. The stolen property was to be restored to the owner or deposited to *bait-ul-mal*. An accomplice of the thief deserved the same punishment. For a third offence, the thief, after *tazir*, was to be kept in prison till he repented. Commitment of any other theft resulted in life imprisonment or punishment by death."[74]

State authorities treated highway robberies and looting as very serious crimes, and intervened routinely to deal with these situations. As has been noted above, these crimes could be punishable by death. Prevention of looting and theft, especially by miscreant groups, had also been ongoing problems for Mughal rulers. If an emperor learned that robbers were ravaging a part of the empire, large armies were sent to subdue them, treating them as rebels in most cases.[75] Sawai Jai Singh, in his capacity as a Mughal *mansabdar,* led many expeditions against rebels and successfully crushed them. Churaman Jat was the most notorious zamindar in the area around Delhi and Jaipur. His activities completely disturbed Mughal trade routes. He was captured with his group at forts controlled by Sawai Jai Singh; afterwards, the area around the state of Jaipur became much safer.[76] In one such expedition against rebels, the Maharaja had to risk his life. A letter from the Mughal court chronicles, "Reporters informed in writing that the Maharaja and Maharao Bhim Singh, etc., had gone to establish a *Thana* in the fort at Sonkh. When they were returning at night, rebels made a sudden attack on Imperial troops and many soldiers were killed or injured. The emperor rejoiced to know that the Maharaja had escaped by dint of his skill and experience."[77]

In order to secure peace and security in their areas the Jaipur rulers took written bonds from their clansmen who resided in neighbouring areas to maintain law and order. In addition, authorities removed troublemakers by force and resettled them in other areas after taking surety from some credible person.[78] *Thanas* (checkposts) were established and soldiers were stationed to patrol the areas. Anup Singh a *Thanadar* informed Sawai Jai Singh that he was taking charge of the area's security.[79] Written bonds were signed with Minas, a hereditary criminal tribe of former petty chieftains, to ensure their cooperation for not creating disturbance and turbulence in the state. Minas were involved in several criminal activities, mostly dealing with robberies and plundering in the *parganas* of Toda Bhim, Tonk, and Malpura. A fortress with a *Thana* was constructed nearby to control their activities. This tribe presumably continued its activities and was referred to as "boldest of the criminal classes" by colonial administrators.[80]

When a robbery was reported, the kotwal or faujdar was required to apprehend the guilty party and recover stolen property. These officers were obliged to discover the real culprits and deal with them sternly to prevent recurrence of the crime. Bhoop Singh Rajawat signed a bond promising to investigate all thefts in return for being granted the posts of faujdar and kotwal of pargana Jaipur.[81] Officers were also responsible for prevention of theft and other crimes. The faujdar's duties in Jaipur were very similar to this description of Bengal by Gholam Husain: "In the general Fodjdary, which in these days means preservation of the country from highwaymen and house-breakers, and power of pronouncing final judgement upon crimes of house-breaking, thieving, murder and fornication."[82] Evidence available from the *arhsatta* documents shows that the faujdar or his officials looked after most criminal activities. Few crimes were reported to the *qazi's* court, and more serious cases were reported directly to the Maharaja.

Fines were collected from culprits in only very few cases of highway robbery. In one looting case on the highway between *pargana* Chatsu and Jaipur, authorities apprehended Prabhat Mina and his companions. Officials seised the goods from the robbers, who had to pay a high fine of Rs 200.[83] Other cases report a marriage party looted in a village (*pargana* Lalsot) and a fight between government officials and Naruka Rajputs, who belonged to the Kachchwaha clan. The faujdar was injured and four of his companions died in the incident.[84] These Rajputs were later caught, fined, and imprisoned on the orders of Maharaja Sawai Jai Singh.

Arhsatta records mention many cases of thefts; fines collected from these offences constituted approximately 35 per cent of the total income under the *Farohi* section.[85] Theft, robbery, and highway looting were considered serious threats to a state's authority and had to be controlled effectively.

Petty Theft

Thefts reported in the documents can be broadly categorised as petty thefts, stealing grain, thefts in homes, and pick-pocketing. Additionally, records enumerate several other types: buying stolen goods, stealing or using animals, cutting wood without permission, and assisting thieves in any way.

Thefts most commonly occurred in the marketplace. Most thefts in Jaipur were reported from Mahajans; thieves were fined and reprimanded even after returning the stolen articles. The following examples illustrate that fines were imposed on everyone regardless of caste or class, varying according to a thief's ability to make payments. The majority of complaints came from shopkeepers who reported thefts to authorities and named culprits when possible. The following cases were recorded in the *chabutra kotwali* of Jaipur city in different years. Bhera Mahajan reported that Vadul Bhujar stole some pounds of wheat from his shop; Vadul paid a fine of Rs 6.50. Similar cases were reported by Tula, Gogha Ajaba, and Chaina Mahajans in their grain shops. Culprits were apprehended by shopkeepers and handed over to authorities. Thieves were fined and the stolen grain was confiscated.[86] Women were also involved in stealing grain: Shobha

Gujari was fined Rs 8 and Chaitra Darjan was fined Rs 5 for stealing from Jetmal Khatri's shop.[87] Miscellaneous thefts were also reported to authorities, such as shoplifting small items (not specified), stealing money (which was reported by Kisaram Mahajan), or stealing five pounds of iron from Nura Lohar. Records show the amount of fines and identity of each offender by his/her caste and name.[88]

City officials patrolled markets continuously and caught thieves red-handed. Faujdar Bhoop Singh caught three people stealing in Chautra Ram Ganj of Jaipur. He apprehended the items and returned them to shopkeepers.[89] Details of the crimes indicate that markets and commercial activities were actively watched and supervised by state authorities. Documents specify exact amounts of stolen grain. For example, Basto Mina stole 34 pounds of wheat from Parsa Mahajan and was fined Rs 25.[90] Likewise, Harda Ahir stole 2 pounds of barley and was fined Rs 11.[91] Miscreants reported as *lucha* (petty criminals) were the most common thieves in markets.[92] Mobile carts were looted for their goods,[93] and merchants or shopkeepers stole from each other's shops and businesses.[94]

States fined individuals who were caught, or even accused, of stealing.[95] The following cases were reported from Kishan Ganj Bazaar (city of Jaipur). Officials caught Veernam Bhujar (*sarkar*) and fined him Rs 9.5; Jeevan Darji was fined Rs 3. Lajja Manhihar was caught stealing from a shop (not specified), and the items were confiscated from her.[96] In another case, Moti Mahajan caught Rudra Mina stealing from his shop and handed him over to authorities.[97] Authorities caught Hari Mina stealing and fined him Rs 5.5.[98] Sobha Chand Khatri was caught stealing from Jewni Brahmin's house and was fined Rs 11.[99] These cases are all reported from the kotwal's office in Jaipur city; most thieves were caught red-handed in their acts. These incidents illustrate that state officials kept a close watch on activities to maintain law and order and ensure smooth transactions in trade and commerce.

Individual cases of household theft were also investigated. Culprits were incarcerated, reprimanded, verbally chastised, and fined. Thieves were often caught by householders and then handed over to authorities. Even people of high caste did not deal with culprits directly, depending instead on state authorities to deal with them. Some thieves tried to outsmart authorities by shaving their heads to conceal their identities, as did Nathu chamar of *pargana* Saganer, who stole from Dungar Ahir and then fled. Dungar was later caught by officials and was ordered to return the stolen money to

Nathu. Dungar paid a fine to cover fees of the faujdar and his men for solving the case.[100]

Not only was theft a punishable offence, but assisting thieves, sheltering them, or keeping stolen things were also regarded as crimes. Merely talking to a thief was an offence. Setaram Ahir was fined Rs 11 for having a conversation with a thief who was being detained by officials in the chabutra kotwali, Jaipur.[101] Thefts reported in Jaipur records indicate that Mughal policies continued in the state. It is useful to study charted criminal activities and analyse the state's initiatives to deal with those situations.

People found guilty of any crime were fined and later incarcerated if they were unable to pay. If a thief could not be apprehended, his relatives were questioned and fined, in some cases. The following cases are reported from the city of Jaipur: Heera Brahmin s' brother fled with stolen things worth Rs 1,161. Due to his brothers absence, the kotwal's office of Jaipur fined Heera Rs 391 and questioned him about his brother's whereabouts.[102] Abetting a crime was also a punishable offence. When his partner (name not mentioned) fled with stolen articles, Rewaram Khatri was detained and questioned about the missing man's whereabouts. Rewaram Khatri was then fined Rs 5.[103] Vepukapri Ahir and Dayaram Ahir assisted in a theft and were fined by authorities.[104] In another case the officials caught Ram Sant Bhujar in possession of stolen ornaments and allowed him to secure his freedom by paying a fine of Rs 51.[105] Chajja Gujar kept stolen items without informing government authorities; he was released after investigation and fined Rs 5.[106] Kesaram and Sukha Baniya caught a thief, but kept the stolen goods in their house. They were ordered to pay a fine of Rs 801 for withholding information from government officials.[107] Failure to report theft or return stolen goods was considered as offences meriting a fine.[108]

Pickpockets had to pay fines and replace the money they stole and it is interesting to note that the cases of pickpocketing were reported only in early decades of the 18th century, which may indicate that Jaipur officials were not as efficient at apprehending criminal activities as they were during Sawai Jai Singh's reign (1744, CE).[109]

Buying stolen articles from thieves or shopkeepers was also an offence. Records note individuals who purchased and sold stolen items such as ornaments, cloth, wood, etc., along with details of their fines.[110] The documents even contain accounts of people who stole or diluted oil from street lamps.[111, 112]

Stealing wood, fruits, and vegetables from orchards belonging to the government (*sarkar*) or private individuals was another punishable offence. Fines for these transgressions ranged from 11 to 101 rupees; individuals who stole from government properties had to pay a heavier fine.[113] For example, Mahakka and Janhilya Gujar were fined Rs 39 for stealing wood from the Sarkar (government) of Kishan Bagh in 1743,[114] whereas Govardhana Ahir had to pay only Rs 13 for cutting wood from Aghat Ahir's place (both cases were reported by the Kotwal of Jaipur).[115] Cutting or stealing expensive wood like timber and teak led to high fines ranging from 60 to 81 rupees.[116] Cases of cutting trees considered to have therapeutic or religious significance, like the pipal[117] or neem[118] tree, are few; in those cases fines ranged from 33 to 66 rupees.[119]

People convicted of stealing and using stolen animals were interrogated and punished, with fines averaging around 51 rupees. Workers and labourers from fields, orchards, and farms were the usual offenders in these types of crimes. Castes involved in stolen animal offences were mostly Jats, Ahirs, Khummars, and Chamars.[120] Merely using animals without their owner's permission led to fine assessment and chastisement from the faujdar. Allah Baksha Mussalman[121] tried to steal Todo Kummar[122] bulls from a field, but another farmer caught him and took him to the faujdar near the Jaipur city.[123] Bhema stole a pair of oxen from state property (Jaipur) and was fined Rs 11.[124] People who stole buffaloes, goats, and oxen were fined; the animals were then returned to their rightful owners.[125]

It is interesting to note that the fine amount for animal theft was uniform, which was not the case with other offences.[126]

Killing of Animals

Use of religious rhetoric in Jaipur legitimised rules that prohibited, discouraged, and severely curtailed slaughter of animals. Rulers were careful to protect religious beliefs of the majority of their subjects, especially elite populations of Jainas, Vaishnavites, and others.[127] Mughal emperors prohibited the slaughter of cows, buffaloes, bulls, and peacocks on certain days and months. During Aurangzeb's reign this policy was abandoned, but several instances were related in which non-Muslim subjects protested and took the law into their own hands when they saw animals being slaughtered. A Persian merchant was brutally killed by villagers in Dantivar (Gujarat) after he shot a peacock with his gun.[128] Manucci, an Italian traveller, was able to save his life with great difficulty when he tried to kill a peacock near Burhanpur (Deccan).[129] Slaughter of cows during the Muslim festival of Bak-id led to several skirmishes in the city of Ahmedabad and other parts of Gujarat.[130] Eighteenth and early 19th century successor states followed a strict policy forbidding the slaughter of cows. Evidence from Jaipur shows that animals were also protected from being injured. Fines related to animal killing were collected throughout the 18th century; those in and around the city of Jaipur ranged from Rs 551 for killing a cow to Rs 2 for injuring a peacock.[131]

Drinking

Drinking alcohol and selling liquor were criminal offences in Jaipur state, as a continuance of Mughal policy. Mughal emperors forbade people from drinking alcohol or any intoxicants, and instructed their officials to punish drunkards, wine-sellers, and distillers in such a way that it serves as a warning to others.[132] In spite of these orders, drinking was still quite common during that period. The state only succeeded in regulating the consumption and selling of alcohol. However, the king and his nobility were exceptions. Jahangir himself was an alcoholic, as he confessed to one of his Farman: "Wine should neither be distilled nor sold. Even though I have issued this order, I am very much inclined to it. I started drinking wine from the age of 16 years … . It has become so predominant over my mind that if I do not drink for an hour, my hands begin to shake. I have no power to sit."[133] According to European travellers, everyone had access to wine, and it was frequently sold and distilled.[134] Sawai Jai Singh also became addicted to locally made liquor towards the end of his career. He instructed his officials not to involve him in any official work when he was in a state of intoxication.[135]

Aurangzeb, known for his puritan measures, ordered severe penalties for selling wine. For the first offence, a wine seller was to be severely whipped but if there was a repetition of the same offence then the person was sent to the prison until he repented. Wine merchants and other assistants were also to be reprimanded and fined.[136] Imperial officials were chastised if they were reported or caught drinking alcohol. In many cases the Mughal official's mansab was reduced on account of drinking. Fatehullah's excessive drinking habit deprived him of his mansab of 250 *zat*/80 *sawar*. Mohammad Ali and Mohammad Ishaq had to pay fines and had their mansabs reduced when their alcoholic habits were reported to the emperor. Adbul Karim was accused of drinking, and his rank of 900zat/900 sawar was reduced to 400zat/200sawar.[137] Thevenot, a French traveller in the 17th century, reports an interesting incident from Qandhar: "A Moor who has both drunk wine and committed any scandal is set upon an ass, with his face to the tail, and led about the town, attended by officers of the Cotoual who beat a little drum, and they are followed by the children of the neighbourhood, who whoop and hallow after them."[138]

Jaipur state officials chastised people involved in either selling or making wine. Similar and sometimes more severe punishments were given in other states for the same offences. Mysore records mention that Tipu Sultan ordered his officials to cut off the hands of individuals who were involved in activities related to selling, growing, or distilling any intoxicants: wine, liquor, or opium.[139] Individuals caught selling wine were penalised severely, and fines for this offence were extremely high. Authorities caught Gangaram Mahajan of Jaipur selling wine; his shop was confiscated, and he had to pay a fine of Rs 501.[140] In another case, Khema Lal Gujarati (living in the city of Jaipur) was fined Rs 401 for selling liquor; Sada Mohan Agarwal of Pargana Jaipur was caught buying it and had to pay authorities Rs 22.[141] A barrel of wine was confiscated from Kheja Jat, who had to pay a fine of Rs 51.[142] Lalchand Mahajan, a wine seller, was imprisoned in Jhawda fort after receiving severe whippings and a penalty.[143]

The cases reported are usually about people who created a disturbance in the city of Jaipur after drinking liquor. Overall, the problem of drinking was taken as a matter of disturbing peace and order. The following cases will explicate this point. Godha Thakur and his group were fined Rs 17 for drinking. Jeva Chamar was caught drinking and was fined Rs 9 by the faujdar.[144] Lokha Ahir was fined Rs 16.5 for the same offence.[145] Differences in fines for the same offence were due to various reasons. Fines were less for individuals caught drinking alone. The main determiner of fine amount, however, was the ability of individuals to pay. Higher caste people usually had to pay higher fines than lower caste people. For example, Mudra Rajput became intoxicated and created a scene on the streets near Chaura Rasta; for that offence he was fined Rs 11[146] whereas Chipa Teli was fined just Rs 4 for the same offence.[147] Other recorded cases of drinking and creating a disturbance in the city were reported against Lalsuni Thakur, Narabala Jat, Gangaram Mahajan and Chajju Gujar.[148] Drinking, which was a favourite pastime and leisure for nobles, royal princes, and kings, was a carefully monitored activity as far as their subjects were concerned.

Recreational Gambling

Recreational gambling was prevalent in pre-colonial India and has been reported by many sources. Although the practice started as a royal pastime, it gradually came to be enjoyed by the common people. Rulers never tried to abolish the practice, but most of them brought it under state control. Regulations regarding gambling in pre-colonial

India were measures to control public order. Most importantly, these laws were a way of legitimising authority through a morally ethical code of behaviour. Jaipur records hold no references to commercial gambling, which became a major issue in colonial cities of Calcutta and Bombay. Jaipur's official policy against gambling is discussed here in context of the nature and extent of state control. Gambling was considered a crime against the state, and officials, especially the faujdar and kotwals, were authorised to punish gamblers. Although Mughals prohibited gambling, there are still a few instances of penalties for common people on gambling charges in 17th century records.

In Jaipur state, people found gambling either in groups or private houses were fined. Most reported cases concern groups of gamblers who were fined according to the amount of money they won in the game. For example, Gangaram Mahajan and three of his associates had to pay 16 rupees and 8 *annas* as a fine; Modi Jat and his four friends each paid authorities Rs 4.[149] Records refer to individuals being penalised for merely sitting in the company of gamblers; Chajju Gujar, Mukka Chamar and Hemashu Ahir were fined on the same day for this offence near Johri Bazaar.[150] It is interesting to note that women were also penalised for gambling in the privacy of their homes. In one case, Chandu Mahajan's wife was fined Rs 36, which she had pay to the faujdar after her husband was questioned and warned to take care of the situation at home.[151] Gambling fines continued to be recorded from 1728 to 1761, but these were less common than reports of theft, fights, and creating disturbances in Jaipur city.[152] Most fines for gambling were collected from Mahajans (traders). This community was targeted for various reasons. First, they were an important part of the economy, and their commercial practices brought economic prosperity to the state; second, they could afford to pay the fines. Additionally, they led a public life and their activities were closely observed by other sections of the population. Regulation of their commercial and social activities represented the extent of state control over daily lives of common people. Orientalist critiques of Indian rulers' inabilities are challenged here with examples from the state of Jaipur, where regulating moral and ethical behaviour also came under the realm of state affairs.

Problems of Law and Order

Problems of law and order have always been chief priorities of any civilised society, closely related to control of unlawful and illegal activities. Political authorities initiated and implemented administrative policies to combat disturbing elements in their domains. Rulers' administrative acumen facilitated their success and fostered their right to rule over their subjects. Jaipur, Awadh, Bengal, Mysore, and Hyderabad became predominant states in the 18th century based on their rulers' abilities to control and consolidate their kingdoms efficiently after Mughal authority weakened. The *arhsatta* documents about Jaipur should be taken as examples of how cases of misconduct, unlawful activities, or disturbance of peace were dealt by state officials without intervention of local authorities. Evidence of attempts to centralise rule can also be discerned from the following cases. For problems of law and order the state detained, penalised, and imprisoned people from all sections of society. This argument resonates with the broader perspective of this paper explicating the nature and extent of state control in 18th century Jaipur.

Cases of Creating Disturbance

There are numerous references to people fighting and creating disturbance in the city or its nearby areas. The state intervened to punish individuals by imposing penalties, incarceration, and fines. No discrimination was made between high or low caste people who tried to break the law, disrupt, or challenge state administrative machinery in any way. High profile cases included people from the upper castes like Rajputs, Thakurs, Patels, and Mahajans. For example, Sardar Singh (Rajput) and his group were arrested on charges on looting and harassing[153] the public on highways between the city of Jaipur and pargana Chatsu. They were intercepted by faujdar Harnam Roop Chand and jailed for several days; they were released after paying fines and agreeing to not to create any problems in the future.[154] In another case, Khairnath Thakur and Manu Patel were arrested for fighting and creating a disturbance near *chabutra kotwali* (police headquarters) in Jaipur.[155] The state intervened to check fighting between groups by making people sort out their differences mutually, sign legal documents, or pay fines. Gukhal Ram Thakur and his group of pargana Dausa signed a razinama (reconciliation letter) and gave a guarantee of their good behaviour to Girdhar Das faujdar.[156] Sukhram Gujarati was taken into custody by Kishor Das faujdar in Jaipur for fighting aggressively with Ughrah Singh Gumashta (a revenue official). Both men had come to Jaipur from the city of Kotla and Sukhram Singh was found guilty of assault, for which he was sent to jail and later released on payment of security.[157]

Skirmishes between people were regarded as offences and it is evident that Jaipur rulers evolved a policy of discipline and control for all sections of society, and established their authority. Harla Mahajan and Bala Agarwal of qasba Saganer had to sign a *razinama* (reconciliation letter) in front of the Faujdar for getting involved in a heated and violent argument.[158] Dehra Ahir and Rudra Bhujar of Toda Bhim got into a fight in which Dehra was injured[159] with an axe. Both men were questioned and fined.[160] Fighting with edged weapons was a common occurrence in Jaipur and its neighbouring areas.[161] Lalchand Rajput and Bala Brahmin of Tappa Khoh were involved in a sword fight; the faujdar had to intervene to end the conflict.[162] Chera and Panch, both Mahajans of Ram Ganj Bazaar (Jaipur city), were fined Rs 51 for fighting with swords in the marketplace.[163] Khushla Sunar attacked Gangaram Purohit[164] with a sword during an argument in Jaipur city. Gangaram was slightly injured in the clash, so he went to the authorities and lodged a complaint. After the investigation, Khushla was found guilty and had to pay a fine.[165] Jaipur was not the only state to punish individuals responsible for violent behaviour. Stewart Gordon cites examples of how the Marathas imposed fines on people engaged in sword fights in the province of Malwa.[166]

Fines were collected from people who showed violent behaviour[167] without reason, regardless of who started the fight or behaved aggressively. For example, Mahaseri Mahajan fought with Bhema Agarwal without any apparent reason and received a fine.[168] Chitra (a woman) got into a verbal brawl with other women at the city's well (place not specified in the document) and was fined Re 1.[169] Dewla Bhujar was also fined Rs 14 for starting a fight with Shreekishan Mali in the marketplace.[170] Nirakha Chamar and Harma Mina quarrelled without any reason; both were fined Rs 16.50.[171]

Verbal Harassment

The state authorities regarded snide remarks and verbal accusations as acts of punishable misbehaviour. Fines collected under this category were not very high; individuals were usually fined between one to two rupees for each offense. Any public behaviour that disrupted others' lawful activities fell under jurisdiction of state authority. Individuals were fined and incarcerated if they caused a fight by verbally abusing someone; Koda Mina of Tappa Khoh a spent a night in jail for picking a fight with Soma Sunar.[172] People in the marketplace were generally targeted for such types of transgressions. Many references were made to fine collection from individuals involved in verbal harassment, comments, and remarks involving shopkeepers and their customers.[173] Marketing skills were taken seriously, and anyone found misusing them or creating disturbances was fined. One Gulla Mahajan of Ram Ganj Bazaar in Jaipur city was fined for interrupting a neighbouring shopkeeper's jingle as he called to his customers. The kotwal was informed of this act, and Gulla Mahajan had to appear in the kotwali for questioning. He was released after being reprimanded and fined.[174]

Even if a person hit someone by mistake or hurt him unknowingly, authorities investigated the matter and treated it as an offence. For example, Khushla Sunar slapped Rupo's face, and Khema Mina hit somebody by mistake in the city of Jaipur. Fines were collected from both men. In other incidents, Kheta Patel hurt someone with a sword[175] and Dewa Gujar was accused of poisoning someone.[176] Tulna Bhujar hit Madho Chamar on the head with an iron tool,[177] and Chetek Patel broke Kallu's julaha axe in a brawl.[178] All these cases were reported to the faujdar in areas around the city of Jaipur, and fines were collected from the culprits.

State intervention in verbal or physical brawls between individuals indicates that the state closely monitored activities of the Jaipur. This fact also reinforces the argument that 18th century states were ruled by increasingly centralised administrative structures, even though they could not continue due to various political and social changes.

Disorderly Conduct Toward Government Officials

Disorderly conduct or misbehaviour (*sarkar ke admi se lariyu aur shokhi kiyo*) toward government authorities was an offence for which individuals were continually charged with fines and punishments. Such types of criminal activities were reported nearly every year of the period under study here (from 1728 to 1761 CE). This is the only category of offence which involved mainly rich and high caste people, and fines collected were quite high, ranging from Rs 45 to Rs 300.[179]

Acts Against State Authority

The *arhsatta* records document acts against state authority, such as bringing false witnesses to testify, wrongly accusing someone without proper proof, tampering with official papers, non-payment of taxes, unlawful possession of government property, and unauthorised employment. The government dealt with these infractions with stern warnings, seizing properties in some cases and imposing fines in all other categories of offence. The following categories of criminal activities represent state intervention in aspects of the law and its execution. Individuals who were apprehended for either abusing or taking advantage of the system were universally penalised, mostly through fines.

Generally, on being informed that an offence had been committed, the faujdar sent his subordinates to make necessary inquiries. Witnesses, usually two males, were required to either establish that a crime was committed or dismiss the claim. Evidence gathered was oral, and close relations' testimonies were not accepted. Individuals involved in an offence was required to produce their own witnesses in front of the authorities.

Sometimes witnesses gave false evidence or told lies to win the culprits' freedom. False witnesses, if apprehended, were fined by the faujdar and his officials. Khema Mina produced false witnesses to clear himself of charges. However, he was arrested again and had to pay a fine of Rs 78 before he was released.[180] A similar case was brought in the Ram Ganj kotwali of Jaipur, where Nanhu Sunar produced a witness to testify that he was not present at a crime scene. Later, the witness (not identified) confessed that Nanhu bribed him to testify on his behalf. The faujdar demanded a fine from Nanhu for bringing a false witness and lying to authorities.[181]

The next sets of offences are related to giving false statements or misleading information, which were both regarded as punishable acts. These offenders challenged state authority either by producing incorrect information or providing wrong statements about their activities or those of others. Lying to government officials or misleading them about criminal behaviour was perceived as act against the state's authority. Individuals guilty of such crimes were heavily fined and sometimes put in jail for several months. The cases mentioned below illustrate the variety of offences throughout this period. One Ghasi Khema of Saganer had given a false statement to get an official document *(patta*, or sale deed) for his land from the government.[182] Pratap Singh and Nahar Singh got into a fight, gave erroneous statements, and were fined Rs 20 each.[183] Khushla Sunar of Jaipur gave a false statement to government authorities about his income and received a fine.[184] Giving a wrong testimony in cases being tried in the *darbar* (court) or faujdar's office was a punishable act.[185] Even when cases were dismissed out of the courts, if officials found out about fabricated testimonies, the individuals responsible were fined and sometimes jailed.[186]

Offences such as tampering with or destroying official documents were criminal offences. In one instance, Manha Balahi of Tappa Khoh did not write an official document properly and changed the wording;

he had to pay Rs 5.50.[187] Hera Patel mutilated an important official grant paper (*sanad*)[188] belonging to Alari *Bhujar* by dropping some ink on it. He was required to pay an official fee for the paper and also compensate Alari.[189] Janna Chamar was fined for tampering and changing some lines written by the faujdar.[190] Evidence coming from archives of Jaipur and other 18th century states contradicts the idea of the states' limited control over their subjects.

Unlawful possession of land or government property is elucidated here. These offences resulted in confiscation of properties, imprisonment, and fines. The Jaipur state established its control over issues arising from rural and urban properties. Any person occupying unassigned property or land was ordered to leave the property immediately and pay a fine. Ram Singh Rajput occupied a piece of land next to his field near the city of Jaipur, although it did not belong to him. He was fined Rs 50 and the land was confiscated.[191] In another case, Sukhla Patel took possession of government property in Jaipur and was fined Rs 151.[192] In a related case of misuse of government property, Ram Krishna and his friends were fined Rs 1.75 each for taking government horses from their stables.[193]

This concludes the discussion on Jaipur rulers' administrative practices and accounts of crime categories reported. It is important to establish that these policies organised the state's administrative structure and effectively enforced rulers' laws over their subjects.

Conclusion

Jaipur rulers' administrative practices discussed in this paper poignantly point out the extent of state control. In addition, a study of the policies negates the powerful critique that pre-colonial states failed to centralise their rule or cogently legitimise their power. This view, presented by colonial rulers in the early 18th century, focused primarily on two areas. The first was the system of fines which led to venal practices. Rich and influential people could bribe the ministers of justice to buy freedom, while the poor and less fortunate could be imprisoned for life if they were unable to pay. Second, the British criticised Jaipur's mild laws, which were full of loopholes and allowed criminals to be inadequately punished. Cruelty was evident in mutilation sanctioned by religious law (both Islamic and Shastric laws prescribed this form of punishment). However, if these criticisms are reassessed in the light of available evidence, it becomes apparent that mutilations for crimes such as petty thefts were always discouraged.[194] Jaipur records indicate that most criminals were liable to fines or imprisonment. In Bengal, as late as 1791, offenders were imprisoned for crimes such as highway robbery without murder, breaking and entering, and even petty thefts.[195]

Jorg Fisch makes the significant point that British rationalisation of law was motivated by the needs of a foreign power wanting to replace the extra legal and illegal elements of extraordinary justice.[196] This analysis adds to the existing historiography reassessing the development of state formations in 18th century India. These states were not remarkably different from their predecessors, but definitely had more cohesive centres of administration. They could not crystallise into elaborate bureaucratic structures because of various political reasons—not because the pre-colonial states were devoid of administrative institutions or their rulers lacked the acumen to establish a centralised state.

Notes

1. This revised edition of the paper presented in the 5th Conference on Rajasthan is influenced by the encouraging comments of the colleagues present there. I am especially indebted to Prof. Dilbagh Singh and Prof. Lloyd Rudolph for their comments and suggestions on ways to improve this paper.
2. This notion was developed through the writings of 17th century European travellers, especially Francois Bernier. Several books have been written on the autocratic nature of Asian states: Marshall Hodgson, *Venture of Islam*, (3 vols.), Chicago, 1974; Max Weber, *Economy and Society*, ed. Guenther Roth and Claus Wittich, (3 vols.); Perry Anderson, *Lineages of the Absolutist State,* London, 1974; and Karl Wittfogel, *Oriental Despotism,* New Haven, 1959. Historians working on Mughal India have refuted the oriental despotism theories put forward by these authors, especially by Irfan Habib in "An examination of Wittfogel's Theory of Oriental Despotism," *Enquiry*, 6, 1961. However, these criticisms do not include 18th century states, and this paper attempts to address that issue.
3. Bernard Cohn, *Colonialism and its forms of Knowledge,* Princeton, 1996, p. 62.
4. Cohn, *Colonialism*, p. 62.
5. Cohn, *Colonialism*, p. 64.
6. Orme, Robert, "Historical Fragments of the Mogul Empire, of the Morattoes, and of the British Concerns" in *Indostan*, ed. J.P. Guha, Associated Press, New Delhi, Reprint, 1974 (first published in 1792), p. 280.
7. This paper showcases the establishment of political authority and explains how rulers were capable of controlling different sections of the society and their activities.

8. Bernard Cohn, *Colonialism and its forms of Knowledge,* Thomas Metcalf, *Ideologies of Raj,* Cambridge, 2006; Jorg Fisch, *Cheap Lives and Dear Limbs: The British Transformation of Bengal Criminal Law 1769–1817,* F. Steiner, 1983; Radhika Singha, *A Despotism of Law: Crime and Justice in Early Colonial India,* Oxford, 1998.
9. All Mughal historians: Ibn Ahmad, Sangar, Sarkar, and Ishtiaq Ahmad Siddiqui.
10. J.F. Richards, *The Mughal Empire,* Cambridge, 1993; Andrea Hintze, *The Mughal Empire and its Decline: An Interpretation of the Sources of Social Power,* Ashgate, 1997.
11. Chris Bayly, *Rulers, Townsmen and Bazaar: North Indian Society in the Age of British Expansion 1770–1870,* pp. 10–11.
12. For Mysore: Hasan, Mohibul, *The History of Tipu Sultan,* Calcutta, 1971; Stein, Burton, "Fiscal Centralisation in Mysore," *South Asia Researcher,* Vol. 2. For Maratha: Edward Thompson, G.T. Garrett, *Rise and Fulfillment of British Rule in India,* London, 1934, p. 63.
13. Gordon, Stewart, "The Slow Conquest: Administrative Integration into the Maratha Empire, 1720–60", *Modern Asian Studies,* Vol. II, No. 1, 1977, pp. 36–37.
14. Narendra Wagle, "Women in the Kotwal's Papers", Pune, 1767–91, in Anne Feldhaus (ed.), *Images of Women in Maharashtrian Society,* New York, 1998; Narendra Wagle, "The Government, the Jati and the Individual: Rights, Discipline and Control in the Pune Kotwal Papers", 1766–94, Contribution of *Indian Sociology,* (Nos.) 34, 3, 2000.
15. Two books edited by Irfan Habib, *Confrontation Colonialism: Resistance and Modernisation under Haider Ali & Tipu Sultan,* Anthem, 2000; *State and Diplomacy under Tipu Sultan,* Tulika, 2001 Sumit Guha and M.R. Anderson (eds.), *Changing Concepts of Rights and Justice in South Asia,* Oxford, 1998.
16. I.G. Khan, *State and Diplomacy* (ed.) Irfan Habib, pp. 66–118.
17. Norbert Peabody, *Hindu Kingship and Politics in Pre-colonial India,* Cambridge, 2003; Gyan Prakash Pilania, *Enlightened Government in Modern India: Heritage of Sawai Jai Singh,* Manohar, 2002.
18. Ibid.
19. Inden, Ronald, *Ritual, Authority and Cyclic Time in Hindu Kingship, Kingship and Authority in South Asia,* ed. J.F. Richards, Cambridge University Press, 1982, p. 42.
20. The archival records maintained by the Amber state are more detailed in content than most Mughal documents.
21. Narendra Wagle and Gordon Stewart for Marathas, Muzaffar Alam for Awadh: *Crisis of the Empire in Mughal North India; Awadh and Punjab 1707–1748,* Oxford, 1986; Yullampalli Vaikuntham, "State, economy and Social Transformation of Hyderabad State 1724–1948", Manohar, 2002; Dilbagh Singh, "State and Society in Medieval Rajasthan" in J S Grewal (ed.); *The State and Society in Medieval India,* Oxford, 2005; and Madhu Sethia, *Rajput Polity, Warriors, Peasants, and Merchants 1700–1800,* Rawat Publications, 2002 and

Nirmal Kumar, "Camel in 18th Century Rajasthan: Some Observations", in this volume (chapter 16).

22. For example, Vijaynagar rulers were not regarded as worthy models by non-Muslim North Indian rulers (no indication of their presence exists in the sources of Jaipur).
23. J.F. Richards, *The Mughal Empire,* Cambridge, 1993, pp. 282–84.
24. J.F. Richards, p. 284.
25. All official orders are preserved in the Jaipur State Museum, Jaipur, and are known as the *Kapadwara* Collection.
26. The official record of *eighteenth* century states reinforces Romila Thapar's argument about the imagined religious communities. For more details: Romila Thapar, "Imagined Religious communities: Ancient History and the Modern Search for a Hindu Identity", *Modern Asian Studies,* Vol. 23, No. 2. 1989, pp. 209–31.
27. Examples are taken from Mysore, Maratha state (Malwa & Pune), Jodhpur.
28. Orme, p. 290.
29. For murder cases, officials requested the Maharaja's intervention.
30. *Arzdasht* # 574/109, undated, RSA, Bikaner.
31. *Arhsatta pargana* Sawai Jaipur, Year, 1758, p. 1450.
32. *Arhsatta pargana* Sawai Jaipur, Year 1758, p. 1484.
33. Jorg Fisch, p. 120: for criticism and collection of fines by the Nawab of Bengal.
34. Khan, Mohammad Ali, *Mirat-I-Ahmadi,* A History of Gujarat, trans. M.F. Lokhandwala, Oriental Institute, Baroda, 1965, p. 261.
35. *Mirat,* p. 343.
36. For details: Fish, p. 56.
37. Wagle, Narendra's article on Pune records of the Marathas, and Gordon Stewart for Malwa.
38. As can be seen by the data presented in this paper.
39. Burton Stein, "State Formation Reconsidered", *Modern Asian Studies,* 19, n. 3 (1985), pp. 387–413; For more details see Partha Chatterjee, *The Nation and Its Fragments,* Princeton, 1993, pp. 25–29.
40. Fine collections in various crimes are evidence of this fact.
41. Fisch, p. 5.
42. Satya Prakash Sangar, *Crime and Punishment in Mughal India,* New Delhi, 1998, chapter 1.
43. Fisch, p. 2.
44. Mansura Haider, *Insha-i-Abul Fazl: Farman and Letters of Emperor Akbar (1556–1605),* New Delhi, 1998, chapter 3.
45. Hintze, Mughal Empire, see Introduction.
46. Aiyangar, K.V., Indian Cameralism, p. 47 cf. Derrett, Duncan, *Religion, Law, and the State in India,* Oxford, 1968, Reprint, 1999, p. 201, "In politics the two (*dharma/ artha*) are balanced, and if the loss of *artha* would be greater than the gain of dharma, *artha* is to be pursued and if necessary, a penance

performed for the breach of *dharma*." (Medhathithi on Manu vi 26 cf. Manu iv 176).

47. Manu ix, 249 and Medhatithi, 280, 289 cf. Derrett, pp. 213–14.
48. There was no change in official policies of the later rulers.
49. Derrett, p. 215.
50. Fisch, pp. 26–30, "Capital punishment was possible only if an instrument was used which was normally served for shedding blood. Thus, killing a man with the wooden part of an axe was no capital offence, while killing him with the iron part was. Sometimes the restriction went a step further—the crime was capital only if death was inflicted with a sharp edge of the iron, not with its other sides."
51. Singha, p. 56.
52. Fisch, p. 24, He quotes Radzinowicz's list of capital punishments which included murder, homicide, counterfeiting, false impersonating another with intention to defraud, simple larceny, pick pocketing of a value of 12 pence, and all kinds of arson (pp. 611–59).
53. James Forbes, *Oriental Memoirs,* Vol. 2, London, 1812, p. 25.
54. H.L.O Garrett and G.L. Chopra, *Events at the Court of Ranjit Singh,* Manohar, 2002, pp. 10–14.
55. For details: See Sangar, chapter 6.
56. *Arzdasht* from Diwan Bhikari Das to Jai Singh, (# 32/1345), 18 January. 1709 CE.
57. Ibid., Year 1762, p. 827.
58. *Mirat*, p. 261 & 281.
59. *Fatawat-I-Alamgiri*, cf. Sangar, chapter 6.
60. Singha, p. 53.
61. *Arhsatta pargana* Sawai Jaipur, 1745 A.D. p. 466. ibid., Year, 1734 A.D., (# 2085).
62. *Chitthi* (letter) of Bhagi Ram to Maharaja Sawai Jai Singh (# 320/309, 12 November, 1712 CE), RSA, Bikaner.
63. *Arhsatta pargana Sawai Jaipur,* pargana, Jaipur, 1740 A.D., p. 381.
64. Ibid.
65. *Chitthi from Diwan Bhikari to Maharaja Sawai Jai Singh, undated.*
66. *Arhsatta pargana* Sawai Jaipur, Year 1745, p. 466.
67. *Arhsatta pargana* Sawai Jaipur, Year 1761, p. 1429.
68. Ibid., Year 1763, p. 725.
69. Letter of Diwan Kirpa Ram to Vidhyadhar (1737), cf. V.S. Bhatnagar: *Sawai Jai Singh and His Times,* Jaipur, 1974, p. 306.
70. The Mughal policy is explained in the following paragraphs.
71. Fisch, pp. 14–15; Sangar, chapter 4.
72. *Mirat*, p. 145: reproduction of Akbar's *Farman*.
73. *Mirat*, p. 160.
74. Sangar, pp. 77–78.

75. Sangar, pp. 85–90 has given several examples of such expeditions during the 17th century.
76. There are many *farmans* related to the actions taken by Sawai Jai Singh against Churaman Jat: *Kharita* # 48 From the Mughal court to Sawai Jai Singh, undated, where he has sent Shyam Singh Khangarot to devastate the Jats; *Kharita* # 54 From the Mughal court to Sawai Jai Singh, undated, "It is good that Maharaja has vanquished the rebels and culprits; rains and cyclones have also been helpful in his efforts."
77. *Kharita,* # 107, From the Mughal court to Sawai Jai Singh, 7 February, 1718, Kapadwara Collection, Sawai Man Singh Museum, Jaipur, cf. Bahura and Singh, p. 15.
78. Mauji Ram Mishra was removed from Utagirgarh and settled in Dhodharpur on the surety of Raja Gopal Singh and Padam Chand Jadam, *Arzis*, # 903 & 904, December 14 and 15, 1745, Kapadwara Collection, Sawai Man Singh II Museum, Jaipur.
79. Letter, #905, From Anup Singh to Sawai Jai Singh, July 22, 1728, Kapadwara Collection, Sawai Man Singh II Museum, Jaipur.
80. Sarkar, p. 11.
81. Bond, # 1302 signed by Bhoop Singh Rajawat to Sawai Jai Singh, Dated 21 August, 1743, Kapadwara Collection, Sawai Man Singh II Museum, Jaipur. Bhoop Singh was the faujdar of pargana Jaipur from 1743–45
82. Ghulam Husain Tabatabai, *Seirul Mutaquerin*, printed, James White, Calcutta, 1789–90, Vol. 3, p. 80.
83. *Arhsatta Pargana* Sawai Jaipur, Year 1741, p. 357.
84. Letter from Shyam Singh to Jai Singh (#453, 1703 A.D.).
85. The *Arhsatta* records from 1728–1796.
86. *Arhsatta pargana* Sawai Jaipur, Year 1739, p. 266; Year 1743, p. 292, p. 268; Year 1734, pp. 2075–2083.
87. Ibid., Year.
88. Ibid., Year 1738, p. 250; Year 1739, p. 270; Year 1739, p. 270; Year 1790, No page numbers; Year 1737, p. 324. ibid.
89. Ibid., Year 1736, p. 2018.
90. *Arhsatta pargana* Sawai Jaipur, Year 1739, pp. 271–72.
91. Ibid., Year 1739, pp. 271–72.
92. Ibid, Year 1738, p. 234.
93. Ibid, Year 1743, p. 259, Nathu stole from a tobacco cart and was fined Rs 1.25; Year 1744, p. 420, Fatah Kutbah looted Subhan's cart and was fined Rs 17.
94. Jetu (Mahajan) stole money from Rupa (Mahajan) Arhsatta pargana Sawai Jaipur, SJ (Sawai Jaipur), Year 1734, p. 134; Year 1734, p. 2088, Narhar (Mahajan) accused Ram Singh for theft; the fine was Rs 51; Year 1737, p. 333, Shatru (Agarwal) fined for theft Rs 91.
95. Ibid., Jamin (Muslim) accused Jafar of stealing.
96. Ibid., Year 1736, pp. 2019–20.
97. Ibid., Year 1738, p. 237.

98. Ibid., Year 1739, p. 274.
99. Ibid., Year 1741, p. 363.
100. *Arhsatta pargana* Sawai Jaipur, Year 1739, p. 272.
101. Ibid., 1740, p. 393.
102. Ibid., Year, 1736, p. 2018.
103. *Arhsatta pargana* Sawai Jaipur Year 1737, p. 328.
104. Ibid., Year 1739, p. 274.
105. Ibid., p. 394.
106. Ibid., Year 1741, p. 343.
107. Ibid., p. 348.
108. Ibid., Year 1737, p. 327.
109. Ibid., Year 1737, p. 2078; Year 1743, p. 277; Year 1744, p. 415 & 423; Year 1745, p. 464.
110. Ibid., Year 1740, p. 393; pp. 396–97; p. 405; Year 1744, p. 445.
111. Ibid., Year, 1737, p. 325, Govardhan Ahir stole oil from a street lamp, fine was Re. 1.
112. Ibid., p. 327, Harji Gujar mixed something into street lamp oil (lantern), fine was Re 1.
113. *Arhsatta pargana* Sawai Jaipur, Year 1738, p. 244; Year 1737, pp. 328, 337, Year 1740, p. 372; Year 1741, pp. 327, 340 & 342; Year 1743, pp. 278; 291; Year 1744, p. 413, Year 1762, p. 831, Year 1797, p. 6.
114. Ibid., Year 1743, p. 291.
115. Ibid., Year 1741, p. 327.
116. Ibid., Year 1762, p. 831; Year 1797, p. 6.
117. In Sanskrit it is spelled as *pipali*, a species of fig tree noted for its great size and longevity; lacks the prop roots of the banyan; regarded as sacred by Buddhists.
118. Neem or margosa tree, a fast-growing broad-leaved evergreen, *Azadirachta indica*, native to India and Myanmar. Its extracts have been used for centuries in Asia as pesticides, toothpaste, medicines, and health tonics.
119. *Arhsatta pargana* Sawai Jaipur Sawai Jaipur, Year 1744, p. 413.
120. Most of the cases were reported from Pargana Jaipur.
121. Muslims are referred to by their religion and not by their caste in these records.
122. Caste of earthen utensil makers.
123. *Arhsatta pargana Sawai* Jaipur, Year 1743, p. 291.
124. Ibid., Year 1738, p. 240.
125. Ibid., Year 1740, p. 383; Year 1743, pp. 277 & 291; Year 1763, p. 723.
126. Of course, records gave no explanation, but it seems that the crimes related to agricultural activities were done by more well-to-do castes like Jats and khummars, who were able to pay the higher fines.
127. This letter of invitation praised the ruler and his two Jaina *dewans* (finance ministers) for sponsoring the event. The letter described Jaipur in this way, "about the city, it lacks seven things. This is to say; in the city you would not find wine sellers, butchers and prostitutes. Also, the killing of animals is prohibited.

The raja's name is Madho Singh. In this kingdom you would not find sinful activities, which are prohibited by the raja. And there are many Jaina residents here. All-important courtiers are Jainas. There are others, but they are in the minority, not majority.

128. Bean Baptise Tavernier, *Travels in India,* (ed.) V. Ball, London, 1977, Vol. 1, pp. 71–72.

129. Niccolao Manucci, *Storia Do Mogor,* trans. W. Irvine, London, 1966, Vol. I, p. 67.

130. *Mirat*, p. 145.

131. Gomal Ahir had to pay Rs 1,401 for killing a bull. This is the highest fine mentioned in Jaipur documents for killing an animal. Parla Jat was fined Rs 206 for killing a buffalo. Mallu mina was fined Rs 551 for killing a cow; Chauka Jat was fined Rs 141 for the same crime. In 1762, Dharma patel paid Rs 300 for killing a cow by beating it ferociously. Sultan Mussalman killed a goat on Bakai'd and was fined Rs 11. Bala Mussalman killed a goat to eat its meat. In addition, some people were fined for physically hurting animals. Khema Ahir had to pay Rs 11 for hurting a cow; Lallu Gujar was fined for beating a cow with a stick so hard that it died; he had to pay authorities Rs 31. Kirpa Ahir was fined Rs 5.50 for beating a bull with a stick, similarly Dula Mali was fined Re 1 for hurting a cow. Harji's (Ahir) daughter in law hurt her animals by beating them with a stick in rage. When it was reported to the authorities she was called for questioning and later fined. Khemla Ahir was accused of injuring a pregnant cow and had to pay a of penalty of Rs 11; and Nanak Mali was fined Rs 2 for injuring a peacock.

132. *Mirat*, pp. 145, 161, & 223.

133. *Mirat*, p. 161.

134. Many references are quoted by Sangar, pp. 168–72.

135. Tod, pp. 84 & 296.

136. *Mirat*, p. 280, cf. Sangar, p. 166.

137. All these cases were reported in *Darbar-I-Maulla*, cf. Sangar, pp. 171–72.

138. Jean de Thevenot, Account of India, in *Indian Travels of Thevenot and Careri*, tr. & ed., S.N. Sinha, Delhi, 1949, p. 79.

139. Khan, I.G., State and Diplomacy (ed. Irfan Habib), p. 78 order # 55 (a).

140. *Arhsatta pargana* Sawai Jaipur, Year 1734, p. 344.

141. Ibid., Year, 1740, pp. 353–54.

142. Ibid., Year, 1743, p. 261.

143. *Parwana* # 836, Kapadwara Collection, Sawai Jai Singh II Museum, Jaipur.

144. *Arhsatta pargana* Sawai Jaipur, Year 1737, p. 271.

145. Ibid., Year 1739, p. 344.

146. Ibid., Year, 1740, p. 395.

147. Ibid., Year, 1740, p. 395, & Year 1745.

148. *Arhsatta pargana* Sawai Jaipur, Year 1743, pp. 291, 93, 58 & 63.

149. Ibid., Year 1736, p. 234; Year 1737, p. 339.

150. *Arhsatta pargana* Sawai Jaipur, Year 1736, p. 268; Year 1737, pp. 324 & 339.
151. Ibid.
152. Ibid., the gambling fines: In 1728, Panchdhan Mahajan was fined 14 rupees; in 1736, 32 people were fined for gambling; most of them belonged to the trading community. In 1737, 12 out of 205 crimes recorded were for gambling; in 1738, only 3 instances of gambling were reported. In the *Arhsattas pargana* Sawai Jaipur from 1739 to 1764, only 3 or 4 cases of gambling fines were reported each year.
153. Original letter mentions that the men of Sardar Singh *ke admi ne looto aur maaryu pargana Chatsu ke raaste par.*
154. Letter from Harnam Roop Chand to Maharaja Sawai Jai Singh, Year 1700, RSA, Bikaner.
155. *Arhsatta pargana* Sawai Jaipur, Year 1734, p. 2088. The document language is *lariyu aur tofail kiyu.*
156. Letter from Girdhar Das to Maharaja Bishan Singh, Year 1695, Preserved in RSA, Bikaner.
157. Letter from Kishor Das to Maharaja Bishan Singh, Year 1695, Preserved in RSA, Bikaner.
158. *Arhsatta pargana* Sawai Jaipur, Year 1738, p. 232.
159. *maar lagayu kulhari so.*
160. *Arhsatta pargana* Sawai Jaipur, p. 335.
161. As mentioned in the sources.
162. *Arhsatta Pargana* Sawai Jaipur, Year 1741, p. 359. Both were fined Rs 33.
163. Ibid., p. 252.
164. A priest by profession and a Brahmin.
165. *Arhsatta pargana* Sawai Jaipur, Year 1764, p. 1320.
166. For details see Stewart Gordon, *The Slow Conquest*, p. 28.
167. *pehle lariyu kariyu.*
168. *Arhsatta pargana* Sawai Jaipur, Year 1741, p. 338.
169. Ibid., Year 1763, p. 762.
170. Ibid., Year, 1764, p. 1317. He was fined Rs 14.
171. Ibid., Year 1761, p. 1428.
172. *Arhsatta pargana* Sawai Jaipur, 1764, p. 1334, RSA, Bikaner.
173. There was continuous collection of fines for verbal harassment from 1734 to 1761 in the state of Jaipur.
174. *Arhsatta pargana* Sawai Jaipur, Year 1743, p. 274.
175. *Arhsatta pargana* Sawai Jaipur, Year, 1758, p. 1487.
176. Ibid., Year 1762, p. 827.
177. Ibid., Year 1764, p. 1319.
178. Ibid., Year 1761, p. 1426.

179.

#	Year	Name	Fines (Rs)	Reference/page no.
1	1740	Khema Mina	45	*Arhsatta pargana* Sawai Jaipur, p. 341
2	1741	Narak Singh	211	Ibid., p. 346
3	1741	Ganga Singh	5	Ibid., p. 327
4	1741	Hardam Patel	101	Ibid., p. 101
6	1743	Gridhar Singh	30	Ibid., p. 266
7	1743	Kesni Brahmini	11	Ibid., p. 270
8	1744	Harji Jat	5.50	Ibid., p. 413
9	1746	Manohar	13	Ibid., p. 381
10	1764	Malsa Rajput	331	Ibid., p. 1326
11	1795	Palta	41	Ibid., No page #

180. *Arhsatta pargana* Sawai Jaipur, Year 1728, p. 2018: Manorath lied about the camels owned by Gegla. Manorath testified that Gegla had 40 camels, but it was established that he had only 10. Manorath was fined for giving the wrong number of camels.
181. Ibid., Year 1794: Joshidevi was fined Rs 40 for giving false testimony for Dewla.
182. Ibid., Year 1740, p. 391. He had to pay Rs 101.
183. Ibid., Year 1758, p. 1490.
184. Ibid., Year 1794.
185. Ibid., Year 1736, p. 2018.
186. Ibid., Year 1744, p. 469.
187. Ibid., Year 1755, p. 254.
188. Official letter issued to a person showing an appointment, allotment of land etc.
189. *Arhsatta pargana* Sawai Jaipur, Year 1755, p. 252.
190. Ibid., Year 1744, p. 412.
191. *Arhsatta pargana* Sawai Jaipur, Year, 1734, p. 2086.
192. Ibid., Year, 1738, p. 242.
193. Ibid., Year 1740, p. 400, the total fine was Rs 8.50.
194. Akbar forbade his *mansabdars* from punishing offenders by skinning, trampling them under the feet of the elephants ... *Mirat*, p. 141 (original *Farman* is reproduced). Jahangir ordered that officials should not blind people or cut off their ears and noses for punishment. *Mirat*, p. 166 (original *Farman* is reproduced).
195. Fisch, pp. 118–19, Mohammad Reza Khan (responsible for criminal justice) describes different cases of imprisonment for petty crimes in Bengal.
196. Fisch, pp. 134–35.

8

Forms of Resistance in 18th Century Villages of Rajasthan

Madhu Sethia

This paper examines the forms of resistance adopted by various sections of the village society in the Hadauti (south-eastern Rajasthan) region. The reason for this academic exercise is to test the opinion that high fertility of land, low subsistence level and free peasant production had created relative stability in India's society and economy and that there was hardly any concentrated social effort to change completely the means, the methods and the relations of production and that a kind of equilibrium in the village society helped the state to appropriate the peasant's surplus.[1] The present paper focuses on the reaction of peasants, artisans and menials to an unequal distribution of economic resources, power and position. Since the big dramatic uprisings or movements have already been highlighted and studied in detail by many leading historians I felt that now there is a need to explore the day-to-day resistance within or outside the process of production in various forms.[2]

It has already been established that forms of resistance vary according to the conditions and constraints under which they are generated. Accordingly, a composite although somewhat elastic concept of resistance has been suggested which assumes that resistance begins from the point where compliance ends. Consequently, almost every act and even thought of a member of a subordinate class which is not that of compliance can be interpreted as an act of resistance even if it is clothed in the language of conformity.[3] In my opinion forms of resistance also depend upon the objectives of resistance. Going by this wide-ranging concept of resistance, I have tried to explore the forms of resistance adopted by various sections of society and individuals in the process of coming to grips with the reality of their existence at that point of time.

My study of the forms of resistance adopted by the ordinary peasants, artisans and menials shows that their primary objective was to create better conditions to live within the existing Hada (the dominant Rajput clan in this region) state system. Consequently, sending petitions to state collectively or individually always remained their first choice. Most of the petitions were sent through the recognised leaders of the village like the patel and patwari (the customary leader of the peasants and the village record keeper recognised by the state as such) but sometimes the state was also approached directly, if the issue concerned only a particular section or an individual and not the village or town as a whole. The petitions revolved around revenue matters, conduct of local officials or *jagirdar*, or the general economic plight and concessions and remissions. Most of the individual petitions were sent with a hope to get personal grievances redressed.

The underlying assumption was that once the situation was brought to the notice of the state it would take a positive action. For instance, the peasants of a village reported the name of the artisans and menials who in spite of living in the village were abstaining and their strips of land were lying unploughed.[4] Obviously, some of the artisans and menials residing in this village had decided for some reason not to cooperate with the peasants of the village. Since, it was the peasants and the patel who were collectively held responsible for maintaining cultivation, they decided to report the matter to the state. As a routine the state expected the village patel and patwari to furnish the names of artisans and menials living in the village for the purpose of realising the customary cesses from them. Therefore, at the beginning of agricultural operations for the season all such names were entered in the village records along with an undertaking that the same have been entered correctly and no names have been hidden or suppressed.[5] Any local unity between the peasants, artisans and menials on this count could harm the state interests in two ways. It could result in loss of the cesses to be realised from artisans and menials and it would also give a valid excuse to the peasants for not cultivating the entire village land due to shortage of labour supplied by the menials during certain agricultural operations. As a result when the artisans and menials decided not to cultivate the land given to them by the village, the matter was reported to the state. The expectation was that the state would provide necessary support to peasants either to compel the artisans and menials to cultivate as usual or allow them to deal with the artisans and menials in a befitting manner or at least they would have a valid explanation for non-cultivation of the entire land. It also shows that the artisans and menials could also decide to resist the pressures or harassment by the peasants in their own way.

In another petition some of the peasants complained against the patel and patwari for realising rupees ten on each plough unit in the name of various contingency levies, over and above the assessed revenue. As a result they were unable to carry on cultivation and therefore their uncultivated land had been allocated to some others for being cultivated. They requested to be relieved of the extortions of such officials and to be allowed to deposit the revenue directly to any place specified by the state.[6] So, they approached the state to resist the high-handedness of the local revenue officials. However, their lack of confidence was only in the intermediaries and not in the state as such, whom they expected to intervene in their favour. Thus, sending petitions was not only the safest method to resist against the oppressive village hierarchy but also a demonstration of their loyalty as subjects in the hope to getting some relief from the state.

Sometimes instead of sending a petition it was found necessary to resist on the spot which could even assume a violent form. In one of the disputes between the patels and the peasants some of the peasants got killed. The details of the dispute, however, are not known except that the patel was made to pay a fine afterwards by the state.[7] It shows that the relations between peasants and patels who were often from the same cast were also not free from tensions and conflicts. Sometimes, on the spot resistance could be in the form of *gatya,* which was used only as a last resort. It implied that an aggrieved person kept sitting at the door of the house of the offender to demand undoing of the wrong. This form of resistance was generally used by the lower castes against members of the upper castes to pressurise them for justice. The reason to resort to *gatya* could be extreme despair due to violation of the customary norms followed by the upper castes in dealing with the member of the lower caste. The chamars of a village had resorted to *gatya* against patel although the specific reason for resorting to this extreme form of protest has not been recorded. The patel felt so helpless against this act of the chamars that he committed suicide out of shame.[8] The state held the entire village as well as the Chamars responsible for this episode and imposed a penalty upon both the Chamars and the rest of the village. It can be inferred from this episode that even the lowest sections could adopt open and direct forms of resistance against violation of customary norms by the village hierarchy. It is not clear whether these violent forms were spontaneous outbursts of anger or were caused by the frustration created by failure in securing a positive response from the state.

The complaints of the villagers were not only against the village hierarchy but at times also against the state policy. One such major issue was repeated realisation of various contingency levies. An official recommended postponement of realisation of such a levy in some of the villages.[9] Conveying the feelings of the subjects he wrote that they were not ready to pay and were adopting defying tactics. The amount to be realised had been assigned to one *bohra* (money-lender) Kisan Ram for repayment of a loan taken by the state. In fact one instalment had already been realised against this levy but the amount collected did not correspond to the outstanding amount of the bohra. Therefore, fresh orders had been issued to raise another instalment of the same levy. As a result, the peasants decided not to pay the same levy twice. Thus whenever the subjects had a legitimate ground to resist they resorted to defiance and evasion. At times instead of refusing directly they adopted time gaining tactics. One of the officers reported, that although the people were feeling annoyed and burdened but were paying gradually when given some concessions.[10] Others were furnishing written undertakings to pay it after a few days or were bringing *chithis* of bohras (a letter of promise to pay) to be cashed after ten or fifteen days. However, if no concession was offered they were not prepared to pay even a penny. Obviously, the people were not in a position to pay and felt overburdened because of recurring levies but instead of defying openly they were pleading to gain time because they did not have a valid excuse as in the case of realising the same levy twice. The reasons for not resisting openly emanated from the general perception of nature of state and authority. The right of the state to realise various levies over and above the normal revenue demand had become quite established by now. This legitimisation of the right to realise levies even if it was found to be burdensome compelled them to adopt only time gaining tactics instead of simply refusing to pay.

Sometimes the villagers even adopted pressure tactics against the state. For instance, in Digodh the state was not able to realise rupees 377.50 against the levy on village houses although the reasons for non-payment have not been mentioned. The local officials recommended to wave off this amount and informed the higher authorities that the weavers were saying that if they were not exempted from this imposition, they would not allow anyone else also to enjoy the exemption.[11] It shows that asking to be treated on par with others could also be used as a form of resistance. In some cases the peasants tried to resist the heavy state demand by leaving part of their land unploughed, although it harmed their interests as well. It was a silent mode of protest because either, the state suffered a loss of revenue or tried to reallocate the land to someone else in order to maintain the production cycle and revenue flow. If the state tried to make any new arrangement for such land the peasants the peasants questioned it and demanded that not only the land be given back to them for cultivation but also a reduction in the ever increasing state demand by way of imposing contingency levies, etc.[12] Thus, it got transformed into an open form of resistance. The peasants who were not in a position to leave their fields uncultivated chose another method. They asked the state to set up a *sarkari hawala* (state farm) on their land and offered to work as *halis* (seasonal labourers) for a fixed share of the produce.[13] Thus, the resistance against heavy state demand could be in several forms and at times could lead to disruption of the production cycle itself.

Besides, a hidden form of resistance was (or an easy individual method to ensure survival) cheating the system by taking advantage of its complexities such as the differences in the rate of assessment for various categories of land and variety of crops. Thc patels often tried to get the entire land under their ploughs assessed at concessional rate in order to pay less although they were given such concession only on a certain portion of their land.[14] At times, it worked, but at times, it was caught and subjected to penalty. Even the poorest of the poor in the village took such individual risks of paying heavy penalty if caught. In c.1765 a fight amongst the chamars of a village lead to a disclosure of pilferage of *chana* (gram) from the standing crops of the village by one of them. It was recovered by the village authorities, but for stealing just one *seer* of *chana*, chamar Champa had to pay rupees eleven as penalty.[15] Some of the peasants tried to sell grains from the field itself before the actual division of crops between the state and the peasants. Dhakar Sanga and Para who had sold wheat from their fields had to pay rupees four each as penalty.[16] At times, to take advantage of the variation in rate for different crops, instead of the actual crops sown in the field, a crop on which revenue rate was comparatively lower, was shown as sown with the connivance of the patel and patwari.[17] Another individual solution to which the peasants resorted was stealing the state's share of grains. In c. 1714 a warning had to be sent to the watchmen appointed to guard the standing crops for their failure in checking pilferage of grains in a village.[18] The peasants also tried to take advantage of the time, which the state share of grains required to be transported to the local grain market centre or state store. In a town when the state share of grains was being transported to the local fort for storage, it was found to be short. It had been pilfered on the way.[19] Thus, cheating the state in various ways was a common practice. Tod had also observed that "the means peasants adopted to perplex and cheat the state in assessment and collection of revenue were varied, at the time of the reaping they left something for the gleaners" then 'tithe for the khoorpi', then during threshing, "though they muzzle the ox who treads on the corn, they do not their own mouths, or those of their family". If not convertible into coin, and was stored up, "the rats are sure to get into the pits". In spite of the village watchman "all is insufficient to check the system of pillage". Thus, it was asserted that 'one-fourth of the crop' or even 'a third' was frequently made away before the government share could be fixed.[20] Tod's observation obviously suffered from exaggeration as he called it 'pillage'. However, the evidence of pilferage in state records of 18th century suggests that it was not baseless.

Selling the village's trees was another source for making some quick money. In Mundala village patel Dama sold the Khejra tree of his field, without the permission in c. 1709.[21] Mali Ganga Ram quietly sold a Keekar tree of a state garden in c. 1695.[22] Some tried to catch fish, like Dhobi (washermen) Mahaulya. Since, it was his job to be on the bank of the river, he could do it without being noticed.[23] Not only the state but even the villagers had to suffer it at times. One of the Malis sold vegetables from the fields of others.[24] Sukhya and Sulya of Tekhra village lifted cattle from the village and sold it.[25] The state tried to deal with individual methods of cheating the system and causing a loss of revenue for making life easier by imposing heavy penalties. In the case of cheating the state the penalty could be much higher for a patel as compared to an ordinary peasants or menial. The underlying assumption being that to maintain the channel of surplus extraction a strong hold was necessary on the local administrative machinery. However, in offences committed against an individual a discriminatory system was adopted. A Brahmin could be treated lightly than a low caste person. However, if he treated the watchmen appointed by the state to guard the standing crops roughly, he was shown no consideration. A Gujargaud Pandit was ordered to leave the village for being harsh to these men.[26]

In certain situations, threat of migration was also used as a form of protest, although it was actually undertaken only as a last resort. In many cases, peasants, artisans and menials threatened to migrate but agreed to stay back if their grievances were removed. A peasant Beniram decided to migrate because he had been subjected to *khainchal* of *baithi-begar* inspite of being exempt from it.[27] The barbers of various villages of *pargana* Baran threatened to migrate due to *khanichal* of various types.[28] However, in both these cases, no actual migration took place after reassurance against such *khainchal.* A scrutiny of actual migrations (as a form of protest) shows that these were of different types and for different reasons. In some cases the state was informed in advance about the migration, especially when the need to migrate was genuine. For instance, a patel had migrated away because the returns of pateli in that village were too low in comparison to the amount payable as *peshkash* for pateli.[29] Obviously he had resorted to migration only when all other efforts to convince the state to reduce the *peshkash* must have failed. However, he was soon called back on the assurance of reduction in the amount of *peshkash*. Such migrations were generally to a nearby village. Another type of migration was to an unknown destination in order to avoid open confrontation. It was generally in the form of flight. Such migration was resorted to, generally to avoid payment of *'dand'* for committing some offence against state or village society. For instance, a Dhakar peasant found guilty of concealment of his crops was caught and ordered to pay rupees 20 as fine but he fled away from the village. As a punishment, the amount of fine was to be realised from the village. The village itself was in distress and therefore, not in a position to pay, but the amount of penalty was neither reduced nor set aside.[30] An order that was sent to a *bohra* to give subsistence loans to the peasants of this village shows that, the state extended help to the village but made it pay the full amount of penalty. It can be inferred from this case that, it was the situation of extreme distress, which, compelled one of the peasants to resort to concealment of crops, and unable to pay the penalty for it he resorted to flight. Thus, individual solutions to common problems were not unknown. Many of the patels also resorted to flight to escape from an unacceptable situation. For instance, patel of Gugalhedi fled away to avoid paying the penalty imposed upon him. Although, the cause of penalty has not been mentioned in the documents.[31] His *zamins* (guarantors) were asked to produce him. They made him surrender some of his moveable possession in order to settle the penalty. Obviously he had managed to reach a place where the orders of Kota chiefs were not directly enforceable but for the sake of his guarantors agreed to pay. Similarly, patel Bachu fled away due to fear of penalty and punishment in such a haste that most of his assets were left behind and were confiscated.

The villagers were instructed not to conceal his assets or to give him shelter in any way.[32] Thus, if any excess on part of state or local officials caused the migration, process of reconciliation and resettlement was initiated, to avoid escalation of the situation any further and to retain the confidence of the people. However, if the migration was in the form of flight to escape punishment for violation of customary norms or for cheating the state, it was treated severely to prevent it from becoming a general trend. It needs to be noted that there are no references of collective migration against any form of harassment.

The most visible and violent forms of resistance were adopted primarily by the Meenas and Bheels, whose position in the region had suffered as a result of consolidation of Hada polity. In spite of some efforts made by the Hada polity to assimilate and pacify them, the two could never be completely reconciled to the Hada rule. However, the forms of resistance adopted by them varied because of the difference in their economic interests and mode of subsistence. Establishment of Hada rule in 14th century by subjugating Meenas of Bundi and Bheels of Kota had lead to colonisation of new areas and spread of agriculture. It spear-headed appearance of many new peasant communities such as Dhakar, Kirad, Keer, Thori, Jat and a shift towards agriculture by Gujar and Ahir pastoralist in the region. The Hada polity was able to provide political protection to the peasants who had the means to clear forests and required skill to develop new agricultural settlements. The process appears to be a fairly long one and went on even up to early 18th century. Therefore, assertion of the right of Hadas to rule, intricately related to the process of spread of agricultural mode of resource utilisation in the region had three broad implications. First, it facilitated emergence of a large class of peasant proprietors and patels involved in agricultural production as well as a class of *himayatis* (literally meaning the favoured ones) through the process of redistribution of agricultural surplus. Second, it lead to marginalisation of the *bhumia* claims of the Meenas who had started shifting to agriculture prior to the Hada conquest of the region. Third, it posed a serious threat to the tribal mode of resource use due to extensive deforestation in the process of agricultural expansion.

The Meenas had started shifting towards agricultural mode of resource use much before the Hada conquest. Therefore, they considered themselves to be the *bhumias* and had begun to claim the *ksatriya* status by 14th century.[33] Subjugation of Meena polity by the Hadas graphically described by Nainsi as "*bhumia sara kut maria*" (all the *bhumias* were annhiliated) wiped out their so called claim to *ksatriya* status and marginalised their position in the region.[34] The Hada conquest paved the way for new agricultural settlement by other castes and communities in the areas dominated by the Meenas so far. It does not mean that Meenas lost their hold on land completely. They continued to live in the region as peasant proprietors and were in a dominant position in scores of village of *pargana* Baran and to a lesser extent in *pargana* Nandgaon. Their representatives enjoyed pateli right and played an important role in the process of colonisation and expansion of area under cultivation.[35] In spite of these efforts to conciliate the Meenas, they could never be completely pacified by the Hadas.

The British administrators noted that the Meenas were "expert plunderers" and dacoity was their "pleasure and past time".[36] Tod on his journey from Bundi to Jehazpur, has observed about the Meenas of Khairad that, they were "for ages terror of the country" and "had studded the plains with cenotaphs of Haras fallen in defending their goods and chattels against their inroads".[37] He felt that, these conflicts with Meenas were an assertion of the axiom that " the right in the soil belongs to him who first cleared and tilled the land".[38] The Rajput conquerors "claimed and received tribute but if he tried to enforce more he was brought to his senses by various mode of self defense, incendiaries, or abandonment of the lands in a body".[39] Though, this observation was about the Meenas of Khairad but such methods of resistance were far more widespread a century ago. Even those who lived within Hadauti as peasant proprietors and patels tried to resist the process of marginalisation by challenging the Hada supremacy in various ways.

Kheeva Meena was notorious for his regular network of lifting cattle from the villages of *pargana* Digodh to be sold in the villages situated in the basin of river Parwan.[40] Raja Salim Singh, a powerful *thakur* of the area shielded his activity, and he had succeeded in gaining considerable assets and position in his own village. The support of a local *thakur* combined with the caste and genealogical ties had entrenched him to the extent of ignoring the order sent by the Kota chief warning him against theft. Ultimately, some of the local Hada *jagirdars* and *kotwal* of the *pargana* planned an operation against Kheeva Meena, in which he was killed and his assets were seised. The report which was sent by the *kotwal* shows that the village sympathy was clearly with Kheeva, although, outwardly they all expressed regrets for his activities. Therefore, the local officials recommended that a *pagh* (turban) should be sent for his brother along with a letter of reassurance for him and the villagers so that normal agricultural operations for the season could start. It was necessary to conciliate Kheeva's family and relatives. Kheeva's killers also deterred from arresting Kheeva's mother inspite of her raising an alarm to rally help for Kheeva at the time of attack. The attack on Kheeva had taken place in the middle of night just before dawn, but no one from the village dared to come out to help him, except one of Kheeva's brother-in-law, perhaps because they could foresee the futility of such an effort. However, they made no secret of their relations with Kheeva nor pretended to disown him. Many of them even claimed the goods confiscated from Kheeva's house on the pretext of having lent them to Kheeva. Since, there was no way to ascertain the truth, the officials sought orders from above. Laying claims genuine or motivated on the seized assets of Kheeva by the villagers was also a form of resistance, as it amounted to harassing the killers of Kheeva. They wanted to take advantage of a situation in which they could gain petty items without paying for them, for example the Malis of the village demanded two *kudals* and one *phavra* (agricultural implements) a Meena demanded his cattle, his brother demanded one of the cots, and an iron drum.[41] Thus, not only the Meenas of Khairad but even of Kota were involved in dacoity and plunder in 18th century. This involvement was not just as 'pleasure and past time', because Kheeva's episode shows that he had succeeded in developing a regular network for carrying out theft and dacoity, taking advantage of the contradictions between the local *thakurs*, as well as by rallying local support. It was an effort to develop some kind of local authority and power by gaining resources through theft and dacoity. However the Meenas could never go beyond 'banditry' (unlike the Bheels who rose in a riot) because of their stakes in the agrarian economy. They could not think of survival without agriculture and settled village life. Acceptance of the broad frame work of Hada polity by the majority was in order to maintain hold on the fertile land under their ploughs, and to retain the institutional means of access to agrarian resources in the form of pateli and *bhom*, inspite of suppressed political ambitions.[42] As a result the restlessness of a Meena's mind, at times posed a threat to the peace and order of an entire village. Meena Rewa of *mauza* Neewali was declared to be an *'oot'* (vagabound) and his possessions were seized which consisted of a cot, a cow, some food grains and *khurpa* and *dantli* etc.[43] It implied that the fellow had become a threat not only to the family and village also to the authorities, although he had not committed any offence, which was punishable. Therefore, to discredit him and to check the people from paying any attention to what he said or did was declared to be an *'oot'* which amounted to be branded as irresponsible and worthless. Thus, the Meenas whose majority was peasant proprietors and some of them even held pateli rights did not adopt any open and collective form of resistance against the state.

The case of the Bheels was different. They inhabited the hill range from Kota to Manohar Thana in Hadauti, although, the actual extent of Bheel area was far more beginning from the hills of Mewar to the hills spread upto Narmada river. They lived in scattered settlements known as *pal*. A Bheel considered himself to be the lord of a large area, which included the jungle around his small field, and the hill top where he had his hut. Several such areas occupied by Bheel households combined to make a '*phala*' and several such *phalas* combined to make a village known as '*pal*'. Each '*phala*' had a hereditary headman known as *phalvi*, while the headman of each '*pal*' was known as *Gameti*.[44] Thus a Bheel village had a different physiography. Instead of being a small cluster it was quite a spread out settlement. This difference was mainly due to the difference in the mode of resource utilisation between the Bheels and the other peasants. Even as late as 19th century the main forms of agriculture which majority of the Bheels practiced was '*walar*' or '*walra*'.[45] Some of the Bheels had taken up to full time cultivation in the low lands by 18th century. *Walar* consisted of "cutting down a patch of forest and burning the trees on ground in order to clear room for field which is mannered by ashes. After an year or two the soil is exhausted and another felling takes place".[46] They grew small crops for subsistence through *walar* field but depended largely on jungle produce for a living. The contrast between the Bheels and other peasants is embodied in a popular saying that, when a Bheel walks his eyes are fixed at a hill while a patel walks with his eyes upon the land under his feet.[47]

This mode of resources use was severely affected in process of development of settled agriculture on the fringes of Bheels dominated areas. The bloodshed accompanying this process is testified by the several commemoration stones of the Hada warriors who died fighting against the original inhabitants of the region, between 14th to 17th centuries, in the villages adjacent to the hill range dominated by the Bheels. These stones are still held in reverence by the village population suggesting that it was through such encounters that the land could be cleared of forests and used for agriculture. The Kota fort itself is situated at a sight, which was associated with the slaughter of Kotea Bheel. One of the main peasant communities who settled down in the Bheel dominated areas was Dhakars. A branch of Dhakars is still known as Malwa Dhakars, suggesting that they had migrated from Malwa towards these new areas.[48] Dhakar cultivators who were found not only in Hadauti but also in Mewar were akin to the Meenas according to Shyamal Das.[49] So these Dhakar peasants could have been those Meena groups who took up cultivation between 14th to 17th centuries on the land snatched from the Bheels. Significantly, the Meenas consider themselves to be superior to the Dhakars.[50]

Even after the repression which followed the killing of Kotea Bheel in 14th century, the Bheels of Khatakheri (Manohar Thana) had rallied in c. 1660 under the leadership of Chakrsen Bheel who was hounded by Bhagwant Singh and the Bheel fortress of Ekelgarh was captured, though, Chakrsen managed to escape.[51] Yet, the Bheels could not be completely subjugated. The areas where the Bheels continued to resist were Chechat, Awa, Suket, Kanwas, Ralaita, Bakaini and Durra. Barely after two decades, the Bheels were reported to be looting and even murdering the traders passing through Manoharpura ravines.[52] By c. 1727 dacoities by Bheels were reported not only from jungles but even from villages of *pargana* Awa. They dared to reach up to the inner ring of fields in some of the villages.[53] Some of the Bheels who were caught by the local Rajput *jagirdars* were made to give an undertaking against theft.[54] The political overtones behind such acts come out clearly from this undertaking. The Bheels vouched not to harm Hadauti or to nurture any will against it as if Hadauti was an alien political entity. They further stated that they would expect *'dad'* (justice) only if they rendered *' chakari'* (service) and in lieu of this service even if they were given handful of floor like alms, they would receive it with both hands stretched out. They would be content to live on leftover of horse feed from a stable, that too if they serve the people. They would consider the 'Maharao' (chief of Kota) to be the lord of their family and it would be up to him who is their *'data'* (the one who gives) to feed or to starve them. The undertaking ended with 'Long live the greatness of *Maharao'*.[55] The political overtones of Bheel resistance emerge clearly in this undertaking. First that they had neither, been able to accept Hadauti as a state, nor did they consider themselves to be the subjects with any kind of defined social status. The very tone of this undertaking was different from the petitions sent by various other sections of the population, which contained an appeal for justice against something which was considered to be a deviation or violation of the customary norms. There was always an underlying expectation that the state would uphold these norms and claims and would not to allow the situation to drift. Whereas in the undertaking given by the Bheels the tone was that of the people who had been vanquished and who had no claim to put forward nor any expectation to be nurtured.

The language was that of acceptance of anything and everything. Whether it was drafted for them by the officials or was their own statement it could not have been heart felt. It was a show they had decided to put up in order to survive a situation in which they had been caught. The whole ethos was to deceive the enemy, to gain time and to wait for an appropriate moment for challenging the enemy once again. The different stages of Bheel resistance also confirm that the Bheels had decided not to succumb. In late 17th century they looted only on the dense hilly forest routes, in early 18th century they dared to reach up to the villages of Hadauti but in the later half of 18th century they rose up in what was described as a *danga* (riot), in the records.[56]

The Hadas had tried to win over the Bheels by giving them land for cultivation in lieu of *chakri* of protecting '*rahbat*' and *khed-bahar*[57] (roads and halting points and village exteriors). A person rendering such *chakri* was known as *sasri*.[58] As a privilege, the wells sunk by Bheels on their fields were also granted to them,[59] but the Bheels could never be appeased. Their customary right to collect *chauki-ki-kaudi* (a customary realisation from the travellers passing through the Bheel areas) had also been upheld. Yet, at times they disallowed any traveller in the Durra (pass), even if an order to this effect had been issued by the Kota chief.[60] It was a common practice for a Bheel not to pay the cesses or levies, to indulge in thefts,[61] to give up service and to disappear in the forest.[62] Some of them who disappeared after living as agriculturist for a while, incited trouble in the villages which they had deserted. Some migrated towards a non-Hada territory, like Khinchiwada to trouble the village of Hada territory.[63] The climax of Bheel resistance was the *danga* in late 18th century. In c. 1790, the Bheels were up in arms against the Hadas at Ralaita.[64] This *danga* coincided with the policy of expansion of area under cultivation, pursued vigorously by Zalim Singh.

Resistance of the Bheels against the Hada state was directed against its policy of agricultural expansion, which deprived them of their natural habitat and mode of survival. It compelled them to resort to theft as a mode of subsistence on many occasions. However, disallowing travellers in the Durra, and the attacks on the security points were clearly a manifestation of their hostility to the Hada state. They were not resisting the heavy state demand or an oppressive state official but the very claim of the Hadas to rule over them. The state took a strong view of both the thefts committed by the Bheels as well as their repeated armed uprising against the Hada rule. To check the thefts the *thakurs* were asked to take strong steps to catch the Bheel and to hand over them to the village authorities. The undertaking given by *thakurs* to this effect were couched in language of physical assault of "breaking hands, legs and neck, of the Bheels".[65] To suppress the Bheel resistance troops of fifty gunmen were posted at several places, with instruction to call more from nearby security posts if required. Thus, the Bheels succeeded in combining their everyday resistance with open struggle against the Hadas on many occasions. The Bheel resistance shows that the state could never completely wipe out the divergent and conflicting value systems, which continued to survive and several such heroes and symbols who represented a different value system, continued to be revered and eulogised.

Conclusion

Thus, the people resisted high-handedness and transgression of authority in various ways and the state found itself increasingly answerable to resolve the issues confronting the people. However, the forms of protest except in the case of Bheels hardly questioned the basis of state power. Most of the time forms of resistance adopted by settled peasants and artisans were non-violent with an underlying hope of getting justice. The methods and ways of cheating the system, as survival strategy show beyond doubt that it was not easy to survive and the system was certainly questionable but individual solutions were practised instead of non-compliance. But it would not be fair to think that everything or anything was acceptable as is clear from the threatened or real migrations. The state was by and large able to check discontentment and anger by making timely intervention and necessary adjustments.

Notes

1. H. Mukhia, "Was There Feudalism in Indian History", *Perspectives on Medieval History*, New Delhi, 1994, p. 123.
2. Mukhia thinks that these features of historical change have been relegated to secondary significance and only the dramatic uprisings have been taken note of. "Peasants Production and Medieval Indian Society", *Perspectives on Medieval History*, op. cit., pp. 152–84.
3. For a discussion of these aspects, see, James Scott, *Weapons of the Weak*, Delhi, 1990.
4. *Likhant* of patel patwari *mauza* Dhapa (undated) s. 1788, Kota Bhandar no. (hereafter K.B.) 1/126.
5. *Adhsatta, mauza* Babli and *mauza* Budana contains such undertakings by the patel and patwari, s. 1784, K.B. 1/121–33.

6. Petition sent by some Dhakar peasants of *mauza* Badoli, (undated) s. 1840, K.B 3/3.
7. *Toji Kotwali Chautra shahar* Kota, K.B. 1/19, considering the consequences of such violence, the state imposed a fine of rupees 22 on the patel.
8. *Pargana* Barod *ki Firohi*, op. cit.
9. Narsingh Das to Zalim Singh, Magh sudi 7, s. 1837, K.B 7/1.
10. Ibid.
11. *Saha* Bihari and others to *Chaudhary* Hargovind, Jeth vadi 11, s. 1771, *Jama Mahusuli mauza* Digodh,, K.B. 1/276, Kota.
12. *Araz* of Dhakar peasants of *mauza* Badoli, op. cit.
13. *Likhant* patel patwari,*karsa* of *mauza* Khabula, Jeth sudi 3, s. 1852, *Toji Parwana*, K.B. 21/1.
14. *Likhant* of patel Khambha, Aghan sudi 8, s. 1766, K.B. 1/66 and of patel Rupa, Jeth sudi 13, s. 1762, K.B. 1/61.
15. *Firohi hasil* of *mauza* Dungarjya, Jeth sudi 6, s. 1762, K.B. 1–61.
16. *Firohi hasil* of *mauza* Digodh, s. 1762, K.B. 1/61.
17. *Likhant* of patel patwari of Borina, Magh vadi 2 s.1784, K.B.1/121–133; note of patel patwari of Rajpura Asadh sudi 15, s. 1798, K.B. 1/135.
18. *Roznamcha Phagun ki tapni ka,* s. 1771, K.B. 1/276 (Kota).
19. Ibid.
20. J. Tod, *Annals and Antiquities*, Vol. II, New Delhi, 1978 p. 434.
21. *Firohi hasil*, s. 1766, K.B. 1/66; *Likhant* of patel Deva of *mauza* Gandhipali, Asadh vadi 7, s. 1767, K.B. 1/67.
22. *Toji kotwali chautra shahar* Kota, s. 1752, K.B. 1/19.
23. *Toji kotwali chautra shahar* Rampura, s. 1827, K.B. 15/1.
24. *Toji shahar* Kota, op. cit.
25. Ibid.
26. *Likhant* of *Pandit* Teela, Jeth sudi 7, s. 1789, K.B. 1/127; a *sahna* was posted in the village to guard the standing crops in order to ensure that peasants did not cheat the state by stealing the grains before *lata*.
27. Durjan Sal to *hawalgir* of Digodh, Asadh vadi 7, s. 1787, K.B. 1/124.
28. Umed Singh to *nais* of *kasba* Baran, Chait vadi 4, s. 1846, K.B. 3/3.
29. Durjan Sal to patel of *mauza* Sanija Bawri, Asadh sudi 9, s. 1808, K.B. 1/135.
30. Bheem Singh to *hawalgir* of *mauza* Digodh and patel Lakha, Asadh vedi 10, s. 1771, K.B 1/276 (Kota).
31. *Likhant* of patel Pura of *mauza* Gugalhedi, Asadh sudi 4, s. 1761, K.B. 1/47.
32. *Likhant* of patel, patwari of *mauza* Kurahad, Aghan vadi 5, s. 1766, K.B. 1/66.
33. Madhu Tandon Sethia, *Rajput Polity*, Jaipur, 2002, pp. 178–229 for detailed discussion.
34. Nainsi, *Khyat,* Vol. I, ed. N.S. Bhatti, Jodhpur, 1974, p. 100.
35. Bheem Singh to patel of *mauza* Barohalya for conferring pateli 10 *biswas* on Tara meena of Sadhalya *gotra*, Jeth vadi 9, s. 1766, K.B. 1/61; *Khate-pargana* Barsanaa *ka Agor ke hawala ka,* K.B. 3 contain many orders for conferring pateli on meenas.

36. *Imperial Gazetteer of India,* 1908 Provincial Series, Rajputana, pp. 288–89 and 372.
37. J. Tod, II, op. cit. pp. 539–40.
38. Ibid.
39. Ibid.
40. The report sent by *Pandit* Binayag Ram and *Kotwal* Akhram to *Khawas* Sri Ramji and *Chaudhary* Hargovind, Phagun vadi 9, s. 1782, K.B. 1/115.
41. Ibid.
42. The political ambition of Meenas was reflected in their love for *pol,* (a massive entrance gate of a fort or palace) and horse, considered to be symbol of power and prestige.
43. *Pargana* Barod *ka Chautra ki Firohi,* s. 1760–62, K.B. 1/37.
44. Shyamal Das, *Veer Vinod,* I, Delhi, 1986, p. 191.
45. *Imperial Gazeteer,* op. cit., p. 43.
46. Ibid.
47. Interview, D.C. Meena from Baran district, General Secretary of Rajasthan unit of All India Kisan Sabha.
48. Interview, D.C. Meena.
49. *Veer Vinod,* I, op. cit.
50. Interview, D.C. Meena.
51. *Khyat* I, op. cit p. 103, *A A R* II, op. cit., p. 411.
52. *Likhant* of *Cheepa* Kisna's wife and son, Chait sudi 3, s. 1755, K.B. 1/30.
53. *Likhant* of *Bhai* Nawal Singh, Baisakh sudi 4, s. 1784, of Raja Hari Singh, Baisakh vadi 7, s. 1784, K.B. 1/121–133.
54. *Likhant* of *Rawat* Ajbo, Bapa and Gaga Bheel, Baisakh vadi 14, s. 1784, K.B. 1/121–133.
55. Ibid.
56. Zalim Sing to *Paswan* Kesho Rai, Bhadva sudi 15, s. 1847, K.B. 1/68.
57. Umed Singh to Bheel Jassa, Sawan sudi 15, s. 1845, K.B. 3/2.
58. Umed Singh to patel patwari of *kasba* Digodh, Bhadva sudi 15, s. 1845, K.B. 3; Bheels were often appointed as *sasri,* see, Durjan Sal to *hawalgir* of *pargana* Ghati, Jeth sudi 12, s. 1799, K.B. 1/135.
59. Umed Singh's order to patel patwari *kasba* Digodh, op. cit.
60. Umed Singh to *hawalgir* of Bakaini *ka talaka,* Asadh sudi 9, s. 1846, K.B. 3/2.
61. Umed Singh to Bheel Cheetarya, Phagun vadi 7, s. 1845, K.B. 3/2.
62. Umed Singh to Rav Nadya Ram, Jeth sudi 5, s. 1845, it warned him to disappear in Jhamra forest valley when called for service in *faujfata,* K.B. 3/1.
63. Umed Singh to Cholya Bheel's son, Sawan vadi 6, s. 1846, K.B. 3/2; *Araz pargana Suket ki* s. 1840, K.B. 3/1, stated that Bheel Sama had 200 *beeghas* of land as *sasri* but pays not even a *kaudi* and incites thefts.
64. Zalim Singh to *Paswan* Keso Rai, op. cit.
65. *Likhant* of *Bhai* Nawal Singh and Raja Hari Singh, op. cit.

Section II

Culture and Tradition

9

Six Incarnations of Mirabai

Frances Taft

This brief contribution should be read together with my earlier essay on the historical Mirabai (Taft, 2002). I was drawn to the subject originally because it seemed to me that recent writers from other fields were failing to recognise that historians around the turn of the 19th century had provided us with a basic framework for the historical Mirabai. At this point I would like to note recent work from the *bhakti* side that provides important evidence for the historical Mirabai. I will also provide an update on my efforts to address unresolved questions concerning the sources used by Shyamal Das, one of the early historians, in his monumental history of Mewar, *Vir Vinod*.

Six Incarnations

It is truly astonishing that a woman who lived in the first half of 16th century and was largely obscure in her own times has become almost a household name in early 21st century India. She is now known to us in many overlapping, and contradictory incarnations, of which I will cite six here: the *bhakti* Mira, the literary Mira, the media Mira; the socio-political protest Mira, Gandhi's ideal Hindu wife Mira, and my own particular interest, the historical Mira. I mention these because although they are far from exhaustive, they serve to illustrate how wide are the interests and concerns of those who invoke her name.

Bhakti Mira is too broad a topic to more than allude to here; suffice it to say that *bhakti* Mira herself is not one but many, a splintering that reflects, among other things, complicated and bitter sectarian disputes among devotees over the centuries. The importance of literary Mira is undisputed: there is no history of Hindi literature that does not mention her *padavali*. Media Mira is of course a modern phenomenon. The Indian film industry has produced no fewer than ten movies about Mira, while comparable male saints have together rated only three or four (Hawley, 2005: 117). There are tape cassettes and CDs. And there is the Amar Chitra Katha *Mirabai* comic, originally published in 1972, which states plainly that "the story of Mira, as narrated in this book, is based on legends about her and not on historical facts". We owe to Jack Hawley a fascinating account identifying which elements of the legends were selected, and why, and how they were manipulated in response to a number of pressures (Hawley, 2005).

Both Parita Mukta and Nancy Martin have published examples of the appropriation of Mira's name and story by lower caste groups for purposes of social and political protest. On the face of it, this is perhaps surprising, but Mira has been associated with rejection of social and family pieties since at least Nabha Das's *Bhaktmal* of early 17th century, and this theme is abundantly evident in the verses of her *padavali*. It would be interesting to know how far back it is possible to trace this sort of use of Mira.

The case of Gandhi, as documented by Mukta (1997: 182–220), is stranger yet. Although Gandhi knew a few of Mira's *bhajans* from his South African days, he evidently did not know much about her story. She appealed to him for what he understood to be her defiance of authority in pursuit of what she believed to be right, and her adoption of a simple life, but at the same time he saw her as a model Hindu wife who never forsook her duty to reconcile her husband ('the Rana') to love for Krishna, and by extension as a foremost *satyagrahi*. In pursuit of his vision he did not hesitate to take liberties with her *pads*, and in what Mukta regards as one of his greatest travesties expunged Mira's rejection of her widowhood from one of her well-known songs (Mukta, 1997: 191).

I come finally to the historical Mira, and I want to turn first to some recent scholarship that adds significantly to our historical understanding.

New Insights from Bhakti Sources

New insights from *bhakti* sources contemporary and near-contemporary to Mira have become available through the work of Heidi Pauwels (forthcoming). Interestingly, they concern not only Mira herself but also her cousin-brother Rao Jaimal Viramdevot of Merta. The Mertiya rulers were well known as Vaishnava devotees. Rao Duda Jodhavat (1440–1497), the founder of the Mertiya lineage, built a temple to Chaturbhuj in Merta that still stands, and to this day the Mertiyas regard Chaturbhuj as their particular deity. Although it is not widely realised, Rao Jaimal also appears in the *bhakti* sources as a devotee and the author of *pads*.

There are references to Mira and to Rao Jaimal, both grand-children of Rao Duda Jodhavat, in verses of Hariram Vyas of Orccha, a contemporary of both Mira and Rao Jaimal. Hariram was a Vaishnava devotee who settled in Vrindavan. In verses likely composed in the 1570s or 1580s, Hariram, who had a long life, laments the passing of a number of his contemporaries. Included are linked references to Mirabai and to Jaimal, "for whom God-interest was self-interest". This was likely a reference to a Mertiya tradition concerning the confrontation between the Mertiyas and a force of Rao Maldev of Jodhpur in 1554, from which Rao Jaimal emerged victorious (see Saran and Ziegler, 2001: 171).[1] From the sense of the verses, it is not impossible that Hariram met Mira in Vrindavan, and perhaps Jaimal as well.

Both Mira and Rao Jaimal were among the devotees mentioned by Nabha Das in his well-known *Bhaktmal* of c.1600. Nabha Das remembered Jaimal as an exemplary devotee and a ruler who respected *bhaktas*, saying that he supported *bhaktas* in Merta[2] extremely well. In another *chappaya* (stanza) of his *Bhaktmal*, on the theme of how the Lord is true to his *bhaktas* in all ages, in a reference to the same tradition that Hariram Vyas knew, Nabha Das related that in battle the Lord mounted Jaimal's horse and personally rode to assist him.

There is also a further reference to Mira in Nabha Das's *Bhaktmal*. The verse (Chappaya, 145) is about a dancer Narayan Das, a devotee, who in performance danced to a "famous song in which love is (declared) a strong bond" which included the phrase "dyed in Krishna's passion"; the reference is undoubtedly to one of Mira's *pads*.

Tracking the Sources

> It is written in Mewar, by the Mertiyas, and in the Jodhpur histories that Miranbai was the rani of Bhojraj (VV2: 2 fn. 2.4).

Shyamal Das was particularly interested in Mira's identity and that of her husband because Tod had written in his *Annals* that she was the wife of Rana Kumbha, and on chronological grounds Shyamal Das knew that this was not correct. I therefore set out to see what I could discover about sources on which Shyamal Das might have based his statement. The results are not quite what I expected.

Vamshavalis and Khyats: I looked first at the genealogical *(vamshavali)* and chronicle (*khyat*) sources for Jodhpur, the Mertiyas, and Mewar. A *khyat* usually generally has broader scope than a *vamshavali*, relating the important events of successive reigns. However, these distinctions are not hard and fast, and the terms are used somewhat arbitrarily and interchangeably. *Vamshavalis* often include historical notes, and *khyats* invariably contain genealogical information. New information could be added to earlier compilations or, drawing on existing material, a new document could be created *de novo*. *Vamshavalis* and *khyats* appear to have been compiled, by Bhats, Charans, Brahmins, and even Jains, for every generation of Rajputs who ruled states and estates since at least the 17th century.

Jodhpur: In Jodhpur, a number of *khyats* compiled before the Mughal interregnum of 1680–1707 have been preserved and have come down to us. There is no systematic Jodhpur or Mertiya genealogy in Nainsi's *Khyat*; these are available instead in *Rao Udaybhan Champavat ri Khyat*, a 17th century Jodhpur *khyat* that has been preserved. This *khyat* is an extensive Rathor genealogy compiled between 1643 and 1678 that provides information on all of the brothers and sons of Rao Jodha of Jodhpur and their descendants, which of course includes the Mertiyas.[3] The information in this *khyat* on Rao Jodha himself and his descendants who ruled Jodhpur is quite detailed; that concerning collateral and other descendant much less so. There is no mention of daughters or their marriages for any of the Mertiyas.

It seems likely that when he spoke of "written in the Jodhpur histories" Shyamal Das had in mind the Mewar section of Nainsi's *Khyat*. Nainsi's *Khyat* is probably unique in that although Nainsi himself was from Jodhpur and was a senior official of the Jodhpur *darbar*, the *khyat* that he compiled includes material on many of the Rajput kingdoms and clans. The mention of Mira occurs in the list of the sons of Rana Sanga; the text reads "Bhojraj—it is said that Rathor Miranbai was married to him" (NK1: 21). It is not unreasonable to read this line as a comment attached to the name of Bhoj Raj by the compiler of the *khyat*. However, there is a textual complication.[4] Almost all of the *vamshavali* and *khyat* manuscripts that have been preserved exist in a single version. In the case of Nainsi's *Khyat*, there are a good number of manuscripts to be found in various libraries and research institutions in Rajasthan. However, they can all be traced back to a single manuscript in the Anup Sanskrit Library in Bikaner, which was copied from an earlier manuscript in 1843 that cannot now be traced (Ranawat, 1987: 5). It is not unlikely that the 17th century compiler of the *khyat* added the comment about Mira; but it is perhaps equally possible that the comment was inserted by the 19th century copyist.

There is mention of Mira as the daughter of Ratan Singh Dudavat and rani of Bhoj Raj, son of Rana Sanga of Mewar, in a document included in the published text of Nainsi's *Vigat* by the editor as Annex 4. However, this document is not contemporary with the *Vigat;* internal evidence indicates that it was compiled after 1832 (NV2: 469).

Merta: The Mertiya[5] lineage to which Mira was born goes back to her paternal grandfather Rao Duda Jodhavat, who in 1495 became ruler of Merta, a town and area roughly midway between Nagor and Ajmer. There is a Mertiya *khyat (Mertiya Khamp Khulasa)* now in the Rajasthan State Archives that lists Ratan Singh as a son of Viramdev and says his daughter Mira was married to Rana Bhojraj of Udaipur. However, this *khyat* dates from the late 19th or early 20th century and was probably compiled after Shyamal Das's time.

Mertiya *thikana* sources are of much more interest. There is no doubt that Badnor,[6] the senior Mertiya thikana in Mewar, had extensive records. Thakur Gopal Singh of Badnor published a history of his Mertiya lineage in 1932 (Gopal, 1932) which he titled *Jaimal Vamsh Prakash* in commemoration of his most famous ancestor, the Rao Jaimal mentioned in Heidi Pauwels' *bhakti* sources, who died heroically in the Mughal seige of Chittor in 1568. He lists "old manuscript *khyats* and *khyats* of the Barwas, Rani-Mangas and Kul-gurus, etc." (JVP1: vii) as among the sources he consulted, and when he gives genealogical information for Rao Duda Jodhavat, Mira's paternal grandfather, and for Rao Viramdev Dudavat, her paternal uncle, he specifically cites "the *khyats* of our Bhats and Rani-Mangas (Bhats who recorded the genealogies of the women of the family)" (JVP 1: 71; 106).

In the process of gathering materials for *Vir Vinod*, Shyamal Das was in touch with all of the Mewar *thikanedars*, including Thakur Kesri Singh, Gopal Singh's grandfather, as well as the *thakur* of Rupaheli, an early 18th century offshoot of Badnor, and in all likelihood asked both of them about Mertiya records of Mira. Is this perhaps what Shyamal Das meant by "written by the Mertiyas"?

Mewar: We have at least two Mewar *khyats* that date from the second half of the 17th century,[7] a number from the 18th century, and even more from the 19th century.[8] It is clear that successive maharanas ordered new compilations—for the six Mewar maharanas who ruled from 1778 to 1884, for example, we have *khyats* compiled in each reign. All of these sources mention Bhoj Raj as a son of Rana Sanga, and most of them include the information that he predeceased his father.

However, none of the 17th or 18th century *khyats* includes Mira. The earliest Mewar *khyat* that I have been able to trace that mentions Mira as the rani of Bhoj Raj, son of Rana Sanga, was compiled during or after the reign of Maharana Javan Singh (d. 1838).[9] A second Mewar *khyat* from the first half of the 19th century that mentions Mira was completed in 1853.[10] She is mentioned as the rani of Bhoj Raj in later 19th century *khyats* as well.

The Bottom Line: In sum, although my search has hardly been exhaustive, I was able to locate *vamshavali* and *khyat* sources for Jodhpur, Mewar, and the Mertiyas mentioning Mira as the wife of Bhoj Raj, son of Rana Sanga of Mewar, that would have been available to Shyamal Das when he compiled *Vir Vinod* in the 1880s (Shyamal, 1886). The dates of these sources, however, are another story. Since Nainsi's *Khyat* dates from about the middle of the 17th century, I had hoped to find mention of Mira in 17th century Mewar *khyats* as well. As noted above, the Mewar *khyats* I consulted list Bhoj Raj as the son of Rana Sanga, but with the possible exception of the Mewar portion of Nainsi's *Khyat* there are no mentions of Mira until the first half of the 19th century. Then we find her in Mewar *khyats*, a Jodhpur *darbar* document from after 1832, and the Bikaner copy of Nainsi's *Khyat* from 1843. Tod must have collected his information, including his reference to Mira, before he left India in 1822. This raises an obvious question: why is 16th century Mira first mentioned in Mewar and probably Jodhpur sources from the first half of the 19th century? It should be noted that Jack Hawley, writing from the *bhakti* side about Mira's *pads*, also concluded that "Mira's efflorescence would seem best dated to the 19th century" (Hawley, 2005: 118).

In sum, while we cannot identify Shyamal Das's sources precisely, he clearly made an effort to find out what information was available, and his conclusions are reflected in what he wrote in *Vir Vinod*: Mira was the daughter of Mertiya Ratan Singh Dudavat and was married to Bhojraj, the son of Rana Sanga of Chittor.

'Life and Times'

If we are limited in what we can say about the life of the historical Mirabai, we do know a good deal about her time—about the Rajput world she lived in and the complicated politics of Merta and Mewar in the first part of the 16th century. Mira would have been married quite young, perhaps when she was not more than about 13 or even younger (Taft, 2002: 325–27). The marriage, as with all such elite Rajput marriages, was a political alliance. Mewar was the dominant Rajput kingdom at the time. The ruler of Merta, Rao Viramdev Dudavat, Mira's paternal uncle, had married a sister of Rana Sanga, and the marriage of a Merta daughter to Rana Sanga's heir offered a means to strengthen Merta's links to Mewar and the advantageous prospect of Merta influence in the Mewar royal establishment in the years to come.

The political situation was complicated and treacherous. There were (Muslim) centres of power in Gujarat, Malwa, and Delhi. However, the Rathors of Jodhpur, who had dominated the Chittor Sisodiyas in the previous century, did not pose a threat at this point, and Rana Sanga was largely successful in expanding his power and influence. In the years following the marriage, which took place around 1516, the involvement of Rao Viramdev in the affairs of Mewar appears to have increased. We know that in 1519 he joined Rana Sanga in a successful attack against the forces of Sultan Mahmud Khalji of Malwa, which had taken control of the fort of Gagraun (modern-day Jhalawar district) from an ally of the rana. In 1520, both Rao Viramdev and Rao Ganga Rathor, ruler of Jodhpur, joined Rana Sanga in support of the raja of Idar (in Gujarat), who had been driven from Idar by the forces of Sultan Muzaffar Shah of Gujarat. And in 1527 Rao Viramdev and several of his sons answered the call from Rana Sanga and joined a Rajput confederation seeking to halt the advance of the Mughal invader Babur.

Rana Sanga's large *zanana*—he had some 28 ranis, a surprising number even for a Rajput ruler—can be understood as a form of conspicuous consumption on the part of the most powerful Rajput raja of the time. At the time of Mira's marriage, the dominant figure in the Chittor *zanana* was likely Rana Sanga's mother, a Jhali identified in *bhakti* sources as a devotee who travelled to Benares to take initiation from the untouchable guru Ravidas (Hawley and Juergensmeyer 1988: 13–14). It is known that the ruling Mertiya family were devoted Vaishnavas, and both Rajasthan and Vaishnava traditions portray the young Mira as particularly devout.

For the child-bride, probably the privileged first wife of the heir, life in the Chittor *zanana* was most likely pleasant. But then fate struck her a series of terrible blows. The first and most devastating was the death of her young husband, leaving her a young childless widow and turning her status in the *zanana* upside down. At some point her likely patron, the Jhali rani who was Rana Sanga's mother, must have gone as well. Then followed the defeat of her father-in-law Rana Sanga at the great battle against Babur at Khanua in 1527, the deaths of her father and one of his brothers in the battle, and the subsequent death of Rana Sanga in the following year. Rana Sanga was succeeded by his eldest surviving son, Rana Ratan Singh, whose mother was from the ruling Rathor family of Jodhpur, and by this time the Mertiyas and the Jodhpur Rathors were on bad terms. It is obvious from her *pads* that Mira was persecuted by one of her brothers-in-law; although Ratan Singh's half-brother and successor Rana Vikramaditya is usually named, the chronology suggests that it was Ratan Singh.[11]

It is perhaps not surprising that the young widow whose family were devout Vaishnavas and who was herself pious from childhood should turn to her lord Krishna Giridhar in her bereavement and reduced circumstances. But her path was different from that of so many other Rajput widows. We know her today in her various modern incarnations because in her own time she had the courage to defy her in-laws, ignore social disapproval, associate with other devotees of whatever origin, leave Chittor, and dedicate the rest of her life to singing the praise of her lord Giridhar and her devotion to him.

Acknowledgements

My grateful thanks are owed to the many colleagues who have continued to contribute to my efforts to expand our understanding of the historical Mirabai; errors, of course, remain my own. I would particularly like to acknowledge the assistance of Shri Indu Shekhar Sharma of Jaipur, without whom it would not have been possible to carry this work forward. Richard Saran of the University of Michigan has continued over many years to share his great knowledge of all things related to the history of Rajasthan and to provide invaluable bibliographic assistance.

Notes

1. There were a number of encounters between Rao Maldev and the Mertiyas; why is this particular one associated with divine intervention in Mertiya tradition? Richard Saran has suggested to me that the explanation is that the Mertiyas were not expected to win—Rao Maldev's forces were stronger than those of the Mertiyas. When something unexpected occurs, look for divine involvement.

2. This reference to Merta conclusively identifies the Jaimal whom Hariram Vyas linked with Mira, and it also provides one more piece of evidence, if that is necessary, for the identification of Mira herself as a Mertiya.
3. The story of the preservation of *Rao Udaybhan Champavat ri Khyat* is dramatic: when Mughal forces invaded Jodhpur in 1680, the compilers of the *khyat* obviously feared for its preservation and walled it up in their house, where it remained forgotten until the late 19th century. The original manuscript and a copy made at the time of its discovery are preserved in the Shri Natnagar Shodh-Sansthan at Sitamau (MP). A copy of a typescript prepared at Sitamau for Vol. I (genealogies of the Rinmalots excluding Rao Jodha) and edited by Raghubir Sinh is available in the US through Inter-Library Loan; Vol. II (Rao Jodha Rinmalot and his descendants), edited by Richard Saran, is forthcoming. A Hindi translation of part of the original made in the 19th century is available at the Rajasthan Prachyavidya Pratishthan (RORI) in Jodhpur (ms. no. 15672). The translator has made certain additions that can be identified only by comparison with the original text.
4. I am grateful to Jack Hawley for first raising with me the question of the text of Nainsi's *Khyat*.
5. The Mertiya lineage is referred to by the name of the town and area ruled by the lineage, Merta. This is unusual; most lineages are referred to by the name of a distinguished forebear. In Mira's time Merta was in effect an independent entity. In 1562 it came into Mughal hands and later became part of Jodhpur state.
6. The *thikana* of Badnor was first granted to Rao Jaimal by Rana Udai Singh of Mewar after Rao Maldev of Jodhpur drove Jaimal from Merta in 1557 and Jaimal sought refuge with the Rana. After Jaimal's death at Chittor in 1568, one of his younger sons retained Badnor. Jaimal's chosen successor and other Mertiyas were able to obtain Merta as a *jagir* from the Mughal Emperor Akbar but lost it to the Jodhpur ruler early in the 17th century, Merta in effect becoming a part of the Jodhpur state. With the end of Mertiya control of Merta, Badnor in Mewar became the leading Mertiya holding.
7. *Suryavamsh* (RORI ms. no. 2637), first compiled in the reign of Maharana Raj Singh (d. 1680), was subsequently continued in other hands, the last additions carrying it to the reign of Maharana Hammir Singh (d. 1778). *Raval Ranaji ri Vat* (RORI ms. no. 2685) was compiled in the reign of Maharana Jai Singh (d. 1698).
8. Most of these manuscripts are currently located in the Rajasthan Prachyavidya Pratishthan (RORI), Udaipur. Others are in private hands.
9. Doc. No. 95, Kaviraj Collection, Rajasthan State Archives, Bikaner.
10. *Barva Gyana ri Pothi*, in the personal collection of Dr Rajendranath Purohit, grandson of Mewar Rajpurohit Swami Devnath Purohit. This *khyat* was compiled at the command of Maharana Swarup Singh and finished in VS 1910 (1853 A.D.). See Devilal Paliwal's introduction to the *Khyat* of Barwa Devi Dan.
11. At the time Ratan Singh succeeded his father Rana Sanga after the latter's death in 1528, Vikramaditya was about 10 years old. See Ojha's *Udaipur Rajya ka Itihas* 1: 401.

Abbreviations

JVP *Jaimal Vamsh Prakash* of Gopal Singh
MJC *Mirabai ka Jivancharitra* of Munshi Devi Prasad
NK Nainsi, *Khyat*
NV Nainsi, *Vigat*
VV *Vir Vinod* of Shyamal Das

References

Devi Dan, Barwa (1985) *Mevar ke Rajaon ki Raniyon, Kunvaron aur Kunvarion ki Hal,* (ed.) Devilal Paliwal, Udaipur: Sahitya Sansthan, Rajasthan Vidhyapith.

Devi Prasad, Munshi (1954) *Miranbai ka Jivancharitra*, 2nd ed., Calcutta: Bangiya Hindi Parishad (first published 1898).

Hawley, John (2005) *Three Bhakti Voices*, Delhi: Oxford University Press.

Hawley, John Stratton and Mark Juergensmeyer (1988) *Songs of the Saints of India,* New York: Oxford University Press.

Martin, Nancy (1999) "Mira Janma Patri: A Tale of Resistance and Appropriation" in *Religion, Ritual and Royalty*, (ed.) N.K. Singhi and Rajendra Joshi, Jaipur: Rawat Publications.

Mukta, Parita (1997) *Upholding the Common Life*, Delhi: Oxford University Press (first published 1994).

Nainsi, Munhata (1960–67) *Nainsi ri Khyat,* 4 vols. (ed.) B. Sakariya, Jodhpur: Rajasthan Oriental Research Institute.

——. (1968) Nainsi ra Parganan ri Vigat. 2 vols. (ed.) N.S. Bhati, Jodhpur: Rajasthan Oriental Research Institute.

Ojha, Gaurishankar, (1928) *Udaipur Rayja ka Itihas*, 2nd ed., Jodhpur: Rajasthani Granthagar (first published, 1928).

Pauwels, Heidi (forthcoming) "Rathauri Mira: Two Neglected Rathaur Connections of Mira: Jaimal Mertiyo and Nagridas" in *Mirabai: Hindu Saint for a Global World* (ed.) Nancy Martin.

Ranawat, M.S. (1987) *Muhnot Nainsi ki Khyat*, Sitamau: Shri Natnagar Shodh-Sansthan.

Saran, Richard D. and Norman P. Ziegler (2001) *The Mertiyo Rathors of Merta, Rajasthan: Select Translations Bearing on the History of a Rajput Family, 1462–1660,* 2 vols. Ann Arbor: University of Michigan Press.

Shyamal Das (1886), *Vir Vinod*, Udaipur: privately published, 1893.

Singh, Chatur (1902), *Chaturkul Charitra*, 2 vols. Nasirabad: privately published.

Singh, Gopal (1932), *Jaimal Vamsh Prakash*, 2 vols. Ajmer: Vedic Yantralaya Press, 1974.

Taft, Frances (2002) "The Elusive Historical Mirabai: A Note" in *Multiple Histories: Culture and Society in the Study of Rajasthan* (ed.) Lawrence A. Babb et al., Jaipur: Rawat Publications.

10

Is the *Dhola-Maru ra duha* Only a Poetic Composition?

Aleksandra Szyszko

One of the earliest forms of Rajasthani literature was developed in the region of Marwar. Dingal—a literary form of Marwari dialect is one of the oldest new Indo-Aryan literary languages.[1] The contribution of Rajasthani works, e.g., rasp poems, to the rise of the Hindi literary tradition is well known though this subject still requires a serious research. Apart from the literary activity of charans in the medieval Rajasthan, poems based on local folktales were also composed, very often by Jain poets. Here I would like to discuss one such poem, which originates from a folktale popular in the medieval Marwar—the *Dhola-Maru ra duha.*

Although written versions of the Dhola-Maru are available only from the 16th century (e.g., the most famous version of the poem composed by the Jain poet Kushallabh is dated 1561),[2] according to Hazari Prasad Dvivedi, the oral transmission of this story dates back to the 11th or 12th century.[3]

The Dhola-Maru belongs to the rich tradition of Rajasthani love-stories. It is very probable that in the beginning the story was popular in a form of *muktaka*, i.e., a short, independent verse, which was transmitted orally.[4] Later, as the story gained popularity with the passage of time, poems narrating the love of Dhola and Maru were composed in Rajasthani courts according to the rules of *prabandha kavya* style.

In the following text I will try to show that the poem *Dhola-Maru* can be treated not only as a poetic composition but as a source of information about medieval Rajasthan, as well. The *Dhola-Maru* is rich of Rajasthani folk motifs and an analysis of the leading characters of the poem can be contributive to better understanding of interrelations among people from different regions of medieval Rajasthan. But before we proceed further, let us summarise the outline of the story.[5]

Once upon a time, the Pugal kingdom faced a severe famine. The king of Pugal—Raja Pingal—had to leave his country with his family. Looking for shelter, he arrived in the Narvar kingdom, which was ruled by Raja Nal. The king Nal gave his guests a warm welcome. Raja Pingal had a daughter, Maru (also known as Marvani), and the king Nal had a son—a three-year-old Dhola. The two royal families decided to arrange a marriage of their children. Both sides gladly accepted the proposal, and the wedding of Dhola and Maru was duly organised. After some time, when the period of drought was over in Pugal, Pingal returned to his kingdom. As Maru was still a child—she was only one and a half years old—Pingal did not leave his daughter with her husband and in-laws, but took her back to Pugal.

The years passed by and Maru became a young and a beautiful woman. One night she saw her husband in a dream and began to long for him. Day by day Maru suffered more and more due to her separation from her beloved. But she did not know that Dhola's father had decided not to reveal to him the fact of his marriage with Maru. Thus Dhola, unaware of the fact that he had been married in his childhood, married another charming princess—Malvani from the Malva kingdom—and was spending his time happily with her. In the meantime, messages from Pugal kingdom were being sent, requesting that Dhola should come to Pugal to take his wife Maru with him. There was no response because the second wife of Dhola, the princess Malvani, knew about his previous marriage. She did not want him to be re-united with Maru; therefore, she ordered that every messenger from Pugal sent to Narvar should be killed.

One day, horse traders visited Pugal and told Raja Pingal the news about the second marriage of prince Dhola. A decision was made to send a group of Dhadhis (*dhadhi*), i.e., a wandering caste of beggar-singers, to Narvar kingdom to deliver the message of Dhola's child-marriage with Maru. The Dhadhis were able to enter Narvar as messengers of Maru unrecognised by the guards put by the second wife of Dhola and at night they approached Dhola's palace and under pretence of singing a song, they passed on a message from Maru to Dhola. After listening to the heart-rending song all night, the prince summoned the Dhadhis and inquired about the details of the story. Thus, he came to know about his childhood bride. Moved by the description of Maru's beauty, he desired to meet her and announced that he would soon visit Pugal and bring Maru to Narvar.

The second wife of Dhola did not let him go. Using various pretexts to stop her husband from leaving, Malvani managed to delay Dhola's journey. She forced him to stay at home during the summer and monsoon seasons. She persuaded him to stay until Dussehra, but Dhola finally put his foot down and began making arrangements for his trip to Pugal. Malvani frustrated, requested Dhola's camel not to take her beloved to a foreign country. She asked the camel to become lame. Finally, Malvani forced Dhola to keep a promise that he would not depart until she fell asleep. The princess did not sleep for 15 days but eventually she closed her eyes and fell asleep. Then Dhola mounted his wonderful, super fast camel, which could even speak, and set off for Pugal. As he left Narvar, the camel roared. Malvani heard the sound and woke up but it was too late to stop Dhola. Once again she tried to make him return by sending a parrot, which was to tell Dhola that Malvani, unable to bear the separation from her beloved husband, had died and he should go back home immediately. However, Dhola guessed that it was not true.

He continued his journey experiencing several adventures on the way. The prince stopped for a while when he crossed the Aravali hills. His next stop was in Pushkar. There he gave water to his camel and went on. Later on, he met on his way a charan of Umar Sumra, who told Dhola that Maru had grown old. *Dhola* hesitated whether he should give up his journey or to continue it. Then he met another wandering bard named Visu. When he was describing Maru's breath-taking beauty, Dhola's mind cleared and he sped his camel towards Pugal.

The night before Dhola's arrival, Maru saw him in a dream. The next day, the prince reached Pugal. Dhola and Maru met and the entire kingdom joyfully celebrated the reunion of the couple. Dhola stayed at Maru's home for 15 days. After that, he set out for a returning journey to Narvar with his wife he had married in childhood.

One night, when they stopped to take rest during their journey, a snake bit Maru. The next morning when *Dhola* got up, he found that Maru was dead. He wept while sitting with her body. After some time a couple of the Jogi caste were passing by (in other versions of the Dhola-Maru it was Shiva and Parvati). The prince of Narvar told them the story of his misfortune. Then the Jogi poured some magic water on Maru's body and she came back to life miraculously. Brimming with joy, Dhola and his beloved wife resumed their journey.

However, they soon had to face another difficulty. Once again, Dhola met Umar Sumra, who invited the prince to spend an evening with him and Dhola accepted the proposal. A singer woman of the Dom caste, who came from Maru's paternal home, was in Umar Sumra party. She gave the couple a hint about Umar Sumra's wicked plan. Thus, Dhola and Maru were able to run away on their camel. Umar Sumra started chasing them but his horse could not match the speed of Dhola's camel. When Umar Sumra learned that the prince and his wife had already crossed Aravali hills, he gave up chasing them. Dhola and Maru reached Narvar happily.

According to the editors of the first printed version of the *Dhola-Maru,* this was probably the end of the original story. However, some other verses concerning a dispute between Maru and Malvani were added, even to the oldest versions of the poem. The princess of Malva, being jealous of her co-wife, began criticising Marwar—the homeland of Maru. In response, the princess Maru found fault with the Malva region. Dhola took Maru's side and confirmed the beauty of the Marwar country. The last *doha* (no. 674) of the poem informs us that finally they all lived happily together.

Although the *Dhola-Maru ra duha* seems to be a typical love-story organised according to the poetic conventions characteristic of the classical Indian love poetry (e.g., in a poem *srngara rasa* dominates; a standard theme of the heroine's suffering because of a separation with the beloved; a conventional use of similes and metaphors in the description of a heroine's beauty, etc.), it also contains folk motifs and depicts the society and culture of the medieval Rajasthan. In such a situation, the *Dhola-Maru ra duha* is not only a story about love but also a poem strongly connected with the region in which it was created, a region with characteristic features and self-identity.

Apart from the poem's leading characters—Maru and Dhola—we find there two more important characters: Malvani and Umar Sumra. Four of them represent four different regions of the medieval Rajasthan. Maru, or Marvani represents Marwar, as her name indicates. She is presented as 'the beauty of Marwar' (Raj. padmini). The princess from Pugal kingdom in general is understood as the symbol of Marwar. Such statement is confirmed in another oral story. In the Sindhi oral tradition, we find *Sumra-Marvi* story,[6] which tells us that Umar Sumra fell in love with Maru/Marvi after hearing that she is the most beautiful woman of Maru region. He kidnapped her and imprisoned her in his fortress in Umarkot. But Maru prefers to die than to live far away from her homeland, which she values as the most beautiful region with the best people whose language is the sweetest one. Finally Umar Sumra realises this fact and decides to send Maru back to Marwar. It seems that till today the heroine Maru connotes the most beautiful woman representing Marwar. In January 2005, I have visited the Camel Festival in Bikaner. To my surprise there was the Dhola-Maru competition. The most beautiful girl wearing traditional Rajasthani clothes got the title of *Maru* instead of the title of the *miss of Bikaner*. Despite of a commercial aspect of such events, in my opinion, it is another example that modern Marwaris still know very well what the term '*Maru*' designates.

It is more difficult to say, however, where the prince Dhola comes from? The poem informs us only that Dhola was a son of Nal, the king of Narvar. If we follow the poem's editors, we should localise Narvar near Gwaliyar (in modern Madhya Pradesh). But R.S. McGregor, for example, states that in the beginning Dhola probably belonged to a small kingdom situated somewhere in Marwar. That is why he was able to reach Pugal on his camel within just one day.[7] However, if we relied on the poem, Dhola would come from a kingdom outside the region of Marwar.

The third character, i.e., Umar Sumra, most probably is a representative of Sindh. Although he appears in the story just a few times, he is a very important character not only for the plot of the story but also for the understanding of the relations between different Rajput clans in the region of the medieval Rajasthan. In order to establish Umar Sumra's background we have to investigate other sources. J. Tod wrote that the region of Sindh (at present in Pakistan) was known under the name of Umar Sumra, with a capital in Umarkot.[8] In the Arabic chronicles the Sumra people are presented as Muslim but according to Indian sources they belonged to the Rajput clan of Bhattis, who in the 10th century converted to Islam. When they became independent from the Muslim sultans, they established their own kingdom in Sindh.[9] In *doha* no. 640 of the poem it is mentioned that Umar Sumra collected an army with 'Khurasani' swords in order to chase Dhola and Maru. An adjective 'khurasani' means not only a particular region in Iran but in the Rajasthani language it has also a general meaning 'a Muslim'.[10] Thus, Umar Sumra name itself is significant and on the basis of the meaning of 'khurasani' weapon we can presume that it may be an allusion to his Muslim orientation.

Although at first glance the story gives the impression that Umar Sumra is Dhola's enemy, he is, in fact, much more opposed to the princess Maru. We should not forget that the *dohas* of Dhola and Maru were based on popular folklore, hence the poem did not need to explain the entire story, as the details were well known to the audiences of the medieval Rajasthan. In order to understand why Umar Sumra was Maru's and not Dhola's enemy, we must also refer to a wider context. It seems that the Rajasthani scholars who worked on the poem are also well familiar with this wider context, as almost each of them states in the commentary that Umar Sumra wanted the princess Maru for himself, therefore he impeded Dhola's journey. Such statements can be corroborated by the evidence found in other stories known in the oral tradition, i.e., in mentioned above the Sindhi oral story—Sumra-Marvi. It should be also noted here that the Dhola-Maru itself is popular in Sindh, as well. In one version of this narrative from Sindh we find Umar Sumra sending a proposal of marriage to Maru's parents. They refuse so Umar-Sumra chases Dhola in order to kidnap Maru.[11] In yet another love-story popular in Marwar—the *Mumal Mahendra* story[12]—Umar Sumra plays the same role. He wants the heroine of the story, the princess Mumal. Keeping in view all these stories, we can hazard a guess that a character of Umar Sumra from the Dhola-Maru poem can be an echo of interrelations among Sindhi Rajputs and Rajputs of other regions of the medieval Rajasthan.

However, the most evidently contrasted regions in the poem are Marwar and Malva. When both wives of Dhola meet this is not only a meeting of two women quarreling over a man but also a confrontation of two different cultures. When the representatives of two distinct cultures meet, in each of them there arises a need to confirm/reconfirm their self-identity. That is the way we learn about the characteristic features of the Marwar and Malva kingdoms from the argument of the two princesses. Maru, representing an arid desert region with nomadic culture, is opposed to Malvani who comes from the green, agricultural Malva, where the centres of culture have been present since ancient times. Malvani, for example, describes Marwar in the following way:

> "O Lord, (please) do not send me to Maru country,
> even if I (had) to become a spinster!
> A bowl in my hands, a pot on my head,
> And I will die pulling (water from a well)!
>
> (*doha* no. 659)

(Marwar is a region) of poisonous snakes,
(where) thorny shrubs are (meant to be) trees,
(where) (only) bushes of ,*k* and *phog* give shade,
(and from) hunger (only) a thorny grass (is a) release!"

(*doha* no. 661)

In Maru's reply, we find the following description of the Malva region:

"O Lord, I will burn the country,
where the scum is over waters,
(where) no groups of water carriers are (present)
nor the (*paniharis*') melodious sound at the well."

(*doha* no. 664)

We should not forget that during the dispute between Maru and Malvani, Dhola took Maru's side. In my opinion Marwar in the poem is contrasted with another region on purpose. Just in order to confirm that Marwar is highly valued region. In 18th or at the beginning of 19th century a song was composed, which is a dialogue between *Maru* and *Mevari*. In the same way as in the poem, in this song *Maru* disputes with a woman from Mewar (Southern Rajasthan) so again Marwar is contrasted to another different region, in this case to Mewar, which similarly to Malva represents separate tradition.[13] But it seems that the most important is to emphasise the significance of Marwar by contrasting it with another region.

The branch of the Aravali hills divides Rajasthan into two geographical zones: the northern-western part and the southern-eastern part. In the poem, we find a reflection of such a general division of a country, as well. It is reflected not only in the confrontation between Maru and Malvani but also in the description of Dhola's journey. *Doha* no. 424 informs us that the prince of Narvar, on his way to Pugal, crossed the Aravali hills. From *dohas* no. 647 and 650 we learn that Umar Sumra gave up his attempt to capture Dhola and Maru when he came to know that they had already passed the Aravali mountains. Such remarks give us also an insight into the folk perception of space including its centres, borders, peripheries, roads, etc.; this perception is often imbued with elements of magic and superstition. The prince Dhola had to face danger only on the western side of the Aravali hills, i.e. in a region he was not familiar with. On the other hand, Umar Sumra did not dare to cross that somehow magic border either. The poem informs us that Dhola stopped for a while in Pushkar (*doha* no. 425). In my opinion, it was not accidental—Pushkar is important here not only as a holy town but also as a place situated on the borderline formed of the mountains and as such, it is a neutral space according to folk perception.

In the poem we find mentions of people from various social strata. Not only ruling Rajputs (in fact this is much more discussible problem—do the leading characters of the poem really belong to Rajputs or rather to folk?) but also people, who belong to castes considered having a very low social status (e.g., Dom, Dhadhi, Banjara, Jogi and Rebari). One episode of the story is worth mentioning here. When Maru bit by a snake is back to life by miracles done by the Jogi. Although a death of a heroine caused by a poisonous snake and then bringing her back to life is a common motif in Rajasthani folktales, however in this case it can have a broader context. The Jogis are devotees of guru Gorakhnath. This caste created also another separate narrative tradition of *Nihalde-Sultan* story, which is much more later than the *Dhola-Maru*.[14] In the Nihalde-Sultan we find episodes from the Dhola-Maru, as well. The hero of the story—Sultan is a disciple of guru Gorakhnath and Maru becomes Sultan's sister in religion (*dharam ki bahin*) and she worships Gorakhnath, too. In this story Sultan's wife—Nihalde—dies by a snake bite. She is back to life due to wonders done by a man of Banjara caste, who is also a Gorakhnath's disciple. Keeping in mind those episodes from the *Dhola-Maru* put in the *Nihalde-Sultan* narrative and the information from the *Dhola-Maru ra duha* that the Jogi—a worshipper of guru Gorakhnath gave the life back to Maru—we can risk to say that maybe the Dhola-Maru was a story, which in medieval times was used also as a medium for spreading ideas of the Gorakhnath panth. We can find a support of this theory in Dhola tradition in the region of Braj *bhasa* where in the whole story two doctrines dominate—Gorakhnath panth and shaktism.[15] These words written above are rather a proposal for a discussion because as I know till now there was not any research about the connection of the *Dhola-Maru* with Nath Jogis or with any other religious doctrines. If in medieval times, e.g., Jains were using Rajasthani folktales as a vehicle to spread their religion (and due to them many such folktales were preserved), we can suspect that other religious groups or sects were doing the same.

Summing up, the *Dhola-Maru ra duha* is an interesting work on at least two levels—as a poem, which occupies an important place in both the Rajasthani and Hindi literatures and as a surviving image of the society and culture of the medieval Rajasthan. In the poem, there are mentions of the multiple Rajasthani cultures, there are also descriptions of different folk beliefs, but also of the fauna and flora of Rajasthan, etc. The *Dhola-Maru* can be used as an additional source of knowledge about Rajasthan as the story is deeply rooted in Rajasthani culture and its background is in the folklore of the region. The *Dhola-Maru* is alive in two traditions—literary and oral, and the latter is still very popular today. But it is another multiple history.

Notes

1. C.P. Masica, *The Indo-Aryan Languages*, Department of South Asian Languages and Civilisations, University of Chicago, Cambridge University Press, 1991, p. 427; Bholanath Tivari, *Hindi Bhasa,* Allahabad 1986, p. 60; Govardhan Simh Sekhavat, *Rajasthani Sahitya ka samshipt Iithas,* The Student Book Company, Jaipur, 1999, p. 10.
2. Ramsinh, Suyakaran Parik, Narottamdas Svami, *Dhola-Maru ra duha. Rajasthani ka supradiddh pracin lokgit,* Rajasthani Grantagar, Jodhpur 1995, a prologue; Charlotte Vaudeville, *Myths, Saints and Legends of Medieval India*, Oxford University Press, Delhi, 1996, p. 276.
3. Hazari Prasad Dvivedi, *Hindi Sahitya ka Adikar,* Bihar Rastrabhasa Parisad, Patna, 1980, p. 8.
4. Ibid., p. 101.
5. Summary of the story on the basis of the edition by Ramsinh, Suryakaran Parik, Marottamdas Svami; op. cit.
6. Kisani Phulvani Khemani, *Barat ke Sindhi geya premakhyan,* Alpha Computers and Printers, 2003.
7. R.S. McGregor, *Hindi Literature from its Beginnings to the Nineteenth Century,* Wiesbaden, 1984, p. 14.
8. James Tod, *Annals and Antiquities of Rajasthan or Central and Western Rajpoot States of India*, Routledge and Kegan Paul Ltd., London 1997 (1st ed. 1829), Vol. I, p. 236 and Vol. II, pp. 250–52.
9. Ramsinh and others, op. cit., p. 19.
10. Badri Prasad Sakriya, Bhupatiray Sakriya, *Rajasthatni-Hindi Sabda kos,* Panchsheel Prakasan, Jaipur, 1993, p. 209; Kalika Prasad, *Brhat Hindi kos,* Jnanmandal Limited, Varanasi 1997, p. 298.
11. Salim Agha, *Dhola-Maru*, Lok Virsa Asait Ghar, Islamabad 1985, p. 7.
12. Kanhaiyalal Sahal, *Mumal ki katha ke katipay rupantar,* (in) K. Sahal (ed.), *Maru-Bharati* (October, 1964), Vol. 3, Sodh-vibhag, Birla Education Trust, Pilani, pp. 33–43.
13. Agarcand Nahata, Marvani—*Mevari samivad,* (w:) Badri Prasad Sakiya, Nathuram Khargavat (ed.), *Rajasthan Bharati,* July 1953, Bikaner, pp. 101–105.
14. Kanhaiyalal Sahal (ed.), *Maru-Bharati, Nihalde-Sultan*. op. cit., Vol. I, II, 1960 and Vol. III, 1961.
15. Satyendra, *Braj-lok-sahitya ka adhyayan*, Sahitya Ratna Bhandar, Agra 1949, p. 374.

11

The Music of Western Rajasthan

A Wider Regional Context

Vijay Verma

The Region

The music and the musicians of Western Rajasthan have justly won international acclaim. But the music, particularly that of the Barmer and Jaisalmer districts, which form the southern half of a belt along the borders, cannot be properly understood and the significance of some of its features cannot be fully appreciated without reference to a wider regional context represented by the sub-regions of Gujarat, Sindh (now in Pakistan) and the Punjab (now divided between Pakistan and India).

Gujarat and Rajasthan have had a close relationship from very early times. The historic *Gurjarade'sa* up to c.10th century A.D. included more of present day Rajasthan than it did of present day Gujarat. The *pratiharas* of Mandore got the appellation *'Gurjara'* when a branch of their's got to rule from Jalore. Present day Rajasthani and Gujarati are both descended from a *Gurjari-apbhrm'sa*. Mirabai as much belongs to Gujarat as Narsi Mehta does to Rajasthan. Ramadevji enjoys as much of a following in Gujarat as he does in Rajasthan. In the popular song *'Lakhi-banjara'*, requests to take the singer to Gujarat or to Marwar form alternate refrains. In a *Kathiawari* song, the beloved is being requested for a rendezvous in the fair at Sancore in district Jalore.

On another plane, M.A. Dhaky's theory of a *Maha-Maru* style of architecture having interacted with a *Maha-Gurjara* one to yield the *Maru-Gurjara* will appear to have a link with these circumstances.

The cultural and economic ties between Kathiawad, Kutch, Barmer and Jaisalmer on the one hand and Sindh on the other, have been very strong. In his *History of Sindhi Literature*' (Sahitya Akademy, N.D.), L.H. Ajwani speaks of the 'greater Sindh' which once extended to Kashmir and Kannauj and incorporated Makran in Baluchistan, Saurastra in Gujarat and Barmer and Jaisalmer in Rajasthan. The famous peregrinations of Sah Latif (1689–1752), the great Sufi saint-poet of Sindh, ranging from Hinglaj in Baluchistan to Dwarka, Junagadh and Kotesar in Gujarat to Barmer and Ludarwa in Rajasthan sort of symbolise the cultural thread running through this region. Testimony to this cultural affinity lies spread over many fields, and music is not the least of them. The avidness with which the compositions of the Sah in his *Risalo* and, though less frequently, of other Sufi saint-poets of Sindh like Sacala and Rohil Sain are sung by the professional singers of Barmer-Jaisalmer and the keenness with which the legends such as those of *Sorath-Ra Khengar, Mumal-Mahendra* and *Lakha Phulani* are still followed in Gujarat, Barmer-Jaisalmer and Sindh further underscore the cultural bond in question. If, in popular lore, Pabuji of Kolu in district Jodhpur went to Umarkot in Sindh to wed where Mumal of Ludarwa, Jaisalmer, enthralled Mahendra of Umarkot. The economic inter-dependence used to be just as significant.

Contiguity with the pre-partition Punjab had extended right up to the north-western tip of the then Jaisalmer State and the compositions of Sufis like Ghulam Farid (1173–1265) and Bulle Sah (1680–1758) and the legends of Hir Ranjha and Laila-Majnun have enjoyed prevalence in western Rajasthan as well. Many professional singers of the districts of Jaisalmer and Barmer can be found singing this couplet as a prelude: "Ghulam Farid ke dohe ko tabiz banakar dalun" (I will put a couplet of Ghulam Farid like a talisman round my neck). The legendary Gogaji of Daderwa is as much revered in the Punjab (and in Himachal, Haryana and western Uttar Pradesh) as he is in Rajasthan while the cycle of stories about Raja Risalu of Sialkot is quite well known in North-western Rajasthan.

It has to be remembered that the *'Surs'* (literally, musical notes, but denoting 'sarga' or chapter-headings in the 'Risalo') of Sah Latif, the *'Suruds'* (modes of singing) of Sah Inat (c. 1623–1712), the *Kafis* of Seikh Farid, Sah Hussain (1538–1601) and Bulle Sah and the importance given to the ragas in the Guru Granth Sahib all testify to the happy interlacing of spirituality with music in Sindh and the Punjab. Music is similarly found in forming the outpourings of both the Nirguna and Vaisnava saint-poets of Gujarat, Rajasthan and the *Braj* and Western Rajasthan has been benefitted by both these streams.

Here we shall be attempting a preliminary study of some musical features which Barmer and Jaisalmer, in particular, are found sharing with Gujarat, Sindh and the Punjab. For, it may be mentioned at the very outset these two South-western districts, along with parts of Jalore and Jodhpur, have a musical portfolio quite distinct from that of the north-west: while the professional music of the former is dominated by the *Manganiyars, Langas and Dhadhis, Dholis*, known by various names, and *Mirasis* dominate the latter; while *Sorath* and other 'folk-ragas', including the many cousins of the *Mand*, the *Kamayaca* and the folk-*Sarangis* are prominent in the former, the '*sastric*' or *Rajwadi Mand*, the classical *Sarangi* and the folk *Pabu-Matas* (two pitchers played in tandem) and the *Derun* (hourglass-shaped twin-faced drum) dominate the latter. However, the *Bhopas* of *Pabuji* with their *Rawana/hatthas*, and the *Kalbeliyas* with their *pungis* are common to both the north and the south.[1] Similar is the case with women's folk-songs, singing of devotional music to the accompaniment of the *Tandura*, also called *Nisana*, or *Cautara*, and the music going with the various stick-dances and the '*Rammat*' folk-operas.

The Music and the Musicians

There is, thus, available to us a wide variety of musical types out of which we have to choose samples most suited to our purpose of inter-sub-regional comparisons. For such comparisons, the ideal tool is that of the popular '*lok ragas*' or folk melodies in currency in the sub-regions concerned.

From this point of view, the most rewarding area is neither that of purely classical nor that of the purely folk, but that where folk music meets classical music. Correspondingly, the musicians who can be of maximum help are those still rooted in folk traditions but with honed capabilities, which make their art pseudo-classical in performance. This fascinating topic of the mid-range of musical frequencies, as we may call it, will bear same elaboration.

Folk music employs simple tunes or *dhuns* some of which, over time, come to be identified as *lok-raga* because of their distinctive character and potential. Then, in turn, some of these *lok-ragas* are picked up by classical musicians who fine-tune and 'discipline' the melody concerned which, thereby, emerges and gets acceptance as a major or a minor '*sastric*' (classical) *raga* or *ragini*. At times the unadumbrated folk version and its classicised kin may be found to be in parallel currency. The well-known minor *raga, pahadi*, offers an example.

Sometimes a folk-melody may be discerned in simple folk *ditties* as well as in the performances of professional performers who do not either have the impulse or the capabilities for elaborating this inhering *raga* element. On the other hand there are folk musicians like the *Manganiyars* and *Langas* who though lacking classical training, knowledge and rigour, have definite names for these folk *ragas* and who consciously try to render them as distinctive musical entities: the virtuosity and the in-depth treatment converts, what remains under other conditions only a tantalising glimpse, into a firmly outlined and fully crystallised manifestation.[2]

Luckily for us, the sub-regions of the region in question have some major living traditions of poetic pieces with preferred-*raga* indications being often rendered in the 'prescribed' *ragas*. These prescribed *ragas* include those, which are at least now, fully-fledged classical *ragas* and *raginis* as well as those, which are in the category of *lok-ragas*. Thus, for example, while some of the 30 '*Surs*' of the *Risalo* have *ragas* like *Ramkali* and *Kalyana* serving as '*sarga*' or chapter-headings, showing an implied preference for the compositions ('*Baits*' and '*Wais*') of the chapter concerned being rendered in the *raga* concerned, there are other chapters named after *lok-ragas* like *Asa*, while, even in respect of chapters named after the heroine, place or theme concerned, there are definite conventions regarding the use of *lok-ragas* like *Rano, Manjh, Kuhiyari* and Jog.

In the case of the Guru Granth Sahib (1604 A.D.), it has been called 'a meticulously arranged musical collection', with the songs arranged under 31 *raga*-name chapter-headings along with further classification according to some other criteria concerning authorship, poetic structure, tunes and hybrid ragas. Notwithstanding the possibility of variant practices being there, conscious attempts at singing the '*sabads*' as per the *raga*-prescriptions are also there.[3]

Maharaja Man Singh '*Rasilairaj*' (1742–1843) of Jodhpur was a prolific poet and a versatile composer and his compositions carry many interesting *lok-raga* name tags. Unfortunately, however, no living tradition of singing his compositions as per such prescriptions now seems to be existing.[4]

Thus, very interesting comparative studies can be made by pursuing, in particular, the existence and treatment of the *lok-ragas* in the sub-regions of the region in question, primarily at the level where the folk and the classical traditions meet, yielding a fuller precipitation, and, secondarily, at that of the unevolved folk, and the results should be of interest not only to the musicologist but also to the social scientist who appreciates the value of music as a socio-cultural index. For such investigation, it will be ideal to take recourse to living traditions, but if none are there or the investigator has not (yet) been able to reach out to them, then one has, naturally, to fall back upon such secondary data as the raga-name tags and descriptions in various treatises. The hazards of going by *raga*—name tags are, of course, many and they may be summarised as follows:

1. The prescription may have varied from one collection to another and from one singing tradition to another;
2. The same *raga*-name may have had different musical 'meanings' over time and in different areas;
3. Notwithstanding the prescription, the song concerned may have actually been sung in a different *raga* or *dhun*.

For a discussion of the oral musical tradition, which generally preceded the stage of a song being committed to writing, which, latter, was subject to its own 'accidents', reference may be made to the Hindi *'Padavali* of *Namdev'* by Winand M. Callewaert and Mukund Lath.[5]

The *Mand* and its Kindred

Mand as it has developed in Rajasthan is the most enigmatic and the most sumptuous of the products of the mating of the folk with the classical. As a minor or *ksudra raga* it is fairly well known throughout North-India, but it is in Rajasthan that it has been invested with a special grandeur. It is not, by any means, a proprietory item of western Rajasthan, the area we are concerned with here, but Bikaner, Jodhpur and Jaisalmer in western Rajasthan have been three of its principal citadels and each has sired a sub-school thereof.

Mand is enigmatic because it incorporates three personalities. In the first place, it is a minor *raga* of the *Bilawal* that using all 7, all *suddha swaras* in both ascent and descent. However, some will ascribe it to *khamaj,* that because of the occasional use of *komal Ni*.

In the second place, at least in Rajasthan, *Mand* also represents a '*gayaki*' or style of singing, the chief cognisances of which are the intermittent use of *duhas* (couplets) and a grand sensuous and expansive manner.

And, in the third place, I-land also represents specific compositions, either in the standardised, *suddha* (pure) or *taksali* form of it or each with a blend of some other *raga*. Thus, we have compositions with admixture of *Des, Pilu, Kalingda* etc. The difference between a *Thumri* in a *misra raga* and a *Mand* composition of this type is this: whereas in the former the *misrana* (admixture) is on an impromptu basis, depending on the taste and the talent of the artist, here we have the blend fixed for all time and every performer will render it in that set manner.

The appellation '*Rajwadi*' (having to do with royalty) is rightly added to the style and the compositions in question because they were obviously developed and composed by talented artists attached to courts, big and small. And just as the style was courtly, so were the themes: it is love, often voluptuous, separation, valour, hunting and drinking which the '*Mands*' or the *Mand* compositions mostly celebrate.

Everybody now sings *Mands*, but it has mostly been a preserve of *Dholis* and *Mirasis, Paturs* and *Bhagtans* of a higher order—'*kalawants*' with grounding in classical music. *Langas* and *Manganiyars* also sing *Mand* compositions but it is obviously not native to them—their forte lies elsewhere and includes the more folksy kindred of the *Mand*.

For, obviously, the standardised, *sastric Mand* has been distilled by the *Kalawants* from the many *Mand*-like folk melodies: the *manjh* of Sindh, the *Mewado*, and, of course, *Asa, Sameri* and *Sub*, just to name a few. It is significant that '*Mand*' does not figure in the hackneyed '*Chairaga, chattis ragini*'—schemes or the *Ragamala* paintings. The prefatory *duhas* (couplets) of the *Langas* and *Manganiyars* include those about the *ragas*: I have never heard a *duha* about *Mand*.

It is typical that whereas the *Langas* and *Manganiyars* swear by *Asa, Sameri* and *Sub* and hold that there are four *Mands—the suddha* one and these three-artists in the rest of Rajasthan are hardly even aware of these three. Perhaps, these three have been subsumed in the *Mand* compositions. For example, *Sub* is very much like *Kalingda* and we do have compositions with admixture of *Mand* and *Kalingda: 'Phulani nai kaio ji, lakho awai chhai parbhat'* is an example. Some even hold that it is *Asa,* which has been adapted as *Mand* and it is significant that while *Rana Manganiyar* describes *Manjh* as the *Mand* of Sindh, in Sindh *Manjh* is perceived as *Asa.*

Before we go on to *Asa, Sameri* and *Sub,* it would be appropriate to mention of the *Manjh*[6] as sung by *Rana Manganiyar* of Satto, Jaisalmer (a composition of Sah Latif); and Jaisalmeri *Mand* sung by Choti Bai of Jodhpur/ Jaisalmer, known for its serene manner and slow tempo and, finally a composition with admixture of *Pilu-Mand* sung by Wazir Khan Kalawant (old 78 RPM record) is superb rendering and reminiscent of *Mand's* glorious heyday.

Asa, the Ascetic

Asa is a very distinctive, straightforward *raga* and has enjoyed a big empire although we are not as conscious of it as we ought to be. It, too, has been recognised as a *k'sudra ragini,* belongs to the *Bilawal* that is, *audhava—sampurna*—omitting *Ga Ni* in the ascent, and, like *Mand,* has an all *suddha* scale. The accent is on *Re* and *Dha* and, as in *Durga*, the important notes are *Sa Re Ma Pa Dha Sa*. It is counted among the *Udasi* or *bairagi ragas,* i.e., those with a touch of pathos and detachment, and, as is typical of this genre, shows a characteristic throw (*ter*) in the upper-register.

In Sindh, Sah Latif gave voice to his religious convictions through '*Sur Asa'* in his '*Risalo*'. In the Punjab, *Asa* has been a favourite vehicle for sacred as well as profane music. If, on the one hand, it features very prominently in the Guru Granth Sahib, it was a favourite of the professional female singers, on the other. A *Ragamala* depiction in the *Pahadi* style from *Himacala Pradesa* depicts *raga Gunkali-Asa*.

In Gujarat, *Asa* has been present in *Bhavai ve' sas* (episodes)[7] as also in other varieties of popular music.

Asa has had its votaries even in an area as far away as Bengal. An old 78 RPH record features *Asa* as rendered by the famous singer, Pt. Bhisma Dev Catterji. Nidhu Babu (1741–1839 A.D.), the famous composer, had used *Asa-Bhairvi* as one of the several composite melodies to which his compositions were set. There are other instances, too, of the recourse to *Asa* by classical musicians. Pt. Ravi Sanker has played *Asa-Bhairava*. A recording of late Ustad Rajab Ali Khan of Dewas, features *Asa Sarang*. Pt. Mani Ram had sung *Asa* but there is too much of *Durga* in his version.

As already noted, *Asa* has been one of the favourites with the *Langas* and *Manganiyars* but by careful observation its presence can be discerned in other areas of Rajasthan also, of which we will soon have an example. Maharaja Man Singh '*Rasilai-raj*' will also appear to have been an *Asa* addict as he has used not only *Asa* but also its compounds like *Asa-Jogiya, Asa-Maru* and *Sindhu-Asa.*[8] *Asa-Sindhu* occurs in '*Narsi ji ro Mahero*' ascribed to Mirabai, also.[9]

This mention of Sindhu here leads us to another area of great interest: in addition to a possible connection with Sindh, there is the suggestion that Sindhu *Raga* is the same as '*Badraga*' or '*Vadairaga*' (big, i.e., major) in which '*Bada duha*' were meant to be sung and which was to be played as marching song or martial music for the armies. It will be worthwhile to investigate this '*Bada raga*' further in the context of the region as a whole and also to ascertain the famous process of '*Sindhu dena*' or '*Sindhu dalna*' and its connection, if any, with the singing of the '*vars*' or *pawadas* concerning Sikh religious history by the *Dhadhis.*[10]

'Rasilai-raj' also composed in 'Sindhdua' and '*Sindhdi ra bhelra*' (*raga* showing a blend of *Sindhdi*) names at once pointing to Sindh and calling for further investigation. Interestingly, again, most of the compositions in *Sindh-dau* are in Punjabi and speak of *Hir-Ranjha.*[11] There clear examples of *Asa* viz., the authentic rendering by Cimme Khan Manganiyar of Raimala, Jaisalmer, the second a more folksy version as heard in the course of a narration of Pabuji's (*Asa* in *Parbhati Dhal* by Mohan Ram, Pabu Bhopa, Pabusar, Churu), the third is a rendering of a *vani* from Guru Granth Sahib (*har ka bilovna bilo mere bhai*), while the fourth (*Asa* heard in a *vesa* regarding *Krisna-lila* performed by a troupe from Morvi at Dhundlod, Jhunjhunu in 1982) and fifth are from Gujarat (*Asa* used, *inter alia*, by a *balladeer* narrating the story of *Nal-Damyanti*, seen on TV).

Sameri, the Mellower Cousin of *Asa*

Sameri will appear to have enjoyed a good deal of popularity from a fairly early period. Agarchand Nahta has traced the (prescribed) use of *Malhara-Sameri, Sameri-Kafi* and *Sameri-Sorath-Kafi* in some folk songs committed to writing in 1603 A.D.[12] *Sameri* also features in 'Sri Karamchanda Mantri Vansa Prabandha' written by Muni Gunavinaya in 1598 A.D.[13]

Another pointer in the same direction is the prescription of this raga for singing a *Barahmasa* (song against the background of the 12 months of the year) written by Muni Jinasoma in the later half of the 18th century.[14] *Sameri* is also known to the *Bhavai vesas* of Gujarat, as evidenced by its presence in the *vesa* of *Ratna-Hamir* and several other *vesas.*[15]

In Sindh, *Sameri* is, perhaps, known as *Samundi* which is also the name of the *'Sur'* in the *'Risalo'* in which the *Sah* speaks of the seafarers and the travails of their loved ones.

Sameri is also found as the prescribed raga for singing some *padas* of the Vaisnava saint-poets Kumbhandas, Caturbhuj Soordas Madan Mohan, Mirabai and Narsi Mehta[16] (*Sameri* has been sung by the *Langas* and *Manganiyars).*

Of *Sub* and of *Jog*

Sub, the 'fourth *Mand*' of south-western Rajasthan has a more distinctive presence as compared to *Sameri* which the uninitiated may be hard put to distinguish from *Asa*. However, there seem to be no references to *Sub* beyond the *Langa-Manganiyar* domain, may be because it, or melodies similar to it, were known by other names there as the case of *'Jog',* to which we shall soon turn, may suggest.[17]

Sub with its *komal Re* and *Dha* is of the *Bhairava* family and resembles *Kalingda* though the occasional use of *tivra Ma* also by some may give it a whiff of Lalit.

In addition to *Sub,* south-western Rajasthan as well as Sindh have a folk melody known as *'Jog'*. It has nothing to do, however, with the *Jog* of the *Kafi* that of Hindustani music and may have got this name, in Sindh at least, because of its association in the *'Risalo'* with *Jogis* and *Kapdis Nath yogies* and *sanya-sis* or asceties. But, interestingly, it also has a lot of *Jogiya,* also of the *Bhairava that* and with *komal Re* and *Dha* in it, giving rise to the possibility that the folk got the classical *Jogiya* rubbed down into *Jog (Sub* by late Bhungar Khan Manganiyar of Jaisalmer, Barmer, *Jog* by Cakar-Candiya and *Jog* by Bhungar Khan are examples from either side of the border).

The Elusive: Pervasive *Maru*

Maru is, by far, the most intriguing of the folk melodies of this region. Its classical namesake is rather obscure, too. Let us try and take up the strands one by one.

First, as far as western Rajasthan is concerned, we come across the *Maru* moored in the legend of *Dhola-Maru,* which speaks of the betrothal of Maru or Marwani of *Pugal* near Bikaner, with *Dhola* of Narwar near Gwalior in infancy and their tribulant reunion as adults.

The message which *Maru* sends to *Dhola* through the Dhadhi messengers is supposed to have been in *raga Maru*:

> *Maruvani bhagtavia Maru raga nipai,*
> *Duha sandesa tanan, diya tiyan sikhai*
> (*Dhola-Maru ra duha*, No. 109)

Mahavir Singh Gehlot observes that in illustrated manuscripts of the story as well as in some *Raga-malas* the associated depiction features a couple on camelback.[18]

Similarly, the name of the *raga* is found traced to '*maru*', signifying desert (*marubhumi*) where the *raga* was born, just as the name *Mand* is traced to the ancient name for the Jaisalmer region. But, obviously, all this involves more of poetic fancy than musical logic because all along the border the '*Duhas*' can be heard sung in a lilting variant of the *Mand* whereas Pandit Bhatkhange is quite emphatic that the '*Maru' raga* of the ancients is not *Mand.*[19]

Then, there is the *raga Maru* of Sindh, which is said to be a '*sok-raga*' (associated with sadness and mourning) and, quite significantly, the sample is the *Marwi's* lament during her confinement by *Umar* at Umarkot. It seems, therefore, that in both these cases, the heroine has lent her name to the melody to which songs about her have been set, just as songs about *Sorath* of *Saurastra* may have caused the initial naming of the *lok-raga* concerned which has since also made the classical grade.

The legend of *Dhola-Maru* is familiar in Gujarat too. For example, verses dealing with *Dhola-Maru* form an essential part of the *Bhavai* folk-opera. *Raga Maru*, too, features in some of its *ves-as.*[20]

Before we come to Punjab, let us take note of some of the numerous other references to and usage concerning *Maru:*

1. Prescribed use of *Maru* and *Marudin* in some *Jaina stava-nas.*[21]
2. Prescriptions for singing the *padas* or devotional hymns of saint poets like Kabir, Mira, Parmanand, Govind, Harirama, Tulsi, Nandadasa, Caturbhuj, Krisnadasa and Narsi in *Maru.*[22]
3. Presence of *Maru* in the *gayaki* of the *Jasnathi's* of western Rajasthan and the use of the well-known couplet, with an obvious *Dhola-Maru* connection, as a '*sirlok*' (*sloka*, couplet) for it:

'Maru thara des men 'upje tin ratarma,
Ik Dhola, biji Marwana, karvo (camel) kunkun-baran'.[23]

4. Two out of the fifty-nine compositions of Ibrahim Adil Sah of Bijapur collected in his '*Kitab-e-Nauras*' (1599 A.D.) are in *Maru*. Interestingly, both the language shows a tinge of Rajasthani.[24]
5. A number of '*Rasilai raj's*' compositions are in *Maru*, alongside those in *Manjh* and *Mand*, establishing their separate existence.[25]
6. The martial drums have often been called '*maru baja*': could there be a link between the death (*marna*) of the valiant ones, the name of the orchestra urging them on and the tune played by it?
7. Then there are the classical *Marus* of Hindustani Music. There is the *Maru* of *Yaman* that which goes into *Maru-Behag* and there is also the *Maru* of the *Purbi* that which is now in desuetude and has (or had) no resemblance with the *Maru* of *Maru Behag*.[26]
8. Reputed classical musicians like Ustad Alauddin Khan and Ro'sanara Begum have played/ sung compounds like *Maru-Khamaj, Muru-Sarang, Maru-Kalyana with Maru-Vasant*.

Amidst this profusion, or, rather, confusion, when we turn to Punjab we find it mentioned that *raga Maru* is usually sung at the time of cremation and we also come across a very complex and, obviously, classical mode heard used for the singing, of the Guru Granth. This latter employs both forms of *Dha* and *Ni* and also occasionally, *tivra Ma* in addition to that *suddha*. No wonder, it is regarded as a very '*aukha*' (difficult) *raga* to sing.[27]

Obviously, here we have an area, which is as challenging as it deserves in terms of further research. Part of the problem will seem to be stemming from the simultaneous existence of folk airs called '*Maru*' because of subject-association, as well as more than one classical *Marus* (One can quote some examples of *Maru* as: *Dhola-maru ra duha* by Subhan Khan Mirasi of Pugal; *Maru* by Lakhe Khan Manganiyar on Pyaledar Sarangi; *Maru* by Master Candar, (Tips No.TC 1189, 1992) and *Sabad-gayan* in *Raga Maru* by Raj Birender Singh).

Prabhati: Song Type or *Raga*

One of the '*Surs*' of the '*Risalo*' is called *Prabhati*. It is a short one but one of the most quoted ones. The rendering of '*Jago ri jago...*' by the legendary Bhagat Kanwar Ram is in *Mand*. In Punjab, *Prabhati* occurs quite often in the Guru Granth Sahib and the example available to us is in the well-known morning *raga Deskar*. A beautiful devotional song also by Kanwar Ram, '*Ram sumir parbhat mere man*', and obviously meant for being sung in the morning, is also in *Deskar*.

In the Gujarati-Rajasthani tradition we come across instructions for the singing of some *Jaina Stavanas* in *Ragas Prabhati* or *Prabhati-Velaul* (*Bilawal*).[28] *Prabhat* or *Prabhati* is also known to the *Bhavai ve'sas* of Gujarat.[29] The devotional *padas* (verses) of Nars Mehta (1414–80 A.D.) in the *Jhulna* metre are also called *Prabhati*. A '*Prabhatiyun*' sung by Abhayaram Bhagat included in 'folk music of Gujarat" (HMV, ECLP 2262) broadly conforms to *Khamaj*. Rukma Devi Manganiyar of Barmer sang two '*Prabhatis*' for me—one in *Asa* and the other in *Asa* with an admixture of *Deskar*.

While more of this genre has, perhaps, to be listened before a conclusion is reached but at this stage it appears that *Prabhati* in the given context denotes a song suitable for being sung in the morning rather than a *raga* although morning *ragas* may often be found employed.

Some Other Pointers, Noted in Passing

The Sindhi tune of *Rano* in *Kafi* that used for rendering *Sah's* compositions in '*Sur Mumal*' is quite popular with the Langas and Manganiyars and is present in Gujarat also as *kutchi Kafi* and *Sankar Rao Vyas* had used it for the well-known song '*Bharat ki ek sannari ki hum …*' in the old Hindi film '*Ramarajya*'. Sah Latif celebrates the brief but exquisite rainy season of the desert in his '*Sur Sarang*', where lightening becomes the flash of divine grace and wisdom. In Rajasthan, too, *Sarang* or, rather, *Salang* as the folk musicians pronounce it, has an association with the rainy season.[30] Ramlal Mathur informs us that the use of (the prohibited) *Dha* in *Vrindavani*, and occasional use of *kamal Ga* yields Rajasthan's own special variety—*Lur Sarang.*[31] In Punjab, the ballad of '*Sassi-Punnu*' is usually sung in *Sarang* while '*Mirza-Sahiban*' is sung in *Tilang* or *Sarang*.

High Grade Poetry for High-End Singing

In addition to the singing of common folk songs, ballads as that of *Dhola-Maru* and the devotional lyrics of saint-poets, the Langas and Manganiyars have also had the opportunity of singing the poetry of accomplished *Caran* poets while some gifted ones in their own ranks have also been good versifiers. Such high-grade poetry has often joined hands with a specially demanding and rewarding style of singing called *Jangda*. These singers have variously described the style as '*tayyari ka gana*' (virtuoso singing), '*Jangalpetha ka gana*' (raw music of the desert), '*Durbar ki sobha ka gana*' (ode to the grandeur of the court), *'Mardon ka gana'* (manly music for men), and so on. It is indeed a zestful, masculine style, calling for more than ordinary talent the classical folk music, if such an expression were permissible. And the song-types rendered in this style are—*Sola* (*subh ro git,* i.e., auspicious, ceremonial song), *Bhawan* (song of eulogy) and *Dodha* (involving a play with rhythm).[32] *Jangdas* are usually sung in *ragas* like *Bilawal, Khamaj, Sarang, Sub* and *Sorath* and often employ intriguing seven-beat rhythms.

Gujarat, too, has had *Caranas* known for their *chandas, vartas* and *duhas.* However, it will be worth finding out if Gujarat and Sindh, have had any traditions resembling *Jangda*-singing (as an example, Lakhe Khan's recital of *chandas* and then sings them as a *Jangda* in Bilawal and recital of *chandas* in praise of Bhagwan Singh of *Randha* by late Jiye Khan).

Conclusion

What has been said here is still only the scratching of a vast subject-area. So many other lines of enquiry, touching so many other aspects could be thought of. For example, the types of instruments used; the ubiquitous *Tandura,* the type of songs sung with it and the *Durga* which often surfaces in them; the highly evolved art of *Manjira* (cymbals)—playing in Gujarat and its adaptation in the *Terahtali* 'dance' of Rajasthan, the popularity of the *Derun* in north-west Rajasthan and the use by the *Dhadhis* of Punjab of a diminutive *Derun*; the musician communities and their numbers and role in the various sub-regions; vestiges, if any, of the seemingly lost art of *Kadkha*-singing by the *Kadkait-bards*, and so on. Perhaps, there is need for a larger, coordinated, cooperative effort.

Notes

* I am grateful to Dr Mukund Lath and Sarvasri Raman Sarma, Sunder Agnani, Krisna Mohan Bhatt, Laksman Bhambhani and Dholan Rahi, and Sardar Rajendra Singh for their advice and help.

1. Ref. worship of Pabuji in lower Sindh, John D. Smith (1991), *The Epic of Pabuji*, Cambridge University Press, pp. 82–83.
2. It must, however, be remembered that a *raga* is still, basically, a '*dhun*' or '*dhala*' for these musicians and often they cannot readily say as to which *raga* they are performing. They may say that there are 3 or 7 types of *Bilawal* but be hard put to demonstrate more than one. They will say, *'Is raga ka ghar yahan hai'* (This is the most important note in this *raga*) and *'Is raga ki chut yahan hai'* (This *raga*

spends itself here, i.e., this is the point of '*vis-ranti*' or rest) but will not be able to name the notes thus indicated. Their dexterity and tunefulness rival that *of* a classical musician but the lack of classical rigour and consistency do often result in the use of aberrant notes. Their virtuosity represents the highest reach of folk music rather than the starting point of that classical.

Between the two, while the art of the *Langas* can be brighter and sprightlier, that of the *Manganiyars* is more warm and wistful, to which fact the use by them of the *Kamayaca* and the *Pyale dar Sarangi* largely contributes. The *Langas* have mostly had Muslim clients, the *Manganiyas*, the Hindus. The *Langas*, or a fair number of them, are immigrant Muslims while the *Manganiyars* are converted local minstrels. Instruments like *Murla* and *Surinda* and the practice of playing instruments other than as accompaniment used to be a preserve of the *Langas* just as castanets used to be that of the *Manganiyars*.

3. The series of *Gurmat Samagamas* initiated by Baba Succa Singh in 1991 will appear to represent such an attempt. All examples of singing of the songs (*shabads*) in the Guru Granth Sahib, cited hereafter, are, unless indicated otherwise, from the *Gurmat Samagama*, perhaps the fourteenth in this series, held in *Gurudwara* Teg Bahadur *Thath Nanaksar* (Jalmahal), Jaipur, in December 2004.
4. '*Rasilai raj ra Git*', '*Parampara*' 18–19, Rajasthani Sodha Sansthan, Caupasni, Jodhpur. Other published or unpublished works also exist.
5. Moti Lal Banarasidas Publications Pvt. Ltd., Delhi, 1989. Regarding similar questions specific to the singing of the Guru Granth, one may refer to '*Madhyakalin Dharmon me Sastriya Sangit ka Tulnatmak Adhyayan*' by Jatindra Singh Khanna, Abhisek Publications, Chandigarh, 1992.
6. *Manjh* is well known in Punjab also and is used, *inter alia*, for singing the Guru Granth too, but there it will appear to be closer to *Kafi* (Paramjot Singh's rendering in the *Samagama*) or *Des* (Gurinder Kaur's rendering in '*Baramah Manj*', Magnasound, C 4 HV, 2327).
7. '*Bhavai*', Sudha R. Desai, Gujarat University, 1972, pp. 44, 517. She, however, is mistaken in taking *Asa* to be the same as *Asavari*. Incidentally, *Mewado*, mentioned earlier here in connection with the *Mand* also features on pp. 45, 525 in Desai's work.
8. '*Rasilairaj ra Git*', op, cit., pp. 22–26, 249–50, etc.
9. Rajasthan Oriental Research Institute, Jodhpur, 1972, p. 97. *Asa* Sindhu is found used by *Ruprasik Devacarya* also. Khanna, quoting Rakesh Bala Saxena, op. cit., p. 235.
10. Reference is invited to Surya Sankar Parik's article, '*Siddhon ki Gayaki aur uska raga-rup*'in *Kalanusandhana Patrika*, Bikaner, 9–10, p. 32. For the use of *Bada aur Tunveri Duhos* by Sah Latif one may refer to Motilal Jotwani's '*Sufis* of Sindh', Publications Division, New Delhi, 1986, pp. 67–68. As regards 'Sindhu *dena*', G.L. Dangi writes that it was rendered without rhythmic accompaniment—one will sing a word or two and follow up with a torrent of 'tanas' (*Gagh Git*, Th. Sivaprakasa Singh, Siwad, 1967, Introduction, p. '*da*').

11. The *'Raga-kosa'*, Sangit Karyalaya, Hathras, 1962, includes *ragas* Sindhu, Sindhu *Dhanasri* and Sindhvi among the lesser *ragas* of Hindustani (north-Indian) music. And, of course, we should not forget the 'Sindhi' *Bhairvi*.
12. *'Rajasthan ke katipaya mahatvapurna pracina lokgit', Kalanusandhan Patrika*, Bikaner, June, 1969, pp. 23–24.
13. *'Mantri* Karamchandra *Van-savali prabandha'*, Bhartiya Vidya Bhawan, Mumbai, 1980, p. 95.
14. *'Baramasa Sangraha'*, Gurjara Grantharatna Karyalaya, Ahmedabad, 1974, pp. 153–54.
15. Desai, op. cit. p. 44.
16. *'Bhaktikalin Kavya men raga aur ras'*, D.C. Gupta, Bharti Prakasan, Lucknow, 1970, pp. 50, 75, 77; *'Narsiji ro Mahero'*, op. cit., p. 157; *'Mira-Brhatpadavali'* Part 2, Rajasthan Oriental Research Institute, Jodhpur, 1975, p. 140, and *'Narsi Mehta na Aprakasit Pad'*, Sambodhi, Ahmedabad, 9, pp. 1–4.
17. Surya Sankar Parik has spoken of four varieties of *raga Subh* in the *gayaki* of the *Jasnathi Siddhas*, viz., *Choti, Badi, Padhri* and *Wud*, but it remains to be ascertained if *Subh* is the same as *Sub*, op. cit. p. 33.
18. *'Dhola-Maru ra duha'*, Rajasthani Granthagar, Jodhpur, 1986, pp. 8, 48–49. In his *'Ragmala* Painting', Ravi Kumar Gallery, New Delhi, 1973, Klaus Ebeling, too, refers to a depiction of *Dhola* and *Maru* on camelback in a *Ragamala* miniature of c. 1650 A.D. from Mewar, now in the National Museum. However, the illustration of Maru in the *Pahadi Ragamala* in the Berlin Museum of Indian Art shows warriors in action, thus pointing to the *ragas* martial and, derivatively, perhaps, dirgic associations (Miniatures of Musical Inspiration, Ernst and Rose Leonore Waldschmidt, Part–I, Popular Prakasana, Mumbai, 1967, Figure 67, pp. 154–55. The book also describes the mode *Suhavi* or *Suhi*, also much mentioned in the Guru Granth Sahib).

    Dr Gehlot also thinks that the induction of Umar Sumra, ruler of the Thar from 1355 to 1390 A.D. and the villain of the Sindhi legend of *'Umar-Marvi'* in a similar role into the ballad of *'Dhola-Maru'*, supposed to have originally been composed also in the 14th century, is only a story teller's ploy (pp. 124–25, 170–75).

    However, there is an unmistakable connection between Maru and Marwi on the one hand and Dhola and the Marus of Malir for whom and for which Marwi pines while in Umar's bondage. In his *'Sur Marui'* the Sah makes the link even clearer when he speaks of the Dhola of Narwar having come with the flock of goats, of Marwi's request to the Dhadhi to remind Dhola of her, in case he chances to come upon him, and of the travails of Raja Ranmal after leaving Narwar (pp. 865–68 in the 1997 edn. of the *'Risalo'*, edited by Mirza Kalica Beg, and published by the Sindhi Akademy, New Delhi). This, incidentally, is another proof of the cultural affinity between Sindh and western Rajasthan.

    'Dhola Maru ra duha' and the style of singing them have to be distinguished from the *'Dhola'*, or, rather *'Dholas'* of the *Braj* and their *gayaki*. In *'Dhola'*, the story of *'Dhola-Maru'* has been appended to that of *Nala*. *Dhola-Maru* also appears in the epic *'Nihal de Sultan'*. In fact their story is known in regions even as far away as Chattisgarh.

19. *'Bhatkhande Sangit Sastra'* Vol.1, Sangit Karyalaya, Hathras, 1981, pp. 219–20. However, Lakhe Khan Manganiyar of Raneri near Phalodi did try to distinguish between *Maru* and *Mand* saying that *Maru* goes only up to *Ni* as opposed to *Mand*, which is of the full *'Saptak'*. But it was said simultaneously that *'Mand, Maru, Manjh, Asa aur Karhal*—meaning swan or peacock, title of one of the *'Surs'* of the *'Risalo-ka ghar ek hi hai'*.
20. Desai, op. cit. pp. 41–42.
21. *'Dadaguru Bhajnawali'*, Prakrit Bharti, Jaipur, 1993, pp. 281, 376, 414.
22. Gupta, op. cit. pp 46, 48, 63, etc. and *'Mira Brhatpadavali'* and *'Narsiji ro Mahero'*, op cit., pp. 17, 23, 92, 141, 146, 155 and 41, 112 respectively.
23. Parik, op. cit., pp. 9–10.
24. Nazir Ahmed, ed., Bhartiya Kala Kendra, New Delhi, 1956, p. 62.
25. op. cit., pp. 139–48.
26. As an interesting aside it may be mentioned that the signature tune in the folk songs sung by the *Mirasis* of Alwar and Mewat is a form of *Maru-Behag*.
27. As regards the dirgic association see Khanna, quoting Gita Paintal, op. cit. p. 42.

    No wonder the subject of Maru has puzzled many scholars. In 'Cirmi' (Sangit Natak Akademy, Jodhpur, 1967, *Maru* of the *Langas* is said to resemble the *'Sastric Maru'* (p. 40), but the illustrative example/ notation (pp. 96–97) does not bear this out. In her *'Rajasthan ka Lok Sangit'*, Siddharth Publications, New Delhi, 1995; Sanno Khurana quotes the classical *Marus 'calana'* (p. 19) but does not illustrate it with a folk song. In Sri Dadu Anubhava Vani, Dadu Mandir, Badagaon, Jhunjhnun, 1996, the editor on p. 298 equates *Maru* with *Marwa*.

    A disciple of a guru in the regular lineage of a senior court musician of *'Rasilai-raj'* gives the sargam (notation) of a composition of the Maharaja: with its use of *komal Re, komal Dha* and *tivra Ma*, the sargam is fairly suggestive of the classical *Maru* of the *Purbi* that (*Raga-kosa*, op. cit. No. 395 p. 30), but, inexplicably, the *raga* in question is, again, said to be *Marwa* which is entirely different from all the *Marus* (Vaidya Buddhi Prakasa Acarya: 'Maharaja Man Singh as Musician and a patron of Musicians', in 'Maharaja Mansingh—the Mystic Monarch of Marwar', Maharaja Mansingh Pustak Prakasa, Fort, Jodhpur, 1991, pp. 56–57, 61).
28. *'Dadaguru Bhajanawali'* op. cit. pp. 247, 253–54. etc.
29. Desai, op. cit. p. 48.
30. 'Cirmi', Komal Kothari Sudha Rajhans, Sangit Natak Akademy, Jodhpur, 1967, pp. 15–45.
31. *'Rajasthan ki Lok-ragniyan', Lok-Rang*, Jawahar Kala Kendra, Jaipur, pp. 58–62.
32. The nature of this 'play' is not yet fully clear to me: it will be worthwhile to get to the bottom of late Bhungar Khan's related expression, viz., *'ek dum ad men cala jana – ad men chut sai ghar mukai hai, ghar awai hai ... jaise 'sastriya sangit men'*.

12

Changing Profiles of Crafts in Rajasthan

Varsha Joshi

Two different ideologies have been prevalent in India regarding the role of crafts and small-scale industries in planning and industrialisation of India from the colonial days. The traditional ideology always blamed the foreign rulers for pursuing the colonial policy of promoting the sale of cheap machine-made goods, which according to them proved ruinous to the indigenous rural crafts. Gandhi was the chief proponent of this view said that the "villages are on the verge of destruction owing to the disappearance of village industries. They can be revived only by a revival of village industries" (Gandhi, 1952: 4). The modernist believed that the colonial policies failed to promote an industrial revolution in India, and hence the economic structure remained static, backward and largely untouched by the stimuli needed for the development of modern industries. Although, traditional manufacturing decreased, it certainly did not disappear completely. According to Myrdal (1968), the vast majority of workers employed in manufacturing are in traditional crafts represented by family based cottage industries. These crafts survive, not because of any intrinsic merit of theirs that enables them to compete with the modern industrial products, but mainly because of the low social mobility rate of growth of economy and industrialisation; of course, an additional reason is the fact that such traditional crafts supply the need of the local rural populations. Unfortunately in India as Acharya and Mitra (2000) point out that rural industrialisation has never been fully planned in the same manner as it is in China and Japan. In these countries there has always been attempt to preserve and protect relics of the past, presumably to postpone a major restructuring necessary to put them on a dynamic growth path. Yet, today the handicrafts sectors stands distinctly apart from other cottage industries because of the major economic benefit it imparts to the economy through substantial foreign exchange earnings and also as an employment generation sector. A benefit which is not only limited to South Asia but also South-East Asian countries are seeing off-farm and non-farm activities as a major zone for employment (DAN, 2003).

The Context

Development of the handicraft sector is not only significant in its capacity to earn foreign exchange but is, also, important as a provider of employment to nearly four million artisans spread mainly in rural and semi-urban areas of the country, who are among the weaker sections of society. Historically, artisans have contributed a significant proportion of rural non-agricultural workforce in India. Their production process has been typically organised as a household enterprise carried on with help of family labour with traditional tool and locally available raw materials.

In the last half of the 20th century there have been fundamental shifts in the world economy and in the structures of societies. The growth in size and proportion of the informal economy has been one part of the overall change in the nature of the work that has accompanied globalisation. Various studies indicate number of reasons for the decline of crafts. SRUTI, an NGO, points out to range of factors involved in the decline of artisans. One of the important causes is the decline of demand for rural artefacts due to the fact that artisanal products are unable to compete with modern substitutes. Apart from this, cultural factors have also been responsible. Some of them are shifts in "tastes and preferences", demands and new occupations are being created, withdrawal of traditionally skilled labour as a reaction to the low social status attached to the practice of these occupations and also the collapse of the *jajmani* system (Saith, 2000). Even Tirthankar Roy's work suggests break of communities, the communal pooling of labour and the loosening of caste—work correspondence in the textile industry (Roy, 1993). Certainly, in communities with a history of independent craft production for exchange (for sale) that maintains non-capitalist economic and social institutions, as well as a relatively high level of ritual activity, the commoditisation of an externally defined indigenous identity can result in reinforcement of community institutions. Such cases of craft production are important examples for development planners seeking to foster productive projects that are consistent with a self-defined indigenous identity and economic self-management (Stephen, 1991). Moreover, psychological theories of entrepreneurship provide another example of how potentially modern features of traditional Indian society have been hidden from view. New historical and anthropological research suggests that the ethic and character of traditional merchant castes could be channelled into behaviour appropriate to capitalist entrepreneurship within the framework of continuing familial and community obligation (Rudolph and Rudolph, 1967).

Studies indicate that wherever both men and women participate in it along with family farming, women's status is better. Where the family's men turn to wage work and women are predominantly working on the craft their condition seems less satisfactory and they have less control over household matters. At skill level the products done by women in rural areas happen to be those that require intricate, delicate, laborious, time consuming work whereas men specialise in high value items (Krishnaraj and Deshmukh, 1989). Being often invisible, women in the informal sector find it difficult to access formal credit programmes. Women do not have collaterals and therefore have no guarantee. For this reason, they are considered by financial institutions to be a high credit risk, so they are less likely to have access to credit through formal or legal institutions. This is immensely precarious, because they have to seek alternative and less reliable sources of credit, which often forces them into a more vicious cycle of poverty. Moreover, with the introduction of new technology in various fields of handicrafts especially the printing sector, we find that home-based units are now transformed into larger units. With the change in nature of structure there is also shift in work pattern also. For example, there is displacement of women from certain jobs. In Rajasthan through cluster formation RUDA (Rajasthan Rural Non-farm Development Agency—a state agency for promotion of rural non-farm activities) has played an important role in providing training, marketing linkages and credit to the craftsmen in some sectors of this industry. This in turn has led to incorporation of new techniques and design of products especially in leather industry and stonework.

The past policies of government have been more concerned with subsidy rather than direct promotion of crafts. Certainly, political expediencies have always prevailed upon well-guided result orientation policy regime. Moreover, the history of policy intervention in India shows that initiatives have been "too-much-care" in certain cases and "too-little-attention" in others (Chadha, 2003). Though, since independence numerous committees, commissions and task forces, both government and non-government have evaluated and strategised the future of Indian crafts.

> But unfortunately there has not been a meshing together of all the different perspectives related to this sector. The questions related to roles and recognition of the rights of the crafts' persons who have been marginalised, more so because the crafts' people themselves—despite there being over 4 million of them—are not active players either in policy making or marketing crafts. Historical processes like the craft activities cannot be treated with a flat universal policy approach but a distinct promotional effort that is sustainable.

Work, its definition, recording and measurement in different cultural context, is now an important focus of concern in several disciplines, including in particular, the non-wage and household activities of women. Anthropologists have been among those social scientist who have been guilty of representing only one half of the world's population. They now share a widespread concern both to improve the conceptualisation and documentation of work and production processes and to give due regard to women as well as men. Which in turn should facilitate better understanding of the nature of culture and the relationship between 'traditional' society and present processes of change. According to Rudolph and Rudolph "If tradition and modernity are seen as continuous rather than separated by an abyss, if they are dialectically rather than dichotomously related, and if internal variations are attended to and taken seriously, then those sectors of traditional society that contain or express potentialities for change from dominant norms and structures become critical for understanding the nature and process of modernisation" (1967).

Rajasthan's Context

The study is confined to the state of Rajasthan, which is one of the major states in handicraft productions. Rajasthan is a major manufacturer and exporter of traditional handicrafts where 0.13 million households are involved in handicrafts and 0.47 million handicraft artisans are engaged in various handicrafts (Vijayagopalan, 1993). Rajasthan has a rich tradition of handicrafts. Tie and dye, block printing, wood crafts, blue pottery, pottery, stone work, embroidery, weaving and jewellery making, etc., are some of the leading crafts of Rajasthan for centuries. References to artisans and the craft practised by them are found in the epigraphs, sculptures, documents and the rich oral tradition of the region. The East India Company records also refer to the textiles printing of Rajasthan. Each craft was practised by a particular caste. Within a caste also because of the skill being imparted on a hereditary basis some families were able to develop the skill to the level of art and become master craftsmen. Some skills were practised by more than one caste, for instances, weaving was done by *julahas, balahi-bunker* as well as *kolis*. Within the same occupational caste also there was differentiation on the basis of specialisation, such as, the carpenters were known as *Suthars* and *Khatis,* each practising a different branch of woodwork.

In Rajasthan the craftsmen were not only involved in production but enjoyed a special place in the society. Their craft endowed them a place in the rituals and ceremonies performed even in the elite households. For instance, a *Maniharan* (bangle maker) was called to give blessings to the newly married bride in the Rajput households. Besides, irrespective of the caste and religious differences among the craft producers as well as their clientage it posed no problems in their dealings with each other. For example, till today the sacred thread used at the time of religious rituals by the Hindus is produced by Muslim dyers.

Organisation of Production

Indian artisans have been considered to be independent commodity producers with the artisan's family acting as a unit of production. As a result women and children also actively participated in the process of production. Thus, the classical concept of village community was in existence in Rajasthan. The artisan family was the basic unit of production except when the artisan was hired by some agency for a specified job. Historically, we find that women and children have had active involvement in the production of craft (Sethia, 2003). Within this broad framework there were two categories of the artisans: (i) The artisans living in a village supplied goods and services to the village clientage on a customary basis in lieu of which they received the share of village produce. With passage of time these customary ties got crystallised as jajmani system as understood in the context of Maharashtra. (ii) Some craftsmen were engaged by the state and the elite to work in their *kharkhanas* set up to meet its conspicuous demand. They received a meagre daily allowance as wage. However, some of the highly skilled artisans were engaged by the state and the *thikanas* on a permanent basis and were given land grants and extended various privileges as patronage. Consequently, they came to enjoy a higher status within their own caste. A common thread in the two categories is that artisans had a dependency relationship with promoters of crafts. According to Bhadani, Craft production for the market seems to have been largely organised in two forms; first as domestic industry in varying degrees of association with agriculture; and, secondly, as full-fledged autonomous production mainly in towns. (Bhadani, 1999) "The historical evidence clearly indicates that members of the craft community continued agriculture with their own caste occupations".

Sociology of the Demand for Craft

Since demand for craft was governed primarily by the local needs, each area had its special designs and patterns reflecting the local specific requirements. Local customs, festivals and rituals governed these requirements. Several folk songs and proverbs portray the demand for the various goods produced by the artisans This phenomenon can be observed very clearly in the case of different types of headgears (*phagh-phenta*), saris, *odhanas, lahengas* dyed and printed for different occasions. For instance, women through innumerable folk songs articulate the desire to obtain colourful clothes, ornaments, etc., from father, husband and brother. Similarly, design and patterns of clothing were made differently for specific castes. The *bahis* also throw light on the specific requirements at specific festivals, which were taken care by the artisans (Viagt, 18). Thus, it is clear that the demand for the various items was created primarily by the community patronage extended to the local artisans. Therefore, the local demand was stable and regular while the external demand was incidental and fluctuating.

Tools and Raw Materials

The tools and raw materials used by the artisans were simple, locally manufactured and owned by them. Most of the cloth used by the dyers and printers was produced locally. The natural dye products such as indigo, *al, kasumal,* etc., were also locally produced (Sethia, 2003). In some cases the *Neelgars* and *Rangrez* were engaged in cultivation and processing of indigo and *al.* Use of locally produced raw material enabled the artisans to carry on production in spite of slow means of transport.

Localisation and Specialisation of Production

Although, craft production was widespread and not confined to a few centres but by the 17th century certain towns in Rajasthan had become well known for a particular style of craft. For instance, the Sanganer was known for it *bhandej* and block-printing. There are references to its product being sent to the wider markets. It suggests that although the craft was embedded in the local community demand but its growing links with the wider were leading to a gradual concentration of artisans in a particular place and specialisation in a style. The artisans living and working in such townships had better access to market and were more prone to change in their product than their rural counterparts.

Women Craft-workers

Women's occupational involvement in rural manufacture is not a recent development. Historically, they have participated in production for domestic consumption. Within the caste-based specialisation of functions they have evolved gender specific occupations. Even though mostly they remain invisible to the market they form a significant element in the production process. In recent years, the development of a national and export market has highlighted their role in commodity production. This is a direct consequence of the indispensability of women to the family for survival as well as to the market for low-cost production. Home based workers, 80 per cent of whom are women, are the most 'invisible' of all unorganised sector workers. Home-based work is found in many different forms in both rural and urban areas. Traditional handicrafts are one such work, which is often carried out in the home. Much of the traditional crafts work done at home is also carried out under putting out system whereby the worker is supplied with material and designs and is paid for her labour, without taking in marketing or sharing in the profits of the business (Singh and Kelles-Vlltanam, 1987). It is characteristic of this sector that some of the products produced by women were items traditionally produced for the consumption of the community, that is, they had no exchange value but only a use value. With the integration of such goods into an external market system, these items become commodities and the producers become commodity producers, even if they maintain the same form of production.

Although these factors can be seen as providing employment opportunities, it can be argued that the forms of mercantile control imposed by export markets determine the relations of production. The work of women in the informal economy is commonly viewed as marginal, temporary and supplemental—whereas it is a source of security, combined with other non-monetary strategies used by women to cope. Women's contribution in production of handicrafts is quite high. A lot of tedious fine handwork in handicrafts is done by female labour; at times constituting a division of labour such that they remain invisible when credit for final product is given. Women, it appears, have been grossly undercounted even in those crafts, which employ them throughout the stages of production right up to the final stages (Lynch and Falny, 1984). It is at times believed that the participation of women in paid labour will facilitate healthy development and lower birth rates. On the other hand, some question these assumptions on the grounds that sources are very inconsistent and sometimes conflicting. Independence and the creation of an 'open economy', villagers felt needs and aspirations rose, their socially accepted standard of living increased, and village communities became underdeveloped. Thus, at this point the need is to balance the discourse on the value of home-based industries to household and community development.

Changing Caste Composition in the Crafts Sector

Interestingly, where traditionally, crafts were restricted to particular and specific castes, there is certainly a change in the caste compositions. We find different castes are taking up occupations, which were traditionally not confined, to their caste groups. Thus, leading to change in the caste hierarchy. These changes in the caste composition can be attributed to two apparent reasons: (1) opening of markets, (2) government interventions. With the opening up of markets we find that employment has increased in this sector. It is both in skilled workers and business. These changes are particularly visible in textiles, pottery, jewellery, woodwork and carpet. Along with the change in caste composition we also find that there is change in gender composition also. Such changes have been visible in other states, especially like Gujarat where in Surat, diamond industry, new caste have displaced the traditional diamond workers. In sectors like textile where on one hand women have been displaced from block printing work on the other hand there is an increase in educated and management trained women who do not belong to *Cheepa* caste, have entered the textile sector as entrepreneurs. But again this change is only in few sectors only.

Role of NGOs

In order to generate employment in the rural sector some of the NGOs in Rajasthan have developed programmes of providing training especially to women in this sector. Apart from this, they also are helping in developing linkages with the market for which further improvisation of designs is also taken care of. The National Institutes of Fashion and Craft designs are some institutions, which are being involved by the NGOs.

Influence of Market on Traditional Designs and Colours

With the opening of market economy one sector which is undergoing major changes if the crafts industry. Handicrafts which were originally catered the domestic demand it s designs and shapes were also based on the usage of the particular craft. Now with the shift from domestic use to commercial purchase of the crafts the patterns and use of the items is now based on the international demand. The most prominent sector in this is Blue Pottery and Block Printing.

Conclusion

Certainly, crafts sector is undergoing changes with need and demand in the market. Though on one hand the handicrafts industry has been treated as a neglected industry in the government policies yet on the other hand it is proving to be one of the major sectors of employment and financial gain. This has brought about another change where professionalism has also entered this sector. Unfortunately, what is happening is that we are loosing on the traditional skills, designs and colours. There is certainly now a need to preserve the traditional handicrafts and this could be done primarily through government interventions in the form of crafts museums etc.

Bibliography

Acharya, S. and A. Mitra (2000), "The Potential of Rural Industries and Trade to provide Decent Work Conditions: A Data Reconnaissance in India", ILO-SAAT working paper, New Delhi.

Bhadani, B.L. (1999), *Peasants, Artisans and Enterpreneurs,* Jaipur: Rawat Publications.

Chadha, G.K. (2003), *Rural Industry in India,* ILO-SAAT, New Delhi.

Chambers, R. (1995), "Paradigm Shifts and the Practice of Participatory Research and Development", in N. Nelson and S. Write (eds.) *Power and Participatory Development*. London: Intermediate Technology Publications.

Chambers, R. and G. Conway (1992), "Sustainable Rural Livelihoods: Practical Concepts for the 21st Century", IDS Discussion Paper 296. Brighton: IDS.

DAN (2003), *Off-Farm and Non-Farm Employment in South-East Asian Transitional Economies and Thailand,* Cambodia.

Dhaliwal, Spinder (1998), "Silent Contributors: Asian Female Entrepreneurs and Women in Business", in *Women's Studies International Forum,* Vol. 21, No, 5, pp. 463–74.

Downing, J. (1992), *The Growing Dynamics of Women Entrepreneurs in Southern Africa.* Bethesda MD: Growth and Equity through Microenterprise Investment and Institutions (GEMINI) Project.

Fals-Borda, Orlando and Mohammad Anisur Rahman (eds.) (1991), *Action and Knowledge: Breaking the Monopoly with Participatory Action Research,* London, Intermediate Technology Publications.

Fanon, Franz (1961), *The Wretched of the Earth,* New York: Grove Press.

Gandhi, M.K. (1952), *Rebuilding our Villages,* Ahmedabad: Navjivan Publishing House.

Krishnaraj Maittreyi and J.P. Deshmukh (1989), *Women in Handicrafts: An All India Study for Data Base and Policy Analysis",* Bombay: SNDT University.

Lynch, Patricia O. and H. Falny (1984), "Craftswomen in Kerdessa, Egypt: Household Production and Reproduction", *Women and Work and Development*, Geneva: ILO.

Memmi, Albert (1991), *The Colonizer and the Colonized* (expanded edition). Boston: Beacon Press.

Myrdal, Gunnar (1968), *Asian Drama*, 3 Vols., Harmondsworth: Penguin Books.

Roy, T. (1993), *Artisans and Industrialisation: Indian Weaving in the Twentieth Century,* Delhi: OUP.

Rudolph, L. and S. Rudolph (1967), *The Modernity of Tradition: Political Development in India,* New Delhi: Orient Longman.

Saith, A. (2000), *Rural Industrialisation in India: Some Policy Perspectives,* New Delhi: ILO-SAAT.

Sen, Amartya (2000), *Development as Freedom.* New York: Anchor Books.

Sethia, Madhu Tandon (2003), *Rajput Polity: Warriors, Peasants and Merchants (1700-1800)*, Jaipur: Rawat Publications.

Singh, A. and A. Kelies-Vlltanam (1987), *Invisible Hands: Women in Home-based Production*, New Delhi: Sage Publication.

Smith, S.E., D.G. Williams, and N. Johnson (eds.) (1997), *Nurtured by Knowledge: Learning to do a Participatory Action Research,* Ottawa: IDRC/The Apex Press.

Stephen, L. (1991), "Culture as a Resource: Four Cases of Self-managed Indigenous Craft Production in Latin America", in *Economic Development and Cultural Change*, 40, October.

Vijayagoplan, S. (1993), *'Economic Status of Handicraft Artisans*, New Delhi: NCAER.

Section III

Environment and Institutions

13

Protecting Wolves from Sheep

People and Wildlife in the Rajasthani Aravalli

Paul Robbins and Anil K. Chhangani

In the year 2004, the Supreme Court of India, under advisement of its Central Empowered Committee reinterpreted rules of access to all game sanctuaries and parks in the country, and officially banned and criminalised all human activity in every wildlife reserve in the nation. Order 14 February, 2000 makes illegal:

"the removal of dead, diseased, dying or wind-fallen trees, drift wood and grasses, etc., from any national park or game sanctuary .... In view of this, rights and concessions cannot be enjoyed in the Protected Areas (PAs)."

— Ministry of Environment and Forests "Handbook of FCA, 1980
— FC Rules, 2004 and Guidelines and Clarifications" (June, 2004).

The order was further interpreted by the Ministry of Environment and Forests to also include the grazing of any livestock, large or small, in any and all sanctuaries. As such, order 14.2 reverses decades (indeed centuries) of local practice in game reserve areas and truncates the previously interpreted rights of local residents for use of resources in sanctuary forest areas.

The order was predicated on a variety of conservation failures in recent decades throughout India, including especially the failure of Project Tiger; in the most recent survey of wildlife for Sariska, for example, not a *single* tiger could be found to count. In the face of what is perhaps rightly described as a crisis, the Supreme Court acted with a bold move to stave off the decline of key endemic non-human species, Rajasthan's patrimony, including Blue Bull, Wolves, Panthers, Hyena, and myriad birds of prey.

Based on an ongoing three-year study of the structure and ecological function of human activity at the Kumbhalgarh Wildlife Sanctuary in Southern Pali district Rajasthan however, preliminary findings suggest that most historic forest uses *do not* discourage the protection of many important species and that the key to future management of these areas will be *context-specific* rules, negotiated within the social and ecological realities of specific places, with proper attention to the human role in not only harming, but also *sustaining* wildlife.

Does Human Density and Activity Retard Wildlife Conservation

Order 14.2 is based on the fairly sound assumption that high densities of human beings are inversely correlated with the populations of top predators and other 'keystone' species, animals that not only provide an index of ecosystem health but actually play a key role in the maintenance of ecosystems.

In one of the few studies of its kind, Woodroffe et al., (2000) regressed proximate human population densities against those of wolves, panthers, wild dogs, and a host of other important endemic animal species. Their findings are deceptively straightforward. In every case, across Africa and Asia, higher numbers of people significantly correlate with lower numbers of 'top dogs' and 'cats'. In this sense, a general effort to curb and all human presence in areas of conservation concern makes intuitive sense. More people appears to equal fewer animals.

There are three reasons, however, to treat the simplicity of this relationship with caution. First, as Woodfruffe and his co-authors urge in the interpretation of their findings, it is essential to treat each management area and species separately, since the adaptive qualities of differing animals and the ecological behaviours of differing user groups vary immensely. For the Indian case this is essential, since many predator and grazing species have long lived alongside rural (and sometimes even urban) people, making the unique circumstances of differing species crucial to understand. Many animal species living over long periods in highly humanised environments (e.g., panther) have passed through an 'extinction filter' (Balmford, 1996) and may be intrinsically less vulnerable to human impacts and influences compared with others (e.g., tiger).

More trenchantly, there is reason in conservation theory to believe that the presence of human activity may be a boon rather than a bane for the preservation of species diversity. Ecologists have long recognised that local species diversity is enhanced by periodic, non-catastrophic disturbances, such as fires, windstorms, or herbivory (Huston, 1979; Petraitis, Latham et al., 1989). As long as the interval between disturbances is less than or equal to the recovery time, transient communities, which typically comprise more species per area than non-disturbed communities, will dominate a given area. According to the 'Intermediate Disturbance Hypothesis' moreover, a theory vindicated in a number of recent studies, it is the presence of various ecological disturbances (e.g., fire, rockfall, hurricanes, grazing, cutting, etc.) that maintains ecological diversity in many disturbance-evolved systems. Such systems (and they are more the role than the exception), must not receive too much sustained disturbance, but neither can they thrive with too little. This is because disturbance opens ecological and spatial gaps in species composition, creates patches, and allows a net increase in habit variability at the landscape scale (Figure 1).

Figure 1

The Intermediate Disturbance Hypothesis

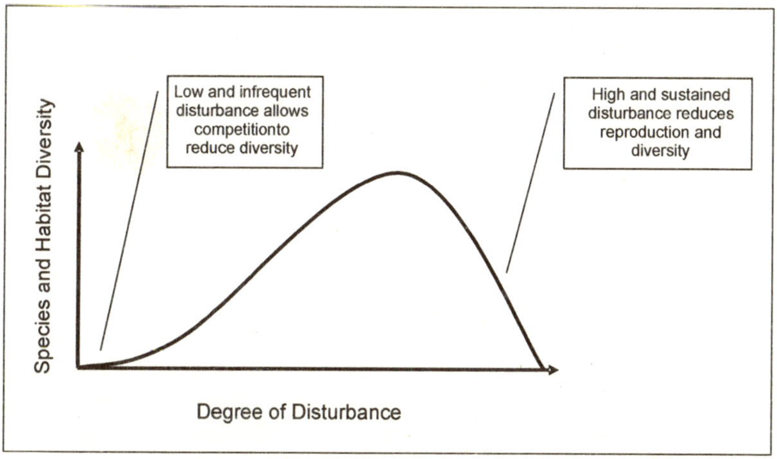

Ideally, such disturbance should be uneven over space and time, moving around the landscape so as to create maximum diversity and not drive any specific location to a condition from which it cannot recover. This, 'shifting mosaic' allows for areas of regrowth in varying stages of ecological succession. In other words, where diverse systems have co-evolved under long-term influences (as they have throughout much of India and especially Rajasthan), long established human activities may *encourage* rather than discourage biological diversity and the protection of key species. Considerable work has shown that anthropogenic disturbances can mimic in both their nature and effect so-called 'natural' disturbances (Huston, 1994; Blumler, 1998; Turner, 1998; Oba, Stenseth et al., 2000; Fuhlendorf and Engle, 2001).

Also, the political ecology of wildlife enclosures around the world have consistently shown the fruitlessness of bans on human activity in areas, especially where adjacent users have historically had rights to these areas and where these activities are essential to livelihood and survival. Whether it is in the use of fire to create agricultural plots in restricted areas in Madagascar (Kull, 2002; Laney, 2002), the practice of fruit harvesting from ancestral fallows in Kalimantan (Peluso, 1992), the general non-compliance with rules of use in Nicaraguan biological reserves (Nygren, 2004), woodcutting in conserved forests in Michoacan, Mexico (Klooster, 2002), or breaches of land use restrictions in the wildlife zones of Kenya (Akama, Lant et al., 1996), it has consistently been shown that conservation rules are made to be broken (Robbins, McSweeny et al., 2006).

The Case and Methods at Kumbhalgarh

As a practical as well as theoretical question, therefore, the enclosure of historically used areas to preserve wildlife might conceivably reduce rather than increase the opportunities of important endemic wild species. Such a proposition, however, can only be assessed empirically, by exploring the practices of user communities, measuring landscape change, and examining the relationships between these activities and landscapes against the conditions of species of concern.

The case of the Kumbhalgarh Wildlife Sanctuary (Figure 2) provides a paradigmatic example of such conditions, and a laboratory for such and assessment. Though founded as a Reserved Forest in the late 1800s, and managed in the post-independence era as an extractive forest reserve, the park was established as a game sanctuary in 1986. Across the long period prior, therefore, the forest was used to extract resources to supplement household subsistence by neighbouring communities, though under constantly changing institutional conditions. Even after the establishment of the reserve, rights for local households were maintained for collection of fallen wood for fuel, coppicing of trees for fodder, collection of fodder grasses, and grazing of both small and large stock.

Figure 2

The Kumbhalgarh Wildlife Sanctuary in Rajasthan

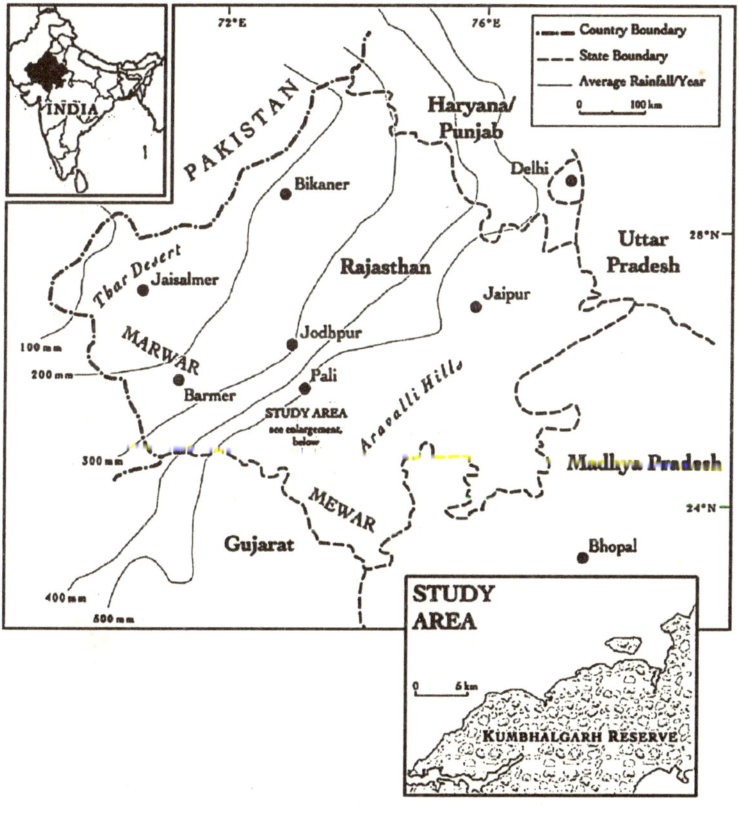

These uses were sustained along with an increasing mandate for biodiversity preservation. With a warden, rangers, foresters and a number of forest guards, rules against poaching, harassing, and trapping animals were instituted, along with an annual census of key species of concern. Though the last tiger in the region was likely shot in the early 1960s, the reserve is home to a great diversity of animals, including Langur monkeys (*Presbytis entellus*), Sloth Bear (*Melwasus ursinus*), Blue Bull (*B. tragocamelus*), Sambar (*Cervas unicolor*), Jackal (*Canis aureas*), Hyena (*Hyaena hyeana*), Four-horned Antelope (*T.c. qudtricormis*), Chinkara gazelle (*Gazella bennetti*), and a host of bird species and small mammals. Of particular conservation interest are the top endemic dog and cat of the area, the Leopard (*Panthera pardus*) and Wolf (*Canis lupus*). This region provides some of the last breeding range for both of these increasingly rare animals.

The spatial characteristics of the reserve are notable in this regard. Hundreds of kilometres in length, but as thin as eight to twelve kilometres thick in some areas, the reserve spans the spine of the Aravalli hills across the central part of Rajasthan. It therefore further serves as a long corridor, connecting diverse habitats and sources of food and shelter. It is also flanked on either side by dozens of villages, home to hundreds of thousands of people and livestock who have historically utilised the area in the reserve to a greater or lesser degree.

To assess the use of the area by locals, the structure and variability of the reserve's flora and fauna, and the impact of human beings and livestock on the reserve in the period prior to the order of the Supreme Court, a three-year study, funded by the US National Science Foundation (#0351037), has been undertaken by a joint interdisciplinary research team, which includes ecologists, zoologists, and geographers from research institutions both from India and the US. The work, conducted in cooperation with the Rajasthan Forest Department, includes household surveys, census counts of resource users, satellite image analysis, botanical survey, and assessment of wild animal activity and predation patterns.

The 400 village surveys were designed to elicit: 1) general demographic data, 2) specific plant resources used by differing households, 3) the general location of resource extraction, and 4) household responses to changing resource availability. These are being conducted across a stratified sample of households in 12 study villages between March 2005 and April 2006, to determine how, whether, and where crucial forest inputs into household production and reproduction are extracted.

Resource mapping entailed three simultaneous techniques to identify extraction locations and densities of forest product use: sketch mapping, trail mapping, and extraction mapping. The data were collected with geographic identifiers using a standardised grid system, between June and November 2005.

Wildlife mapping was performed by direct observation of key species, as well as indirect evidence including pug marks and fecal matter. Each data point (e.g., scat or paw prints) collected between October 2005 to April 2006, was tagged with a geographic identifier to produce a map of the distribution of wildlife within the reserve for comparison with human impact/use data.

Image analysis was performed on satellite data from the winters of 1986 and 1999 to determine the location and direction of forest cover change and determine whether and where gaps were opening in the forest canopy and where regrowth, succession, and canopy closure might also be occurring.

These data are to be integrated with the results of a botanical survey of the forest. This method uses stratified random sampling, following standard methods for tropical dry deciduous forests, examining 500 quadrats across the forest to determine the spatial variability of local conditions, plant species diversity, canopy cover, and herbaceous ground cover, as well as the relationship between these conditions and the spatial pattern of human use.

In sum, the work will empirically assess whether historic human use, which is to be brought to a halt by Supreme Court order, actually retards floral and faunal diversity, or rather, enhances it.

Results: A Translated World

Preliminary findings suggest a great deal of socio-ecological complexity. While human use seems to have resulted in canopy opening and deforestation in some areas, it also seems to have encouraged or allowed regrowth of forest cover in others. Based on current data, therefore, a strong case can be made that exclusion of some human activities from the forest may hurt, rather then help, conservation goals. More than this, it seems that local human uses, labour and resources, have to a degree actually served as a subsidy to the conservation mandate, often with unremunerated losses for households only one harvest away from migration or starvation. These results might give pause to supporters of the one-size-fits-all enclosure policy for conservation in India.

The Shifting Mosaic

Satellite imagery of forest between 1986 and 1999, a period of high and sustained human access to the reserve, shows a great deal of dynamism in forest cover, especially in areas proximate to, and impacted by, adjacent user communities. Figures 3 shows areas of forest opening and closing over the period. Most notably, all areas of change, in either direction, occur predominantly in the edge area of the reserve, along its north-western flank, in areas proximate to human populations, and more specifically in areas that coincide with human use and extraction of fodder materials and along grazing paths in the lower hills. Clearly, change in forest cover status over the period depends heavily on whether or not the forest area experiences human impacts. People and livestock influence forest canopy quite directly.

Figure 3

Conversion of forest cover to states of decreasing density (opening) and increasing density (closing)

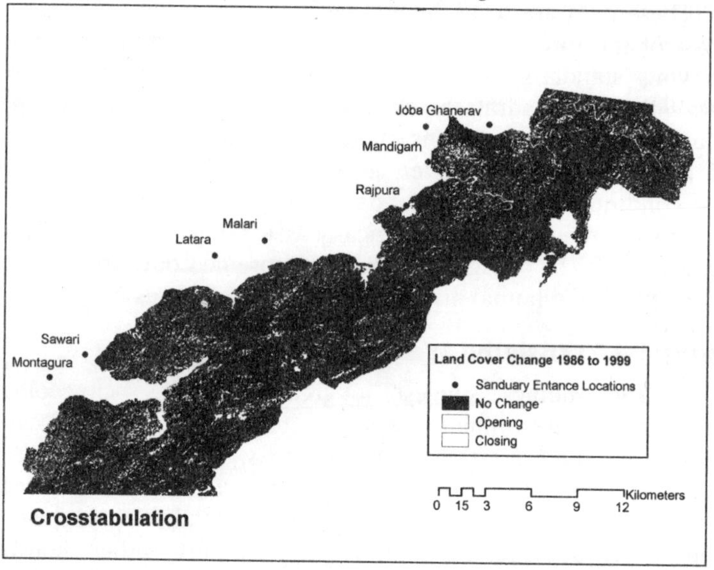

The nature of change, however, does not seem to be exclusively in the direction of deforestation, however. Indeed some areas in which the canopy is opening are directly adjacent to those areas where it is closing. This pattern of simultaneous and multidirectional patchy changes is commonly described as a *shifting mosaic* in the ecological literature. Sometimes encouraged through intentional forestry management practices, this pattern typically results in a maximum diversity of coverage, ranging from open gaps that encourage some herbaceous ground covers, to closed cover of tree canopy and multiple stages of succession between.

In this case, however, the effect is created by the uneven use of the forest by adjacent communities and households, rather than by intentional state management design. What causes this spatially uneven use is yet unclear, but it seems that a number of influences may be at work. First, it is likely that enforcement of restrictions in some areas is stricter than others, with Forest Department control of some enclosures within the reserve keeping higher pressure uses concentrated in other areas. Second, it is possible that that some areas that are heavily used are intentionally allowed by locals to rest and recover.

In any case, while the net effect of this dynamic change is an overall decrease in the density of forest cover, a significant component of change is increasing density. As shown in Figure 4, the total conversion rate between open, mixed, and closed canopy, while highly symmetrical in both directions, is bi-directional, this during a period of intensive use of the forest for a range of resources, and large populations of livestock making seasonal use of the area.

Figure 4

Land Cover Change in the Kumbhalgarh Sanctuary 1986–1999 (km²)

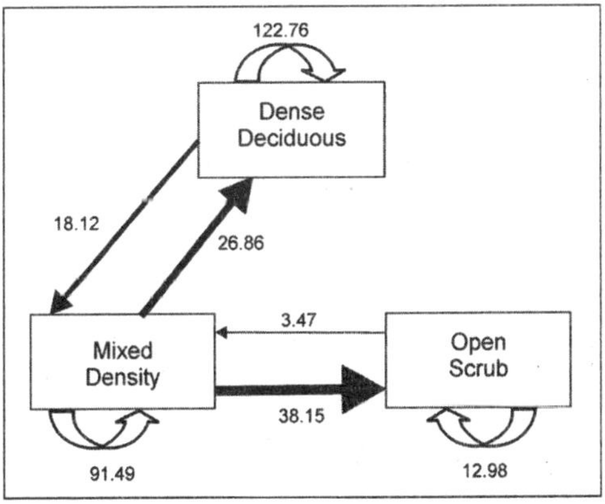

In sum, despite high and sustained uses, or indeed because of them, forest cover has experienced a complex bidirectional change in the Kumbhalgarh Sanctuary in the period prior to the Supreme Court decision. On the other hand, forest cover has, either incidentally, or through a compromise of interests, been guided into a pattern of shifting mosaic, potentially resulting in higher floral diversity across the reserve than could have been afforded in the absence of human activity.

The Ecological Subsidy from the Poor

The implications of this use of the forest and concomitant habitat change on faunal species, especially those animals of key conservation concern are less clear. Based on preliminary assessment of official Forest Department data, however, it appears that while some species are having difficulty adapting to human forest use, many seem to be taking advantage of it, with implications for the effect of restrictions of human access on wildlife survival. Table 1 shows the most dramatic trends in species population change in the sanctuary since 1991. Because Forest Department data are somewhat unreliable and because middle and long-term wildlife population fluctuations are a natural part of inter-species competition and predation, only the most dramatic and unidirectional trends are considered significant (increases of >50% of 1991 populations).

Table 1

Population trends for species experiencing highest levels of change in the Kumbhalgarh Sanctuary, 1991–2005

Species		*1991*	*2005*	Δ
Langur	*Presbytis entellus*	3071	4894	59%
Blue Bull	*B. tragocamelus*	604	931	54%
Leopard	*Panthera pardus*	54	82	52%
Sloth Bear	*Melwasus ursinus*	105	162	54%
4-H Antelope	*T.c. qudtricormis*	211	106	–50%
Chinkara	*Gazella bennetti*	37	10	–73%

Clearly, some species, especially small grazing and browsing antelope and gazelle, have adapted poorly to current conditions in the reserve. Likely, the heavy competition with goats and sheep for available fodder in the reserve, coupled with predation by increasing leopard populations, represents a serious threat to these animals. Having said this, gazelle and antelope have never been found in large numbers in this region and their densest populations are historically found elsewhere in the state.

More remarkably, several of the keystone species for which the reserve was designed and implemented, especially leopards/panthers, are clearly experiencing dramatic population growth in the recent past. This steady and sustained growth (Figure 5) is mirrored by the growth of other large mammals, including both browsers and omnivores.

Figure 5

Growth of Leopard (Panthera pardus) populations in the Kumbhalgarh Sanctuary, 1991–2005

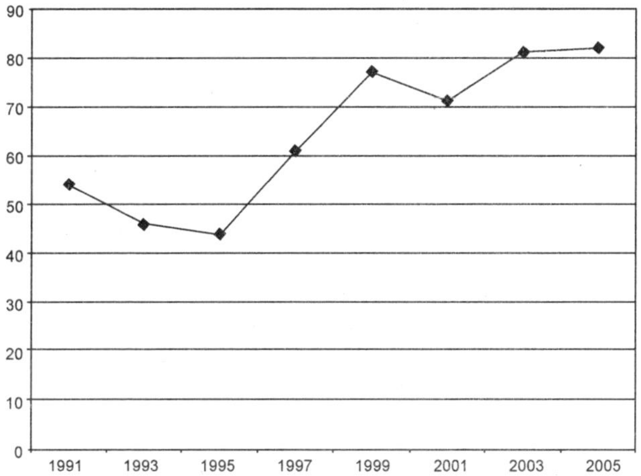

The driving force in this population growth is at first glance somewhat unclear. As their prey base dwindles, sustained growth of a predator population like leopards is unlikely. Preliminary survey data results, however, suggest that the roots of their population success lie outside rather inside the reserve. Herders from both specialist castes (*raika*) and other communities report high levels of predation on livestock by panthers both inside the reserve and outside. Estimates of herd predation during the dry season suggest approximately a 1 to 2 per cent attrition rate for herds entering the reserve to graze every month. With a minimum of 25,000 sheep and goats (of 76,816 year-round population) entering the park during that season, some 250 to 500 animals can conservatively be estimated to be taken monthly, enough to easily support a relatively small population of 129 predators. Such a pattern is by no means unprecedented. Jethva and Jhala (2004) describe a significant proportion of the prey base of wolves in their area of study to be cattle. Edgoankar and Chellam (2002) report similar findings for panthers, which have been shown to thrive on buffalo and dogs.

Similarly, the success of Indian Blue Bull is as much a product of human proximity as it is of ecosystem dynamics within the reserve.

Most households in the 20+ villages adjacent to the north side of the reserve report constant serious problems with crop raiding by forest animals, especially Blue Bull. Clearly these animals supplement their caloric intake through browsing of domesticated maize and wheat crops. Their rise in population depends heavily on resources created and maintained by people.

The central lesson of these wildlife-related findings is that, to the degree that conservation goals of the sanctuary are being met, they are doing so as a result of, rather than despite, human presence and influence. More to the point, however, these outcomes are largely the effect of a direct subsidy towards national and international conservation goals from some of the world's poorest people, coming in the form of both livestock and crops. Considering that many of these households are no more than one failed crop away from migration or starvation, this subsidy comes with extremely high unremunerated costs and risks for the communities involved. The removal of human beings from the forest resource base as suggested by the Central Empowered Committee of the Supreme Court is therefore somewhat ironic, in both social and ecological terms.

Conclusion

The problem at Kumbhalgarh, put simply, is that a co-evolved ecological system cannot be suddenly turned into a wilderness, either in practical terms or ecological ones. The fundamental issue more generally is the problem inherent in the insistence on enforcing an *ecological misunderstanding,* one which presupposes a case of people versus wildlife, a zero-sum choice, with limited historical precedent. This understanding (commonly based on little rigorous assessment), proffers: 1) a one-size-fits-all rule for ecologically diverse areas and, 2) an unstable ontological distinction between 'human beings" and 'nature.' This latte problem, fundamental to conservation conflicts and failures elsewhere in the world is one deeply rooted in modernist partitions of the world that tend not only to lead to poor science, but also impoverished democracy (Latour, 2004). Nor does it by any means necessarily fit the indigenous cosmologies of Rajasthan. Based on our fieldwork, conducted in cooperation with the Forest Department of Rajasthan, we believe that enforcement of the Supreme Court's order may lead to an increasing rate of conservation failures in many areas: a decline in the species it is designed to protect, a deterioration in the potential for participatory ecological democracy, and an erasure of dynamic cultural practice.

To be absolutely clear, our findings do not suggest that totally free and open use of forests is ecologically sustainable. On the contrary, the historical elimination of encroachments on forest areas, a crack-down on commercial exploitation of these areas, and a full effort to halt poaching, are all prerequisites to the survival of key endemic species, including wolves, panthers and a host of other fauna. Nor do the data suggest that the plantation, protection, and enclosure practices of the Forest Department are wholly inappropriate; at least not where they (like local subsistence practices) follow a rotational 'shifting mosaic' that mimics historical disturbance patterns. The Rajasthan Forest Department, it would not be an exaggeration to say, has performed heroically in attempting to implement crucial conservation efforts with extremely constrained budgets and limited operational opportunities.

What we do suggest, however, is that the success of some recent conservation efforts has largely been afforded by subsidies provided by some of the country's poorest and most politically marginal people, and that the temporal and spatial variability afforded by extant (pre–2004) local practices is likely essential to the conservation of the region's flora and fauna. In the absence of ecologically and politically sensitive planning and practice, a wholesale ban on human disturbance will likely do more harm than good. The future of Rajasthan's wildlife heritage hangs in the balance.

Acknowledgments

This research was made possible by a grant from the United States National Science Foundation (#0351037) and through the collaboration of researchers at The School for Desert Sciences in Jodhpur, Ohio State University, and the University of Arizona. Thanks go to S.M. Mohnot, R.N. Malhotra, PCCF, and Bhopal Singh, ACF, KWS, Government of Rajasthan, for granting permission to work in KWS and providing valuable information.

References

Akama, J.S., C.L. Lant, et al. (1996) "A Political-ecology Approach to Wildlife Conservation in Kenya", *Environmental Values,* 5(4): 335–47.

Balmford, A. (1996), "Extinction Filters and Current Resilience: The Significance of Past Selection Pressures for Conservation Biology", *Trends in Ecology and Evolution,* 11: 193–96.

Blumler, M.A. (1998), "Biogeography of Land-use Impacts in the Near East", K.S. Zimmerer and K.R. Young *Nature's Geography: New Lessons for Conservation in Developing Countries*, 215–36. Madison, WI, University of Wisconsin Press.

Edgaonkar, A. and R. Chellam (2002), "Food Habit of the Leopard, Panthera Pardus, in the Sanjay Gandhi National Park, Maharashtra, India", *Mammalia,* 66(3): 353–60.

Fuhlendorf, S.D. and D.M. Engle (2001), "Restoring Heterogeneity on Rangelands: Ecosystem Management Based on Evolutionary Grazing Patterns", *Bio-Science,* 51(8): 625–32.

Huston, M.A. (1979), "A General Hypothesis of Species Diversity", *The American Naturalist,* 113(1): 81–101.

Huston, M.A. (1994), *Biological Diversity: the Coexistence of Species on Changing Landscapes,* Cambridge, UK, Cambridge University Press.

Jethva, B.D. and Y.V. Jhala (2004), "Foraging Ecology, Economics and Conservation of Indian Wolves in the Bhal Region of Gujarat, Western India", *Biological Conservation,* 116(3): 351–57.

Klooster, D.J. (2002). "Toward Adaptive Community Forest Management: Integrating Local Forest Knowledge with Scientific forestry", *Economic Geography,* 78(1): 43–70.

Kull, C.A. (2002) "Madagascar Aflame: Landscape Burning as Peasant Protest, Resistance, or a Resource Management Tool?" *Political Geography,* 21(7): 927–53.

Laney, R. (2002), "Disaggregating Induced Intensification: A Case Study from Madagascar", *Annals of the Association of American Geographers* 92(4): 702–26.

Latour, B. (2004), *Politics of Nature: How to Bring the Sciences into Democracy,* Cambridge, Harvard University Press.

Nygren, A. (2004), "Contested Lands and Incompatible Images: The political Ecology of Struggles Over Resources in Nicaragua's Indio-Maiz Reserve", *Society and Natural Resources,* 17(3): 189–205.

Oba, G., N.C. Stenseth, et al. (2000), "New Perspectives on Sustainable Grazing Management in Arid Zones of Sub-Saharan Africa", *Bio-Science,* 50(1): 35–51.

Peluso, N.L. (1992), *Rich Forests, Poor People: Resource Control and Resistance in Java,* Berkeley, University of California Press.

Petraitis, P.S., R.E. Latham, et al. (1989), "The maintenance of Species Diversity by Disturbance", *The Quarterly Review of Biology*, 64(4): 393–416.

Robbins, P., K. McSweeny, et al. (2006), "Even Conservation Rules are Made to be Broken: Implications for Biodiversity." *Environmental Management,* 37(2): 162–69.

Turner, M.D. (1998), "The Interaction of Grazing History with Rainfall and its Influence on Annual Rangeland Dynamics" in Sahel. K.S. Zimmerer and K.R. Young *Nature's Geography: New Lessons for Conservation in Developing Countries*, 237–61. Madison, WI, University of Wisconsin Press.

Woodroffe, R. et al. (2000), "Predators and People: Using Human Densities to Interpret Declines of Large Carnivores", *Animal Conservation*, 3: 165–73.

14

Murky Waters

Mediating Local Institutions for Demand Side Solutions in Rajasthani Irrigation Systems

Trevor Birkenholtz

The people of Rajasthan have a long history of harnessing groundwater for domestic and irrigation purposes. For example, writing in 1894, Munshi Hardyan Singh identifies the Beldar caste of Marwar as historically devoted to "digging the earth, quarrying stones, and the like" (Singh, 1894: 210). The Beldar claim descent from Bhagirat, who "vowed never to drink water twice out of the same well, and so dug a fresh one every day till one day he dug down and down, and never came up again" (ibid.). In imitation of him, the Beldar are said to bury their dead even though they are Hindu.

Embodied in this long history are traditional groundwater and irrigation knowledges, practices and institutions of use (where institutions are standardised practises and rules of procedure), such as drawing on Hindu beliefs for determining well location or performing flood irrigation for non-paddy crops. But Rajasthan also has a recent history of rapid technological change and adaptation. Since the late 1960s, Rajasthani farmers have adopted over 13,30,000 tube-wells to irrigate nearly 70 per cent of the state's irrigated area, equal to 4.0 million hectares (Directorate of Economics and Statistics, 2003; Government of Rajasthan Groundwater Board, 2003). Traditional knowledge and practices of groundwater, however, haven't simply disappeared with the proliferation of the tube-well. It is therefore not likely that they will disappear (and nor should they) with the introduction of new technologies by the State to mitigate demand management in the area, such as drip or sprinkler irrigation systems. Thus, there is a potential conflict between local-traditional methods of irrigation, and husbandry more generally, and technical or bureaucratic methods of the same. This is of serious concern as groundwater extraction currently surpasses recharge in the state by 409.65 million m^3 per year (Directorate of Economics and Statistics, 2003).

Furthermore, the State of Rajasthan, working with multiple development agencies such as the World Bank and European Commission, and the Jal Bhagirathi Foundation founded by the Maharaja of Jodhpur, has formed an 'Expert Committee' that is preparing new regulations to address the discrepancy between groundwater use and recharge, which is currently regulated by local people and not the State. But somewhat unsurprisingly, this 'Expert Committee' has a myopic and at times hubristic view of what the problems and solutions are. For example, the proposed regulation, titled the "Rajasthan Groundwater Rational Use and Management Act of 2005", currently rests on a model of resource privatisation that is in contradiction with: 1) local thinking about groundwater as a common property, and 2) the practice of sharing tube-wells between farms for irrigation. In other words, the regulation proposes to regulate tube-well construction and groundwater withdrawal as if the resource is finite and easily converted into a commodity, and as if the tube-well is used and owned by individual users. Neither happens to be the case. On the contrary, my research shows that due to high construction costs and high probability of failure, 83 per cent of tube-wells are jointly owned, sometimes by as many as 11 families.

The future, therefore, of developing effective and coordinated management institutions rests on the rift between the interaction of local and technical groundwater knowledges and practices, and the divergence between actual conditions of groundwater use and the policies being written to address them. The question becomes: How does understanding the interaction of local and technical irrigation knowledges, practices and technologies inform the future of groundwater demand side management, such as efficiency enhancing irrigation technologies?

The goals of this paper are twofold. First, I evaluate the potential success of future groundwater management in Rajasthan by comparing and contrasting existing local and technical groundwater knowledges, and irrigation practices and institutions. Specifically, I will draw out the tensions and contradictions between local and bureaucratic ways of thinking and doing. I begin with a short history of the tube-well in Rajasthan and the problem of groundwater management as seen through the eyes of the State and the World Bank. Second, I will illustrate how the current bureaucratic and so-called expert thinking on groundwater regulation mirrors British Colonial policies on the same issue. Using tube-well location techniques as an example, I compare local understandings on this subject to that of the Government of Rajasthan Groundwater Board and Public Health Engineering Department, the two state institutions responsible for public water supply and who are involved in drafting future legislation. At the same time, I discuss the tensions between 'expert' and local expertise on groundwater use and management and illustrate how these tensions could be barriers to the future creation of equitable, efficient and effective groundwater management. Finally, I contrast the proposed legislation with British Colonial thinking on water management and caution that we ought to be cognisant of the continuities between them before proceeding down a market led path.

Background

Tube-wells tap underground aquifers of varying depth, volume and recharge capacity. It is widely accepted that they were introduced into India in the late 1960s through Green Revolution development programmes by UNICEF, the Ford Foundation and other development agencies (Shiva, 2002; Black and Talbot, 2005). This is false, however. The British introduced them as early as the late 1890s as 'preventative irrigation' systems to supplement surface water irrigation in drought years to reduce the possibility of famine (Scottish Mission in India, 1905). Tube-wells were, therefore, initially thought of as merely supplemental to the large scale, surface water irrigation systems of the Raj. The Raj administrators did not encourage their widespread adoption because they thought that due to low population density and poor electrical infrastructure tube-wells could not be profitable (Citation). Then in the late 1960s, after 20 years of five-year development plans, the Indian Central Government recognised the huge cost of building and maintaining surface water systems, noting that their overall cost did not meet their benefit (Narayanamoorthy and Deshpande, 2005) (Government Pub. Citation). This in turn, along with other political economic factors, propelled the Central Government in Delhi to nationalise the banking system in 1969 to provide low interest loans for tube-well construction and to focus on updating and expanding the national electrical grid to encourage the private adoption of tube-wells.

This strategy was and continues to be wildly successful. Since the late 1960s, Indian farmers have adopted 20 million tube-wells and nearly 2 million in the State of Rajasthan alone (Shah, 2005; Government of Rajasthan Groundwater Board, 2006). And even though groundwater is rapidly declining, tube-well construction is on the rise with 33 per cent growth between 1999 and 2001 (Government of Rajasthan Groundwater Board, 2003). As mentioned in the introduction, this has resulted in a serious state of groundwater overdraft and calls for both regulation and more efficient irrigation practices. Surface water and groundwater regulation under the Indian Constitution, however, is under the purview of individual states and like most states, Rajasthan does not have any *de jure* regulation of groundwater, though it is heavily managed locally under de facto property regimes.

Before outlining the proposed regulation, I would like to briefly draw attention to one issue, namely, the everyday vilification of the Indian farmer. I discuss this issue at length elsewhere, but it is important here to understand that Indian farmers are identified as the main culprit of groundwater overuse, for doing exactly what the State and their backers, beginning in the 1960s, wanted: adopting tube-wells without major government investment in irrigation (other than electricity) and expanding agricultural production through capital intensive means using High Yielding Seed Varieties (HYVs), and chemical fertilisers and pesticides. They wanted farmers to 'modernise'. In the absence of regulation, the state achieved exactly what they wanted.

The Problem and Solutions of Groundwater Use and Regulation

According to the World Bank, groundwater demand is expected to exceed supply in India by 2020 (World Bank, 2005). A recent World Bank report, "India: Bracing for a Turbulent Water Future", identifies two major problems exacerbating the groundwater problem: 1) indiscriminate groundwater pumping for irrigation by farmers, and 2) free electricity in the agricultural sector. In Rajasthan, farmers actually pay INR 750 (20 US $) per month for electricity, which is a large percentage of their monthly net income (Survey Citation). Electricity is therefore not free in Rajasthan, even though it is in some states.

The solutions are straightforward and based on four market-based principles. The first is defining and setting water entitlements. 'Entitlements' is a very benign term that stands for a much contested process of defining transferable rights over water. Closely related to entitlements is the second principle of clearly defining property rights over water. The third is "increasing supply and efficiency through technological expansion", including more efficient irrigation systems and surface water dams. And the fourth is establishing water user associations, thereby localising governance. The World Bank plans to carry forward these plans by increasing their water sector loaning from $ 250 million between 1999 and 2004, to $ 1,400 million between 2005 and 2008 (World Bank, 2005).

The recommendations of the Expert Committee, embodied in the "Rajasthan Groundwater Rational Use and Management Act of 2005", also follow these four principles emphasising ownership, pricing, local user groups and technological expansion, while acknowledging the importance of regulation. Therefore, both the Expert Committee and the World Bank are in agreement. But the Act also calls for the formation of a three tiered hierarchical groundwater Authority: the first tier is the "Rajasthan Groundwater Authority" at the state level and composed of 7 elected officials and 15 appointed members; the second tier is the "District Groundwater Authority" at the district level and is composed of 2 elected officials and 10 appointed members; and the third tier is the "Block Ground Water Authority" at the block level and is composed of 1 elected official and 8 appointed members. These new Authorities are proposed not to replace the current bureaucracies charged with groundwater management but are in addition to them. The Authorities are charged with 28 duties, functions, or powers including regulating tube-well construction, implementing conservation measures including new technologies, monitoring withdrawal and recharge, ensuring equitable distribution, and creating groundwater user associations. The Act neither lays out how these objectives will be accomplished, nor does it address how local people's concerns and ways of practicing groundwater management or irrigation will be incorporated into the Act. It is to this tension, between government expertise and local knowledge and practices that I now wish to turn. In the following section, I illustrate these divergences by focusing on the variations between local and government tube-well location techniques, to illustrate a broader argument about both the tensions between local and state forms of knowledge, and also the level of distrust that local people have for government expertise and authority.

Divergent Expertise: Government 'Truths' Versus Local Know-how

In the scorching June heat of 2005, I surveyed over 150 land managers of Bassi Tehsil, around 50 km from Rajasthan's capital city of Jaipur. I chose six villages near the city of Bassi for their social and ecological diversity. The villages are comprised of low and high caste Hindus, small, medium and large landholders, and slowly to rapidly declining groundwater levels. This allowed me to understand the impacts of differential risk ecology on variously situated individuals distinguished by caste and class, categories which are known to be reliable and discernible social characteristics (Jeffrey, 2001). Over the next several months I followed up on these surveys with in-depth interviews and group discussions with over 78 land managers, multiple government technocrats, and several tube-well drilling firms.

The Rajasthan Groundwater Board, in addition to monitoring groundwater quality and quantity, provides well location services to land managers. They base their recommendations on historical hydro-geological maps and monitoring wells in the area, from which they predict areas of relative groundwater abundance. For them, it is these maps and techniques on which their authority rests.

For example, I queried land managers about who they would seek advice from before digging an expensive tube-well, knowing that their primary consultancy options included the following: (1) government engineers, who base their recommendations on historical hydro-geological maps and monitoring wells in the area, from which they predict areas of relative groundwater abundance and on which their authority rests; (2) tube-well drilling firms, who base their recommendations on accumulated experience in the area; and (3) Sunghas, who are local water diviners, that utilise traditional Hindu astrological principles.

So I asked land managers: "Who would you consult before constructing a tube-well?" I was intrigued but not surprised by their responses. None indicated that they would consult a government engineer 25 per cent indicated that they would consult a Sungha (a Hindu groundwater diviner), 64 per cent indicated that they would consult a tube-well drilling firm, and 12 per cent indicated that they would consult both the Sungha and the tube-well drilling firm. Nobody would consult the government engineer. Personified by the

Central and Rajasthan Groundwater Boards, the Public Health Engineering Department, and the proposed Groundwater Authorities, the government engineer (in the abstract) are the future purveyors of irrigation efficiency enhancing technologies. The question is why. Why do land managers choose to rely on tube-well drilling firms and Hindu spiritual experts rather than government expertise? Part of the answer lies in the following land manager quote:

> If we hire the government engineer (for tube-well placement), they don't know our area and we pay them rupees 2,000 and they don't come back. Also, they have all these formalities that we don't understand.
>
> The Sungha is more accurate and cheaper. The Sungha is only charging rupees 50. The Sungha is better than the engineer because the engineer doesn't care or know about the cost of drilling a tube-well, where the Sungha cares more and is more sympathetic.
>
> The engineer relies on physical methods that are not good for all areas. Sungha's methods are not only for this area, they are more universal and could be used anywhere; he could find water in Ajmer, for example (Land Manager, July 22, 2005).

This quote brings to life four issues that land managers have with government engineers and the particular form of expertise they embody. The first is that the government is unreliable, not in their methods or results, but in their actual presence and in their ability to finish the job. Their methods require multiple visits and they cannot be depended upon to follow through. This is a serious issue because when land managers need a new tube-well, they need it quickly because their crops, their livestock and their domestic needs rely on it. Second, the engineer is simply more expensive. They charge the equivalent of $50 for their services, plus sometimes an equivalent bribe. Third, the engineer's methods are thought to be less accurate because their knowledge is believed to be particular, where the Sunghas' knowledge is believed to be universal. This indicates that land managers do not believe in the engineers' methods and, while not represented in this quote, they do not believe their results to be as reliable either. For instance, of those surveyed, 80 per cent responded that the Sungha's results were better than the engineers'. Fourth, there is a perception that the engineer and the government more generally do not care about the problems or plight of rural farmers, nor do they understand the stakes involved in drilling a tube-well.

Tube-well drilling is risky due to rapidly declining groundwater levels and tube-well drillers demand payment even if the tube-well does not produce water.

This rift if further exemplified, but in the reverse, through the words of two engineers with the Groundwater Board and PHED:

> They (land managers) hire these Sunghas who walk around the field until they get the *feeling* and then they tell them to place the well there. There is no science in this. Their wells work sometimes, but they are not the most productive wells. *It's luck*. (Groundwater Board Engineer, May 20, 2005. Speaker's emphasis.)

> Farmers don't understand technical language (PHED Technocrat, August 02, 2005).

> This is of great concern because if the government wishes to encourage the adoption of efficiency enhancing technologies,—and I think they should—land managers and government engineers and/or technocrats need to cooperate. But not only are land managers not willing to place their trust in government engineers, they are skeptical of the new technologies.

> (The) sprinkler isn't successful because it splashes the sandy soil onto the leaves of the plants and damages them (Land Manager, July 25, 2005).

> Sprinklers aren't as productive as flooding (Land Manager, July 25, 2005).

> (Regarding drip irrigation) one drop of water will dry in the sun before it ever reaches the plant (Land Manager, August, 2005).

These sentiments further exemplify the persistence of traditional methods and a general historical lack in the transfer of technology, and knowledge of technologies transfer. But they also signal an uphill battle for the future adoption of efficiency enhancing technologies. This has important implications for the future coordination of effective management institutions and the implementation of new demand side technologies. But the 'Expert Committee', working through the new Groundwater Authorities, does not want to only integrate more efficient technologies, which as I have shown is problematic in itself. They also want to bring about a change in the way local people think about groundwater, while crafting neo-liberal institutions for the management of the resource. While space does not permit me to interrogate the differences between the principles of common property management to those of market-led approaches, I hope to draw out the dangers of accepting the principles embodied in the proposed Act and made explicit by the World Bank. In the next section, I illustrate the parallels between the proposals of the 'Expert Committee' with that of 19th and 20th century British Colonial Administrators.

From Contradictory Perceptions to Contradictory Solutions

Rajasthan's 'Expert Committee', hoping to establish a three-tiered 'Groundwater Authority', emphasises four main principles on which the future of groundwater management ought to rest. Following the World Bank, as stated above, the committee outlines ownership, pricing, local user groups, technological expansion, and regulation as central features for the future of water related state-led (and World Bank funded) development. State acceptance of desperately needed loans ensures that these principles will be followed. But these principles are not new.

Early 20th century colonial administrators and engineers in the Irrigation Department outlined three basic strategies for the administration of surface water irrigation systems. First and second, they recommended pricing schemes, built on clearly articulated access rights, as a way to regulate demand and to increase efficiency. Third, they promoted decentralising the government through the creation of user groups to relieve the government of those responsibilities. Much like the World Bank's latest recommendations, they gain their legitimacy for decentralisation from the past by indicating that the people of India had effectively managed their own water for millennia and should be able to continue to do so. While this is true, local politics do not always produce equitable outcomes. So too, decentralisation in India as shown by Agrawal, can be a means for the state or colonial administration to exert their authority over localities by shaping local politics, and social and environmental outcomes to the detriment of most local working people (Agrawal, 2005).

Moreover, pricing appears to be a sensible solution to increase the efficient use of water, but the difficulty is in how pricing actually functions. If metres are installed on individual tube-wells, what will people actually be paying for? Today, when we pay for water we are paying for the treatment, distribution, and delivery of water. But what service would farmers receive by paying for water that they pump themselves? What if they cannot afford to pay? In other parts of the world, pricing used as a tool to increase efficiency has resulted in the most marginal communities, where service infrastructure is in the poorest condition and is therefore expensive to serve, paying the most for water (Bakker, 2001, 2002, 2005; Perreault, 2005). A final consideration is that India's economy depends on the availability of inexpensive, locally produced food and increasing the cost to farmers would presumably increase the cost of food.

The proposals are misguided not just because they mirror colonial policies, but because privatising water resources is a preconceived remedy to a set of conditions that do not exist. That is to say, it is the wrong solution to the wrong question. Privatisation and entitlements do not follow logically from the need to increase efficiency. On the contrary, they will result in the poor and powerless trading their rights to mediate short-term economic difficulties, while large and powerful landholders act to consolidate landholdings and water entitlements. The state set of institutions and appointed officials proposed by the 'Expert Committee', rather than elected bodies, ensures this. Efficiency gains in the agricultural sector can be met through incentives for technology adoption. According to Narayanamoorthy and Deshpande (2005), sprinkler irrigation results in roughly 40 per cent gains in water efficiency, while drip irrigation yields up to 65 per cent. But the expansion of scarcity reducing technologies, such as drip and sprinkler irrigation, has been shown to reduce relative scarcity unevenly (Citation).

In other words, local elites are better able to harness the productive power of technologies, such as tube-wells, to increase their beneficial political economic position. As previously mentioned, the design of the proposed regulation through its top down approach with appointed representatives and symbolic local elected members, who are at best local tools for implementing state policies (as in Agrawal's work in northern India), will not ensure equity or efficiency. As with recommendation of the colonial administration, localising governance under the proposed Act does not equate to democratising governance.

Conclusion

In this paper, I demonstrated that the future of developing effective and coordinated groundwater management institutions rests on the tension between local and technical groundwater knowledges and practices, and the divergence between actual conditions of groundwater use and the policies being written to address them. I also highlighted the continuities between the proposed "Rajasthan Groundwater Rational Use and Management Act of 2005" and British Colonial recommendations on irrigation management.

The World Bank-inspired Act seeks to improve water user efficiency by recommending the privatisation of groundwater resources through the creation of entitlements so that the resource may be priced. It also recommends the devolution of governance to local user groups and the expansion of efficiency enhancing irrigation technologies, such as drip and sprinkler irrigation systems.

But resource privatisation as the remedy for demand side management is a forgone conclusion. The State's acceptance of funding from the World Bank ensures that the problem of groundwater is framed so that privatisation is the solution, because the World Bank's solutions to natural resource management rest on an ideology of market based or neo-liberal approaches. Yet local people conceive of groundwater not as something to be privately held but as something to be collectively managed, as illustrated by the cooperative use of tube-wells.

Moreover, the localisation of governance is problematic because the three-tiered Groundwater Authorities set up through the Act consist of appointed consultants at every level of governance rather than democratically elected representatives. The localising of governance in this way will simply result in a more efficient means to subject local people to state control, while reproducing the beneficial political economic positions of local elites.

Furthermore, technological expansion is of concern for several reasons. First, local distrust in government expertise and past government failures to follow though on projects frustrates both local land managers and hinders the prospect of future collaboration. Whereas, on the other hand, the knowledge and techniques of tube-well drilling firms and that of the Sungha hold more currency for locals because they are more accessible, both in terms of the approach and method of implementation. Additionally, technologies, such as tube-wells, are historically not adopted neutrally but benefit those with the ability to adopt them and to control the political apparatus.

Research does show, however, that sprinkler and drip irrigation technologies can significantly increase irrigation water use efficiency. But the successful dissemination of technologies to ensure long-term equity and efficiency in their adoption and implementation depends on the cultivation of local institutions through democratic government intervention.

References

Agrawal, A. (2005), *Environmentality: Technologies of Government and the Making of Subjects,* Durham and London: Duke University Press.

Bakker, K. (2001), "Paying for Water: Water Pricing and Equity in England and Wales", *Transactions of the Institute of British Geographers,* 26: 143–64.

Bakker, K. (2002), "From State to Market?: Water Mercantilization in Spain". *Environment and Planning,* A 34: 767–90.

Bakker, K. (2005), "Neoliberalizing Nature? Market Environmentalism in Water Supply in England and Wales". *Annals of the Association of American Geographers,* 95(3): 542–65.

Black, M. and R. Talbot (2005), *Water—A Matter of Life and Health: Water Supply and Sanitation in Village India,* New Delhi: Oxford University Press.

Directorate of Economics and Statistics (2003), *Statistical Abstract—Rajasthan, 2001*, Jaipur, Directorate of Economics and Statistics.

Government of Rajasthan Groundwater Board (2003), *Personal Communication*, T. Birkenholtz. Jaipur.

Government of Rajasthan Groundwater Board (2006), *Personal Communication*, T. Birkenholtz. Jaipur.

Jeffrey, C. (2001), "A Fist is Stronger than Five Fingers': Caste and Dominance in Rural North India", *Transactions of the Institute of British Geographers*, 26: 217–36.

Narayanamoorthy, A. and R.S. Deshpande (2005), *Where Water Seeps!: Towards a New Phase in India's Irrigation Reforms*, New Delhi: Academic Foundation.

Perreault, T. (2005), "State Restructuring and the scale politics of rural Water Governance in Bolivia", *Environment and Planning,* A 37(2): 263–84.

Scottish Mission in India (1905), *Note on Irrigation in Rajputana: A Brief Summary of the Investigations made during 1903–05, with Suggestions by the Consulting Engineer*, Ajmer: Scottish Mission Industries, Ltd.

Shah, T. (2005), "Groundwater and Human Development: Challenges and Opportunities in Livelihoods and Environment", *Water Science and Technology*, 51(8): 27–37.

Shiva, V. (2002), *Water Wars: Privatisation, Pollution and Profit*, New Delhi: India Research Press.

Singh, M.H. (1894), *The Castes of Marwar* (1993, 2nd ed.), Jodhpur: Books Treasure.

World Bank (2005), "India: Bracing for a Turbulent Water Future", http://www.worldbank.org.in/WBSITE/EXTERNAL/COUNTRIES/SOUTHASIAEXT/INDIAEXTN/0,contentMDK:20668501~pagePK:141137~piPK:141127~theSitePK:295584,00.html. Accessed: January 3, 2005.

15

The Camel in Rajasthan

Agricultural Biodiversity Under Threat

Ilse Köhler-Rollefson and Hanwant Singh Rathore

The camel population of Rajasthan, and of India as a whole, is experiencing a steep decline. While water-intensive animals, such as buffalo, have skyrocketed in numbers, camel breeding is rapidly being abandoned. This trend, if it is allowed to continue, will make Rajasthan more vulnerable to droughts, increase dependence on non-renewable energy and have severe negative impacts on the livelihoods of many poor families depending on working camels as a source of livelihood.

This paper argues that in order to prevent a further decline and eventual near-extinction of this species in India, it is necessary, for one, to adopt participatory approaches and focus research and development efforts on the needs and worries of the people whose livelihoods depend on camels, especially the Raika camel breeding community. Equally or even more important, the government urgently needs to create a supportive policy framework by providing secure access to grazing areas and encouraging the marketing of camel products.

Camel Population Trend in India

India was once proud of having the third largest camel population in the world, after Somalia and Sudan, and numbering well over one million head. By 1997, the overall camel population of India had dropped to 9,11,000, according to the official data of the government, and it had been surpassed by Pakistan and Mauritania. In Rajasthan, camel numbers decreased from 7,56,088 to 6,68,237 head between 1992 and 1997, amounting to a decrease of 11.6 per cent (while all other types of livestock, especially goats and buffaloes increased their numbers). The number of young camels decreased by 50 per cent during this time period—a development that indicates a drop in camel breeding activities.

The results of the official livestock census conducted in 2003 are not yet available, but the decline seems to have accelerated since 1997 as indicated by our own household surveys. In two Tehsils of Pali District, the camel population was reduced by almost 50 per cent between 1995 and 2004.

Table 1

Camel Population in Bali and Desuri Tehsils of Pali District, in 1995 and 2004.

	Desuri Tehsil	*Bali Tehsil*	*Combined*
1995	1026	783	1809
2004	556	396	952
Reduction	45.8%	49.4%	47.4%

Another crucial observation concerns the fact that thousands of camels (at least 50% of them female) were sold for slaughter at the Pushkar Fair in November 2003. Ten years ago, selling of camels for meat was unheard of in Rajasthan, and there were deeply ingrained social restrictions against this among the Raika, the traditional camel breeding caste, which own ca. 80 per cent of female camels. Now the sense of custodianship that obtained in this community is rapidly breaking down, and this is probably the greatest reason for concern.

Sale of Female Camels for Slaughter

Ten years ago the slaughter of camels was unheard of, and abhorred by Hindus and Muslim alike. Furthermore, the Raika did not even sell female camels to anybody outside the community, well aware that this would erode the foundation of their existence. It is tragic that in recent years, these social restrictions that served to preserve Rajasthan's camel population have crumbled away. Purchase of female camels for slaughter from Pushkar began in a clandestine fashion several years ago. The authorities did not even believe this until newspaper clippings from Bangladesh provided incontrovertible evidence. Then, in 2003, thousands of female camels were openly sold for meat at Pushkar. In 2004, because of the timing of the Eid, transactions between breeders and meat purveyors took place well before the Pushkar Mela. The reason why it is mostly female camels that go for slaughter is the fact that they are cheap by comparison with the male camels that are favoured as work animals. At the Pushkar Fair in 2005, an estimated 50 per cent of the camels were sold for slaughter. Demand was so strong that camels were snapped up as soon as they arrived on the mela ground. Prices had risen steeply, so that many farmers who had wanted to purchase a camel for agricultural work, could not afford to buy. While in earlier years, selling camels for meat happened in a clandestine fashion, and nobody would admit to be involved in it, now there is hardly a trace of embarrassment left.

If this process of a gradual, but rapid, sell-out of Rajasthan's female camel population is not brought under control, then the end of camel breeding is surely in sight, unless efforts are made to address the issue.

Socio-economic Significance of the Camel in Rajasthan

The camel is often regarded as emblematic of Rajasthan. In Rajasthani folklore it symbolises love, and ownership of a camel once signalled status and wealth. It was used for warfare by the Maharajahs and played an important role in desert communication, transportation and trade. Historically, camels were thus a valuable commodity used by the ruling classes and by the business community (Srivastava, 1991).

The breeding and supply of the camels required by the elite for battle and commerce was, and is, the traditional occupation of a Hindu caste known as Raika. The human-camel relationship and camel culture of Rajasthan is unique from a global perspective, since the Raika are probably the only camel pastoralists in the world who have developed a deeply ingrained prohibition against the use of camels for meat. Earlier, there was also a religious bar against the sale of milk and wool. Raika identity was traditionally based on the belief that they were created by God to take care of the camel. Therefore they regarded themselves as guardians of the camel in the true sense of the word, feeling responsible for the well-being of this animal. The community outlawed the sale of female camels, female camels were part of the dowry and for the marriage ritual the bridegroom had to be seated on a camel (Köhler-Rollefson, 1992a). Due to this intimate association with the camel over the centuries, the Raika also accumulated a large body of indigenous knowledge related to camel management, breeding, disease treatment, and behaviour. For this reason, they were referred to as "native camel doctors" by colonial veterinarians (Köhler-Rollefson, 1994a).

Despite their continuing emotional linkage with the camel, it is now only a small minority of Raika for whom this animal forms the basis of subsistence. The majority of the Raika still involved in animal husbandry keep sheep and/or goats, serve as village cattle and buffalo herders, work as caretakers in *gaushalas* (cow sanctuaries) or as traditional animal healers. Although such animal related occupations are still typical for the Raikas, many of them have severed all connections with livestock and invested profits from the sale of their herds in agricultural land, in the purchase of shops, or made fixed deposits in the bank.

The majority of young men now seek wage labour outside Rajasthan, mostly in menial jobs which usually pay little more than room and board. Typically, they go to Surat, Mumbai or other big towns in South India where they work in the houses of Marwari (trader) families, a caste with which they have long-standing ties.

The Significance of the Camel for Livelihoods

Conventional analysis has attributed the decline in the camel population to a diminishing demand of these animals for work, due to their replacement by tractors and trucks. This may be true in some parts of Rajasthan, such as Ganganagar district where wealthy farmers can afford tractors. But participatory evaluation of the situation with Raika camel breeders reveals that lack of pasture and impact of disease is rendering camel breeding not only uneconomical, but almost impossible; this forces them to abandon their hereditary activity. In Pali district, continuous pressure by forest officials for bribes and abuse by landowners make camel breeding an extremely unattractive option for the younger generation. Raika camel herders in Pali district unanimously feel that they are the last generation involved in this occupation and that their children will search for employment in the cities.

Nonetheless, the significance of the camel as basis of the livelihoods of some very poor and marginal communities remains undiminished.

These camel dependent communities include:

- Around 20,000 families from the Raika caste who own herds of female camels and make a living from selling the young animals. Some of these families (in Mewar, Malva and Godwar) generate additional income by selling camel milk, alleviating the chronic milk shortages typical of many rural areas.

- An estimated 250,000 people and their families who own a male working camel plus cart and make their living from providing short and medium distance transportation in large cities, in remote desert areas and in the hilly areas of the Aravalli range.
- Entire villages in the Thar Desert depend on a camel to lift water from deep wells.
- Many Untouchable castes receive income from the processing of camel products. Although poorly documented, these secondary industries include leather and bone work.
- The population of Rajasthan as a whole benefits from the camel as an eco-friendly source of energy. In some parts of Rajasthan, such as the Godwar area, camel dung is exchanged with grain and makes an important contribution to upholding soil fertility. Most significantly, during the recent droughts camels have thrived by comparison with other livestock underscoring their superb adaptation to the local conditions. From the perspective of environmental sustainability camels with their minimal impact on vegetation and low water requirements are definitely preferable to goats and buffaloes.
- Finally, without the camel, Rajasthan would lose much of its attraction as a tourist destination.

Economic Role of the Camel in Rajasthan

Transport

Throughout much of its distribution area, the dromedary camel is an important source of food (Farah and Fischer, 2004). But in India the camel is traditionally regarded as a draught animal and means of transportation, while its food potential is largely ignored. In the Thar desert, camel carts are still popular and remain a frequent means of transportation. They fulfil this function not only in remote rural areas, but also in the major cities. In Bikaner, Jodhpur and Jaipur, camel-drawn carts are ubiquitous. They move goods of all kinds, especially wood, fodder, gas cylinders, fabrics, bricks, etc. The typical two-wheeled carts are a relatively recent invention dating back to the 1950s.

Ownership of a camel and a cart is a solid source of income, sufficient to support a family. For this reason, development agencies (such as Heifer Project International) and regional banks support loans for the purchase of a camel cart. According to studies by the National Research Centre on Camel, the average daily income from camel carting was Rs 300 and Rs 140 in city and village areas, respectively, versus a daily expenditure of Rs 40/camel/day. The income from camel carting was estimated to be higher in city areas as compared to rural areas because camel keepers in the city area had more opportunities to transport different agricultural commodities and construction materials than those operating in the rural areas (NRCC, 2004).

In the hilly parts of the state (Aravalli range and southern Rajasthan), the camel continues to be used as beast of burden, notably for the transportation of harvested crops, such as chili peppers, *chara*, etc. It can carry loads weighing 150–300 kg over long distances and 450 kg over short distances. Other chores performed by camels include threshing, lifting of water and powering of oil mills.

The camel is used as riding animals mainly in the Jaisalmer area, where it exerts considerable draw on tourists. This is utilised by the Department of Tourism which organises a Camel Festival in Bikaner and promotes other camel games, such as racing and polo at various festivals (Gahlot and Chada, 2000).

Finally, the camel also maintains some military significance, being used to patrol the desert border. The Border Security Force keeps 1,750 camels for this purpose in Rajasthan and Gujarat.

Camel Milk

Camel milk is a by-product of camel breeding which is consumed primarily by herdsmen (especially on migration) and by their families. In Rajasthan, there are traditional cultural restrictions on the sale and processing of camel milk, and it is not marketed in the core camel breeding areas, such as Bikaner, Jodhpur and Jaisalmer. But in the late 1990s, there was a large 'grey' camel market in the northern tip of Madhya Pradesh (Mandsaur, Jarwa, Ratlam, Indore, Bhopal, and Ujjain) and in parts of southern Rajasthan (Bhilwara, Chittorgarh, Udaipur, Kota, Nimbahera) which proceeded at tea-stalls, to private households, or under the guise of cow/buffalo milk to dairies. The average daily yield of a lactating camel is around 2 kg, although some owners assert that individual yields can be as high as 6 kg or more.

The production system is extensive—camel herds are usually stationed about 10–15 km from the towns and supported exclusively on natural graze, mostly consisting of tree vegetation. Some of the trees include *Acacia nilotica, Prosopis cineraria, Capparis decidua, Balanites aegyptiaca, Zizyphus glabrata, Acacia leucophloea* and *Acacia senegal*. The camels are milked twice or thrice per day, usually during the night, because the milk is collected in the early morning.

The income generated from milk sales can be substantial, exceeding the returns from selling the young male offspring.

Several years ago, the Rajasthan High Court declared camel milk as hazardous to human health and sentenced a Raika camel milk vendor to a monetary fine and jail. This decision was appealed to at the Supreme Court through a Public Interest Litigation initiated by the NGO Lokhit Pashu-Palak Sansthan. The plaintive brought forward evidence about the high esteem for camel milk in other countries, and the Supreme Court decided that camel milk was fit for human consumption.

Yet, to this day, camel milk continues to be discriminated against by the Rajasthan Dairy Federation, which does not accept it. At the same time, research by Indian scientists now also supports the therapeutic value of camel milk in the treatment of several diseases, including tuberculosis. A recent study by the Medical College in Bikaner and the National Research Centre on Camel suggests that camel milk is also useful for the treatment of Type 1 diabetes (Agrawal, et al., 2003).

Camel Meat

Earlier, camels were not slaughtered in India, except in a clandestine fashion. The consumption of camel meat is not acceptable to most castes, and the Raika are unique among camel pastoralist worldwide in rejecting the use of camels for meat. In a small number of cities with large Muslim populations (for instance Tonk), there has been a tradition of sacrificing a camel at the occasion of important Muslim holidays. Within Rajasthan, eating of camel meat is therefore restricted to rare occasions and religious minorities.

However, since the last couple of years, an increasing number of camels are leaving the state to be sold for slaughter in other parts of India, especially West Bengal, but also Bangladesh and purportedly for export to the Middle East. Several thousand camels, mostly females, were sold for this purpose at the Pushkar Fair in 2002 and 2003. In February 2003, camel smuggling across the border between West Bengal and Bangladesh resulted in a shootout between Indian and Bangladeshi border troops (*Daily Star*, Dhaka, 28.2.2003).

Camel Wool

Camel wool is utilised by camel breeders for the manufacture of items to be used in their own household such as rugs, blankets, *charpais* and saddle girths. Similarly to camel milk, there were earlier certain cultural restrictions on the sale of wool. Because of low wool yields and short fibre, there appears to be only limited potential for commercial use of camel wool.

Camel Leather

The skins of camels are especially useful for manufacturing lampshades, toys, drum covers and certain types of containers. They are also used as material for shoes; according to members of the leather working community, there is no tanning facility in Rajasthan and skins have to be transported to South India for this purpose.

A regional specialty used to be the *kuppa* or *kuppi*, painted vessels for oil, ghee and perfume painted in an intricate pattern. Because of lack of demand this artisan industry has now stopped.

Camel Bones

Similar to the bones of other animals, camel bones are processed into fertiliser (bone meal). They are also used in lieu of ivory, for the production of jewellery and ornaments, as well as for manufacturing inlaid furniture. Logistics are complicated by the fact that the nearest facility for cleaning bones is located in Uttar Pradesh, requiring transport to and fro.

Camel Dung

Camel dung represents an important fertiliser and plays, or played, a significant role in the relationship between camel breeders and farmers. Although the fertilising effect of camel dung is not as high as that of goat or sheep dung, it is regarded as better than cow dung. Although its effect is retarded, since it takes longer for camel dung to decompose, it lasts for 3 years. Sedentary camel breeders sell camel dung by the cartload or exchange it for grain. Nomadic camel pastoralists receive compensation in kind from the owners of the land on which their herds stay overnight. Even higher fertilising value is attributed to camel urine.

Ecological Benefits of Camels

Ecologists emphasise that camel grazing has very little, if any, damaging effect on desert vegetation and does not contribute to desertification, for its foraging habits are optimally suited to areas with a low carrying capacity (Köhler-Rollefson, 1994b). Camel herds disperse over huge areas instead of clustering together like sheep. While goats often ravage a whole shrub in one extended feeding session, camels tend to take only one or two bites before moving on to the next bush or tree. In addition, their flat pad-like feet are believed to be gentle on the soil surface and not carve it up like the sharp cloven hooves of small ruminants (Gauthier-Pilters and Dagg, 1981). Camels also have a very efficient feed conversion rate and according to some calculations require only 1.9 kg of dry matter to produce 1 litre of milk, compared with 9.1 kg in cows (Stiles, 1983).

Camel Breeds in India

In India, camel breeds are named after the region in which they have originated, but there is no agreement among authors which regional populations should be regarded as distinct breeds (Köhler-Rollefson, 1992b). Only the Bikaneri and Jaisalmeri camel are universally accepted as discrete, and they have their origin in the breeding herds kept by the Maharajahs of these kingdoms. Rathore (1986) referred to Mewari and Kacchi breeds, while Khanna (1988) mentions Marwari, Mewati, and Kutchi breeds, and in another paper also refers to Shekhawati, Mewari, Sindhi, and Riverine breeds and strains (Khanna and Rai, 1995). Camel breeders also list Sirohi, Jalore, and Sanchori camels as separate breeds. The Malvi camel has been described as a separate and phenotypically very distinct breed with good milk potential (Köhler-Rollefson and Rathore, 1996).

Approaches to Supporting Camel Based Livelihoods

Lokhit Pashu-Palak Sansthan (LPPS), an Indian NGO based in Rajasthan's Pali District, has been working with the Raika camel breeding caste since 1996, helping them to improve economic returns from their hereditary activity, by providing camel health care, assistance with camel milk marketing and other support (Köhler-Rollefson, 1995, 1997; Rathore, 2001).

The work of LPPS developed out of a research project on the socio-economics of camel husbandry in India begun in 1990/91 (Köhler-Rollefson, 1992a). At that time, the Raika from Pali district in central Rajasthan had expressed concern and complaints about the disease problems of their camel herds, mostly early and late miscarriages, as well as difficulties of finding grazing for them. These interactions resulted in an applied research project seeking to verify the information provided by the Raika, to establish data on the reproductive performance of camels under field conditions and to identify the bottlenecks in the system. The research focused on an area known as Godwar, which is composed of Bali and Desuri tehsils of Pali District and extends along the north-western face of the Aravalli Hills, but it also extended into adjacent parts of Pali district. Some of the salient results are summarised here.

Results of Applied Research

Production System and Yearly Cycle

The Godwar camel breeders are sedentary and engage in village-based herding, in contrast to many of the Maru Raika from outside Godwar who are usually migratory and rarely return to their village. Of 156 herds encountered during the project's survey of camel holding families in southern Pali district, 34 (22%) were sedentary and 122 (78%) were nomadic.

Often 2–5 families form herding groups. The herds are grazed on various types of lands, including fallow or harvested fields, *gauchar* (village grazing grounds), *oran* (pasture land devoted to a deity), so-called 'wastelands' (uncultivated land under the jurisdiction of the state) and, during the rainy season, the forests of the Aravalli Hills. For access to the latter, grazing taxes have to be paid, frequently incremented with bribes for the forest officials.

The breeding season falls in the cold months of the year from November to March/April. This is the most work-intensive part of the year. During the rainy season from July to October, the incidence of disease is greatest. In November, the calves born during the previous winter are taken for sale to the Pushkar market, a trek that takes some 10–14 days. Traditionally, this is the time when the whole year's income is realised.

Herd Sizes in Pali District

Herd sizes range between two and 60 head, with holdings of 11–20 camels forming the most frequent category (Table 2).

Table 2
Distribution of Herd Sizes in Pali District

Herd size	1–10	11–20	21–30	31–40	41–50	51–60
Number	15	25	17	8	3	1

There was a definite trend for herds to become smaller. Of the 156 camel holdings surveyed in Godwar and adjoining area, 119 (76%) were said to have decreased in size over the last 20 years; only 28 (18%) had increased, whereas 9 (6%) were said to have remained about the same by their owners.

Income from Camel Breeding

The Raikas predominantly sell young male camels, which represent about two-third of the sold animals. About 25 per cent of the sold camels are young female animals. The rest are adult animals—either female camels that cannot be used for breeding, male riding camels, or male breeding camels.

- In 1994, the average price of 67 camels sold at Pushkar by Raika families from the village of Jojawar (District Pali) amounted to Rs 2,104; male animals obtained an average price of Rs 2,071, compared with Rs 1,661 for females.
- In 1995, prices were slightly higher, with Rs 2,209 for male and Rs 1,700 for female young animals. By some this development was attributed to the project inputs.
- In 1996, prices were not recorded, but the Pushkar Fair witnessed a dramatic rise in prices for good quality camels which were also so much in demand that after the first two days practically all of them were sold.

The price range for calves of weaning age reportedly runs from a few hundred to around Rs 10,000. Camel breeders from other parts of Rajasthan where camels can range unsupervised generally prefer to sell them at the age of 4–5 years, when they fetch the highest prices—of up to Rs 20,000.

Profits

The average annual income of the 'average' family can be calculated as follows. In an average family holding of 13 female breeding camels, 6–7 calves are born, of which 50 per cent (3–4) are male and can be sold. At an average price of Rs 2,200, this amounts to an annual income of Rs 6,600–8,000.

Disease Spectrum

The two infectious diseases of greatest economic importance are trypanosomosis and mange.

Other health problems with significant impact include injuries which are often due to falls. Apparently camels fairly often slip or fall down, especially when grazing in the Aravalli Hills. Fractures occur in both young and adult animals. Poisonings from eating certain plants (*Lantana* sp., *Oleander*) also occur regularly.

Calf Diseases

The mortality of young camels is fairly low. Of 47 camel calves whose births were recorded by the project in 1994–95, five died before weaning, i.e., before they could be sold at Pushkar, amounting to an infant mortality rate of 11 per cent. This sample was small, but analysis of 388 births with the help of the "progeny history method" also showed that 43 (11%) had resulted in infant death.

Of 40 camel calves born to Godwar Raikas in 1995–96 only 2, equivalent to 5 per cent, died before weaning. Causes of death are constipation, diarrhoea and accidents (for instance falling into the well), sometimes also predators (leopards).

Abortions

An analysis of 473 pregnancies compiled by the progeny history method showed that 18 per cent had ended in abortions. The Raika generally attributed the abortions to infection with trypanosomosis, although causal connection was never confirmed scientifically.

Project Interventions

Based on the results of the research and suggestions of the Raika, the project undertook a number of interventions aimed at making camel breeding more economically viable. These included:

- *Camel health services,* notably prophylactic treatment against trypanosomosis and curative treatment for mange.
- *Support for camel milk marketing.* In order to generate additional income, the project supported the initiation of camel milk marketing, which was against traditional social rules of the Raika community. Depending on the situation of the family (sedentary

or nomadic), this can be reasonably profitable, although it requires skilled management if malnourishment of the calves is to be avoided (Köhler-Rollefson, 1997).

- *Provision of superior male breeding camels.* Because the price of camel calves depends very much on their quality, high quality male camels were made available for shared use by the community.
- *Exposure tours for camel breeders.* Linkage was established with the National Research Centre on Camel, and camel herders benefited from exposure to scientific camel breeding.
- *Solution of grazing conflicts.* The most important but also the most difficult aspect of the efforts has been pushing for access to grazing in the Aravalli Hills which constitute the traditional summer grazing grounds of the camel herds, and fighting the corruption of the Forest Department. While there have been some successes these have been temporary, and there are plans to further restrict the access of camels to this area. Lack of grazing areas is actually the most crucial and limiting factor to camel breeding.

Why Camels are Still Needed

Drought Resilience

Rajasthan is a drought-prone area. Average annual rainfall amounts fluctuate wildly between years and in most years. But the policy makers seem to have forgotten this and have supported and subsidised irrigation agriculture in a big way. Already this has led to a depletion of groundwater supplies in many parts of the state, including the immediate area around us. Over the last 20 years or so, the number of bore-wells multiplied exponentially, and the traditional one-crop rainfed agriculture was replaced with an irrigated two or even three-crop cycle. But since the last seven years the majority of fields has lain fallow and so once again can be put to productive use only by means of livestock.

The riots surrounding water distribution in Hanumangarh are another indication that water will become increasingly scarce rather than more abundant in the coming years. An animal, which can thrive on local vegetation that grows without irrigation, is an inestimable asset in such a scenario. It is in the interest of drought-proofing Rajasthan that the camel should have a larger rather than a smaller share of the economy.

Livelihoods for Poor People

In earlier times, camel ownership was a prerogative of the rich and powerful, and camel ownership symbolised wealth, as well as military power. But currently, it is the poor and the voiceless who own camels and for whom they form the basis of their livelihoods. Among camel owners we can distinguish two broad categories: camel breeders who keep herds of female camels, and camel users who own one or two male camels for work. We can estimate that there are about 6,000–10,000 camel breeding families and up to 200,000 families for whom working camels are an important element of their livelihood. These include the camel cart owners in Jaipur and other cities who earn a living by transporting construction materials and other goods, and for whom this business generates enough income to provide education for their children. It also includes poor farmers in the Ganganagar area who can not afford tractors for carrying out agricultural activities. Thirdly, and sadly, there are some sub-sectors of Rajasthan's society for whom the camel cart affords the only means of transportation, since they are not allowed to take advantage of public transportation. One of the participants in the grazing workshop that we just concluded belonged to the Vagri community and related how his people were not allowed to use buses and therefore had to resort to camel carts to get to the hospital, etc.

This livelihood option will remain open only as long as camels are reasonably priced. If they become too scarce and too expensive, an important source of income will disappear and more people become unemployed.

Environmental Protection

As a means of transporting goods, even in cities, camel carts have much to recommend them, being silent, independent of fossil energy, and non-polluting. Instead of being perceived as antiquated, camel carts should be regarded as trademark of Rajasthan and a progressive, because eco-friendly, source of energy. Lifting water is another activity that can easily be performed by camels.

Identity

Eighty per cent of India's camel population is at home in Rajasthan, and the camel is practically symbolic of this state. The word Rajasthan practically conjures up images of camels in most peoples' minds, and everybody knows that camels can be found only in Rajasthan. The camel means deserts, sunsets, turbaned and moustachioed men—even love—and advertising agencies capitalise on this. From mobile phone companies to the Department of Tourism, many businesses exploit the romantic vibrations emanating from the image of a camel and use it in their advertising campaigns.

Tourism

Undoubtedly, it is the possibility of undertaking a camel safari that lures a large proportion of especially young tourists to Jaisalmer and to Rajasthan as a whole. The significance of the camel for Rajasthan's attractiveness as a tourist destination can not be overstated. Some tourism entrepreneurs are already expressing anxiety about the shortage of camels.

Culture and Indigenous Knowledge

From Dhola-Maru to Moomal and Mahendra, Rajasthan's folklore abounds with references to the camel. But apart from that, there is one community for whom it is of special significance: the Raika, who believe they were created by Lord Shiva to take care of the camel and who took care of royal breeding herds. Because until today, this special sense of responsibility towards the camel is retained among the elder generation, the Raika represent the guardians of the camel, replete with an immense store of knowledge on camel management and treatment. The Raika form one of the most fascinating components of Rajasthan's ethnic mosaic, and their indigenous knowledge is a treasure that must not be squandered. Alas, few members of the young generation feel inclined towards a camel herding way of life, and this represents one of the most severe threats to the survival of the camel. The camel culture of India is precious and very distinct to that in other countries because of its Hindu foundation and the prohibition on using camels for meat.

Reasons for the Decline of the Camel Population

Grazing Problems

The most important causal factor for the decline of the camel population is the disappearance of pasture and that can sustain camel breeding herds. For camel breeding to be reasonably profitable, a certain minimum herd size (around 20–30 female camels) is required, which in turn need to have access to sufficient pastureland. Camels are browsers and, in India, primarily depend on trees, especially various slow-growing *Acacia* species.

The causes for the disappearance of grazing opportunities are multi-factorial and include expansion of irrigation agriculture (both through deep wells and the Indira Gandhi Canal), the alienation and neglect of community grazing lands, and the establishment of wildlife sanctuaries and other reserved areas. The Indira Gandhi Canal has eaten into, and cut into half, a prime camel breeding area. Farmers reportedly shoot camels with guns, tie their mouths shut to starve them, and attach thorny shrubs to their tails. Military shooting zones also complicate camel breeding.

In Pali and Udaipur districts, the area that has been turned into the Kumbhalgarh Sanctuary has traditionally represented the rainy season pasture for several thousand camels. Access to this area has become very difficult, and now there is a total ban on grazing in all sanctuaries. In coastal Gujarat, camels have grazed in the mangrove areas, and here too they are now being barred from access. Institution of the Joint Forest Management system has also often led to the exclusion of camels, since their owners are not members of the Village Forest Protection Committees.

In Sanchore, establishment of a *gaushala* has taken away pastures and been accompanied by the destruction of *jal*, a plant that is ideal camel fodder but takes many years if not decades to grow.

Discrimination by Policy Makers

The significance of the camel for Rajasthan's economy is not reflected in the various livestock related laws, legal acts, and support programmes. In fact, reference to the camel is omitted in almost all of them, while cattle are given special consideration.

- Camel milk is not included in the Rajasthan Dairy Act. The rejection of camel milk by the government dairies to accept camel milk creates added hurdles towards the marketing of camel milk and makes it more difficult for them to support their livelihoods.
- There are no provisions for camels in the newly set up Livestock Development Board, which instead caters towards cattle breed improvement and *gaushalas*.
- The programmes of the Central Ministry of Agriculture for the camel are largely inappropriate for addressing the problems of camel population decline.

- Camels, together with sheep and goats, are not included in the Famine Code. However, there are apparently provisions in the National Calamity Relief Fund and the Calamity Relief Fund to assist owners of draught animals with a quarter to a third of the replacement costs. However, this is not widely known.
- Funds are channelled into *gaushalas*, which compete with camels and other livestock for grazing resources.
- Livestock as a whole is not given any attention, as is reflected in the low priority and status of the Department of Animal Husbandry. This is incomprehensible and irresponsible considering the enormous competitive advantage Rajasthan has in livestock production.
- Lack of interest among non-camel specialist researchers and institutions—as is reflected in the scant participation at this conference.

Consequences for Camel-dependent People

Prices for Camels are Up

Because of the added demand for camels by slaughterers, the demand for camels at Pushkar now by far exceeds the supply, and camel prices have risen significantly, may be by close to 50 per cent. This is good news for breeders obviously, but not for camel users who find it more difficult to obtain suitable animals.

Lack of Interest in the Young Generation

Young people have lost interest in the profession of camel breeding because it does not offer the prospect of a reasonable livelihood. Within the Raika community, young women also do not want to marry men who breed livestock.

Need for Action: Recommendations by Camel Breeders

In the grazing workshop that we held recently the participating camel breeders who hailed from all parts of Rajasthan, made the following recommendations to address the issue:

1. Camel grazing areas should be identified and protected. The responsibility for their management should be given to camel herders.
2. Camel milk must be included in the Rajasthan Dairy Act.

3. There should be systematic *camel health care* through vaccinations.
4. There should be a *ban on the slaughter* of fertile and healthy female camels.
5. It must be ensured that the work of the National Research Centre on Camels benefits the camel breeders. For this field centres must be opened.

Additional recommendations pertained to making camel breeders once again proud of their profession so that the young generation would look at it as a viable career option.

I would like to add one recommendation from my own perspective. While the camel population will likely shrink further before the decline can come to a halt, it is important that the process is 'managed' and that loss of the most genetically valuable animal resources is avoided. There is a big degree of genetic variability within the population; for example, it seems as if the camels from Mewar and Malva have relatively high milk potential. Therefore, an effort must be made to save the breeds from this region.

References

Agrawal R.P., Swami S.C., Beniwal R., Kochar D.K., Sahani M.S., Tuteja F.C., Ghouri S.K., (2003), 'Effect of Camel Milk on Glycemic Control, Risk Factors and Diabetes Quality of Life in Type–1 Diabetes: A Randomised Prospective Controlled Study', *J. Camel Res. Pract.*,10, 45–50.

Farah, Z. and Fischer, A. (eds.) (2004) 'Milk and Meat from the Camel', *Handbook on Products and Processing*, Vdf Hochschulverlag AG an der ETH Zürich, Switzerland.

Gahlot, T.K. and Chada, B.P. (2000) 'Training and Sport of the Dromedary Camel', pp. 577–591 in Gahlot, T.K., (ed.) *Selected Topics on Camelids*, The Camelid Publisher, Bikaner.

Gauthier-Pilters and Dagg (1981), *The Camel, Its Evolution, Ecology, Behaviour, and Relationship to Man*, University of Chicago Press.

Jodha, N.S. (1988) 'The Decline of Common Property Resources in Rajasthan, India', *Pastoral Development Network Paper* 22c. Overseas Development Institute, London.

Khanna, N.D. (1988) Traits and Calf Behaviour in Bikaneri Breed of Camel', pp. 73–80 in Hjort, A., (ed.) *Camels in Development*, Scandinavian Institute of African Studies, Uppsala.

Khanna, N.D. and Rai, A.K. (1995) *Perspective and Strategic Plan for Camel Improvement Research Programmes at NRC on Camel at Bikaner (1995–2025)*, National Research Centre on Camel, Bikaner.

Köhler-Rollefson, I. (1992a), 'The Raika Dromedary Breeders of Rajasthan: A Pastoral System in Crisis, *Nomadic Peoples,* 30: 74–83.

——. (1992b) 'The Camels of India in Social and Historical Perspective', *Animal Genetic Resource Information*, 10: 53–64.

——. (1994a), 'Ethnoveterinary Practices of Camel Pastoralists in Northern Africa and India', *Journal of Camel Practice and Research*, 1(2): 75–82.

——. (1994b), 'Camel Pastoralism: An Indigenous Arid Land Exploitation Strategy, *Journal of Camel Practice and Research*, 1(1): 1–6

——. (1995), 'Rajasthan's Camel Pastoralists and NGOs: The View from the Bottom, pp. 115–28 in D. Stiles (ed.) *Social Aspects of Sustainable Dryland Management*, John Wiley & Sons, Chichester.

——. (1997), 'New hope for the Raikas of Rajasthan', *Livestock International,* 1(1): 11–14

Köhler-Rollefson, I. and Rathore, H.S. (1996), 'The Malvi Camel: A Newly discovered Breed from India', *Animal Genetic Resource Information*, 18: 31–42.

Leese, A.S. (1927), *A Treatise on the One-humped Camel in Health and Disease*. Haynes and Son, Stamford.

Malhotra, S.P. et al. (1983), *Population, Lands, Crops and Livestock statistics of Arid Zone of Rajasthan*, CAZRI, Jodhpur.

NRCC, (2004), http://www.icar.org.in/nrccm/bio-main.htm (14.4.04)

Rathore, G.S. (1986), *Camels and their Management,* Indian Council of Agricultural Research, New Delhi.

Rathore, H.S. (2001), 'Saving the Camel in Rajasthan', *Ecology and Farming,* 27 (May–August): 16–17.

Srivastava, V.K. (1991), 'Who are the Raika/Rebaris?' *Man in India,* 71(1): 279–304

Stiles, D. (1983), 'Camel Pastoralism and Desertification in Northern Kenya', *Desertification Control,* 8: 2–15.

16

Camel Theft in 18th Century Rajasthan

Some Observations

Nirmal Kumar

Rajasthan came under severe threat from the sultans of the Sultanate period during the first decade of 14th century.[1] This negates the general notion that the region was generally out of the pale of Sultanate state. But definitely, the Islamic influence was more pronounced once it came under the Mughal suzerainty after being defeated and then accommodated by Akbar. "In theory, once a Rajput ruler accepted *mansab* and became *banda-i-dargah* (slave of the court), he lost all his suzerainty; and indeed even the Rajput rulers within their own domains were bound to carry out the orders of the Emperor".[2] In fact, the extent of the Mughal influence on Rajputana was so considerable that though free to govern internal matters by themselves, their entire administration betrayed an unmistakable Mughal imprint. S.P. Gupta opines that the main lines of the agrarian system is indistinguishable from those of the Mughal type, as come to us from the *dastur-ul-amal, amal-dastur, taqsim*, etc. The differences, if any, are minor and secondary. The heavy Persian vocabulary and identical names for documents of particular kinds suggest that the Mughal influence permeated details of administration.[3] G.D. Sharma concurred with this conclusion in his exhaustive work on Rajput polity.[4] Going by the prevailing trend in Rajasthan historiography, it would be only expected to presuppose a wholly Mughal type judicial administration and crime situation in the state. Beginning here we would try to test this assumption in this paper and see for ourselves if it holds good, and, if not, then we shall try to explore and suggest alternatives.

Camel in Rajasthan

In all pre-industrial economy the most efficient and economical power comes from animals. Whether it was in transportation, agriculture, dairy purposes or industries like shoe-making all depended upon livestock. Incidentally in India, the animal waste was not used as manure in the agricultural fields mainly because the dung-cakes were used as fuel for domestic cooking.[5] It has been strongly suggested that compared to 20th century there were more cattle in the Mughal period, around c.1595 A.D. when Abul Fazl completed his celebrated *Ain-i-Akbari.*[6] Naturally animals made a very lucrative object of theft. It usually became a subject of dispute between two or more individuals or villages. They could be stolen from the shed, pasture or even while travelling on highway. They could be taken away at night but sometimes could be snatched forcibly, very much before the eyes of its owners or attendants. Animals, though mute, have this unique capacity of recognising their herd, shed and owner. Often they react violently or even make noises if handled by strangers. Thus, it would only be natural to argue that most of the cattle thieves were professionals who would possess the requisite knowledge about handling animals. It is so because usually animals are used to their handlers and react to the strangers.

Camel occupies the place of pride in Rajasthan. In the rough and hot terrain of a desert camels are rightly called the "ship of the desert". They may not be the most expensive of all the animals, but certainly were most numerous and useful of all the animals. It is no surprise that all romantic tales and folklores have camels as an integral part of the story. They are used in carts, transportation, travelling and even to pull ploughs. It is no wonder that the greatest number of thefts relate to this animal. People decorate it, flaunt it, love it and steal it.

In his sectional presidential address to Indian History Congress (in 1995), S.P. Gupta has adequately summarised the history and historiography of camel:[7]

> "In recent times the history of the camel has attracted much attention, there being a full-fledged work on it, concentrating on dromedaries, or camels with single humps.[8] It has been recognised that this major beast of transport in tropical desert had not been available to north-western Indian protohistoric and early historic

> communities. Only the double humped Bactrian camel being known, and this animal was useless for Thar transport.[9] The dromedary made his first known appearance within India in the 7th century; the authority is again, Yuan Chwang. In *Sin-tu* (Sind), he says, "the camels are small in size and have only one hump".[10] It is likely that the Arab conquest of Sind led to a further improvement in the breed, yet the breeding of dromedaries in Sind was clearly antecedent to the arrival of the Arabs."
>
> "With the dromedary, desert transport must have expanded very considerably. The lines of trade between Gujarat and the upper Gangetic basin and the Punjab via Marwar could have been thrown open. And so would arise the prosperous merchants of *A-tali*. But the basis of their prosperity would rest on the shoulders of the lowly camel-breeders, necessarily nomadic and pastoral. In present day Sind they belong to the community of jats. The jats appear as a lowly, almost menial, but large community of pastoral people in Sind, in the *Chachnama* (8th century). Yuan Chwang too describes them but leaves them unnamed. These "several hundreds of thousands of families" gave themselves exclusively to tending cattle".

Camel Theft: Some Episodes

The economic usefulness of camels in a desert made them particularly an object of desire for all and sundry. And the fact that they were the main beasts of transportation made them more vulnerable. Moving from one place to another, they were often left unattended or with tired attendants/owners themselves prone to sleep. One Sankhla Chhatu of village Nihasdesar of Bikaner reported that one of his camels was stolen from the caravan (*katar*).[11] But it could have been lifted from one's house, especially when the owner was away.[12] Perhaps the cattle lifter had an information network, which informed them about the owners' absence or the arrival/passage of a caravan. In the ensuing discussion, we shall encounter professional thieves and villages full of thieves who could not have flourished in the absence of such an information network.

It was usual for people including the state to buy camels at different cattle fairs. These fairs presented a unique opportunity to all and sundry to buy and sell animals. Quite often large numbers of animals were purchased and then made to walk long distances to their new homes. This usually entailed risk because of unsafe routes and existence of robbers all the way. Actually the state usually blamed the merchants for the crime as they would ignore the authorities and take a shorter route, which might not have been safe, and also travel without proper escort.[13]

On *Baisakh Bad* 7 v.s. 1822, one Tiku was coming from Mewar after purchasing 38 camels. Somewhere between village Bidhu and Bilada all his 38 camels were looted.[14] He himself conducted a search and found at least one camel, but the owner claimed that he had bought it for Rs 65. Such fast was the network in stolen animals! Still other easy victims on the highway were the traders who would transport goods over long distances. Laden with goods and basically peace loving and business-minded these, people made very soft targets. Mehta Goyand's two camels, three bullocks and the money to buy horse were looted near Chutra by two persons identified by him as Devkaran and Dalkaran of village Talwaada.[15] In yet another case village, Lohawat's Rajputs identified one Rajput Anup Singh who had forcibly taken away five camels laden with grain. Perhaps other goods besides camel and grain were also looted because the royal order instructs the restoration of 'camel, grain, etc.' to the complainant.[16]

Lifting of camel can also be plainly an attack over some person for plunder or revenge. From village Jajhu of Bikaner one Brahman Godhu migrated to village Chakhu of Phalodi to earn a living. Chakhu's *jagirdar* probably upset at his migration sent thirteen camels to Jajhu apparently to collect haystacks. But there his men beat up the Brahman's servant, looted his property, and seized two sets of family of camels comprising one male camel, one female camel and one calf each. The punishing operation also included molestation of the Brahman's wife.[17] While beating of the Brahman's servant and molestation of his wife were to be seen as a part of corporal punishment meted out to the body, looting of camels with other property meant to gain materially. As it is, raids purely to procure camels were also not unknown.

Theft, loss, loot or abduction of camels generated passion and often invited retaliatory actions. One common way was to detain camels or caravans of the same village as that of the thieves. This, of course, presupposes a certain level of intelligence work done. The absence of a dedicated police force also necessitated, quite often, private action. In v.s. 1823, thieves belonging to village Saisar of Bikaner stole 3 camels of one Ghagal Rupe of village Chadarakh. In retaliation, a caravan from village Saisar was detained at Chadrakh.

The men of Bikaner then petitioned the state for the eventual release of their caravan and even promised to locate the camels. This suggested the widespread availability of information about habitual/professional thief. What further proves the general involvement of the village in such criminal activities was their readiness to pay/compensate for the camels, which they did soon thereafter.[18] An interesting information given here is in the last part of the order. It gives a sort of general sanction to such retaliatory measures of the people to settle scores. It so happened the people of Saisar had made a payment for the camels to one Ghagal Surte and the money, it appears, did not reach Rupe Ghagal whose camels were stolen. Such was the ineffectiveness or general indifference of the state coupled with lack of an independent police force that the state instructed the people of Saisar to detain a caravan from Chadrakh and settle the account of Rupe's camels.[19]

At another place a series of retaliatory and counter-retaliatory actions of detaining caravans is reported, which suggests a very low level of state participation in solving the crime-related problems and hence people on their own did much of policing, searching, recovering the lost goods and then punishing the culprits. The state in a way sanctioned such private initiatives to compensate for its lack of police force and positively speaking, it hints towards a greater autonomy to local authorities in dealing with local matters. Such a trend is very visible in caste and other social matters where local *panchayats* and caste/community *nyats* had a very important role to play. One camel was stolen from *qasba* Koliya. It was traced to Fatehpur. In this respect five camels of a *raibari* of village Magluna were detained at Parbatsar. Investigations were made at Fatehpur, but they denied the whole thing and agreed for an ordeal (*dheej*), to prove their innocence. It is one of the ancient forms of investigation that had religious sanction (Even Sita had to undergo a fire ordeal to prove that the demon king Ravana had not outraged her modesty). But they actually did not turn up for that. Later one Jat Daho Har Ram of village Kudi Pipad of Jodhpur had taken his cattle to Dindarpur in Fatehpur for grazing. When he was returning in the month of *asadh* his camels and a daughter were abducted. In retaliation at Kudi Pipad, people detained a caravan belonging to Dindarpur.[20]

Such a series of retaliatory measures by people themselves in spite of the state is a little intriguing. That the state allowed people to settle scores among themselves prompts even a casual observer to argue for a weak state. But it is truer of a state organised on a clannish organisation, which had an incomplete state formation. After the Rajput states came under the well-structured Mughal administration they tried to copy the system at the top level, but at local levels the things remained more or less free of recent administrative changes. The administrative integration of the Gangetic belt-type was difficult in Rajput states not only because of the clannish/feudal set-up, but also because of desert conditions, lack of fertile lands and scattered village settlements. This particular document (in f.n. 20) is also important for some general guidelines enunciated by the state regarding thefts. It instructs the people not to entertain thieves in one's village, to expel them. Further, it enjoins upon authorities to confiscate the property of such thieves. Authorities also have to maintain the safety of roads and highways for the sake of traders.[21] In states of Rajasthan where trade provided essential goods and held the lifeline, a state's sincere concern for their safety is only too obvious to be argued for.

By now, we have noticed that in most of the cases the owner of the camels has been able to identify the thief or we find the thief or thieves mentioned by their names and village they belonged to. In all such cases the state's keenness to investigate the crime and trace the criminal cannot be doubted, though it may have failed due to lack of a full-fledged agency. The state did order the officials to conduct a search, identify the thief, and restore the stolen goods and animals to its rightful owner.[22] Even when lacking an organised agency for policing, the state sometimes took pains to investigate the matter. Repeated reminders to search acted as extra pressure on the local officials to inquire into the matter.[23] Such investigations were carried on for as many as 20 to 22 days before being abandoned. We find that dissatisfied with this, the court ordered the search to be restarted and camels to be restored to its owners.[24]

Camel being the most numerous and popular beast of transportation, its identification became a problem. Its capacity to walk or run fast and tendency to mix easily with other groups made the matter worse. The one way was to go by the footprints, which would lead them to some village or even person, but a clever thief would take care of that and all searches would come to a blind end.[25] The best option open to the people was to depend upon local information network. Indian villages being a small settlement, people would notice a stranger immediately. Even today people in villages know the exact morphology and settlement pattern of scores of neighbouring villages.

Hence, they also know the regular thieves. Victims to trace their stolen goods and animals hired spotters (*khojis*). Almost every region, if not village, was expected to have spotters to help investigate the matter.[26] Even an ascetic (*Bhopi*) could double as a spotter, though he was not much trusted. In many documents we find that the complainant had already searched for and even identified the thief complete with his address. This of course presupposes some amount of private initiative. Sankhla Chhatu of village Nihardesar of Bikaner reported that one of his camels was stolen. He himself conducted a search and found it with one *baniya* of village Devli, who reportedly had bought it from someone.[27] Similarly in a case mentioned above, one person who was coming from Mewar after making a purchase of 38 camels, on the way between villages Bidhu and Bilada his camels were looted. He himself conducted a search and was able to find one camel with one Dhanna Paliwal of village Cherai. But Dhanna Paliwal denied having stolen the camel and claimed to have bought it from one Tulchha Paliwal of village Sadara on *Phagun Sud* 5 for Rs 62!.[28]

What comes out very clearly and most regularly is the existence of professional thieves everywhere. Coming alone or in a group they would indulge in camel lifting with impunity. Theft of camel or any other bigger animal was usually not possible by one thief and would require more than one person to conduct the whole affair smoothly. Eyes would be kept at the prospective target, more persons would take care of any eventual resistance by the owner/attendants, driving the camel(s) away, hiding them to ensure non-detection and its eventual sale to a professional buyer of stolen goods or any unsuspecting customer. All this meant involvement of more than one person in the whole act. While sometimes the victim did not know the identity or the number of thieves, yet another time he could only say that they were many in number.[29] There are instances when the complainant could actually tell the numbers of persons involved in the whole operation, in one case the exact number being eight.[30] In another instance a victim could identify two persons who had stolen his one camel.[31] The whole operation was so smooth and fast that stolen camels disappeared into thin air in no time. The camel was stolen, driven to some distant village, hidden in some group of camels or simply sold to a professional buyer of stolen goods or to some unsuspecting customer. This network was so well oiled that by the time the camel owner tracked his camel down, it had already changed at least two hands.[32] All this obviously indicated towards existence of professional animal lifters. Perhaps they were well known to people and would naturally be the butt of people's suspicion. The promptness with which some accused criminals were recognised and named is confirmed by the documents.[33] Though the concept of criminal tribe took concrete and theoretical shape only under the British, it was not altogether absent in the earlier period. Modern commentators have generally regarded it as a mental and legal construct of the British administrators as much as the concept of 'martial race'.[34] Perhaps it suited the limited penetration of administrative model of the British where they ruled by coercion and segregation. But the fact that even the pre-British Rajput administration considered certain tribes or groups more prone to crime like *Mer, Bawari, Sansi, Meenas* calls for a serious review of the widely accepted historiography on the criminal tribes which generally and unequivocally repudiates the British concept of criminal tribes.

Our sources directly or indirectly refer to some villages, which had large numbers of criminals or were full of them or at least had some criminals who were granted protection. When three camels of one Ghagal Rupe were stolen, he soon identified that the thieves were from village Saisar of Bikaner.[35] In another case the blame for the theft of 5 camels was put on Fatehpur though the people of Fatehpur challenged this and even agreed to undergo ordeal to prove their innocence. But that they did not actually turn up for the said ordeal only proved their complicity in the crime.[36] It should be remembered that in both the instances mentioned it is the village, which is named, and not individuals. The notoriety of these villages would have been such that it made easy to point out to the criminals. The state was well aware of the problem and took strict actions against them.

Reacting to the reported case of theft of a camel of one *Bishnoi Jagu*, the authorities suspected that there might be more thieves in the village, and ordered the troops to expel the entire village.[37] In another very interesting case a communal fine was imposed on a village because it was reported that eight thieves who belonged to this village stole three camels. Though we are not told as to what was the exact fine, we came to know that Rs 25 were still due on the said village.[38] This sort of local communal responsibility towards maintenance of law and order, tracing the criminals or making good the loss was in conformity with the general tendency of the state to entrust local safety to local state and private authority. Special emphasis used to be laid on the safety of the highways and instructions were there not to harass the traders.

Epilogue

The above observations point to the fact that camel theft was in existence in 18th century Rajasthan. The state though aware of the problem, took serious action in limited cases. People used all available methods to retrieve the stolen animal. Caste/ community did play a role in tracing and fining the camel thieves. The discussion also leads us to believe that camel theft was an organised business for many. Retaliations also took place in certain cases when the stolen animal when traced was not returned to owner. Judicial system in the Mughal era was only partially helpful in controlling the crime.

Notes

1. M.S. Ahluwalia, *Muslim Expansion in Rajasthan*, Delhi, 1978, pp. 1–195, as quoted in S.P. Gupta's Sectional Presidential address, Proceedings of Indian History Congress, Delhi, 1995.
2. S.P. Gupta, "Reconstructing the Political and Economic Profile of Rajasthan", Presidential address, Section II, Proceedings of Indian History Congress, Delhi, 1995, p. 165.
3 Ibid., p. 166.
4. G.D. Sharma, *Rajput Polity: A Study of Politics and Administration of the State of Marwar,* 1638–1749, Delhi, 1977, p. 32.
5. W.H. Moreland, *India at the Death of Akbar,* Delhi, 1962, p. 100.
6. W.H. Moreland, ibid., p. 99; also Irfan Habib, "The Systems of Agricultural Production" in Tapan Raychaudhuri and Irfan Habib, (eds.) *The Cambridge Economic History of India*, Vol. I, Hyderabad, 1982, p. 221.
7. S.P. Gupta, op. cit, pp. 160–61.
8. R.W. Bulliet, *The Camel and the Wheel.*
9. R.H. Meadow, "A Camel-Skeleton from Mohenjo-Daro", in B.B. Lal and S.P. Gupta, (eds.) *Frontiers of the Indus Civilisation,* New Delhi, 1984, pp. 133–39, quoted in S.P. Gupta, op. cit, p. 161.
10. S. Beal, *Buddhist Records of the Western World*, London, 1884, p. 272; T. Watters, *On Yuan Chwang Travels in India*, Vol. II, London, 1905, both quoted in S.P. Gupta, op. cit., p. 161.
11. Sanad Parwana Bahi (hereafter referred to as SPB, No. 5, v.s. 1823, f. 227.
12. Ibid., no. 11,v.s.1828, f.18; ibid., No. 5, v.s. 1823, f. 196; ibid., No. 6, v.s. 1824, f. 108.
13. Patta Parwana Bahi, Bedla vigat 17, Kartik sud, v.s. 1923 and Asoj bad 9, v.s. 1924.
14. SPB, No. 2, v.s. 1822, f. 4; ibid., No. 5, v.s. 1823, f. 195 where 10 camels were looted.
15. SPB, No. 5, v.s. 1823, f. 207; ibid., No. 2, v.s. 1822, f. 79.
16. Ibid., No. 6, v.s. 1824, f. 113.

17. Ibid., f. 108.
18. Ibid.
19. Ibid.
20. SPB, No. 9, v.s. 1826, f. 12.
21. Ibid., also No. 5, v.s. 1823, no. 5, v.s. 1823, f. 216.
22. Ibid., No. 5, v.s. 1823, ff. 195 and 207.
23. Ibid., f. 196.
24. Ibid., No. 10, v.s. 1827, f. 42.
25. Ibid., No. 6, v.s. 1824, f. 90.
26. Ibid., No. 5, v.s. 1823, f. 216.
27. Ibid., f. 227.
28. Ibid., No. 2, v.s. 1822, f. 4.
29. Ibid., No. 6, v.s. 1824, f. 90; ibid., No. 5, v.s. 1823, f. 215.
30. Ibid., No. 5, v.s. 1823, f. 214–15.
31. Ibid., No. 2, v.s. 1822, ff. 4 and 79.
32. Ibid.
33. Ibid., No. 9, v.s. 1826, f. 21; *also,* ibid., v.s. No. 2, v.s.1822, f. 79.
34. Sanjay Nigam, "Disciplining and Policing the 'Criminals by Birth': The Making of a Colonial Stereo Type-the Criminal Tribes and Castes of North India", *IESHR,* Vol. 27, No. 2 & 3, 1990; Anand Yang, *Crime and Criminality in British India*, Arizona, 1985.

35 SPB, No. 6, v.s. 1824, f. 108.

36. Ibid., No. 9, v.s. 1826, f. 12.

37 Ibid., No. 5, v.s. 1823, f. 215.

38. Ibid., ff. 214–15.

Section IV

Social and Gender Issues

17

Gendered Participatory Approaches to Drinking Water Supply

Power and Practice

Kathleen O'Reilly

From 1997 until 2005, a joint Indian-German drinking water supply project was being built in northern Rajasthan. The project combined Government of Rajasthan engineers, who built the supply system infrastructure, and the staff of the Project Social Side (PSS), who were charged with facilitating community and women's participation in the project. The women's participation programme was meant to promote project sustainability through village women's inclusion in 'bottom-up' water resource planning, decision-making and control. Over the course of the project, women's participation also came to mean women fieldworkers' equal participation in the planning and management activities of the PSS.

Between 1997 and 2002, I studied the women's participation programme of this drinking water supply project (O'Reilly, 2002; 2003; 2004). My research shows that the result of gendered participatory approaches is a gendered paradox: development organisations are charged to bring women into the social and economic lives of their communities, yet they cannot accept their own women employees as full participants. Women working for Non-governmental Organisations (NGOs) like the PSS find themselves marginalised within these organisations even as they are called upon to bring about empowerment for women in villages. Officially women's participation in the project is 'essential' (PSS *Leporello Leaflet*, 1999), but the reality was that women—both fieldworkers and their clients in villages—did not participate in the project on the same footing as men. For example, when all staff gathered at the main office, men segregated themselves in small offices and planned field activities, while women staff waited for them in the conference room. The paradox surrounding women's participation drives my exploration of participation as a negotiated set of concepts and practices between women fieldworkers, their co-workers and their village clients.

Participation is a widely accepted approach to environmental management that seeks to tap the knowledge and skills of local communities for the good of sustainable development and associated projects. As a precept, participation was codified as Principle 10 during the UN Conference on the Environment and Development (Earth Summit) in 1992. Principle 10 states that "Environmental issues are best handled with the participation of all concerned citizens ..." (www.unep.org). Participation or 'community-based natural resource management' strives to gain input from people at a grass-roots level and facilitate their access, control and management of natural resources. Public participation is often written into projects as a framework for securing the investment of local actors who will be affected by environmental policies. By involving citizens in environmental management and governing institutions, participation is expected to empower local populations. Local involvement can also achieve cost savings and increased efficiency of projects.

Gendered participatory approaches were also codified at the Earth Summit as Principle 20, which states: "Women have a vital role in environmental management and development. Their full participation is therefore essential to achieve sustainable development" (www.unep.org). Women's participation has gained wide acceptance as a critical component of sustainable development and sound environmental management practices. Like community participation in general, women's participation programmes seek to access women's knowledges about locally sustainable environmental practices. They also intend to draw on women's (essentialised) inherent capacity for environmental protection. Planners expect that women as housewives and mothers will maximise the benefits of intended improvements in resource allocation and use. As neoliberal economic policies have found the state an inefficient and expensive service provider (e.g., water supplier), gendered approaches to participation aim to increase local women's self-management of resources and channel their labour toward project goals (see Paley, 2001).

Women's empowerment-through-participation is also sought through an incorporation of women in initial-stage decision-making and planning. Women's participatory approaches often have an agenda promoting social change, e.g., sustainable resource management and social equality through women's participation and empowerment. The PSS's women's participation component followed these general guidelines. Women as the primary water consumers in villages were mobilised to pay for water and maintain the new public taps. Planners expected that women would be empowered through women's participation.

From the outset, the PSS began hiring women to facilitate their women's participation component. Like many NGOs in Rajasthan, PSS management accepted unquestioningly that women fieldworkers were necessary components of a women's participation programme. Women fieldworkers, simply because they were women, were expected to enable local women's participation (O'Reilly, 2004). However, once women joined, they found themselves and their work on the margins of the organisation. Women's participation may not have ensured project sustainability, but it did produce tensions within the organisation over what women's participation was, and where it was going to happen. These tensions ultimately translated into different forms of implementation at the village level (O'Reilly, forthcoming).

In this paper, I specifically explore participatory approaches to development as negotiated practices that encompass: i) women fieldworkers' understanding of the (in)significance of women's participation to project success and ii) their own personal understandings of participation. I argue that participation is a form of power, wielded by women fieldworkers and reflective of tensions between them, their co-workers and their clients. The paper is based on extended field research undertaken between 1997 and 2002 as part of a larger project examining the function of development projects over time and space. Too often, development research is based on short periods of observation that leave the internal workings of NGOs unexplored (Ferguson, 1990; Crewe and Harrison, 2000). But to make sense of why people do what they do, the shifting context of the everyday social relations where they work must be fully explored (Mutersbaugh, 2002). Extended fieldwork provides a depth that cannot be gained any other way.

Below, I have divided my paper into three sections. The first is a brief introduction to my case study. The second section is some theoretical background on power and participation, followed by field examples that illustrate my argument that women's participation is not simply 'put in place' but both derives from and is generative of struggles between staff and villagers. I end with some conclusions. What follows places the research within its Rajasthani context.

Case Study

The drinking water project was established to provide drinking water at German quality standards to local residents of Rajasthan's *khara pani* (saline water) belt. Parts of this belt include Hanumangarh, Jhunjhunu and Churu districts, where groundwater is undrinkable because of its high salt content. The project included 378 villages and two towns, all of which would be covered with a 24-hour drinking water supply. Before the arrival of project water, residents of the area received their water twice daily at public standposts (taps) through a Government of Rajasthan (GoR) pipeline. The work of fetching water from public taps is predominantly the work of women and girls. Water provision by the GoR was both unreliable and unclean, although it was allegedly treated and it was free.

Water's commodification is a global trend (see Page, 2003), but in Rajasthan, the project was the first of its kind. Community participation in maintaining and paying for the system was seen by donors, planners and project staff as a vital part of the water supply's long-term sustainability. In return, it was hoped that the Government of Rajasthan would be more responsive to villagers as supply manager and service provider. Water for the project comes from the Himalaya in northern India via the Indira Gandhi Canal. From there a series of smaller canals and pipelines transport water to treatment facilities before it is piped into villages. Within villages a network of underground pipes were laid that connect to public standposts or taps, the locations of which were to be chosen by villagers themselves. Each village has a metre where the underground pipeline enters its boundary; households pay a portion of the total bill according to their number of members and livestock (*anga*). It was assumed by project planners that villagers desired regularly-supplied, clean water and they were willing to pay a small fee in order to get it.

The Project Social Side drew its staff from five local NGOs, but it strove to act as a cohesive unit. Officially, the PSS was charged to "convince mostly illiterate users, who see at their end only a small fraction of the whole infrastructure, of (1) the need to own and manage their local system and (2) to contribute to the general cost of O&M (Operation and Maintenance)". Approximately 70 Indian staff work for the PSS. There are seven Indian Programme Officers (the only woman Programme Officer is the Women's Participation Programme Officer), one German consultant as required by the donor bank, and approximately 50 fieldstaff—15 of these are women, all of them work on women's participation. PSS members are a diverse group; their home state, first language, socio-economic background, education level, age and marital status vary from person to person. Fieldworkers are divided into teams of one woman and two men; they live and work in area villages. Women fieldworkers assume the task of women's participation, which includes the formation of women's groups and health and hygiene trainings. Male members of the team take responsibility for water management, payment and latrine-building activities.

The work of a PSS fieldworker takes place at a number of different locations: the main office; field offices; and villages. At the main office, monthly meetings of all staff for 'experience sharing' and training sessions are held. At field offices, small teams of fieldworkers live, plan daily activities, and meet with individual villagers. In villages, fieldworkers travel together or separately to conduct activities and meetings. In the words of one fieldworker about conditions in villages: "Villages in (the project area) are very backward. There is no light (electricity), water problems are there; there are no roads." Villages are electrified, but provision is erratic. Unlike many of the neighbouring homes, all field offices have a latrine and bathroom (i.e., room for bathing), courtesy of the PSS. Road conditions can be especially bad—*andhii* (sandstorms) erase existing tracks in the sand between villages and whole sections of *pakka* (paved) roads. Distances from the field offices to the main office vary, between 2–5 hours. Road conditions (both paved and unpaved) alter with the seasons and vary by area. Difficulties of communication and distance give fieldworkers a high degree of independence when implementing project activities.

In any given day, field teams make approximately two village visits by Jeep, depending upon the villages' distance from the field office and each other. A woman fieldworker might meet with a women's savings group at the home of one of the members, give a training on safe water handling practices, or introduce the project to a new group of women. During my own fieldwork, I accompanied these women and their male colleagues as they travelled and worked in the villages of the Project area, taking notes and recording conversations. I conducted interviews assisted by Tasneem Khan in Hindi, English and Marwari with NGO staff and villagers in the main office, field offices and in villages. I also discursively analysed project documents in order to trace the history of women's participation in the project.

The following section delves more deeply into relationships of power and the practices of participation.

A Foucauldian Approach to Participation

There is a large literature both praising and condemning participation as a development strategy but the focus for mainstream development institutions often remains on establishing a definition of women's participation so that technical solutions can be found. By technical solutions, I mean answers to problems that do not require addressing complex social issues (see Ferguson, 1990). An example of a technical solution from the PSS is defining women's participation as the presence of a woman in village level meetings, which requires the election of a woman representative regardless of her actual ability to represent the variety of women living in her village. The social issues neglected in such a solution include attention to class and caste relations and the significance of gender as an element of those relations.

Following Foucault, I theorise participation as a form of power that travels through agents (see Cooke and Kothari, 2001). Foucault does not understand power as something held or possessed by individuals, but rather as something that is exercised through the web of social relations linking individuals together. Individuals both exercise this power and are subjected to it (Foucault, 1980: 98). That means that whether fieldworkers subvert or reproduce women's participation as project planners define it, their activities always carry power with them. I find that fieldworkers play an active role in recreating and subverting meanings of women's participation that circulate alongside each other. Everyday meanings and practices of participation reflect women fieldworkers' personal responses to the socio-political circumstances in which they find themselves (Springer, 2001; O'Reilly, 2002). In contrast to technical solutions to participation, my research shows participation is a form of power whose shape reflects and interconnects with other gendered relations of power within NGOs. To put it plainly, participation is given many meanings over the course of project implementation, and many of these meanings operate to support existing inequalities between men and women (O'Reilly, 2006). For example, women's participation takes a back seat to men's activities in the field because of male fieldworkers' definition of women's participation as a 'great joke'.

In the section below, I use two examples to illustrate how participation takes different forms in villages due to: 1) women fieldworkers' personal views on participation; and 2) the gendered politics of participation that surround them within the PSS. I begin with the example of Kavita, who learned quickly that her co-workers did not value women's participation as she did.

Two Examples from the Field: Kavita and Savitri

A woman fieldworker named Kavita told me that on her first day working in villages, she learned from her co-workers that women's participation was just a programme used to procure funding from the German donor bank (O'Reilly, 2004). It was clear to her that both men and women senior fieldworkers did not take women's participation seriously. But Kavita did not join the PSS to get money out of a foreign donor, she joined to do social work. For her "the primary concern was the village women" (October, 2000 interview). Kavita reacted to the lack of seriousness on the part of her colleagues by refusing to repeat empty promises about what the drinking water supply project might do for women. She decided to tell village women honestly that they were going to receive a 24 hour supply of clean water. Their responsibility was to pay for it and maintain the public taps. When women asked to be paid for cleaning public taps, she told them that this work was their expected contribution to the new supply system. Kavita admitted to me that her decision to present women's participation in a straightforward manner led to fights with her co-workers and that she was not meeting her field targets. Eventually, she quit the PSS citing frustration and arguments with her male co-workers as part of her reason (O'Reilly, 2006).

Kavita's actions demonstrate how women fieldworkers: i) are influenced by the internal politics surrounding women's participation; and ii) react to what they have learned by implementing their own ideas about what constitutes meaningful forms of participation. Having heard from her colleagues that women's participation was not taken seriously, she was empowered to dispense with lies and postponements of solutions. In turn, she believed she was empowering her women clients in villages with the knowledge of what the project would and would not do for them and what was expected of them in return. She also took the time to get to know women and listen to their concerns, offering herself as at least one person willing to hear women's voices. She made it her business to know what women's problems were, and what village politics meant for their everyday lives. Kavita's outsider status within her field team led her to seek closeness with village women and eventually to quit, as part of protecting her own integrity (O'Reilly, 2006).

The brief example of Kavita shows that participatory practices in villages are responses to gendered power dynamics within NGOs. Women fieldworkers' may not perform as their co-workers and supervisors expect, but their actions 'make sense' given their understanding of the insignificance of women's participation in the PSS. Women fieldworkers—because they are project insiders—have learned that women's participation is simultaneously spoken of as essential to project success and denigrated as a minor project element. At the very least, many staff feel ambiguous about women's participation. While undoubtedly aware of project definitions of participation, women fieldworkers redefine participation within a context of their marginalised status within their NGO (O'Reilly, 2006).

In another incident, a woman fieldworker named Savitri, after some initial training began to work on her own in villages. The following passage is from my June 2000 fieldnotes:

> We arrived in *Apnagadh* (village pseudonym) and went directly to a house where we sat on *charpoi* (cot). About 4–5 women and as many girls in this Jat neighbourhood gathered around the *charpoi* and after a little while Savitri began talking with them. The women were cheerful and friendly toward us. After a short time Savitri and I got up and went over to take a look at the latrines. I don't know what her agenda was supposed to be that day, but she covered a range of topics. First, she told them how the latrines much be kept clean with a brush or a stick with some cloth tied around it. I did not learn Savitri's exact criteria for clean, but certainly the presence of "*mitti*" (dirt) was a negative. She did not ask or comment on whether or not the latrine was being used or by whom.

While standing in front of the latrine with the women and girls, she brought up the non-hygienic practice of women putting their unwashed hands into *matkas* (pots). "Wash your hands first," she said, "or lift the *matka* from the bottom. See my hands, they look clean, but they are not. The project gives clean water but if your hands are not clean then they will dirty it." Lots of nodding and agreement by the women. Later that night she said to me proudly, "Didn't I cover all the topics: sanitation, health education, water, and women's participation?"

Savitri did cover all the topics expected of her, and she spoke according to her understanding of what was important in each. This example of Savitri's practices illustrates one common way many women fieldworkers facilitated women's participation—one in which a fieldworker instructed women on what they should do, and expected them to agree with what she was saying. Her interaction with village women was not intended to be a discussion of these topics with them. In Savitri's case, women's participation is a technical solution: she gathers women together to listen to what she has to say about health, sanitation and hygiene. Women's participation, as she understands, it does not encompass the social reasons why women might not be aware of germs (e.g., lack of educational opportunities due to gender and poverty) or might take precautions (e.g., time constraints due to gendered work burden).

Although her women clients assented to what Savitri said at the time, when women fieldworkers were not present, village women across age and caste expressed to me that they had no intention of changing their habits. Village women's agreement with unclean hands and water pots was in keeping with the many trainings that they had about water handling. They knew how and why project staff wanted them to handle water in certain ways, but according to my observations, they were as likely to put their hands in pots as they were not to, and I seldom if ever saw women washing their hands before water collection. For many women, their participation in the project was the fact that they showed up at meetings when women fieldworkers called them. Most did not feel it necessary to follow the instructions that women fieldworkers gave them.

From this example, we see how participation, although implemented as a technical solution, is a negotiated exercise. For Savitri, she relates to village women the ideas that she learned in PSS trainings. For her women clients, they agree with her at the time and then follow their own established practices. Savitri exercises power when she gathers women for a meeting, and part of their 'bargain' with her is to attend when they are called. She is listened to attentively, but when the meeting disbands village women continue their water handling practices as before. Village women understand participation as the necessity of their presence when women fieldworkers hold meetings, but whether they conform or not to Savitri's lesson on water hygiene is an exercise of their power. They know that regardless of how they fill their water pots, the project will provide them with clean water.

Analysis

The practices of Kavita and Savitri illustrate that women fieldworkers' practices of participation encompass their individual responses to the social dynamics in which she is working. Each took what they learned in training and from their co-workers and implemented participation in a way that made the most sense to them. Although they may not be doing their jobs as they were taught in trainings, the words and actions of Savitri and Kavita demonstrate both how power circulates through their practices. Kavita used participation—as she defined it—to give women information that would help them make decisions about their involvement in the project. In doing so, her colleagues felt that she was undermining project goals. For Savitri, participation maintained the status quo, i.e., women gathered, gave their time, and then left the meeting to do as they had done before. Any time a woman fieldworker acts or speaks in the name of women's participation, she exercises power to influence project outcomes.

Additionally, women fieldworkers are influenced by the ways that those around them define participation. Kavita reacts to her co-workers' definition of participation as insignificant by purposely telling women the 'truth' as she knows it. Her choices demonstrate how participatory practices in villages are influenced by gendered power dynamics within NGOs. Savitri knows that some of her colleagues denigrate women's participation as unnecessary to project success, but she sticks to what she learned in training. From their position inside the PSS, women fieldworkers have learned that women's participation is a programme touted as 'essential' to project sustainability, but that many staff feel conflicted about it.

All project actors demonstrate an ability to disrupt dominant meanings of participation as defined in project documents and trainings. Savitri does her best to implement participation as she has been taught in training, but eventually learns that women in villages come to her meetings but do not change their habits. Village women's behaviour might be called 'resistance' (Scott, 1985). But for my purposes, it is more useful to take Crewe and Harrison's (1998) suggestion that 'resistance' is a hybrid resolution to conflict. In the case of village women, they create a hybrid definition of women's participation that includes their attendance at meetings, but omits adopting new hygiene practices. Participatory practices are not pure; instead they include mixed practices that derive from power dynamics (e.g., hierarchy and gendered discrimination) surrounding the work of development project staff. The many hybrid forms of participation indicate that development planners must go beyond searching for technical solutions and move into the messy realm of social relations.

The above examples of field practices show women fieldworkers' and village women's substantial role in recreating, subverting and hybridising meanings of women's participation. I have shown participation as a form of power circulates through women fieldworkers and their clients. Whether they subvert meanings or reproduce project norms of participation, their activities always carry power with them (Foucault, 1980). Women fieldworkers' actions in villages illustrate how meanings of participation may be influenced by an ambivalence within the organisations about the importance of women's participation and women employees (O'Reilly, 2006). From women fieldworkers' and village women's negotiated relationships with each other, multiple meanings of participation emerge and are created. It is clear that both women fieldworkers and their clients exercise power to create women's participation in ways that make individual sense to them.

Conclusion

To conclude, my research demonstrates that development projects are sites of struggle, where the politics between actors impact project outcomes. As the work of a project unfolds, staff and constituents engage in constant negotiations over meanings of terms like 'participation'. The results of these struggles have importance not only for meanings of participation, but project outcomes (e.g., will women become empowered or clean standposts or both?). Shifting meanings of participation cannot be pinned down by training and policies; instead relationships of power between staff and between staff and their constituents provide clues for understanding what meanings emerge, when and why. This paper does not offer easy solutions to development's or NGOs' problems—instead I seek to complicate notions that there are simple solutions. However, by investigating the social complexities of development implementation, my research shows that further research is needed on how meanings and practices of development are worked out within organisations. Given their increasing focus on women, it is critical we move toward a richer understanding of participatory programmes' impacts on meanings, spaces and relationships.

References

Cooke, B. and Kothari, K. (2001), *Participation: The New Tyranny?*, Zed, London.

Crewe, E. and Harrison, E. (2000), *Whose Development?: An Ethnography of Aid*, Zed, London.

Ferguson, J. (1990), *The Anti-Politics Machine: 'Development,' Depoliticisation, and Bureaucratic Power in Lesotho,* Cambridge University Press, Cambridge.

Foucault, M. (1980), *Power/Knowledge*, Pantheon Books, New York.

Mutersbaugh, T. (2002), "Building Co-ops, Constructing Cooperation: Spatial Strategies and Development Politics in a Mexican Village", *Annals of the Association of American Geographers,* v. 92, pp. 756–76.

O'Reilly, K. (2002), "Creating Contradictions, Recreating Women: Struggles Over Meanings and Spaces of Women's Participation in a Rajasthan (India) Drinking Water Supply Project", Ph.D. Dissertation, University of Iowa, Unpublished.

——, (2003), "Competing Logics of Women's Participation in a Rajasthan Development Project", in Surjit Singh and Varsha Joshi (eds.) *Institutions and Social Change*, Rawat Publications, Jaipur, pp. 272–91.

——, (2004), "Developing Contradictions: Women's Participation as a Site of Struggle within an Indian NGO", *The Professional Geographer*, v. 56, pp. 174–84.

——, (2006), "Women Fieldworkers and the Politics of Participation", *Signs: Journal of Women in Culture and Society*, 31: 4.

Page, B. (2003), "Communities as the agents of commodification: The Kumbo Water Authority in Northwest Cameroon", *Geoforum,* 34: 483–98.

Paley, J. (2001), *Marketing Democracy: Power And Social Movements In Post-Dictatorship Chile,* (University of California Press, Berkeley, CA.

Project Social Side (1999), *Leporello Leaflet,* Popular Printers, Jaipur.

Springer, J. (2001), "State Power and Agricultural Transformation in Tamil Nadu", in A. Agrawal, and K. Sivaramakrishnan, (eds.) *Social Nature: Resources, Representations, and Rule in India,* Oxford University Press, India, New Delhi, pp. 86–106.

Scott, J. (1985), *Weapons of the Weak: Everyday Forms of Peasant Resistance*, Yale University Press, New Haven.

United Nations Environment Programme, (www.unep.org), Accessed 3 August 2006.

18

Female Employment in Unorganised Sector in Rajasthan

Surjit Singh

The labour market in developing countries is segmented into formal and informal sectors. Informal sector is taken to be synonymous with unorganised sector in India. The attributes of both these sectors are vastly different. The formal sector or the organised sector employs only small proportion of Indian labour force while the informal/unorganised sector is a refuge for all those who are not able to find jobs in the formal segment of the labour market (Singh, 1994). The work conditions are different in both the sectors. There are gender differences too. Informal sector has major proportion of women compared to the formal sector. There are regional variations too in deployment of labour force in India and activity-wise variations. This paper is an attempt to look at the female workers in Rajasthan with a specific focus on unorganised sector. As data on unorganised sector with gender features is hardly available, we have largely relied on economic census of 1998 on Rajasthan and National Sample Survey Organisation (NSSO) unorganised manufacturing sector survey of 2000–2001.

Female Workforce in Rajasthan

Population census provides us with detailed occupational distribution of workforce. However, we limit ourselves to broad categories of employment. Table 1 shows that in 1981 and 1991, the share of female workers in total main workers (other than cultivators and agricultural labourers) was just 8.29 per cent in 1981 that reduced to 7.82 per cent in 1991. In urban areas, the share of female workers has improved during 1981–91 while it deteriorated in rural areas. Looking at the seven major occupational divisions, we find that at the aggregate level, except for first three divisions (professional, technical and related workers; administrative, executive and managerial workers and; clerical and related workers), in all other divisions the share of female workers has gone down. This means that in Rajasthan during 1981–91, the work participation rate in professional, technical and related works; administrative, executive and managerial works and; clerical and related works has improved and this could be due to improvement in education.

It is also observed that 44.34 per cent of female workers are engaged as production and related workers, transport equipment operators and labourers followed by 19.23 per cent in agriculture related activities (farmers, fisher-women, hunters, loggers and related workers), 15.26 per cent in professional, technical and related works. The other significant activity where women are engaged is service sector. These four activities account for 89 per cent of all female workers in 1981. In 1991, the share of female workers increased in professional and related group, administrative, executive and managerial group and sales workers group, while the share declined in other groups.

It is also observed from the data that in 1981, 85.3 per cent of all female main workers were in clerical and related occupations in urban Rajasthan (while in 1991 this proportion fell to 83.9%) compared to only 14.7 per cent in rural Rajasthan. In case of professional, technical and related workers, 75.4 per cent of all female main workers were in urban Rajasthan (75.1% in 1991), 71.6 per cent in case of administrative, executive and managerial workers (72.8% in 1991), 61.4 per cent in case of service workers (70.3% in 1991), 51.1% in case of sales workers (59.3% in 1991), 38.5 per cent in case of production and related workers, transport equipment operators and labourers (48.5% in 1991) and just (expectedly) 4.3 per cent in farmers, hunters, loggers and related workers groups (5.3% in 1991). At the aggregate level, share of urban Rajasthan in total female main workers has increased from 42.2 per cent in 1981 to 54.7 per cent in 1991. This reveals two things, i.e., there are occupations, which are only urban in nature, and that shift towards rural Rajasthan of such occupation has not taken place except for sales workers group. This also means that increased opportunities are available in urban centres only.

Table 1

Occupational Distribution of Female Main Workers Other than Cultivators and Agricultural Workers: 1981 and 1991

Divisions	Share of female in			Share of female in total female main workers		Distribution of female workers		
	Total	Urban	Rural	Urban	Rural	Total	Urban	Rural
1981								
All Divisions	8.29	6.81	9.85	42.20	57.80	100.00	100.00	100.00
0–1	13.56	18.35	7.53	75.37	24.63	15.26	27.25	6.50
2	1.63	1.90	1.19	71.64	28.36	0.54	0.91	0.26
3	2.16	2.66	1.04	85.27	14.73	2.39	4.83	0.61
4	2.73	2.27	3.47	51.11	48.89	4.63	5.61	3.92
5	11.19	12.08	10.02	61.39	38.61	10.16	14.78	6.79
6	16.90	8.80	17.62	4.27	95.73	19.23	1.94	31.85
7–8–9	8.18	6.15	10.30	38.45	61.55	44.34	40.39	47.21
X	10.07	10.04	10.10	52.17	47.83	3.45	4.27	2.86
1991								
All Divisions	7.82	7.77	7.90	54.68	45.32	100.00	100.00	100.00
0–1	16.31	21.75	9.31	75.06	24.94	23.90	32.81	13.15
2	3.35	3.43	3.14	72.78	27.22	0.96	1.28	0.58
3	3.54	4.43	1.73	83.85	16.15	3.95	6.06	1.41
4	2.59	2.37	2.99	59.30	40.70	5.36	5.81	4.81
5	9.75	11.65	7.02	70.34	29.66	9.07	11.67	5.94
6	15.65	8.80	16.36	5.28	94.72	9.20	0.89	19.22
7–8–9	7.55	6.71	8.57	48.46	51.54	42.84	37.98	48.71
X	7.26	8.58	6.57	40.64	59.36	4.72	3.51	6.18

Note: 0–1 include professional, technical and related workers; 2 include administrative, executive and managerial workers; 3 include clerical and related workers; 4 include sales workers; 5 include service workers; 6 include farmers, fishermen, hunters, loggers and related workers; 7–8–9 include production and related workers, transport equipment operators and labourers; X include workers n.e.c.

Source: Economic Tables of Rajasthan, 1981 and 1991.

Economic reforms have brought in structural changes in nature of employment. It has displaced workers from traditional sectors and provided avenues of employment in new sectors that demand high skills and education (Singh and Sagar, 2004). What was the educational level of female workforce at the time of initiation of economic liberalisation in Rajasthan? Table 2 reveals that 61 per cent of female workers were illiterate and another 9.6 per cent were either having primary or below primary level education. This means that 70 per cent of female workers in Rajasthan were either illiterate or having primary or below primary level education. This is not all, 84 per cent of female workers in Rajasthan, in 1991, had education of higher secondary or below. It is also noticed that higher proportion female workers are illiterate in rural Rajasthan compared to urban Rajasthan. However, in all other educational groups, higher percentage of female workers is in urban Rajasthan. This again reflects on the availability of job opportunities in urban centres. If one considers, the distribution of female workers region-wise in Rajasthan, then one finds that higher percentage of female workers are in urban centres compared to rural centres across the educational groups, except for illiterate workers. As per the NSSO 61st Round Survey (2004–2005), 93 per cent of female non-agricultural workers in the unorganised sector were having education of primary and below, when this proportion at the India level was 77 per cent in the rural areas. The corresponding percentages in urban areas are: Rajasthan 76.3 per cent and India 63.7 per cent. Such figures reflect on poverty ratios as we notice that 31.5 per cent unorganised non-agriculture workers are below poverty line and majority are women.

Table 2

Distribution of Female Workers (Other than Cultivators and Agricultural Workers) by Education in 1991

Education level	*Share in Total Female Workers*			*Region-wise share*	
	Total	*Urban*	*Rural*	*Urban*	*Rural*
Illiterate	60.69	47.21	76.96	42.53	57.47
Below Primary	4.00	4.34	3.60	59.27	40.73
Primary	5.60	5.65	5.54	55.19	44.81
Middle	4.14	4.30	3.93	56.90	43.10
Matric	4.62	6.05	2.89	71.62	28.38
Higher Secondary	4.96	6.66	2.92	73.32	26.68
Diploma non-technical	0.07	0.09	0.05	68.57	31.43
Diploma technical	0.97	1.33	0.55	74.57	25.43
Graduate non-technical	5.20	8.43	1.29	88.77	11.23
PG. Non-technical	6.43	10.84	1.10	92.22	7.78
Eng. & Technology	0.09	0.14	0.03	84.97	15.03
Medicine	0.54	0.93	0.08	93.08	6.92
Agriculture & Dairying	0.02	0.02	0.01	71.43	28.57
Veterinary	0.01	0.01	0.00	75.00	25.00
Teaching	2.65	3.98	1.04	82.28	17.72
Others	0.01	0.02	0.01	65.91	34.09

Source: Population Census, Economic Tables, 1991.

Employment and Unemployment

The National Sample Survey Organisation (NSSO) gives employment and unemployment figures for states for principal status and usual status (includes both principal and subsidiary status). Table 3 shows that in 1999–2000, in Rajasthan female employment rate according to principal status were 27.2 in rural Rajasthan compared to just 9.3 in urban Rajasthan. As per the usual status definition, in rural Rajasthan the female employment rate stood at 38.8 compared to 13.8 per cent in urban Rajasthan. This means that rural Rajasthan has higher employment rate than urban Rajasthan considering both the definitions of work. When one looks at other states in the country, one finds that female employment rate is the highest in rural Andhra Pradesh (44.3%) followed by Meghalaya (41.4%), Tamil Nadu (40.1%) and Maharashtra (39.3%) for principal status work. The lowest employment rate is found in rural Delhi at 2.2 per cent. In case of urban areas, the highest employment rate is in Mizoram at 24.6 per cent and the lowest in J&K at 4.1 per cent. It is also observed that in Assam, Haryana, Punjab, Tripura, Andaman & Nicobar Islands, Chandigarh, Delhi and Lakshdweep the urban female employment rates are higher than rural employment rates. This is probably largely due to social reasons and high rural incomes.

Moreover, all India female employment rates (rural) are not surpassed by Assam, Bihar, Goa, Haryana, J&K, Kerala, Manipur, Orissa, Punjab, Tripura, Uttar Pradesh, West Bengal, Andaman & Nicobar Islands, Chandigarh, Delhi and Lakshadweep in case of principal status employment. In case of urban India, all India female employment rate is surpassed by Andhra Pradesh, Karnataka, Kerala, Madhya Pradesh, Maharashtra, Manipur, Meghalaya, Mizoram, Nagaland, Sikkim, Tamil Nadu, Andaman & Nicobar Islands, Daman & Dui, and Pondicherry. This means that female employment rates are not only low across states, but also below national average in most states.

When we consider usual status definition, then only four states, viz., Tripura, Andaman & Nicobar Islands, Delhi and Lakshadweep have higher female employment rate in urban regions compared to rural regions. The rural female employment rates vary between a low of 2.9 per cent in Delhi and a high of 47.8 per cent in Andhra Pradesh. The urban female employment rate ranges from 6.2 per cent in J&K to 25.9 per cent in Mizoram. The all-India average rural female employment rate is exceeded by 15 of the 32 states/union territories compared to 14 of 32 states/union territories in case of urban employment rates. All this indicates that female employment rates are largely higher in rural India.

Table 3

Distribution of Unemployed and Employed Females in Population according to Principal and Usual Status: 1999–2000

States	*Unemployed Persons in Population according to*				*% of Employed persons in Population according to*			
	Usual Principal Status		*Usual Status excluding those employed in a Subsidiary Status*		*Principal Status*		*Usual Status*	
	Rural	*Urban*	*Rural*	*Urban*	*Rural*	*Urban*	*Rural*	*Urban*
Andhra Pradesh	0.30	0.70	0.20	0.70	44.30	15.90	47.80	17.80
Arunachal Pradesh	0.00	1.00	0.00	1.00	27.80	10.00	31.00	10.00
Assam	1.20	2.80	1.10	2.60	8.70	9.70	15.10	11.20
Bihar	0.10	0.70	0.10	0.70	13.20	6.40	17.30	7.50
Goa	3.40	5.30	3.40	5.30	14.80	9.80	18.10	10.60
Gujarat	0.10	0.30	0.00	0.30	31.10	11.40	41.30	13.50
Haryana	0.00	0.30	0.00	0.30	3.30	5.80	20.20	9.80
Himachal Pradesh	0.50	1.30	0.30	1.10	28.10	9.60	47.10	13.00
J&K	0.30	0.60	0.30	0.60	4.60	4.10	32.70	6.20
Karnataka	0.10	0.80	0.10	0.80	35.40	16.70	38.00	17.80
Kerala	3.90	5.60	3.50	5.10	15.90	15.60	23.80	20.30
Madhya Pradesh	0.10	0.20	0.10	0.20	33.10	12.20	38.20	13.40
Maharashtra	0.40	1.00	0.30	1.00	39.30	12.20	41.80	19.70
Manipur	0.40	1.60	0.40	1.40	15.30	14.20	25.30	21.10
Meghalaya	0.10	1.40	0.10	1.40	41.40	19.60	43.40	13.70
Mizoram	0.20	0.60	0.10	0.60	36.70	24.60	44.00	25.90
Nagaland	1.00	1.90	0.90	1.90	24.50	15.80	44.10	19.90
Orissa	0.30	0.80	0.30	0.80	20.30	11.20	29.90	14.50
Punjab	0.30	0.30	0.30	0.30	4.00	7.30	28.00	12.50

Cont'd...

Cont'd...

Rajasthan	0.10	0.40	0.00	0.30	27.20	9.30	38.80	13.80
Sikkim	0.50	2.50	0.50	2.50	23.40	20.00	24.10	20.00
Tamil Nadu	0.50	1.20	0.40	1.10	40.10	19.70	43.00	21.50
Tripura	0.30	0.70	0.30	0.70	6.90	7.20	7.30	7.50
Uttar Pradesh	0.10	0.30	0.10	0.30	12.20	6.60	20.10	9.40
West Bengal	0.50	1.30	0.50	1.20	11.60	10.20	16.00	11.70
Andaman & Nicobar	1.40	5.40	1.30	4.30	16.00	16.90	18.00	20.60
Chandigarh	0.10	1.90	0.10	1.70	8.10	11.40	12.80	13.60
Dadra Nagar Haveli	0.00	0.00	0.00	0.00	34.70	11.20	35.40	11.20
Daman	0.00	1.70	0.00	1.70	25.90	18.10	30.00	18.60
Delhi	0.80	0.50	0.80	0.40	2.20	8.20	2.90	10.50
Lakshadweep	8.50	4.10	8.50	4.10	8.10	10.30	11.50	17.90
Pondicherry	0.70	1.20	0.70	1.20	28.30	15.90	28.70	16.90
India	4.00	9.00	0.30	0.80	23.10	11.70	29.90	13.90

Note: Usual status is principal and subsidiary status.

Source: Computed from NSSO 56th Round.

Now when we consider female unemployment rates across states in India, we find that as per the principal status definition, 4 per cent female unemployment exists in India compared to 9 per cent in urban India. In Rajasthan, the rural unemployment rate is 0.1 per cent compared to 0.4 per cent urban unemployment rate. There are many states that have no rural or urban female unemployment rates. In rural areas, the unemployment rates vary between a low of 0.1 per cent (8 states) and a high of 8.5 per cent in Lakshadweep. In case of urban areas, the range is 0.2 per cent in Madhya Pradesh to 5.6 per cent in Kerala. Besides, it is only in Delhi and Lakshadweep that female urban unemployment rate is lower than the rural rate.

The usual status female unemployment rates are significantly lower, though rural rates are relatively lower than urban rates except for Delhi and Lakshadweep. Smaller states like Goa, Kerala, Lakshadweep, Assam and Andaman & Nicobar Islands have relatively higher female unemployment rates both in rural and urban areas. This could be due to educated unemployment. These relatively low unemployment rates also reflect that fewer women still looking for work outside the household domain.

The Unorganised Sector

The National Sample Survey Organisation (NSSO) had conducted an integrated survey of households and unorganised manufacturing enterprises in its 56th Round during the period, July 2000 to June 2001. Table 4 provides genderwise distribution of workers across states in 1999–2000 by regions as per NSSO round 56th.

Data reveals that more men than women are engaged in rural and urban unorganised sectors across the states. There are exceptions like Kerala, Manipur and Tamil Nadu. The share of women in rural unorganised workforce ranges from a low of 4.93 per cent in Daman and Dui to a high of 79.3 per cent in Manipur. In Rajasthan, women constitute 30.87 per cent of rural unorganised sector workforce. Andhra Pradesh, Karnataka, Kerala, Orissa, Punjab, Tamil Nadu, Tripura, West Bengal and Lakshadweep have higher percentage of women in rural unorganised sector compared to all India level proportion of 38.69.

The share of female workers in urban unorganised sector varies between 3.26 per cent in Sikkim and 66.51 per cent in Manipur. It is only in Manipur that women outnumber men in urban unorganised sector. In Rajasthan, women constitute 27.31 per cent of urban unorganised sector workforce. Andhra Pradesh, Chattisgarh, Goa, J&K, Karnataka, Kerala, Madhya Pradesh, Manipur, Mizoram, Nagaland, Orissa, Rajasthan, Tamil Nadu, West Bengal, Daman & Dui and Pondicherry have higher percentage of women in urban unorganised sector compared to all India level figure of 24.58 per cent. It is also discernible that women form a higher proportion of unorganised workforce in rural India compared to urban India. This holds true for all states. Exceptions of course are Chattisgarh, Mizoram, Nagaland, Andaman & Nicobar Islands, Daman & Dui and Pondicherry.

At the aggregate level, women constitute 33.71 per cent of unorganised sector workforce. This percentage varies from a low of 4.17 per cent in Delhi to a high of 74.23 per cent in Manipur. It is only in Manipur that women workers outnumber male workers significantly. Andhra Pradesh, Chattisgarh, Goa, Jharkhand, Karnataka, Kerala, Manipur, Nagaland, Orissa, Tamil Nadu, Tripura, West Bengal and Pondicherry have higher percentage of women in unorganised sector compared to all-India figure of 33.71 per cent. In Rajasthan, this percentage is 29.34.

Table 4

Genderwise Percentage Distribution of Workers Across States: 1999–00

States	*Rural*			*Urban*			*Total*		
	Male	*Female*	*All*	*Male*	*Female*	*All*	*Male*	*Female*	*All*
Andhra Pradesh	55.41	44.59	100	66.49	33.51	100	58.48	41.52	100
Arunachal Pradesh	72.19	27.81	100	90.03	9.97	100	82.00	18.00	100
Assam	69.75	30.25	100	81.66	18.34	100	71.86	28.14	100
Bihar	76.13	23.87	100	80.57	19.43	100	76.91	23.09	100
Chattisgarh	66.50	33.50	100	61.09	38.91	100	65.01	34.99	100
Goa	61.37	38.63	100	74.00	26.00	100	64.93	35.07	100
Gujarat	77.97	22.03	100	88.54	11.46	100	84.54	15.46	100
Haryana	85.43	14.57	100	89.18	10.82	100	87.59	12.41	100
Himachal Pradesh	76.54	23.46	100	90.31	9.69	100	78.09	21.91	100
J&K	70.61	29.39	100	71.25	28.75	100	70.83	29.17	100
Jharkhand	61.67	38.33	100	82.54	17.46	100	63.66	36.34	100
Karnataka	50.26	49.74	100	66.25	33.75	100	56.23	43.77	100
Kerala	48.25	51.75	100	62.45	37.55	100	51.20	48.80	100
Madhya Pradesh	66.57	33.43	100	69.92	30.08	100	67.66	32.34	100
Maharashtra	71.96	28.04	100	80.54	19.46	100	76.96	23.04	100
Manipur	20.70	79.30	100	33.49	66.51	100	25.77	74.23	100
Meghalaya	66.11	33.89	100	83.95	16.05	100	67.87	32.13	100
Mizoram	82.43	17.57	100	69.12	30.88	100	75.17	24.83	100
Nagaland	65.28	34.72	100	64.42	35.58	100	64.87	35.13	100
Orissa	55.06	44.94	100	71.79	28.21	100	56.10	43.90	100
Punjab	60.42	39.58	100	89.30	10.70	100	76.40	23.60	100
Rajasthan	69.13	30.87	100	72.69	27.31	100	70.66	29.34	100
Sikkim	94.06	5.94	100	96.74	3.26	100	95.12	4.88	100
Tamil Nadu	46.64	53.36	100	64.73	35.27	100	55.95	44.05	100
Tripura	57.76	42.24	100	85.33	14.67	100	61.74	38.26	100
Uttaranchal	76.42	23.58	100	81.07	18.93	100	77.54	22.46	100
Uttar Pradesh	71.24	28.76	100	76.69	23.31	100	72.97	27.03	100
West Bengal	55.06	44.94	100	69.53	30.47	100	58.65	41.35	100
Andaman & Nicobar	94.64	5.36	100	82.42	17.58	100	89.96	10.04	100
Chandigarh	87.56	12.44	100	89.41	10.59	100	89.29	10.71	100
Dadra Nagar Haveli	89.80	10.20	100	90.45	9.55	100	89.88	10.12	100
Daman	95.07	4.93	100	69.57	30.43	100	90.24	9.76	100
Delhi	84.29	5.71	90	95.88	4.12	100	95.83	4.17	100
Lakshadweep	60.00	40.00	100	76.37	23.63	100	75.63	24.37	100
Pondicherry	66.81	33.19	100	66.34	33.66	100	66.46	33.54	100
India	61.31	38.69	100	75.42	24.58	100	66.29	33.71	100

Source: Computed from NSSO 56th round.

Unorganised Manufacturing Employment

Looking more closely, the Rajasthan situation, Table 5 shows that female workers in unorganised manufacturing sector are 336.4 thousand constituting 29.34 per cent of all workers. Of these 187.5 thousand are working owners (26.3% of all working owners). Women are not generally hired in manufacturing unorganised sector in Rajasthan as only 16.1 thousand women are reportedly hired (8.86% of all hired workers). However, women constitute a significant proportion of other workers implying that they belong to the household of the proprietor or households of the partners who are working in or for the enterprise without regular salary or wages. This is reflected amply in own account enterprises where 315.1 thousand female workers (93.7%) are employed of the total 336.4 thousand female workers. Another 1.6 per cent is in NDMEs and 4.7 per cent in DMEs. It is also interesting to find that 55.1 per cent of all women employed in unorganised manufacturing sector is working owners running own enterprises and another 38.5 per cent is other workers category. This means that almost all the women workers in own account enterprises are either owners or working as unpaid family workers. This is true across regions. Also, more women workers are found in rural enterprises (60%) compared to urban enterprises. A higher proportion of family female labour participates in rural enterprises (46.5%) compared to urban enterprises (29.1%). Here again, own account enterprises dominate in terms of female employment, but the difference is that other female workers out number urban other female workers. Other female workers in own account enterprises are 60.3 per cent of all other workers in rural areas compared to 48.2 per cent in urban areas. This implies that females in the family contribute much greater labour to unorganised own account manufacturing enterprises.

Table 5 also shows that females as working owners in case of non-directory unorganised manufacturing enterprises (NDMEs) constitute around 3 per cent, though this proportion is marginally higher in urban enterprises compared to rural enterprises. Similar is the case with directory enterprises (DMEs). More female workers are hired in rural enterprises compared to urban enterprises. It means that as the size of enterprises, even within unorganised sector increase, the proportion of females as owner declines. However, female participation in such enterprises is significantly higher in rural enterprises as against urban enterprises. The rural urban division is explicit.

Table 5

Estimated Number of Female Workers by Region and Type of Enterprise (00')

Type of Enterprise/ Worker type	*Rural*		*Urban*		*Combined*	
	Number	*Share in All %*	*Number*	*Share in All %*	*Number*	*Share in All %*
OAME						
Working owner	943	22.77	910	40.11	1853	28.90
Hired worker	0		2	22.22	2	8.00
Other worker	916	60.26	380	48.16	1296	56.13
Total	1859	32.74	1292	42.13	3151	36.03
NDME						
Working owner	5	2.96	13	3.51	18	3.34
Hired worker	6	2.42	11	1.90	17	2.05
Other worker	10	23.26	8	9.09	18	13.74
Total	22	4.78	32	3.08	53	3.60
DME						
Working owner	1	2.22	2	1.49	3	1.68
Hired worker	126	39.01	17	2.65	142	14.83
Other worker	11	33.33	2	4.55	14	16.88
Total	138	34.41	21	2.56	159	13.03
Combined						
Working owner	950	21.81	925	33.35	1875	26.30
Hired worker	131	22.32	30	2.44	161	8.86
Other worker	938	58.77	391	42.41	1328	52.78
Total	2019	30.88	1345	27.31	3364	29.34

Note: Totals may not tally because of rounding up of figures.

Source: NSSO 56th Round.

Workforce in unorganised manufacturing sector in Rajasthan is either full-time or part-time. As discussed above, there were 336.4 thousand female workers employed (Table 6). There are 72.5 per cent full-time female workers employed and the remaining are part-time female workers. The proportion of female full-time workers in rural enterprises (75.5%) is higher compared to urban enterprise (68%). Now coming to own account enterprises, 71 per cent of female workers are full-time workers and this proportion is 73.6 per cent in rural enterprises and 67.2 per cent in urban enterprises. It is also observed that female workers constitute a very high proportion of

Table 6

Estimated Number of Female Workers Engaged in Manufacturing Enterprises by Nature of Employment

Type of Enterprise/ Employment	Rural			Urban			Combined		
	Number '00	Share in all %	Per unit female workers	Number '00	Share in all %	Per unit female workers	Number '00	Share in all %	Per unit female workers
OAME									
Full time	1368	27.3	0.37	869	34.1	0.46	2237	29.6	0.40
Part time	491	73.8	0.13	424	81.4	0.22	914	77.1	0.16
All	1859	32.7	0.50	1292	42.1	0.68	3151	36.0	0.56
NDME									
Full time	21	4.7	0.15	26	2.6	0.08	47	3.2	0.10
Part time	1	7.7	neg.	6	15.8	0.02	6	11.8	0.01
All	22	4.8	0.13	32	3.1	0.10	53	3.5	0.12
DME									
Full time	136	34.6	3.43	19	2.4	0.19	155	12.9	1.13
Part time	2	25.0	0.05	2	16.7	0.02	4	20.0	0.03
All	138	34.4	3.48	21	2.6	0.22	159	13.0	1.16
Combined									
Full time	1525	26.1	0.39	914	21.0	0.39	2439	23.9	0.39
Part time	493	71.9	0.13	431	75.4	0.19	925	73.5	0.15

Note: Totals may not tally because of rounding up of figures.
Source: Computed from NSSO 56th Round.

part-time workers in own account enterprises and more so in urban enterprises. This also the case with non-directory enterprises, but the obverse is the case of directory enterprises. Non-directory and directory enterprises have significant full-time female workers, the proportion is higher in rural enterprises compared to urban enterprises. Thus, full-time female employment is sizeable in unorganised manufacturing enterprises in Rajasthan.

Table also shows that per enterprise female employment is only 0.54 in Rajasthan when it is 0.56 in case of own account enterprises, 0.12 in case of non-directory enterprises and 1.16 in case of directory enterprises. The average female employment per rural own account enterprise is 0.5 compared to 0.68 in case of urban enterprises. The non-directory and directory rural enterprises out-score urban enterprises with regard to average female employment, it is 0.13 and 3.48 respectively in rural enterprises. Similar is the case with average full-time female employment. This shows that more women work in rural unorganised manufacturing enterprises' vis-à-vis urban enterprises at least in case of firms hiring workers.

Female Employment through Economic Census

Given the above picture, this section using economic census data looks at the female employment in the unorganised sector. Here we deal with employment in own account enterprises,[1] non-directory enterprises[2] and directory enterprises[3] (large proportion are of small size with employment of less than 9 workers). The last two categories are called establishments in economic census.[4]

In the year 1998, 13.3 lakh non-agricultural enterprises employed 2.97 lakh female workers or about 9.33 per cent. Of these female workers, 54.33 per cent were in rural areas and the remaining in urban areas. The non-agricultural own account enterprise employed 1.01 lakh female workers (7.79% only) with 0.6 lakh in rural areas and 0.41 lakh in urban areas. The non-agricultural establishments employed another 1.97 lakh female workers (10.39%) with 1.02 lakh in rural areas and 0.95 lakh in urban areas. Female employment in agricultural enterprises was 0.93 lakh and out of them 0.81 lakh (87.45%) were employed in rural areas. Further, 0.85 lakh were employed in own account agricultural enterprises and 87.39 per cent were in rural areas. Of the agricultural establishment enterprises female workers (0.08 lakh), 88.07 per cent were in rural areas. At the aggregate level, of the 3.9 lakh female workers, 52.51 per cent were employed in establishments and 76.17 per cent were in non-agricultural enterprises. Of these female workers, 62.22 per cent are in rural areas. Thus, we find that there is concentration of unorganised sector female workers in rural areas, non-agricultural enterprises and establishments.

Table 7 to Table 10 present employment information of these enterprises. Table 7 shows that of the total workers in agricultural unorganised sector, 28.42 per cent are female workers with 2.29 per cent being female child workers. In the non-agricultural enterprises, 9.61 per cent are female workers and only 0.28 per cent female child workers. It is also observed that female child workers proportion is higher in case of agricultural enterprises compared to non-agricultural enterprises. Also, the proportion of male child workers across regions and type of enterprises is higher than female child workers. The proportion of female workers in total workers is higher in urban agricultural enterprises while it is higher in case of rural non-agricultural enterprises. Besides, share in total workforce is lower of female workers in non-agricultural enterprises.

Table 7

Percentage of Persons Usually Working in Unorganised Enterprises

Region	*Female*			*Male*			*Grand Total*
	Adult	*Child*	*Total*	*Child*	*Adult*	*Total*	
			Agricultural				
Rural	25.46	2.38	27.83	5.66	66.51	72.17	100
Urban	32.04	1.55	33.58	2.82	63.59	66.42	100
Total	26.13	2.29	28.42	5.37	66.21	71.58	100
			Non-agricultural				
Rural	10.96	0.45	11.41	1.72	86.87	88.59	100
Urban	7.93	0.15	8.07	0.79	91.13	91.93	100
Total	9.33	0.28	9.61	1.22	89.16	90.39	100
			All				
Rural	13.54	0.79	14.33	2.42	83.25	85.67	100
Urban	8.43	0.18	8.60	0.83	90.56	91.40	100
Total	11.02	0.49	11.50	1.64	86.86	88.50	100

Source: Computed from Economic Census 1998, GoR.

It would be interesting to see where women are employed i.e., which economic activity. Table 8 reveals that in case of own account enterprise (OAE) in Rajasthan, 46.52 per cent female workers are engaged in agricultural activities of which 45.88 per cent are involved in raising of livestock alone. The next important activity is manufacturing which employs around 26.6 per cent of all female OAE workers followed by retail trade (13.5%) and community, social and personal services (9.7%). This means that half the female workers in OAEs are engaged in these three activities. It is found that 57.31 per cent of female child workers are employed in raising of livestock followed by 24.47 per cent in manufacturing, 9.49 per cent in retail trade and 4.99 per cent in community, social and personal services. This implies that these four activities engaged 96.3 per cent of all female child workers. When we consider all workers in OAEs, the share of female workers ranges from a low of 1.41 per cent in storage and warehousing activities to a high of 30.1 per cent in raising of livestock. Women are significant contributors in raising of livestock and manufacturing in

Table 8

Distribution of Female Workers in OAEs

Activities	*Share in All Workers*			*Distribution %*		
	Adult	*Child*	*Total*	*Adult*	*Child*	*Total*
Raising of Livestock	27.65	2.40	30.05	45.10	57.31	45.88
Agriculture service & hunting, etc.	9.81	0.49	10.31	0.65	0.48	0.64
Agriculture activities	26.95	2.33	29.28	45.75	57.79	46.52
Mining & quarrying	6.40	0.87	7.26	0.08	0.15	0.08
Manufacturing	16.57	1.04	17.60	26.73	24.47	26.59
Electricity, gas, water	2.38	0.00	2.38	0.01	0.00	0.01
Construction	2.97	0.36	3.33	0.15	0.27	0.16
Wholesale trade	6.70	0.41	7.11	1.21	1.08	1.21
Retail trade	5.30	0.25	5.55	13.75	9.49	13.48
Restaurants & hotels	3.22	0.26	3.48	0.80	0.93	0.81
Transport	1.96	0.07	2.04	1.11	0.61	1.08
Storage & warehousing	1.36	0.05	1.41	0.01	0.01	0.01
Communications	2.33	0.09	2.42	0.11	0.06	0.11
Financial, etc.	2.62	0.09	2.71	0.31	0.15	0.30
Community, etc.	6.57	0.22	6.79	9.97	4.99	9.66
Non-agricultural	7.79	0.41	8.21	54.25	42.21	53.48
Total	11.55	0.79	12.34	100.00	100.00	100.00

Source: Computed from Economic Census of Rajasthan 1998.

terms of employment share. The other activities where women workers in OAEs are relevant are mining and quarrying, wholesale trade, community, social and personal services and retail trade (above 5% share in total sectoral employment). Female child workers' share is above one per cent in raising of livestock and manufacturing.

In case of non-household enterprises having at least one hired worker (NDE), 0.581 lakh female workers are employed of which 0.569 lakh are adult workers. Here one finds (Table 9), non-agricultural enterprises employing 88.41 per cent female workers and only 11.59 per cent in agricultural enterprises. Community, social and personal services sector employs about 62.3 per cent of all female workers in NDEs followed by 11.2 per cent in manufacturing and 10.34 per cent in raising of livestock. These three together have 84 per cent of all female workers, a very high concentration of female workforce. The two other activities where women are employed are retail trade and transport sectors. When we consider female child workers in NDEs, we find that 34.11 per cent are employed in raising

Table 9

Distribution of Female Workers in NDEs

Activities	*Share in All Workers*			*Distribution %*		
	Adult	*Child*	*Total*	*Adult*	*Child*	*Total*
Raising of Livestock	24.39	1.64	26.04	9.88	34.11	10.34
Agriculture service & hunting, etc.	7.06	0.09	7.15	1.26	0.81	1.26
Agriculture activities	19.08	1.17	20.24	11.14	34.92	11.59
Mining & quarrying	5.93	0.28	6.21	0.60	1.44	0.62
Manufacturing	5.24	0.25	5.49	10.88	26.64	11.18
Electricity, gas, water	1.40	0.00	1.40	0.14	0.00	0.14
Construction	10.06	0.16	10.22	0.79	0.63	0.79
Wholesale trade	1.52	0.03	1.55	0.91	0.90	0.91
Retail trade	2.41	0.14	2.54	6.48	18.63	6.71
Restaurants & hotels	1.70	0.07	1.77	1.03	2.16	1.05
Transport	3.36	0.09	3.45	3.53	4.86	3.56
Storage & warehousing	1.63	0.00	1.63	0.05	0.00	0.05
Communications	1.25	0.01	1.26	0.29	0.09	0.29
Financial, etc.	1.88	0.02	1.90	0.86	0.54	0.86
Community etc.	14.33	0.04	14.37	63.29	9.18	62.25
Non-agricultural	7.14	0.10	7.24	88.86	65.08	88.41
Total	7.67	0.15	7.82	100.00	100.00	100.00

Source: Computed from Economic Census of Rajasthan 1998.

of livestock followed by 26.64 per cent in manufacturing, 18.63 per cent in retail trade and 9.18 per cent in community, social and personal services. This means that these four activities employ about 89 per cent of all female child workers. This again reveals high concentration of female child workforce in a few activities.

Directory enterprises in Rajasthan are around 15.9 per cent of all enterprises and employ 1,194,531 workers. Of this number female workers are 151,415 or 12.68 per cent. Table 10 shows that in all 98.47 per cent female workers in this component of enterprises are in non-agricultural enterprises. The main activities where women workers are engaged in are community, social and personal services (57.66%) and manufacturing (25.33%). The other relevant sector is mining & quarrying sector (5.3%).

Table 10

Distribution of Female Workers in DEs

Activities	*Share in All Workers*			*Distribution %*		
	Adult	*Child*	*Total*	*Adult*	*Child*	*Total*
Raising of Livestock	22.78	7.28	30.07	0.87	11.93	1.12
Agriculture service & hunting, etc.	24.19	1.31	25.50	0.40	0.93	0.41
Agriculture activities	23.21	5.48	28.69	1.27	12.86	1.53
Mining & quarrying	18.49	0.14	18.64	5.38	1.78	5.30
Manufacturing	10.38	0.59	10.97	24.43	59.92	25.23
Electricity, gas, water	2.43	0.00	2.43	0.35	0.00	0.34
Construction	18.74	0.56	19.29	1.39	1.78	1.39
Wholesale trade	6.96	0.33	7.29	0.97	1.98	0.99
Retail trade	9.07	0.74	9.82	3.06	10.83	3.24
Restaurants & hotels	4.95	0.07	5.03	0.66	0.41	0.65
Transport	6.76	0.50	7.26	1.28	4.10	1.35
Storage & Warehousing	2.59	0.08	2.67	0.04	0.06	0.04
Communications	3.15	0.03	3.18	0.23	0.09	0.22
Financial, etc.	7.21	0.01	7.23	2.08	0.17	2.04
Community, etc.	3.89	0.01	3.90	58.86	6.02	57.66
Non-agricultural	12.31	0.25	12.57	98.73	87.14	98.47
Total	12.39	0.29	12.68	100.00	100.00	100.00

Source: Computed from Economic Census of Rajasthan 1998.

However, in case of female child workers, 87.14 per cent are engaged in non-agricultural activities and concentration is in manufacturing sector (59.92%) as against only 24.43 per cent adult female workers. It is followed by raising of livestock activities (11.93%), and retail trade (10.83%) and financial, insurance, real estate and business services (6.02%). Adult female workers are mainly in community, social and personal services (58.86%), manufacturing (24.43%) and mining and quarrying (5.38%). Retail trade is another activity of some significance. Thus, there is concentration of female workers in a few activities. Given the total workforce in directory enterprises, we find that women workers are mainly concentrated in raising of livestock, agriculture service and hunting, etc., construction works, mining and quarrying and manufacturing activities (10% above share of female workers).

Real Wage Earnings

In Rural Labour Enquiry Reports, the earnings mean payments received in cash or kind or both and those that are receivable for the work done during the reference week. The average daily wage earnings are arrived at by dividing the total earnings received for the reference week for all activities by the corresponding number of full intensity employment days in these activities. Therefore, daily average earnings are different than wage rates in that while the former indicates the average earnings for a day, the latter refers to the prevailing daily wage rate. Table 11 presents trend in daily real wage earnings of adult female labour in both agricultural and non-agricultural occupations since 1974–75. The data shows that the real wage earnings of adult female labour increased continuously since 1974–75, except for 1983, both in agricultural and non-agricultural occupations in all the states barring Assam, Haryana and Rajasthan, where these declined between 1987–88 and 1993–94.[5] In Rajasthan, daily real wage earnings of agricultural adult female workers have been higher than all India level wage earnings in agricultural occupations in all the years except for 1983 and gap has tended to widen. The same is the case with wage earnings from non-agricultural occupations with the exception of 1974–75 and 1993–94. In this Rajasthan has performed better than the national situation.

Conclusion

During 1981–91, the share of female workers in total main workers has gone down (0.47% points fall). In urban areas, though, the share

Table 11

Trends in Daily Real Wage Earnings of Agricultural Adult Female Labour in Agricultural and Non-agricultural Occupations (1980–81 = 100)

States	Daily Real Wage Earnings of Agricultural Adult Female Labour in									
	Agricultural Occupations					Non-agricultural Occupations				
	1974/5	1977/8	1983	1987/8	1993/4	1974/5	1977/8	1983	1987/8	1993/4
Andhra Pradesh	2.21	2.92	3.12	4.18	5.20	2.49	3.43	2.30	4.60	5.34
Assam	3.63	5.21	3.52	6.83	7.32	3.08	5.16	3.71	7.25	4.60
Bihar	2.99	3.98	3.18	4.91	5.24	2.53	4.22	2.07	5.08	7.08
Gujarat	2.81	4.53	3.63	5.47	6.62	3.20	4.21	3.34	5.20	6.61
Haryana	5.12	6.31	4.50	4.81	8.29	3.77	4.03	1.35	6.41	5.18
Himachal Pradesh	4.27	6.30	2.51	7.99	8.85	3.17	6.80	1.83		
J&K	4.29	4.98	4.87	4.19	8.35	3.49	4.48	5.32	1.40	
Karnataka	2.09	2.70	2.70	3.90	5.10	2.77	3.40	2.51	4.99	6.65
Kerala	4.24	5.60	6.51	7.23	8.65	2.75	4.16	2.43	5.49	5.52
Madhya Pradesh	2.85	2.77	2.65	4.47	5.24	1.87	2.74	2.72	5.76	6.11
Maharashtra	1.70	2.49	2.50	3.84	4.60	2.09	2.97	3.18	4.93	6.58
Orissa	2.03	2.94	2.47	3.74	4.62	1.98	2.74	1.46	4.24	5.30
Punjab	4.42	6.01	4.12	5.97	11.99	2.47	2.97	1.75	5.06	5.86
Rajasthan	2.97	4.09	2.79	5.87	8.17	2.22	3.67	4.40	5.70	4.08
Tamil Nadu	2.25	2.99	2.73	3.83	5.57	1.95	3.05	2.99	3.73	4.57
Uttar Pradesh	3.01	3.54	2.75	4.57	5.70	2.59	4.18	2.11	4.58	6.15
West Bengal	3.35	4.61	3.54	6.60	7.42	2.20	2.89	1.98	4.63	5.69
India	2.52	3.36	3.04	4.40	5.42	2.36	3.36	2.54	5.01	5.79

Note: Money wages have been deflated by CPIAL and base has been shifted from 1960–61 to 1980–81.
Source: Rural Labour Enquiry: Report on Wages and Earnings, various years.

has improved while it has deteriorated in rural areas. The work participation rate in professional, technical and related works; administrative, executive and managerial works and; clerical and related works has improved. Production and related works, transport equipment operators and labourers; agriculture related activities; professional, technical and related works and; service activities has concentration of female workers (more than 80% women are in these activities). Besides, we find that there are occupations which are only urban in nature and that shift towards rural Rajasthan of such occupation has not taken place except for sales workers group in case female workers. This also means that increased opportunities are available in urban centres only. Around 84 per cent of female workers in Rajasthan have education of higher secondary or below with majority being illiterate (Singh, 2005). More educated female workforce is found in urban areas compared to rural areas.

In 1999–2000, in Rajasthan female employment rate according to principal status were 27.2 in rural Rajasthan compared to just 9.3 in urban Rajasthan. As per the usual status definition, in rural Rajasthan the female employment rate stood at 38.8 compared to 13.8 per cent in urban Rajasthan. Rural Rajasthan has higher employment rate than urban Rajasthan considering both the definitions of work. In Rajasthan, the rural unemployment rate is 0.1 per cent compared to 0.4 per cent urban unemployment rate. In Rajasthan, women constitute 30.87 per cent of rural unorganised sector workforce and 27.31 per cent of urban unorganised sector workforce. At the aggregate level the percentage is 29.43. There is concentration of unorganised sector female workers in rural areas, non-agricultural enterprises and establishments. Female child workers proportion is higher in case of agricultural enterprises compared to non-agricultural enterprises. The proportion of female workers in total workers is higher in urban agricultural enterprises while it is higher in case of rural non-agricultural enterprises. Besides, share in total workforce is lower of female workers in non-agricultural enterprises. Female workers in OAEs are concentrated in three activities, viz., manufacturing, retail trade and community, social and personal services. Women are significant contributors in raising of livestock and manufacturing in terms of employment share. The other activities where women workers in OAEs are relevant are mining and quarrying, wholesale trade, community, social and personal services and retail trade. Community, social and personal services; manufacturing, and raising of livestock in NDE sector employ about 84 per cent of all female workers. In the present context there is dire need for training, especially of rural women (Singh, 1990, 1992) to ensure greater role of women in the labour market. The educational level and achievements of female children also require added attention (Singh and Srivastava, 2006).

Notes

1. These are owned and operated with the help of household labour.
2. These are enterprises, which employ less than 6 workers (including at least one hired worker) daily on fairly regular basis.
3. These are enterprises, which employ 6 or more workers (including at least one hired worker) daily on fairly regular basis.
4. Enterprises, which employ at least one hired worker on fairly regular basis.
5. In 1999–2000, average daily earnings of women in agricultural occupation were Rs 39.12 compared to Rs 28.57 at all-India level. The women's wages as percentage of men's were 76 per cent in Rajasthan and 70 per cent in India. There are social category differences too.

References

NSSO (2002), *Employment, Assets and* 56th round (July, 2000–June, 2001), November.

Singh, Surjit (1990), "Issues in Human Resources Development in India", *Journal of Education and Social Change*, vol. 4, No. 3, pp. 47–69.

——. (1992), "Training and Employment: Some Lessons from Experience", *Journal of Educational Planning and Administration*, Vol. 6, No. 2, pp. 119–32.

——. (1994), *Urban Informal Sector*, Rawat Publications, Jaipur.

——. (2005), "India and the Knowledge Economy: Overview and Global Context", *Indian Journal of Labour Economics*, October–December, Conference volume.

Singh, Surjit and Divya Sagar (2004), "Human Capital Base and Labour Market: Some Regional Features", *Indian Journal of Labour Economics*, October–December, Conference volume.

Singh, Surjit and Komal Srivastava (2006), "Elementary Education in Rajasthan: Emerging Issues and Challenges" IDS, Jaipur (mimeo).

19

Crisis, Food and Nutrition Security

Some Gender Concerns

Varsha Joshi and Surjit Singh

Food security implies several aspects of hunger including famine, energy-deficiency, micronutrient deficiency and nutrients depleting illness. Food security questions are tackled at global, regional, national, household and individual levels. Food security largely depends on access and entitlements to food, which depend on improved incomes for many (Pretty, Thompson and Hinchcliffe, 1996). Women in developing countries are the principal, if not the sole, economic support to themselves and their children and they are increasingly responsible for food security. Women play a crucial role, though constrained and undervalued, in ensuring food availability for household members, in both normal times and in periods of stress. Achieving household food security is concerned with enough food for all members at all times. It implies freedom from future vulnerability to food and other shocks, as well as a guarantee of adequate current consumption (Laier, et al., 1996). World Bank looks at food security in terms of access by all people at all times to enough food for active healthy life. However, nutrition security is broader than food security that requires broadening and diversification of our food base.

At the present juncture, the extent and depth of food security in the developing countries remains unquestionable (Singh, 2002). One-sixth of the developing world's population, mainly children and women, do not have access to sufficient food to lead healthy, productive lives. The progress in tackling food insecurity is slow.[1]

Micronutrient deficiencies (iron, iodine and vitamin A) also remain widespread among children and women, especially poor women[2]. Besides, there is neglect of zinc, riboflavin, and calcium and the global extent and consequences of their deficiencies are unknown. The consequences of micronutrient malnutrition include mortality and morbidity, lower cognitive ability and work production and impaired reproduction. This paper, thus, attempts to look at issues related to gender and food and nutrition security in times of crisis. It also presents nutrition situation in India and Rajasthan.

Crisis, Women and Issues

Women are responsible for generating food security for families in many developing countries. They not only process, purchase, and prepare food, but also play an important role in agricultural production[3]—food and cash crops. Women make sure that household members, particularly the children, get an adequate share of the food that is potentially available, i.e., they are 'gatekeepers' of their household's food security through the allocation of their own time and income.[4] This means greater the share of income in the hands of women, greater is the calories requirement met of the household. In the times of crisis the income flow is constrained that adversely impacts the nutritional intake of the families and more so of women. Thus, greater the degree of autonomous management of household resources exercised by women, the greater is likely to be the availability of household income for food; and for any given level of household income, the greater is the likely to be actual level of food provision. Another aspect of food security is food utilisation, i.e., ensuring that the food consumed contributes to good physical and cognitive development. During the times of economic crisis, it is assumed (women themselves do it) that women will act to absorb shocks to household welfare by expanding their already stretched time schedule.[5] In this context it is argued that women may act as shock absorbers through the liquidation/risking of their own nutritional status. A woman's economic, biological and social roles therefore cause conflicts when resources/food are/is inadequate. It is also argued that poor people economise on food either by buying cheaper or different items, or omitting meals altogether (Dobson, et al., 1994).[6] Activities that act as constraints on woman's time and health also affect household security and nutritional levels of the households through her increased workload. Weight loss has been observed with the onset of food crisis. In Kenya, during drought an increase in the prevalence of severe protein-energy malnutrition in children, non-pregnant women, non-lactating women was found (Neumann, et al., 1989).

Historically, women have been found to be more resilient to crisis situation of any type. Osborne (1850) writes that girls and women bore the Irish famine of 1849 better than the males. Arguments as to women's greater ability to withstand famine are also found in other 19th century famine situations. Sen (1981) too points it out in the context of Bengal famine in India. The Bengal famine observed higher rate of male mortality. In biological or physiological terms, women are usually considered to be "less vulnerable to deprivation, having smaller needs for energy and most nutrients because they are smaller than men, have lower metabolic rate and a higher body fat" (Rivers, 1988). Chatterjee and Lambert (1989) too point out that women have generally lower calorie intake than men and gender differences vary between socio-economic groups in India and Pakistan. Women also have less access to food than men in times of economic crisis. They argue that women's inadequate nutritional status is a reflection of their inferior social status. However, Greenough (1982), Arnold (1988) and Dreze and Sen (1993), point out that such a relative advantage needs to be set against patterns of exploitation and discrimination, especially within family situations, which may value less highly the needs of female members during periods of crisis. Dreze and Sen (1993) argue that we should seek explanation in terms of greater female ability to survive nutritional stress. Fitzpatrick (1997) too supports this argument. Kelleher (1997) points out that superior female capacity is attributed to capacity to store body-fat. Daly (1986) supporting these arguments on famine and women, speculates that the greater vulnerability of men may be due to the pressure of relief works, particularly for bodies deprived of food, or may simply reflect the fact that men have greater calorie requirements than women and thus faced greater difficulties in coping with scarcity. In this context, Sen (1981) argues that in famines there may not occur significant decline in food availability, but person's entitlement or ability to command food may get affected. Here, the pointer is towards rise in food prices and sharp changes in distribution of food and individuals may starve. Fitzpatrick (1997) in this light suggests that women possess other less material or non-monetary resources as 'reproducers and household managers' and as the providers of 'the unquantifiable services of affection and consolation'. These arguments on women and famines really ignore the mobility of women, the fate of widows and female orphans. Famines and crisis situations have observed reduction in fertility, nuptiality and childbirth.

Crises of seasonality and calamity can negatively affect ownership endowments and exchange entitlements as well as the strength of external support systems for both sexes. Men and women respond differently to crisis-coping strategies are centred to the survival of vulnerable groups, but they are highly gendered. It is argued that the household itself is a problematic concept and individual members of a household will experience different food security risks and often follow different food security strategies. People's own perception of vulnerability and risk predominate in food security strategies. Cultural values are important too in determining the quality of food entitlement, rather than just the quantity. However, men and women are affected unequally and it alters their relative intra-family bargaining strengths. A crisis that leads to a total collapse of or even a large decline in the wife's fall-back (break-down) position, while that of the husband sustains in relative terms, could weaken her bargaining power even to a point where non-cooperation is found more beneficial by the man than cooperation, creating a tendency towards the disintegration of families, and the abandonment of spouses (Agarwal, 1997). However, moral considerations may act as cushion to breakdown.

Seasonal variations in climate and crop cycles reflect on variations in employment, wages and food prices. These in turn impact a poor agricultural household's immediate as well as long-term command over food.[7] Rural households in anticipation of such situations may devise ways to overcome them in terms of diversification of sources of income (seasonal migration) and; drawing upon communal resources, social relationships (see Lingam, 1994), household stores and adjusting to current consumption patterns and, assets. In this regard, women are affected more than the men. Women tend to bear responsibility for the early stage of a food crisis and as the situation deteriorates both men and women cope. In the first phase of a crisis, women rely on social networks, as well as reducing their consumption. Also, food intake and nutritional status vary seasonally (Mukherjee and Mukherjee, 1994) and that in normal times intra-household food distribution discriminates against women and children. In case of migration during crisis period, either of male members of the family or the whole family together, women and children put in critical input both in terms of earnings from wage employment and in enabling families to explore additional earning sources (Agarwal, 1997).[8] Women due to their limited control over own labour power and ability to exchange it, as they desire, limits their overall exchange entitlements. There is no doubt that in the times of crisis, woman's contribution to the household increases.[9] Currie (1992) suggests that the social relations of production and reproduction have historically shaped people's food entitlements. Changes in production and distribution by commercialisation, capitalisation and farming techniques have also altered food entitlements.

At the time of crisis, dependence on communal resources gets intensified. It is coupled with variations in availability of products of commons. Poor and women are mainly dependent upon these resources. It has been argued in certain quarters that nearly 30 million people in India are dependent on minor forest produce alone for a livelihood. In a situation of distress, intra-family cooperation becomes critical. Women and children are vital to this cooperation. It has been studied that among central Indian tribals, during normal pre-harvest seasonal shortages, gathered food provides 12 per cent of energy intakes compared to 2 per cent in the post-harvest period (Agarwal, 1997).[10] In some parts of India, common property resources have provided greater employment than even the various anti-poverty government programmes. A rapid decline in and degradation of forest and common property resources do impinge upon food security of women and children.

Patron-client relationship (especially *jajmani* system) provided some security against crisis. The erosion of these institutions have made poor vulnerable and more so the women. Social relationships with kin and with villagers outside the kin network have been serving the poor households. It has been natural for women to draw upon other women for borrowing small amounts of foodstuffs, fuel, fodder, etc. Women have typically played an important role in the cultivation of social relationships. It is important to point out here that women, however, are less able to seek help of their natal kin, than men.[11] However, there is increasing erosion of these support systems. It has been well documented that in the times of crisis and low food availability, children get first preference, then men and finally women (Joshi, 2002).[12] However, the extent and causes of gender biases in food allocation within the family are debatable in the Indian context. There is no doubt that gender differentials tend to increase during crisis.[13] Poor families also resort to sale of productive assets at the time of distress, i.e., drawing upon assets is the effective way of household coping mechanism. The burden of coping the crisis disproportionately falls on women, in terms of work and consumption.[14]

Indian Situation

Food security is reflected in health and nutritional status of people. Lack of food and inadequate nutrition cause ill health. It also leads to lack of resistance to disease and impaired mental capacities. Poverty is central to it. Poor and vulnerable not only lack in adequate food but also nutritious food. That affects their health and performance in the labour market and thereby low income. Just as education, livelihood, or assets are unequally accessi. le to everybody, so also access to food is constrained for some. Human behaviour changes from place to place and from time to time. It adjusts to hostile times too. Food consumption levels are therefore closely related to the standard of living and the environment. The national accounts data shows that the share of private final consumption expenditure at constant prices has been declining over time on food (Bansil, 2003). This means that Indians, on an average, or on a per capita basis are consuming less food now. There is a change in the consumption basket in favour of health care, transport and communication services, etc. There has been steady decline in the per capita consumption of cereals at the All India level (Table 1). There is also shift in consumption pattern as between the various grains both in rural and urban areas. The share of rice, for instance, has remained more or less constant. Wheat on the other hand has replaced coarse grains to a significant extent (Table 2). This has implication for nutrition intake. Joshi (2002) argues that this shift is worrisome on one count that there is a curtailment of fibre content of the diet. Gopalan (1994) argues that when poor ascend the socio-economic scale, they generally tend to discard millets in favour of the more prestigious rice and wheat—an option not particularly beneficial from the point of view of nutrition. Added to this, there is decline in consumption of pulses and legumes. This is to do with the near constancy in production of pulses in India and rising prices. Joshi (2002) also argues that the change in consumption basket implies a change not only in the method of cooking but also in complementary food. For instance, *moong* and *moth* formed a major part of the diet in the bajra-consuming zone and with consumption of wheat these were not necessary. However, the enhanced consumption of leafy vegetables compensated the nutrition loss due to this switching.[15] There is of course regional differentiation in changes observed.

Table 1

State-wise Per Capita Consumption of Cereals

(Kg./month)

State	*1970–71*	*1983–84*	*1987–88*	*1990–91*	*1999–00*	*2004–05*
URBAN						
Andhra Pradesh	13.31	11.95	11.70	11.70	10.94	10.51
Assam	11.91	12.78	12.39	12.08	12.26	11.92
Bihar	13.68	13.44	13.37	12.85	12.70	12.27
Gujarat	10.35	9.61	9.44	9.55	8.49	8.29
Haryana	11.90	11.59	10.98	10.10	19.36	9.15
Karnataka	11.91	11.69	11.06	10.40	10.21	9.71
Kerala	7.55	10.12	9.60	9.60	9.25	8.83
Madhya Pradesh	12.88	12.32	11.89	11.54	11.09	10.35
Maharashtra	9.75	9.90	10.18	9.74	9.35	8.39
Orissa	13.22	14.19	13.74	13.94	14.51	13.11
Punjab	11.25	9.94	9.74	9.06	9.21	9.01
Rajasthan	13.03	12.95	12.73	12.03	11.56	10.84
Tamil Nadu	10.63	10.39	10.14	10.14	9.65	9.48
Uttar Pradesh	11.79	11.66	11.63	11.14	10.79	10.94
West Bengal	10.88	11.80	11.71	11.78	11.17	10.39
India	11.36	11.30	11.19	10.87	10.42	9.94
RURAL						
Andhra Pradesh	16.05	15.37	14.35	13.62	12.65	12.04
Assam	15.70	14.23	14.23	13.63	12.63	13.04
Bihar	16.39	15.77	15.39	16.45	13.75	13.16
Gujarat	15.00	12.56	12.00	11.75	10.19	10.07
Haryana	18.13	14.54	15.02	14.55	11.37	10.66
Karnataka	15.71	15.03	13.75	11.62	11.53	10.73
Kerala	7.99	10.01	10.36	10.73	9.89	9.53
Madhya Pradesh	16.51	15.83	15.39	15.22	12.94	11.76
Maharashtra	12.83	13.79	13.03	11.48	11.32	10.49
Orissa	16.12	15.61	15.72	15.98	15.09	13.98
Punjab	15.46	13.52	12.41	11.69	10.58	9.92
Rajasthan	17.91	17.19	16.62	15.75	14.19	12.68
Tamil Nadu	13.95	13.05	12.24	12.20	10.66	10.88
Uttar Pradesh	16.32	15.17	15.32	14.79	13.62	12.91
West Bengal	13.35	14.28	15.12	15.06	13.59	13.19
India	15.35	14.80	14.47	14.06	12.72	12.11

Source: Bansil (2003) and NSSO *Survey of Consumer Expenditure 2004–05.*

Table 2

Per Capita Consumption Pattern of Cereals in Rural and Urban India (in kg)

NSS round	Year	Rice	%	Wheat	%	Coarse cereals	%	Total cereals	%
				RURAL					
17	1961–62	8.77	50	2.63	15	6.15	35	17.55	100
27	1972–73	8.56	56	3.83	25	4.84	32	15.26	100
28	1973–74	6.90	46	3.52	23	4.67	31	15.09	100
32	1977–78	7.12	45	4.05	26	4.51	29	15.68	100
38	1983	6.63	45	4.46	30	3.71	25	14.80	100
43	1987–88	7.04	49	4.94	34	2.49	17	14.47	100
50	1993–94	7.00	52	4.40	33	2.00	15	13.40	100
55	1999–00	6.78	53	4.55	36	1.39	11	12.72	100
61	2004–05	6.38	53	4.19	35	–	–	12.11	100
				URBAN					
17	1961–62	6.16	50	4.10	33	2.09	17	12.35	100
27	1972–73	4.94	43	4.82	42	1.61	14	11.37	100
28	1973–74	5.38	48	4.32	38	1.62	14	11.32	100
32	1977–78	5.48	47	4.87	42	1.27	11	11.62	100
38	1983	5.32	47	4.82	43	1.16	10	11.30	100
43	1987–88	5.35	48	4.98	45	0.86	8	11.19	100
50	1993–94	5.28	50	4.72	44	0.63	6	10.63	100
55	1999–00	5.22	50	4.77	46	0.43	4	10.42	100
61	2004–05	4.71	47	4.36	44	–	–	9.94	100

Source: *NSSO Survey of Consumer Expenditure*, various rounds. See, Bansil (2003).

Nutritional requirements vary not only with climate, but also with gender, age and activity status. National Institute of Nutrition recommended daily allowance (RDA) of 1875 calories per day for an adult woman engaged in sedentary activity compared to 2400 for adult man. The requirement for moderate work is 2875 and 2225 for man and woman. Table 3 reveals that across the Indian states, during 1983 and 1999–2000, the average calorie intake in rural areas has declined in all states except Jammu & Kashmir, Kerala, Orissa and West Bengal. Also, in 1983, average intakes were below 2400 calories in all but six states and were above the norm only in the northern states. In 1999–2000, except for four states (Haryana, Himachal Pradesh, Jammu & Kashmir and Rajasthan) the calorie intake was below the norm of 2400 calories. There has been, thus, a secular decline in calorie intakes in rural India over 1983 to 1999–2000

Table 3

Calorie Intake and Poverty Across Major States

States	Average Calorie Intake per capita per Day (kcal)		Head Count Ratios (% consuming below 2400 calories per day)		Head Count Ratios of poverty (% with OPL incomes)	
	1983	1999–00	1983	1999–00	1983	1999–00
Andhra Pradesh	2204	2021	68.5	80.7	35.8	11.1
Bihar	2189	2121	67.6	74.9	60.5	44.0
Gujarat	2113	1986	72.6	80.5	39.0	13.2
Haryana	2554	2455	54.1	55.1	27.5	8.3
Himachal Pradesh	2636	2454	44.5	56.5	23.9	8.0
Jammu & Kashmir	2569	2631	44.5	39.7	31.6	4.0
Karnataka	2260	2028	64.0	78.9	40.0	17.4
Kerala	1884	1982	81.5	81.2	48.5	9.4
Madhya Pradesh	2323	2062	62.5	78.4	53.7	37.1
Maharashtra	2144	2012	73.1	83.3	54.6	23.7
Orissa	2103	2119	70.9	74.6	66.2	48.0
Punjab	2677	2381	46.2	62.8	18.5	6.4
Rajasthan	2433	2425	54.2	56.7	46.7	13.7
Tamil Nadu	1861	1826	80.6	86.5	59.1	20.6
Uttar Pradesh	2399	2327	58.4	64.5	50.8	31.2
West Bengal	2027	2095	76.0	75.6	66.7	31.9

Source: Meenakshi and Vishwanathan (2003).

(about 70 calories per capita). These declining or below normal intakes apparently have got translated into increased head count ratios of calorie deprivation. Data shows that as income poverty has declined, calorie poverty appeared to have increased. Not only this, in absolute terms, head count ratios of calorie deprivation much higher than those based on income poverty. Table 4 further presents picture on calorie deprivation across states. During the period 1983/1999–2000, in case of 2400–calorie norm, we find that there is rising deprivation in 15 of 16 states (Meenakshi and Vishwanathan, 2003). In case of 2200–calorie norm, deprivation decreased marginally in 4 states, viz., Jammu & Kashmir, Kerala, Rajasthan and West Bengal. However, increased deprivation is observed in other 12 states. When 1800–calorie norm is considered, HCRs of calorie deprivation declined in 8 states. This does point to not so favourable nutrition situation across the states. In the Indian situation, low calorie intake is associated with low income. High income also does not mean sufficient calorie intake. Deprivation among high-income groups is reflected in the type of food intake. Table 5 shows that average calorie intake among the poorest quintile increased in all states except two (Madhya Pradesh and Maharashtra). The extent of increase in intake among poor is greater in the poorer states like Bihar, Orissa and West Bengal in comparison with states with rural prosperity. However, average calorie intake in case of rich, 20 per cent has fallen significantly across the states. This should be the result of changes in consumption basket of poor and the rich.

The National Family Health Survey–2 recorded the nutritional status of women and children. These estimates show significant impact of factors like caste, gender, region, and standard of living on their nutritional status. The poor women especially are vulnerable to food insecurity. The nutritional status of women in India is discussed below. Despite the fact that women in most communities are treated as producers, gatekeepers and shock absorbers (Brown, et al., 2001), they suffer from poor health. Woman ordained by culture eats last in the family and poverty and times of crisis constrain reflect on her

Table 4

Head Count Ratios of Calorie Deprivation

States	*2200 Norm*		*1800 Norm*	
	1983	*1999–00*	*1983*	*1999–00*
Andhra Pradesh	56.9	69.7	30.0	36.9
Bihar	56.9	62.4	32.4	32.5
Gujarat	63.8	70.4	36.6	41.0
Haryana	42.8	43.5	19.3	18.4
Himachal Pradesh	33.8	42.7	14.8	12.1
Jammu & Kashmir	31.9	28.9	13.0	7.3
Karnataka	55.2	69.9	35.7	41.8
Kerala	74.0	70.3	53.2	42.8
Madhya Pradesh	51.6	68.0	27.9	38.5
Maharashtra	61.6	70.5	34.2	39.2
Orissa	60.6	61.7	35.1	29.1
Punjab	36.8	48.1	19.8	20.6
Rajasthan	43.4	43.0	22.7	15.5
Tamil Nadu	74.6	78.7	54.4	55.4
Uttar Pradesh	47.1	52.0	24.0	23.0
West Bengal	67.3	63.3	43.8	34.1

Source: Meenakshi and Vishwanathan (2003).

Table 5
Average Calorie Intake by Poorest and Richest (Expenditurewise) Groups

States	Poorest Quintile (kcal per day)		Richest Quintile (kcal per day)	
	1983	*1999–00*	*1983*	*1999–00*
Andhra Pradesh	1513	1522	2822	2592
Bihar	1426	1601	3072	2797
Gujarat	1459	1534	2865	2558
Haryana	1671	1713	3654	3156
Himachal Pradesh	1757	1981	3384	3116
Jammu & Kashmir	1838	2228	3295	3266
Karnataka	1362	1464	3076	2676
Kerala	1054	1398	2409	2627
Madhya Pradesh	1592	1528	3243	2703
Maharashtra	1593	1546	2751	2479
Orissa	1300	1578	2910	2684
Punjab	1644	1733	3790	3277
Rajasthan	1233	1836	3622	3182
Tamil Nadu	847	1294	2763	2427
Uttar Pradesh	1646	1758	3352	3091
West Bengal	1148	1550	2994	2712

Source: Meenakshi and Viswanathan (2003).

nutritional status (Table 6). Nearly 52 per cent of women aged 15–49 suffer from anaemia that results from nutritional deficiency of iron, vitamin B or other nutrients in 1998–99 and this proportion increased to 55.3 per cent in 2005–2006 (NFHS-3). This would affect the children born to these women. Gopalan (1995) points out that 30 per cent of all infants born in India are of low birth weight (below 2.5 kg) reflecting maternal malnutrition and consequent intra-uterine growth retardation. Iron deficiency anaemia among reproductive age women is important factor responsible for this. It also is a major factor contributing to maternal morbidity and mortality. That is, there is increased risk for maternal deaths and unhealthy children. Anaemia increases the risk of premature delivery and low birth weight babies.[16]

Table 6 also reveals that 35.8 per cent of women in India as per the NFHS–2 (1998–99), a drought year in most parts of the country,[17] were underweight (with BMI below 18.5 kg/m^2). This percentage was almost the same in 2005–06. Rajasthan, Madhya Pradesh, Bihar, Orissa, West Bengal, Gujarat, Maharashtra, Andhra Pradesh and

Table 6

Nutritional Status of Women in India

State	Per cent of below 18.5 kg/m2		Women with ≥ 25.0 kg/m2		BMI of ≥ 30.0 kg.m2		Per cent of Women age 15–49 with any anaemia	
	1998–99	2005–06	1998–99	2005–06	1998–99	2005–06	1998–99	2005–06
India	35.8	35.6	10.6	12.6	2.2	2.8	51.8	55.3
Delhi	12.0	14.8	33.8	26.4	9.2	7.8	40.5	44.3
Haryana	25.9	31.3	16.6	17.4	3.9	4.4	47.0	56.1
Himachal Pradesh	29.7	29.9	13.1	13.5	2.3	2.1	40.5	43.3
Jammu & Kashmir	26.4	24.6	13.8	16.7	3	3.3	58.7	52.1
Punjab	16.9	18.9	30.2	29.9	9.1	9.1	41.4	38.0
Rajasthan	36.1	36.7	7.1	8.9	1.6	1.8	48.5	53.1
Madhya Pradesh	38.2	41.7	6.1	7.6	1.2	1.4	54.3	56.0
Uttar Pradesh	35.8	36.0	7.5	9.2	1.5	1.7	48.7	49.9
Bihar	39.3	45.1	3.7	4.6	0.5	0.6	63.4	67.4
Orissa	48.0	41.4	4.4	6.6	0.6	1.1	63.0	69.5
West Bengal	43.7	39.1	8.6	11.4	1.3	2.0	62.7	63.2
Arunachal Pradesh	10.7	16.4	5.1	8.8	0.6	1.1	62.5	50.6
Assam	27.1	36.5	4.2	7.8	0.7	0.9	69.7	69.5
Manipur	18.8	14.8	10.8	13.3	1.2	1.9	28.9	35.7

Cont'd...

Contd...

Meghalaya	25.8	14.6	5.8	5.3	1.2	0.8	63.3	47.2
Mizoram	22.6	14.4	5.3	10.6	0.5	1.2	48.0	38.6
Nagaland	18.4	17.4	8.2	6.4	0.7	0.7	38.4	–
Sikkim	11.2	11.2	15.7	15.4	2.5	3.0	61.1	60.0
Goa	27.1	27.9	21.2	20.2	4.3	4.8	36.4	38.0
Gujarat	37.0	36.3	15.8	16.7	4.4	4.6	46.3	55.3
Maharashtra	39.7	36.2	11.7	14.5	2.9	3.6	48.5	48.4
Andhra Pradesh	37.4	33.5	12	15.6	2.2	4.1	49.8	62.9
Karnataka	38.8	35.5	13.6	15.3	2.9	3.7	42.4	51.5
Kerala	18.7	18.0	20.6	18.1	3.8	5.0	22.7	32.8
Tamil Nadu	29.0	28.4	14.7	20.9	2.7	5.1	56.5	53.2

Source: NFHS–2 and NFHS–3.

Karnataka have higher proportion of women with BMI below 18.5 kg/m^2 in 1998–99 compared to India, but in 2005–06, Rajasthan, Madhya Pradesh, Uttar Pradesh, Bihar Orissa, West Bengal, Assam, Gujarat and Maharashtra were in this category. The range is 10.7 per cent in Arunachal Pradesh and 48.0 per cent in Orissa in 1998–99 and the range is 11.2 per cent in Sikkim and 45.1 per cent in Bihar. Except for J&K, Orissa, West Bengal, Manipur, Meghalaya, Mizoram, Nagaland, Gujarat, Maharashtra, Andhra Pradesh, Karnataka, Kerala and Tamil Nadu other states observed deterioration in this indicator. Rajasthan is one of these states. Obesity is becoming a substantial problem among women in India, particularly living in urban areas, well-educated and those from a high standard of living. About one-tenth Indian women have BMI of greater than 25.0 and another 2.2 per cent have BMI of $\geq$ 30.0 in 1998–99 and these proportions were 12.6 and 2.8 in 2005–06. This means that there is increasing trend towards obesity. In Rajasthan, the situation is relatively better compared to the national average. But deterioration is observed. Across states we find that only in Delhi, Punjab, Meghalaya, Nagaland, Goa and Sikkim there is some improvement. North India has higher proportion of obese women. It is less common in north-east, central and east India. However, body's adaptation mechanisms enable those with lower body weights to metabolise a lower amount of calories more efficiently (Sukhatme, 1993).

Rajasthan's Nutrition Profile

It would be interesting to observe the situation in a perpetually drought affected state of India—Rajasthan in the context of crisis and nutrition security. Table 7 shows that in 1999–00 (another drought year in Rajasthan when 23,406 villages and about 64 per cent rural population were affected), food basket predominates with milk and milk products and other food items. This is so across the MCPE classes. Even in a stress year, consumption of food items per se is low; an indication of improvement in the consumption behaviour of the poor too. The state appears to have improved both the availability and the access to food even in a distress year. This should be reflected in nutrition intake of the population. Table 8 presents data on calorie, protein and fat consumption. The average calorie consumption in all the years has been above the recommended calorie intake (RCI). The year 1987–88, the extreme stress year in comparison to other years, turns out to a peak period in calorie consumption. The year 1993–94 was again a drought year in Rajasthan, which observed a marginal decline in calorie consumption and so, did 1999–2000. During these years, however, protein and fat consumption in the state has

Table 7

Value of Consumption (Rs) for a Period of 30 days in Rural Rajasthan (1999–00)

Monthly Per capita Expenditure Rs	Per HH	Value of Consumption (Rs)				
		thousand persons	food grain	milk etc.	other food	total food
up to 340	105	129	86	33	93	180
340–380	61	74	98	54	130	228
380–420	83	97	100	66	149	249
420–470	115	127	105	76	166	271
470–525	123	131	112	94	191	303
525–615	156	156	118	117	226	343
615–775	187	171	123	157	281	404
775–950	84	62	137	194	342	479
Above 950	85	54	157	302	516	672
All	1000	1000	112	110	214	327

Source: NSSO Report (2001), p. 457.

Table 8

Nutritional intake in Rajasthan Over time

Year	Average Calorie	Consumption of Protein	Fat
1983	2433	75	42
1987–88	2493		
1993–94	2470	79	52
1999–00	2425	77	54

Source: Sagar (2003).

marginally improved. But when we observe, regional distribution in calorie consumption in Rajasthan, especially in a severe drought year: 1987–88, we find variations across regions (Table 9). Besides, across regions except for the top two deciles there is a deficit in calorie consumption. As we move from bottom decile to top decile, the deficit is observed to reduce. The southern region is the most deficient region in Rajasthan. This means that poverty and inadequate nutrition are directly related in Rajasthan in severe stress year. As data is not available sex-wise, one can safely presume that women must be more affected (see, Singh, 2007a). However, NFHS–2 and NFHS–3 data shows that there is a visible difference in diet of rural and urban women (Singh, 2007b).

Anthropometric data say a great deal about the adequacy of food and nutritional intake of people. It also is an indicator of their ability

Table 9

Calorie intake at Decile Point—1987–88 (Kcal)

Decile Points	Regions (state sample estimates)					Central Sample
	Western	Northeast	Southern	Southeast	Rajasthan	
I	1737	1802	1191	1936	1655	1853
II	1814	1988	1309	2188	1878	2021
III	2070	2190	1378	2280	2073	2115
IV	2228	2349	1568	2417	2241	2268
V	2306	2473	1744	2730	2395	2452
VII	2409	2637	1904	2963	2567	2631
VII	2493	2600	2392	3114	2593	

Source: Sagar (2003).

to lead healthy and active lives. Mothers who are short are more likely to have low birth weight babies and difficulty in delivering the child. Also those with height of below 140–150 cm are considered nutritionally at risk. The mean height of women in Rajasthan is 154 cm. Only 6 per cent of women are under 145 cm in height. The proportion in urban areas is marginally higher that those in rural areas (Table 10). The proportion of Muslim women at 6.9 per cent is higher than Hindu women and Jain women. Higher proportions of scheduled tribe women have height of lower than 145 cm. South-eastern Rajasthan has higher proportion of women of height of below 145 cm. The body mass index (BMI) is used to assess both thinness and obesity. The mean BMI in Rajasthan is 19.9. Chronic energy deficiency is normally indicated by a BMI of less than 18.5. More than one-third (36%) women in Rajasthan have a BMI of below 18.5, indicating a high prevalence of nutritional deficiency. The situation has only marginally improved in 2005–06 (NFHS-3). Nutritional problems are more serious for scheduled caste women, Muslim women, living in south-eastern region and rural women. About 49 per cent women in Rajasthan have some degree of anaemia. There are differences ascribed to their background (Singh, 2007b). It is slightly higher among rural women, currently married, Muslim women and scheduled tribe women. Poverty, culture, environment (where they are located) apparently has direct relation to nutritional status of women in Rajasthan.

Epilogue

India's nutrition problem is not so much due to lack of food grains, but of lack of adequate access to food in over 30 per cent of poor households whose family incomes are so low that even 70 per cent of that

Table 10

Nutritional Status of Women in Rajasthan (1998–99)

Features	Height			Weight for Height		
	Mean Height (cm)	% below 145 cm	No. of women for height	Mean body mass index (BMI)	% with BMI below 18.5 kg/m sq.	No. of women for BMI
Residence						
Urban	153.2	6.8	1534	21.3	28.5	1432
Rural	153.8	5.3	4798	19.5	38.7	4296
Religion						
Hindu	153.7	5.5	5609	19.9	35.9	5076
Muslim	153.4	6.9	605	19.9	40.7	542
Jain	154.7	1.2	61	23.0	16.5	57
Other Caste	154.8	5.8	58	20.5	36.7	53
Schedule caste	152.9	7.0	1134	19.2	43.7	1002
Schedule tribe	153.1	6.8	788	19.2	39.6	676
OBC	153.5	5.6	1417	19.7	38.3	1289
Other	154.2	4.8	2989	20.4	31.5	2756
Region						
Western	154.8	2.9	1946	20.0	34.1	1740
North-eastern	153.6	6.2	2793	20.0	37.2	2579
Southern	152.2	7.3	825	19.8	35.5	738
South-eastern	152.6	8.6	769	19.7	37.8	701

Source: IIPS (2001b).

family income is spent on food, nutritional needs are not met (Gopalan, 1995). Over time food security problem has been handled effectively, though nutrition security is found wanting. In the context of household food security, that food security is a necessary but not sufficient condition for adequate nutrition, the other conditions being care and health. These two are closely related, not least because of the genetic, physiological and behavioural adaptations people to nutritional stress. Though during the times of crisis in India, improvement is observed, women and poor are still vulnerable. There is no doubt that women are nutrition mediators. To make them more effective in ensuring household food and nutrition security following are suggested:

- Enhance their access to material resources.
- Enhance or facilitate their decision-making power.
- If the strategies to end hunger and alleviate poverty are to be successful, they must include women.

- Flexibility in the division of labour is important for coping, as is the diversification of income. Women usually mix multiple roles. Malnutrition can be tackled to some extent through nutrition education. Educating women about quality of food and providing knowledge of nutrition is important for household food and nutrition security in times of crisis.
- Women should be given priority in employment in drought/ famine works or food for work programmes.[18]
- Assuring woman's access to land and other assets. This may require changes in existing laws.
- Women's saving groups can help tied over the economic crisis situation and thereby ensuring food and nutrition security of the woman and her family.
- State intervention in terms of making public distribution system effective and targeted. A dependable network of PDS does ensure food security if access to food, whether through production, labour, trade or transfer based entitlements is ensured.
- Agricultural crop production strategies need to take adequate care to incorporate gender concerns.
- Making extension available to women, which means it has to be more than training and motivating extension workers to address women farmers' problems and their problems on the farm.
- Take steps to increase women's efficiency in home production. If women can save time and energy through increased efficiency in post harvest agricultural processing, water and fuel wood supply, cooking and cleaning, etc., then they can enhance their nutritional responsibilities.
- The ICDS, mid-day meal, WFP-India mix like programmes can be useful for contributing to children and women's nutritional needs. Such programmes need to be made more effective.
- Provisioning and growth of non-farm employment opportunities in the vicinity can help raise the incomes of women.

Finally, command over food during crisis times should depend not only on entitlement but also on enfranchisement.

Notes

1. The recent projections of FOA reveal that World Food Summit goal of halving the number of food-insecure people from 800 million in 1995 to 400 million by

2015 will not be achieved until 2030 (Pinstrup-Anderson and Pandya-Lorch, 2001).

2. About 2 billion people suffer from iron-deficient anaemia, more than 2 billion are at risk of iodine deficiency disorders, and 250 million children are affected by severe vitamin A deficiency (Pinstrup-Anderson, Pandya-Lorch and Rosegrant, 2001).
3. Aidoo (1988) argues that African food production lagged behind food demand due to neglect of the crucial role-played by women in food production and food security in policies. There is a general consensus that the persisting food crisis in Sub-Saharan Africa is the consequence of a long-run neglect of women's food farming roles, when in these countries women perform 70 per cent of labour in food production (Kabeer, 1990), 65 per cent in Asia, and 45 per cent in Latin American and the Caribbean (Brown, et al., 2001).
4. Studies have shown that real income and who earns it influence the household food security. In this context there is large volume of evidence that female control over income has positive impact on household expenditure, calories intake and anthropometric indicators (Brown, et al., 2001).
5. Women constitute almost 40 per cent of the employed workforce in low-income countries, are sole income earners in one-quarter to one-third of the households (McGuire and Popkin, 1988; 1990).
6. In case of Kenya, Neumann, et al. (1989) points out that during low rainfall periods household food intake declined significantly, households could not even fulfil their basal metabolic needs. They found that during 1984 drought, 63 per cent households ate fewer meals (1.1 per day compared to 2.2 before the drought).
7. As per the Rural Labour Enquiry of 1974–75, female agricultural labourers did not work for 124 days during the year due to want of work and it was 76 for males. The annual real earnings per person in case of females were recorded as Rs 121.90 as against Rs 243.30 for males. There are of course inter-regional variations; there are considerable gender earning differentials.
8. They would tend livestock and poultry and women would also assume additional responsibilities. Ali (1987) argues that in the time of food crisis women's role as food producer changes from gathering wild foods to income earning activities, then to migration and frequently to prostitution. (Kelleher, 1997) too reports it during Irish famine years. In the contemporary world, we do find that women from poor families do foray into begging, prostitution. In India, there have been reports of sale of children.
9. In the normal times, studies have found that wife's earnings from agricultural wage work is half or one-third of husband's earning contribution in absolute terms.
10. In lean seasons, edible herbs, mushrooms, tubers, wild millets, edible leaves and fruits are crucial sources of food for the poorest (also see, Byrne and Baden, 1995).
11. In Bangladesh (Nath, 1979) women have been observed to increase the frequency of their visits to their parental homes during the hungry season (also see, Rozario, 1997).

12. In the traditional society, Fernandes and Menon (1987) state that everyone used to eat together, but in the present times, women have to starve quite often because of food shortages. She gives all that is available to the man and keeps nothing for herself.
13. There is of course a tendency to favour male children during food shortages within the family as against the female child who is in fact nutritionally more vulnerable (see also, Katona-Apte, 1988).
14. Women are required to spend more time in searching, foraging, gleaning and the processing of food; in looking for fodder, fuel, and water; and in tending of animals. Women may also venture into activities traditionally their caste or social status may hinder (Leslie, Pelto and Rasmussen, 1988).
15. Leafy vegetables are rich in carotene, folic acid, vitamin C, calcium and limoleic acid. In Sri Lanka it was found that rice constituted the core of the meal and bread that was more expensive on an energy-basis than rice, was sometimes bought for practical purposes to ease the work of cooking. This could occur when the housewife found it difficult to cook because of sickness or in pregnancy, as well as when labourers or guests had to be fed and there was no help in the kitchen. Besides, green leaves are consumed by households of all strata and traditionally are considered good for body, particularly during special physiological states like pregnancy. The consumption of green leaves is also going down as paddy-growing seasons are becoming long and people avoid picking green leaves that were usually considered the work of women and children. Many women who did not have green leaves on their own garden premises, hesitated or were restricted from walking around by themselves on the paddy fields or in the shrub jungle. When green leaves therefore had to be bought, the consumption was cut down in the poor household. In households where women and children did not pick green leaves because of time constraints, reluctance to pick in the paddy fields due to fear of poisoning, or because of restrictions in women's freedom to move around, the consumption of these may have been significantly reduced (Senauer, Sahn and Alderman, 1986).
16. During the same year, 47.0 per cent children below the age of three were underweight, 45.5 per cent had stunted growth and 15.5 per cent were wasted (IIPS, 2001a).
17. In Rajasthan alone 21.5 million people were affected by drought in 1998–99 in 20069 villages.
18. There is a word of caution here because some evidence does point out that when food or cash has been distributed to household or particular individuals in famine relief programmes, this has not always resulted in the increase in food intake that were expected. This may be due to household strategies at crisis point give priority to purchasing of assets to safeguard their future survival (Corbett, 1988).

References

Agarwal, Bina (1997), "Social Security and the Family: Coping with Seasonality and Calamity in Rural India", *Journal of Peasant Studies*, pp. 341–412.

Aidoo, A.A (1988), "Women and Food Security: The Opportunity for Africa", *Development*, (2–3), pp. 56–62.

Ali, M (1987), "Women in Famine" in B. Currey and G. Hugo (eds.), *Famine as a Geographical Phenomenon,* D. Reidel, Dordrecht, pp. 113–34.

Arnold, David (1988), *Famine: Social Crisis and Historical Change,* Blackwell, London.

Bansil, P.C. (2003), "Demand for Foodgrains by 2020", in S. Mahendra Dev, K.P. Kannan and Nira Ramachandran (eds.), *Towards a Food Secure India: Issues and Policies,* IHD, New Delhi, chapter 3.

Brown, Lynn R., et al. (2001), "Generating Food Security in the Year 2020: Women as Producers, Gatekeepers, and Shock Absorbers", in Per Pinstrup-Andersen and Rajul Pandya-Lorch (eds.), *The Unfinished Agenda: Perspectives on Overcoming Hunger, Poverty and Environmental Degradation,* IFPRI, Washington, D.C., chapter 32.

Byrne, B and S. Baden (1995), *Gender, Emergencies and Humanitarian Assistance,* A report, European Commission, Directorate General for Development, Brussels.

Chatterjee, M and J. Lambert (1989), "Women and Nutrition: Reflections from India and Pakistan", *Food and Nutrition Bulletin*. Vol, 11, No. 4, pp. 13–28.

Corbett, Jane, (1988), "Famine and Household Coping Strategies", *World Development*, Vol. 16, No. 9, pp. 1099–1112.

Currie, B. (1992), "Food Crises and Prevention: An Analysis in the Indian Context", *Contemporary South Asia,* Vol. 1, No. 1, pp. 93–111.

Daly, Mary (1986), *The Great Famine in Ireland,* Dublin Historical Association, Dublin.

Dobson, B,. et al., (1994), "Diet, Choice and Poverty: Social, Cultural and Nutritional Aspects of Food Consumption among Low Income Families" (as quoted by Elizabeth Dowler (1997), "Food Poverty and Food Policy" a paper presented in PRU/IDS Research and Policy Workshop, Sussex, April.

Dreze, Jean and Amartya Sen (1993), *Hunger and Public Action,* OUP, Delhi.

Fernandes, W, and G. Menon (1987), *Tribal Women and Forestry Economy: Deforestation, Exploitation and Social Status,* Indian Social Institute, Delhi.

Fitzpatrick, David (1997), "Women and the Great Famine", in Margaret Kelleher and James H. Murphy (eds.), *Separate Spheres: Gender and Nineteenth Century Ireland*, Irish Academic Press, Dublin.

Gopalan, C. (1994), 'Trends in Food Consumption Patterns" in M. Biswas and M. Gabr (eds.), *Nutrition in the Nineties: Policy Issues,* OUP, Delhi.

——. (1995), "Towards Food Security and Nutrition Security", *Economic and Political Weekly*, December 30, pp. A–134–41.

Greenough, Paul (1982), *Prosperity and Misery in Modern Bengal,* OUP, New York.

IIPS (2001a), *India: National Family Health Survey (NFHS–2),* Mumbai.

——. (2001b), *Rajasthan: National Family Health Survey (NFHS–2),* Mumbai.

Jodha, N.S (1978), "Effectiveness of Farmers' Adjustment to Risk", *Economic and Political Weekly,* Vol. 13, No. 25, pp. A–38–48.

Joshi, Varsha (2002), "Changing Food Habits and Nutrition in India: A Gender Perspective", in S.S. Acharya, Surjit Singh and V. Sagar (eds.), *Sustainable Agriculture, Poverty and Food Security,* Rawat Publications, Jaipur, chapter 40.

——. (2003), *Globalisation and Cultural Imperialism: Gender Identities,* IDS, Jaipur, WP No. 136.

Kabeer, Naila (1990), *Women, Household Food Security and Coping Strategies,* Nutrition Policy Discussion Paper No. 6, ACC/SCN, Geneva.

Katona-Apte, Judit (1988), "Coping Strategies of Destitute Women in Bangladesh", *Food and Nutrition Bulletin,* Vol. 10, No. 3, pp. 42–47.

Kelleher, Margaret (1997), "Women as Famine Victim: The Figure of Women in Irish Famine Narratives", in Ronit Lentin (ed.) *Gender & Catastrophe,* Zed Books, London, chapter 18.

Laier, Julie Koch, et al. (1996), *Gender, Household Food Security and Coping Strategies,* Development Bibliography, 14. June, IDS Sussex.

Leslie, Joanne, Gretel H. Pelto and Kathleen M. Rasmussen (1988), "Nutrition of Women in Developing Countries", *Food and Nutrition Bulletin,* Vol. 10, No. 3, pp. 4–7.

Lingam, Lakshmi (1994), "Women-headed Households: Coping with Caste, Class and Gender Hierarchies", *Economic and Political Weekly,* March 19, pp. 699–704.

McGuire, Judith and Barry M. Popkin (1988), "The Zero-sum Game: A Framework for Examining Women and Nutrition", *Food and Nutrition Bulletin,* Vol. 10, No. 3, pp. 27–32.

——. (1990), "Beating the Zero-sum Game: Women and Nutrition in the Third World", *Food and Nutrition Bulletin.,* Vol. 12, No. 1, pp. 3–11 (Part 2).

Meenakshi, J.V. and Brinda Vishwanathan (2003), "Calorie Deprivation in Rural India, 1983–1999–2000", *Economic and Political Weekly,* January 25, pp. 369–76.

Mukherjee, Neela and Amitabha Mukerjee (1994), "Rural Women and Food Security: What a Food Calendar Reveals", *Economic and Political Weekly,* March 12, pp. 597–99.

Nath, J. (1979), "The Role of Women in Rural Bangladesh: A Study of Nantupur Village", in *Women for Women: Situation of Women in Bangladesh,* BRAC, Dhaka.

Neumann, Charlotte, et al. (1989), "Household Response to the Impact of Drought in Kenya", *Food and Nutrition Bulletin,* Vol. 11, No. 2, pp. 21–33.

Osborne, S.G (1850), *Gleanings in the West of Ireland,* Boone, London (as quoted in Kelleher, 1997).

Pinstrup-Andersen, Per and Rajul Pandya-Lorch (eds.) (2001), *The Unfinished Agenda: Perspectives on Overcoming Hunger, Poverty and Environmental Degradation,* IFPRI, Washington, D.C.

——. and Mark. W. Rosegrant (2001), "Global Food Security: A Review of the Challenges" in Per Pinstrup-Andersen and Rajul Pandya-Lorch (eds.), *The*

Unfinished Agenda: Perspectives on Overcoming Hunger, Poverty and Environmental Degradation, IFPRI, Washington, D.C. chapter 2.

Pretty, Jules N., John Thompson and Fiona Hinchcliffe (1996), *Sustainable Agriculture: Impacts on Food Production and Challenges for Food Security*, Gatekeeper Series No. 60., IIED, London.

Rivers, J.P.W (1988), "The Nutritional Biology" in G. Harrison (ed.), *Famine*, OUP, Oxford.

Rozario, Santi (1997), " 'Disasters' and Bangladeshi Women" in Ronit Lentin (ed.), *Gender & Catastrophe*, Zed Books, London, chapter 19.

Sen, Amartya (1981), *Poverty and Famines: An Essay on Entitlement and Deprivation*, OUP, Oxford.

Senauer, B.D. Sahn, H. Adlerman (1986), "The Effect of the Value of Time on Food Consumption Patterns in Developing Countries: Evidence from Sri Lanka", *American Journal of Agricultural Economics*, Vol. 68, No. 4, pp. 920–27.

Singh, Surjit (2002), "Food Security: Agenda for Asian Economies", *Economic and Political Weekly*, June 22.

——. (2007a), *Household Food Security in the Context of WTO: Reflections from Rajasthan*, unpublished report, Jaipur.

——. (2007b), *Millennium Development Goals in Rajasthan: Status and Future Concerns*, IDS and UNMC, Bangkok Office.

Sukhatme, P.V. (1993), "Note" in *Report of the Expert Group on Estimation of Proportion and Number of Poor*, PPD, Planning Commission, GOI, New Delhi.

Sagar, V. (2003), "Food Security Issues in a State of Large Agricultural Instability: Rajasthan", IDS, Jaipur, WP. No. 128.

MSSRF (2001), *Food Insecurity Atlas of Rural India*, Chennai (with WFP).

Appendix 1

Food grains Consumption during Drought Year in Rajasthan: 1963–64

Food grain Consumption class (gms/day)	*Oct. 1963*	*Nov. 1963*	*Dec. 1963*	*Jan. 1964*	*Feb. 1964*	*Mar. 1964*	*Apr. 1964*
	Percentage of Households in each Consumption Class						
300–450	7.7	21.3	34.6	48.1	57.7	60.5	69.2
			1.9	5.7	3.8	5.7	7.6
451–600	21.2	25.0	38.5	34.6	35.5	32.7	25.0
	67.3	73.0	69.2	74.9	76.8	78.7	78.7
601–750	71.1	53.8	26.9	17.3	5.8	5.8	5.8
	32.7	27.0	28.9	19.4	20.4	15.4	13.9

Note: First row indicates drought year and second row indicates post-drought year.

Source: Jodha (1978).

20

Two-Child Norm in Panchayati Raj

Evidence from Rajasthan

P.R. Sharma and G.S. Narwani

India is a welfare State wedded to democracy and development. The overriding objective of social and economic development is to improve the quality of life of people and to enhance their well-being. With this objective in view, in 1952, India was the first country in the world to launch a national programme, emphasising family planning to the extent necessary for reducing birth rates "to stabilise the population at a level consistent with the requirement of national economy".[1] After 1952, sharp declines in death rates were, however, not accompanied by a similar drop in birth rates. The National Health Policy 1983 stated that replacement levels of total fertility rate (TFR) should be achieved by the year 2000. Though universal awareness of the need for family planning has been generated and total fertility rate has also reduced from 6.0 (1951) to 3.3 (1997), population has continued to increase at an alarming rate. During 1981–91, decadal variation was 28.44 per cent and even after continuous family planning efforts, such decadal increase was 28.33 per cent during 1991–2001. Population of India has crossed one billion mark as per 2001 census.[2]

Rajasthan is one of the larger state in the country with a population of over 56 million (2001). The Census of India 2001 also reveals that Rajasthan has maintained its record of registering one of the highest population growth rates in the country since independence. According to NFHS–2, the current total fertility rate in the state is 3.78 children per woman. According to the Technical group on Population Projections, constituted by the Planning Commission, Government of India, Rajasthan will not achieve the replacement level fertility before 2048. It is interesting to note that the level of unwanted fertility has increased from 22 per cent in 1992–93 to 32 per cent in 1998–99.[3] In short, the state recorded the highest mortality ratio, third highest total fertility rate and fourth highest infant mortality rate among the major state of the India.

Stabilising population is an essential requirement for promoting sustainable development with more equitable distribution. To achieve such objective small family norm is being encouraged. Various incentive schemes have also been promoted for it.

Incentives for Small Family Norm

Balika Smridhi Yojana: It is run by department of Women and Children to promote survival and care of girl child of BPL family. A cash incentive of Rs 500 is awarded at the birth of a girl child up to second living child. It is kept in deposit for payment of scholarship @ Rs 300 to Rs 1,000 per year during school going period from class I to class X.

Maternity Benefit Scheme: It is run by Panchayat and Development department. A cash incentive of Rs 500 is awarded to mothers who have their first child after 19 years of age, for the birth of first and second child of BPL family.

Family Welfare Linked Insurance Plan: In case of death of a woman within 30 days from the date of tubectomy/laproscopy operation, a compensation of Rs 50,000 was paid by United India Insurance Company till 20 August, 2001 which has since been raised to Rs 2.00 lakh.

Reward to Couples: Population Policy 2000 also provides for rewarding couples below poverty line, who marry after the legal age of marriage, register the marriage, have the first child after the mother reaches the age of 21, accept the small family norm and adopt a terminal method after the birth of the second child.

Freezing the number of MPS: 42nd Constitutional Amendment has frozen the number of representatives in the Lok Sabha at 1971 census levels to serve as an incentive for state governments to fearlessly pursue the agenda for population stabilisation. The freeze valid upto 2000 was extended to the year 2006. Planning Commission of India is advocating to extend it till 2026.

Steps by Government of Rajasthan

Rajasthan Family Welfare Pension Scheme 1995: After family planning operation, in case only daughters are left as children in the family due to death of the only male child, pension of Rs 150 per month is payable. BDO of Panchayat Samiti is competent to sanction such pension.[4]

Janani Suraksha Yojana (JSY) 2005: It has been started under National Rural Health Mission (NRHM) to minimise maternal mortality. This scheme is an extended form of Maternity Benefit Scheme for grant of a package of Rs 700 to mother in case she delivers the child in health centre. Rs 500 are payable irrespective of the place of birth. Transport expenses are also borne from residence to the sub-centre where delivery takes place. Additional Rs 200 in rural area or Rs 100 in urban area is an incentive for delivery of a living child of BPL family in a medical sub-centre/dispensary in the interest of safe motherhood. Rs 1,500 are payable if some specialist has to be engaged for scissorean operation in any private nursing home or hospital. ANM keeps an imprest amount of Rs 5,000 for cash payment to the beneficiary.[5]

ASHA Scheme: For providing services to pregnant mother before, during and after delivery, Gram Sabha has selected an ASHA health worker per every 1000 population. *Jan Mangal Workers* are already propagating the message of family planning in rural areas. Trained Mid-wife is also assisting pregnant mothers for safe delivery. All such health workers have to register themselves in the nearest sub-centre/dispensary. Any of these workers will be provided incentive of Rs 600 for each safe delivery for providing following services:

(i) Identify pregnant mother and fill JSY Card 16–20 weeks before delivery.
(ii) Registration of such pregnant mother in health centre in her presence.
(iii) Get Below Poverty Line (BPL) certificate ready in advance.
(iv) Advise and assist pregnant mother for three health check-ups in health centre/dispensary during pregnancy and convince for institutional delivery.
(v) Assist pregnant mother for two TT Injections.
(vi) Accompany pregnant mother for delivery to health centre/dispensary and stay with her till she is relieved from health centre.

(vii) Ensure registration of birth of the child.

(viii) Advise mother for feeding colostrums milk within one hour of delivery and only breast feeding till 3–6 months, and not to give water or ghutti, etc.

(ix) Assist in protection of newly born child upto 10 weeks

In lieu of such services, she gets Rs 300 immediately after delivery and Rs 300 after 3 months. She is also advanced Rs 1500 as imprest for transport or maternity benefit to beneficiary.

Referral Transport: Transport facility is being provided in 19 districts where medical sub-centres are located at far off places. Economically weaker women are ensured safe delivery and other maternity benefits.

Rewards for Best Performance: Panchayati Raj Institutions, NGOs, private hospitals and nursing homes, government hospitals in every district are rewarded and honoured for best performance in universalising the small family norm in Rajasthan.

Details of Rewards	*Amount (Rs in Lakh)*	*No. of Prizes*
Best Panchayat in every Block	1.00	237
Best Panchayat Samiti in every District	5.00	32
Best District in the State	50.00	01
Best NGO in every District	1.00	32
Best Private Hospital/Nursing Home in every District	1.00	32
Best Government Hospital in every District (CHC, Sattelite, District Hospital)	1.00	32

Scheme is in force since 2003–04 in the interest of population stabilisation.

State governments strive for strict enforcement of Child Marriage Restraint Act, 1976 also.

Small Family Norm in Panchayat Raj: Initiatives by States

Since local bodies are in direct contact with the community, they can become the most effective instruments for taking up population stabilisation programme. Elected Panchayats have a great role in this respect. Panchayats can undertake awareness campaign through direct mass contacts to break the traditional resistance to change. Out of 28 states, 7 states of Rajasthan, Madhya Pradesh, Haryana, Andhra Pradesh, Orissa, Gujarat and Himachal Pradesh took the lead and debarred the persons, who do not adopt the two-child family norm, from contesting election to Panchayati Raj Institutions (PRIs). Gujarat is the last state, which has introduced this disqualification only in 2005, when Himachal Pradesh has withdrawn the similar clause.

State	*Relevant Act with Section*	*Remarks*
Rajasthan	Rajasthan Panchayati Raj Act, 1994 Section 1ʕ (L)	* Disqualification if third child born after 27.11.1995 (Nine months after enacting the Act)*Twins born out of single delivery considered as one entity
Madhya Pradesh	MP Panchayati Raj and Gram Swaraj Act, 1993	* Chief Minister had decided to scrap the provision as announced in July 2005. Subsequently withdrawn
Haryana	Haryana Panchayat Raj Act, 1994 Section 175 (1)	* Disqualification if third child born after 24 April 1994, the date of enactment itself. Chief Minister has declared for its withdrawal
Andhra Pradesh	A.P.Panchayat Raj Act, 1994 Section 19 (3)	
Orissa	Orissa Panchayat Raj Act, 1994	
Himachal Pradesh	H.P.Panchayat Raj Act, 1994	* Enforced wef 8 June, 2001 * Withdrawn as per Cabinet Decision Dated 16 February, 2005
Gujarat	Gujarat Panchayat Act	* Act amended as per Panchayati Raj Update, April 2005, p. 1

It is true that people's representatives should become role models for the public to emulate. In Rajasthan itself, there are approximately 1.20 lakh PRI representatives as against only 25 MPs and 200 MLAs. Hence, PRI members can become a formidable force for population stabilisation. It was perhaps with this objective in view that such provision was made in Panchayat law.

Impact of Disqualification in various States

In Haryana, as many as 297 elected Panchayat representatives (24 Sarpanch and 273 Panch) were removed from their posts for having more than 2 children in 2001–02 under Section 175(1)of Haryana Panchayat Raj Act, according to State Election Commission.[6]

In Himachal Pradesh, the restrictive law came into force on 8 June, 2001. In subsequent 4 years, more than 100 Panchayat representatives were dismissed for having a third child. Norm became so unpopular that Himachal Pradesh had to withdraw the provision of 2-child norm in a state cabinet meeting on 16 February, 2005.[7]

In Rajasthan, Section 19(L) Panchayati Raj Act, 1994 provided for qualifications for election as Panch or member of PRI. Member of PRI shall be deemed to become disqualified to contest for election or for holding the post after election, in case third child is born after 27 November, 1995. In any child was born from the date of commencement of the Act i.e., 23 April, 1994 and 27 November, 1995, such person shall not be deemed to be disqualified. Any number of children born out of subsequent single delivery shall be deemed to be one entity. Procedure prescribes for making an enquiry as may be deemed necessary and giving an opportunity of hearing to the delinquent before issue of order for removal. Officer competent for issue of order is Divisional Commissioner though it requires prior approval of the State Government.

In case of Rajasthan, Section 39 provided that cessation of membership of PRI representative suffering from disqualification shall be subject to provisions of Section 40 of the Act. Section 40 read as under:

> S.40(1) Whenever it is alleged that any member of PRI is or has become disqualified and such member does not admit the allegation or whenever any member is himself in doubt whether or not he is or has become disqualified for being a member, such member or the competent authority or any member of PRI concerned may apply to the District Judge having jurisdiction for a decision on the allegation or doubt.
>
> S.40(3) The Judge, after making such enquiry as he considers necessary, shall determine whether or not such member is or has become disqualified and his decision shall be final.
>
> S.40(4) Pending a decision, the member shall be entitled to act as if he were not disqualified.[8]

Hence during the period 1995–2000, it was not possible to remove a disqualified PRI member prior to decision of the court of District Judge. Approximately 1000 cases remained pending in the courts and only 145 PRI representatives could be removed for violating the 2-child norm during 1995–2000. Good sense subsequently prevailed upon the State when Section 40 was deleted by an Ordinance dated 6 January, 2000. Now it became comparatively easier for the competent authority to enquire into the allegation after receipt of the complaint, arrive at the finding after giving him/her an opportunity of hearing under Section 39 (2) of the Act, and get order issued for his removal from office. Hence during the period 2000–2005, as many as 598 PRI representatives were removed for violation of 2-child norm. The details of 743 PRI representatives removed during 1995–2005 are reproduced in Table 1.

Table 1

Tier wise, Genderwise and Postwise PRI Representatives Removed for Violating 2-child Norm During the Period 1995–2005[9]

Post	Male	Per cent	Female	Per cent	Total
Ward Panch	447	82	96	18	543
Up-Sarpanch	40	87	6	13	46
Sarpanch	85	83	18	17	103
Pradhan/Up-Pradhan	7	87	1	13	08
Panchayat Samiti Members	27	79	7	21	34
Pramukh/Up-Pramukh Zila Parishad	2	100	—	—	2
Zila Parishad Members	7	100	—	—	7
Total	615	82.77	128	17.23	743

Analysis: Tier-wise and Genderwise

Tier-wise, it can be seen that no woman candidate was disqualified at Zila Parishad level, whereas 9 males were removed for violating the 2-child norm. At Block Panchayat level, out of 34 members of Panchayat Samitis, only 7 female members were removed on this account. Block Chair persons or vice chair persons removed due to this disqualification, were 7 times the number of females. At Village Panchayat level, also, such number was about 5 times the number of female representatives.

As regards male-female ratio, it is observed that as against one-third reservation of seats for women, only 17.23 per cent women became ineligible for not adhering to 2-child norm after being elected in PRI elections. Similarly as against two-third seats generally of males, 82.77 per cent PRI representatives were removed on this account. It shows that women are not the only victim of this disqualification. Men are sufferers in greater number as compared to females. One of the reasons could be that the enquiry starts only after receipt of a complaint. Complaints are generally made by opposing camps or on account of retaliation by defeated candidates. Complaints against women candidates might have been received in lesser number. Moreover, ladies generally go to their parent's house for delivery as a social practice. By the time they return, things are forgotten or remain unknown. Sometimes, child might have been transferred through adoption by some other family at the place of birth itself.

Castewise, it is difficult to conclude that scheduled caste/tribe (SC/ST) or marginalised classes suffer most on such account. Such percentage varies as per proportion of caste population in different districts. If Meena, Damor, Rot, Ninama (scheduled tribe) were disqualified in tribal districts, Jatav, Meghwal, Bairwa, Rawat, Khatik, Bambi, Gadri, Bunkar, (scheduled caste) were removed in Dausa, Jaipur, etc., Jat, Dhakad, Gurjar, Teli, Barath, Nai, Dhobi, Chowdhri, Dudi, Prajapat, Jangid, Banjara, Saini, Kharadi, Yadav, Mali, Tailor, Potter, Bairagi, Daroga (Other Backward Castes) were removed in a large number in proportion to seats occupied by them, and Rajput, Pareek, Jain, Muslims, Bohra, Naagar, Pande, Vaishnav, Joshi, Patidar, Sikh from general castes were also removed. No caste was an exception.

Literacy and Disqualification in the District

Average literacy of the State is 61.3 per cent. Kota has highest literacy of 74.45 per cent with 17 disqualified PRI representatives but Banswara with low literacy of 44.22 per cent has only 4 PRI representatives removed on this account (Table 2). Small district of Sirohi having 54.39 per cent literacy, has as high a number of 45 PRI representatives having violated small family norm and removed due to it. Banswara and Sirohi both have tribal population as well as almost same size but a large difference of 11 times so far as removed PRI representatives on account of violating the norm is concerned. In Shekhawati area, some correlation is visible in Sikar and Jhunjhunu, which have 71.19 per cent and 73.61 per cent literacy and at the same time 25 and 17 disqualified PRI representatives respectively. Both the districts are almost equal in size. Sri Ganganar is the district having the highest SC population in the State but only 8 PRI representatives were removed due to such reason. Thus, human nature is same irrespective of caste, literacy or any such other factor specially, at the grass-roots level in rural areas.

Table 2
Representative Removed

District	*PRI Representatives removed for violating 2-child norm during 2000–05*	*Percentage Literacy as per 2001 Census*
Ajmer	61	65.06
Alwar	23	62.48
Banswara	4	44.22
Barmer	10	59.65
Baran	4	60.37
Bhilwara	27	51.09
Bikaner	12	57.44
Bundi	9	55.80
Chittorgarh	16	54.37
Churu	11	66.97
Dausa	24	62.75
Dholpur	12	60.77
Doongarpur	36	48.32
Ganganagar	8	64.84
Hanumangarh	3	65.72
Jaipur	31	70.63
Jaisalmer	3	51.40
Jalore	35	46.51
Jhalawar	13	57.98
Jhunjhunu	17	73.61
Jodhpur	7	57.38
Kota	17	74.45
Nagaur	16	58.26
Pali	32	54.92
Rajsamand	14	55.82
Sawai Madhopur	11	57.34
Sikar	25	71.19
Sirohi	45	54.39
Tonk	17	52.39
Udaipur	26	59.26
Karauli	3	64.59
Bharatpur	26	64.24

Review of Sample Studies

Six out of 28 states had enacted such legislation, which disqualifies a person from holding a Panchayat post if she or he had a third child after specified date. The proclaimed aim of such harsh measure was to encourage family planning in rural India. To study the fallout of law during 7 years (1994–2001) of its implementation, the Union Ministry of Health and Family Welfare commissioned studies supported by UNFPA, in 21 districts of Andhra Pradesh, Haryana, Madhya Pradesh, Orissa and Rajasthan. The Mahila Chetna Manch of Bhopal undertook these studies in 2001–02 with a common framework. A total of 262 respondents were interviewed. Findings revealed the following:[10]

- Process of disqualifying starts only after a complaint is received. People are generally uninformed about such provision of 2-child norm. They become aware only on receipt of notice. This happens more often with women.
- 54 per cent of the disqualified candidates were either illiterate or had primary education: 16 per cent were educated upto middle level, 27 per cent were higher secondary and 3 per cent were graduates.
- 78 per cent of disqualified candidates belonged to SC/ST/OBC, which are socially weaker sections of population.
- 30 per cent affected persons were having annual income less than Rs 11,000 of per annum: remaining 70 per cent had also annual income below Rs 30,000.
- Manipulation and misrepresentation of the date of birth, are common because of high prevalence of home deliveries and non-registration of births. Moreover, disqualification was also contested on the basis of false certificate of sterilisation.
- Complaints usually start from opposing camps, in order to settle old scores or to retaliate.
- Prolonged court procedures and stay orders, benefit some PRI members by giving them time to complete their tenure.
- There are many instances of disputing the age or date of birth of last born child, tampering of records and evidence like Anganwadi immunisation records, pulse polio campaign records, procuring false certificates, collusion with local officials and getting stay orders, etc.
- The norm has been used as a strategy to remove potentially promising political rivals from election or remove them after election.

- 95 per cent of disqualified persons belonged to age group 21–39. This defeated the very purpose of reducing the age from 26 years to 21 years for contesting PRI election and encouraging younger generation to participate in the PRIs.
- Issues such as still birth, subsequent infant mortality or birth of twins varied indifferent states. Only Rajasthan covered the issue of twins as one entity.
- 50 per cent of SC and 38 per cent of OBC castes are women. In Orisa, women constituted 55 per cent and in Andhra Pradesh 48 per cent. Thus, women are further marginalised by such legislation.
- Cases have been noticed of abortion, desertion, divorce, extra-marital affairs and giving away of children in adoption. Legal wife was sent to her natal home to hide the third pregnancy or child.
- Benefits of having a son far outweighed the benefits of being a PRI representative.
- Women got discouraged by long drawn court cases and enquiries after birth of a third child.

Survey of 60 Panchayats in 21 districts of Madhya Pradesh was conducted by HARKHA, a Delhi based organisation during October 2003. They collected details about education, health care, other facilities and opinion of elected PRI members on a variety of subjects. Only 12 per cent PRI members approved 2-child norm whereas 88 per cent did not approve it.[11]

The task force on Panchayati Raj, set up by the Rajiv Gandhi Foundation has rejected restrictive provisions like the law on 'two-child norm' as violative of human rights. In a memorandum to the Prime Minister, the task force said that "such a law is against the policy of informed responsible choice for family size and violates human right".[12] Quoting the research on the subject, it said that restrictive provision is leading to malpractices like desertion of women, sex selection test, female foeticide and neglect of girl child. It will particularly discourage young women and disadvantaged sections from entering the Panchayats.

Family Planning Association of India, has also advocated non-coercive strategies for planned parenthood by providing comprehensive quality clinical and non-clinical services.[13] States like Tamilnadu, Kerala, Andhra Pradesh and Karnataka have through non-coercive strategies amply demonstrated declining population growth rates. Coercive measures have not worked in Rajasthan, Madhya Pradesh, Haryana etc. where this rule is in force. Those are most populous states in the country. It shows that development rather than punitive measures is more effective in curbing population growth. The educated among the middle classes have realised that fewer children ensure a better quality of life. This awareness is spreading both in urban as well as rural areas.

Union Health Ministry has also withdrawn the Bill seeking to impose two-child norm on members of Parliament.[14] The Bill had been pending in Parliament for the last 12 years. It has reiterated a fundamental principle that elected representatives are entitled to the same rights as other citizens.

Perhaps it was under such circumstances that Himachal Pradesh withdrew such provision recently through a Cabinet decision dated 16 February, 2005. Babulal Gaur, Chief Minister of Madhya Pradesh stated in Bhopal that "the biggest victims of this Rule have been women and poor people".[15] Village women seldom have a say in how many children they will have and the poor have little access to reproductive health care. Madhya Pradesh is also on way to withdraw provision regarding disqualifying PRI representatives for violating two-child norm.

Karnataka Government turned down a proposal sent by the State Election Commission during 2004 to disqualify people with large families from contesting Panchayat elections.[16]

Some statewise Court decisions regarding Two-Child Norm for Panchayats are:

During September 1999, Andhra Pradesh High Court decided three petitions challenging the Constitutional validity of Section 19(3) A.P.Panchayat Raj Act 1994, which disqualifies persons having more than 2 children, from holding a post in PRIs of the State. Arguments put forward by the petitioners were as under:

1. The impugned provision violates the right of privacy of the petitioners as enshrined under Article 19 and 21 of the Constitution.
2. It has no nexus with the purpose of population control
3. The impugned provision violates Article 14 of the Constitution, which provides equality before law, as members of Parliament and State Legislatures face no such disqualification.

The High Court examined all the three arguments in detail and came to the conclusion that the provision of 2-child norm for the

Panchayat representatives stood the test of law. The Court held that Section 19(3) of the Act does not directly interfere with the right of any citizen to take a decision in the matter of procreation. It only creates a legal disability on the part of a person who has procreated more than 3 children to contest for or hold a public office under the Panchayat Raj Act. Moreover, the right to contest an elected office is not a fundamental right but only a legal right arising out of a statute. That being so, no grievances could be made out on the ground that the right to liberty and right to privacy of an individual are taken away by the impugned legislation. The legislative measure is reasonably connected with the object sought to be achieved. Lastly, the legislature while bringing out a particular enactment need not embrace all categories within its scope. It is for the legislature to determine the categories it wishes to embrace within the scope of legislation. Hence there is no violation of the principle of equality before law.[17]

But Division Bench of Madhya Pradesh (MP) High Court, on 17 May, 2002 stayed the provision of MP Panchayat Raj and Gram Swaraj Act 1993 for removal of elected Panchayat office bearers having more than 2 children, until further orders. The petitioners had contended before the High Court that discrimination against any class of persons violates the right of equality enshrined in the Constitution of India. Petitioner Rukmani Devi also claimed that child birth should be considered as having taken place on the date of conception and not on the date of birth of a child. She was pregnant on the date of filing her nomination.[18]

Haryana High Court had referred to Apex Court two separate writ petitions of Sarpanchs Lakhpatsingh and Dharamvirsingh of the State challenging the Constitutional validity of Section 175(1) of Haryana Panchayat Raj Act, 1994, which bars a person with more than 2 children from contesting Panchayat elections. More than 200 similar petitions were already pending before Supreme Court for decision.

Supreme Court has already decided this issue of disqualification on the right to contest Panchayat election for having more than 2 children in *Javed* vs. *State of Haryana* (2003 SCC 369) and *Rameshwarsingh* vs. *State of Haryana* (2003 SCC 396). While dismissing the appeals, Supreme Court held that "No fault can be found with the State, for having enacted the legislation. The disqualification contained in the Act, is neither arbitrary nor discriminatory ... . Disqualification seeks to achieve socio-economic welfare, health care of the masses and is consistent with national population policy... . Disqualification on the right to contest an election by having more than 2 living children does not contravene any fundamental right." In second case, where Section 175(1)(g) and Section 171(1) of Haryana Panchayat Raj Act 1994 was challenged as being violative of Article 25 and 26 of the Constitution, it was held by the Supreme Court that "... Said condition is not arbitrary and classification is based on intelligible differentia having rational relation to the objects sought to be achieved".[19]

Rajasthan High Court had admitted writ petition of Ram Nivas on 9 February, 2005 challenging constitutional validity of Section 19(L) Rajasthan Panchayati Raj Act, 1994 regarding disqualifying PRI member for having third child after 27 November, 1995. It is still pending for judgment of the court.[20]

But in view of Supreme Court Judgment in 2003, the issue seems to be settled as regards the constitutional validity of small family norm.

Decentralised Model of Population Planning

Though legislation regarding two-child norm has been found legally valid by the Supreme Court, Himachal Pradesh has withdrawn this disqualification in February 2005 itself. Madhya Pradesh has decided in its Cabinet meeting to scrap this clause from Panchayat Act. At the same time Gujarat has amended Panchayat Act in the year 2005 itself by introducing 2-child norm for PRI representatives. States of Andhra Pradesh, Orissa, Haryana, Gujarat and Rajasthan still continue with it. Legislatures can exercise the power to continue or scrap such clause disqualifying PRI members to hold the post in case they bear a third child.

As against it, the Union Health Ministry has recently withdrawn the bill seeking to impose two-child norm on members of Parliament. The Bill had been pending in the Parliament for the last 12 years. Elected representatives are entitled to the same rights.

Rajiv Gandhi Foundation has rejected restrictive provisions like the law on the two-child norm as violative of human rights. Nina Puri, President Family Planning Association of India said that the southern states of Tamil Nadu, Kerala, Karnataka have demonstrated declining population growth rates through non-coercive strategies. Coercive legislation in the states of Haryana, Rajasthan etc. has not shown any declining trend in population 2001 though it is a short period to study its impact. Around 88 per cent PRI members in a study in Madhya Pradesh did not approve this clause of disqualification. National Population Policy 2000 does not prescribe any family norm but stresses on better quality of life and quality family planning services. Hence, it needs a further debate on the issue as to why only PRI representatives, and that too in 7 out of 28 states are expected to become role models in this respect?

Population stabilisation cannot be viewed in isolation from poverty, illiteracy, status of women in society and living conditions. No doubt Panchayats at the grassroots are expected to become effective instruments for population stabilisation. Ten Lakh elected women representatives on the reserved seats along with 20 lakh male representatives can become a formidable force in case they take the issue with desired seriousness. In Rajasthan 82 per cent male and only 18 per cent female PRI representatives have been removed on account of having a third child during last 10 years.

Experience of southern states has shown that education and people's participation are key to success for small family norm. Since divergent views have been expressed in different quarters advocating that PRI representatives should not suffer from coercive measure. In fact, this sort of coercion goes against the national population policy 2000, which does not prescribe any size of the family. We need to strengthen the public health system, create awareness on the merits of the small family and offer couples a variety of contraceptive options. If the government takes care of the people, population will take care of itself. ASHA has been appointed on every 1000 population for safe motherhood and promoting family welfare; Jan Mangal couples are already propagating small family norm at village level, it is necessary to educate and convince the menfolk to change their attitude in favour of small family norm to improve quality of life of their families. However, no programme of national significance can succeed without political will. Looking to declining population growth rates in southern states and even China shifting from compulsion to choices now, disqualification on account of small family norm in 6 states and that too limited only to PRI representatives, as role models for society, can hardly make any visible impact. Education, communication, awareness generation, along with political will can be a model for success in the field of family welfare.

Appendix 1

Main Demographic and Other Indictors of Population (2001)

Total Population	5,64,73,122
Population Density	165
Decadal increase	28.33%
Sex Ratio	922/1000 Male
Total Literacy Rate	61.03%
Male	76.46%
Female	44.34%
Life Expectancy	61.36 years
Gross Fertility Rate	4.9%
Infant Mortality Rate	85 per thousand
Child Mortality Rate (1–5 years)	40 per thousand
Mother Mortality Rate	677per lakh
Average age at Marriage	
Boys	21.3 year
Girls	17.5 year
Total Immunisation	37.1%
Safe Delivery	33.5%
Ante-natal Care	62.3%
Contraceptive Protective Rate	40.5%
Institutional Delivery	22.5%
No. of Hospitals	219
Community Health Centre	263
Primary Health Centre	1693
Sub Centre	9926
M.C.W. Centre	118
Aid Post	13
Aganbadi Centre	36000 approx.

Source: Rajasthan Health Scenario, IIHMR, Jaipur.

Notes

1. National Commission on Population, *National Population Policy*, 2000.
2. *Census of India* 2001, Series 9, Rajasthan.

3. Kothari D., 2001, "Rajasthan Reproductive Health Needs of Women as Emerged from the Recent Findings", paper presented in the seminar on Women and Development in Rajasthan as Seen from the Latest Census and Surveys, organised by Rajasthan State Commission for Women and Forum for Population Action in collaboration with UNICEF, October.
4. *Annual Progress Report,* 2004–05, Medical and Health Department, Government of Rajasthan.
5. *Janani Suraksha Yojana Guide,* 2005, Directorate of NRHM, Medical and Health Services, Government of Rajasthan.
6. *Panchayati Raj Update,* July 2002, Institute of Social Sciences, New Delhi.
7. *Panchayati Raj Update*, February 2005, p. 1, Institute of Social Sciences, New Delhi.
8. *Rajasthan Panchayati Raj Act*, 1994.
9. Commissioner Panchayati Raj, Government of Rajasthan, Jaipur.
10. *Panchayati Raj Update*, February 2003, pp. 1,6, Institute of Social Sciences, New Delhi.
11. *Panchayati Raj Update*, December 2003, p. 7, Institute of Social Sciences, New Delhi.
12. *Panchayati Raj Update*, December 2004, p. 5, Institute of Social Sciences, New Delhi.
13. *The Tribune* Daily, 31 August, 2003.
14. *Times of India* Daily, 24 November, 2004.
15. *Panchayati Raj Update*, July 2005, p. 3, Institute of Social Sciences, New Delhi.
16. *Panchayati Raj Update*, February 2005, p. 1, Institute of Social Sciences, New Delhi.
17. *AIR* 2000 AP156.
18. *Panchayati Raj Update*, May 2002, p. 3, Institute of Social Sciences, New Delhi.
19. A Compendium of Resolutions of the Seven Round Table Conferences of Ministers in Charge of Panchayati Raj, Ministry of Panchayat Raj, Government of India, 2004, pp. 20–21.
20. *Panchayati Raj Update*, April 2005, Institute of Social Sciences, New Delhi.

Contributors

Trevor Birkenholtz, Assistant Professor, Department of Geography, Rutgers University, New Brunswick, New Jersey (USA).

Anil K. Chhangani, Department of Zoology, Faculty of Science, J.N.V. University, Jodhpur (India).

G.S.L. Devra, Former Vice Chancellor, Kota Open University (Kota) and UGC Emeritus Fellow, Department of History and Culture, Jamia Millia Islamia University, New Delhi (India).

Enrico Fasana, Professore di Storia e Istituzioni dell'Asia presso: Università degli Studi di Trieste Facoltà di Scienze Politiche (Italy).

Marco Fattori, Professor of Anthropology of Development at Faculty of Political Sciences, University of Trieste (Italy).

Fatima Imam, Department of History, University of Toronto, 2-86 Cassandra Blvd. Toronto (Canada).

Varsha Joshi, Associate Professor, Institute of Development Studies, Jaipur (India).

Elena Karachkova, currently teaching at Moscow University, Moscow.

Ilse Köhler-Rollefson, Project Coordinator, League for Pastoral Peoples, Pragelatotrasse, Ober-Ramstadt (Germany).

Nirmal Kumar, Reader, Department of History, Sri Venkateswara College, University of Delhi, New Delhi (India).

G.S. Narwani, Former Director, Panchayati Raj Department, Government of Rajasthan, Jaipur, (India).

Kathleen O'Reilly, currently at University of Illinois, USA.

Hanwant Singh Rathore, Director, Lokhit Pashu Sansthan, Sadri, Rajasthan (India).

Paul Robbins, Professor and Interim Head, Department of Geography and Regional Development, University of Arizona, Tucson, Arizona (USA).

Madhu Sethia, Lecturer in History, Kanodia College, Jaipur (India).

P.R. Sharma, Assistant Professor, Institute of Development Studies, Jaipur (India).

Surjit Singh, Honorary Director, Institute of Rajasthan Studies, Jaipur and Director, Institute of Development Studies, Jaipur (India).

Aleksandra Szyszko, Department of South Asian Studies, Institute of Oriental Studies, Warsaw University (Poland).

Frances Taft, Independent Scholar, 1105 D Street, Washington DC (USA).

V.K. Vashishtha, Visiting Professor, Banasthali Vidyapith, Banasthali (India).

Vijay Verma, Freelancer, has written extensively on folk music in Rajasthan. He is retired Registrar and Commissioner, Census of India.